Party Institutionalization and Women's Representation in Democratic Brazil

Brazil's quality of democracy remains limited by enduring obstacles including the weakness of parties and underrepresentation of marginalized groups. *Party Institutionalization and Women's Representation in Democratic Brazil* theorizes the connections across those problems, explaining how weakly institutionalized and male-dominant parties interact to undermine descriptive representation in Brazil. This book draws on an original multilevel database of 27,653 legislative candidacies spanning six election cycles, more than 100 interviews, and field observations from throughout Brazil. Wylie demonstrates that more inclusive participation in candidate-centered elections amidst raced-gendered structural inequities relies on institutionalized parties with the capacity to support women, and the will, heralded by party leadership, to do so. *Party Institutionalization and Women's Representation in Democratic Brazil* illustrates how women leaders in Brazil's more institutionalized parties enable white and Afro-descendant female aspirants to navigate the masculinized terrain of formal politics. It enhances our understanding of how parties mediate electoral rules, as well as institutional and party change in the context of weak but robustly gendered institutions.

Kristin N. Wylie is Assistant Professor of Political Science at James Madison University. She specializes in gender politics, representation, political parties, and Brazilian politics. Her research appears in *Politics & Gender* and the *Journal of Black Studies*.

Cambridge Studies in Gender and Politics

Cambridge Studies in Gender and Politics (CSGP) publishes empirical and theoretical research on gender and politics. The series advances work that addresses key theoretical, normative, and empirical puzzles concerning sex and gender and their mutual impacts, constructions, and consequences regarding the political, comprehensively understood.

General Editors

Karen Beckwith, *Case Western Reserve University (Lead)*
Lisa Baldez, *Dartmouth College*
Christina Wolbrecht, *University of Notre Dame*

Editorial Advisory Board

Nancy Burns, *University of Michigan*
Matthew Evangelista, *Cornell University*
Nancy Hirschmann, *University of Pennsylvania*
Sarah Song, *University of California at Berkeley*
Ann Towns, *University of Gothenburg*
Aili Mari Tripp, *University of Wisconsin at Madison*
Georgina Waylen, *University of Manchester*

Books in the Series

J. Kevin Corder and Christina Wolbrecht, *Counting Women's Ballots*
Mala Htun, *Inclusion without Representation in Latin America*
Aili Mari Tripp, *Women and Power in Postconflict Africa*

Party Institutionalization and Women's Representation in Democratic Brazil

KRISTIN N. WYLIE

James Madison University, Virginia

CAMBRIDGE
UNIVERSITY PRESS

CAMBRIDGE
UNIVERSITY PRESS

University Printing House, Cambridge CB2 8BS, United Kingdom

One Liberty Plaza, 20th Floor, New York, NY 10006, USA

477 Williamstown Road, Port Melbourne, VIC 3207, Australia

314-321, 3rd Floor, Plot 3, Splendor Forum, Jasola District Centre, New Delhi - 110025, India

79 Anson Road, #06-04/06, Singapore 079906

Cambridge University Press is part of the University of Cambridge.

It furthers the University's mission by disseminating knowledge in the pursuit of education, learning and research at the highest international levels of excellence.

www.cambridge.org
Information on this title: www.cambridge.org/9781108453530
DOI: 10.1017/9781108612722

First published 2018
First paperback edition 2020

A catalogue record for this publication is available from the British Library

Library of Congress Cataloging in Publication data
NAMES: Wylie, Kristin, author.
TITLE: Party institutionalization and women's representation in democratic Brazil / Kristin Wylie.
DESCRIPTION: Cambridge, United Kingdom ; New York, NY : Cambridge University Press, 2018. | Series: Cambridge studies in gender and politics | Includes bibliographical references.
IDENTIFIERS: LCCN 2017061462 | ISBN 9781108429795 (hardback)
SUBJECTS: LCSH: Political parties – Brazil. | Political participation – Social aspects – Brazil. | Women – Political activity – Brazil. | Women political candidates – Brazil. | Representative government and representation – Brazil. | Brazil – Politics and government – 2002–
CLASSIFICATION: LCC JL2498.A1 W95 2018 | DDC 324.281–dc23
LC record available at https://lccn.loc.gov/2017061462

ISBN 978-1-108-42979-5 Hardback
ISBN 978-1-108-45353-0 Paperback

Additional resources for this publication at www.cambridge.org/delange

To the late Ana Alice Alcântara Costa, who made this project possible, to the women who shared their stories with me, and to my daughter, Lucy.

Contents

Figures

Tables

Acknowledgments

My first trip to Brazil in 2004 was motivated by my graduate program's requirement that as students of Latin American Studies we should speak at least two languages from the region. I went speaking limited Spanish and just a handful of Portuguese words, moved in with a family, took a language class at the Universidade Federal do Bahia (UFBa), and came to develop a deep connection with Brazil. I have since returned six times for a cumulative thirty months of fieldwork. The last two times I returned to Brasília, women politicians I had interviewed over the years asked me when my work would finally be published as a book. I am delighted to finally present this book to Brazil's female politicians and feminist activists in party politics, without whom this work would not be possible. They were generous with their time and shared countless insights, helping me to document women's political exclusion and identify trajectories affording women the opportunity to overcome the obstacles and win election.

My dissertation advisor, Wendy Hunter, introduced me to Brazilian politics and planted the initial seed for this research. Her enduring support and mentorship throughout my graduate studies provided a stalwart source of encouragement and I am forever grateful to have had the opportunity to work with her. I would also like to thank Robert Moser, Tse-min Lin, Kurt Weyland, Victoria Rodríguez, Tasha Philpot, Raúl Madrid, Dan Brinks, Ken Greene, and Henry Dietz, who each offered valuable contributions to this research. My cohort of fellow govgrads was intellectually abundant and made graduate school enjoyable. I especially thank Danilo Contreras, Austin Hart, Mary Slosar, Randy Uang, Manuel Balán, Daniel Budny, Eduardo Dargent, Paula Muñoz, Rachel Navarre, and Rodrigo Nunes for their feedback and friendship.

I incurred innumerable debts conducting fieldwork throughout Brazil, too extensive to list exhaustively here. I am profoundly grateful for the mentorship of the *guerreira* and feminist stalwart, Ana Alice Alcântara Costa, and the entire team at the Universidade Federal da Bahia's Núcleo de Estudos Interdisciplinares sobre a Mulher. Ana Alice was always there to share ideas, invaluable contacts with scholars and activists across Brazil, and her deep insight on questions of gender and politics. Her work and guidance enriched this project substantially, and I miss her immensely.

It was my dear friend Luis Fujiwara who first introduced me to Ana Alice while assisting me in securing a research affiliation in Brazil. Luis also helped to improve my research instruments and methods at several stages in the project, and put me in contact with his wonderful colleagues at UN Women in Brasília. I want to thank Luis and his amazing family, as well as Vicente, Sol, Renata, Marina, Paula, and the entire *galera mineira* for graciously hosting me during extended stays in Brasília and providing a home away from home. I am thankful for the insights and *cafezinhos* shared by various staffers and activists in the corridors of Congress while scheduling interviews and awaiting committee meetings, especially Sílvia Rita Souza, Mara Paraguassu, Laisy Morière, Regina Adami, Sandro Salazar, Leany Lemos, Mônica Almeida, Rose Barreviera, and Iara Cordero, Joseanes Santos, and the rest of the women's secretariat. The staff and collections at the congressional libraries and the Feminist Center for Advocacy and Studies (CFEMEA) were a wonderful source of information and guidance. Clara Araújo, Luzia Álvares, Lúcia Avelar, Betânia Ávila, Maria do Socorro Braga, Cristina Buarque, José Eustáquio Diniz Alves, Mary Ferreira, Vanda Menezes, Jussara Prá, Patrícia Rangel, Teresa Sachet, and Fanny Tabak each took valuable time to talk with me about this project over the years and have, along with Ana Alice—who first introduced me to most of these amazing feminist activists/scholars—continued to motivate and inspire me with their work enhancing women's sociopolitical reality in Brazil. I would also like to thank Tim Power, David Fleischer, Rachel Meneguello, Octávio Cintra, and David Samuels for sharing with me their data and general insights on Brazilian politics. I extend my deepest gratitude to the women and men who granted me interviews throughout Brazil—elected officials, candidates, party leaders and militants, bureaucrats, activists, and scholars—candidly responding to my questions about their paths to power and the struggles they have confronted.

The gender and politics subfield is an exceptionally welcoming and vibrant academic home. I thank Diana O'Brien, Jennifer Piscopo, and Melody Valdini for their constructive feedback and inspiring work, my wonderful co-authors Pedro dos Santos and Malu Gatto, and Tiffany Barnes, Melanie Hughes, Amy Alexander, Elin Bjarnegärd, Sarah Childs, Kimberly Cowell-Meyers, Kelly Dittmar, Susan Franceschet, Kendall Funk, Magda Hinojosa, Farida Jalalzai, Meryl Kenny, Mona Lena Krook, Fiona Mackay, Michelle Taylor-Robinson, Frank Thames, Gwynn Thomas, Melanee Thomas, Tània Verge, Christina Xydias, and countless others for exchanging thought-provoking ideas and making academia both intellectually stimulating and fun. Greg Schmidt and Paula Muñoz's deep knowledge about the Peruvian case were instructive and helped me to refine my discussion of Peru in the concluding chapter.

Sara Doskow, Danielle Menz, and the entire team at Cambridge have been a joy to work with, at once professional and prompt, and generous and patient. I am deeply grateful to the editors of the Cambridge Studies in Gender and Politics series, Karen Beckwith, Christina Wolbrecht, and Lisa Baldez, who have offered steadfast support for me and this book. I also thank three anonymous reviewers for Cambridge University Press who gave me constructive suggestions for improving the book.

My friends and colleagues at James Madison University have been supportive and provided a remarkably strong intellectual community. I want to thank my wonderful colleagues and especially Chris Blake, Melinda Adams, Kerry Crawford, and Keith Grant for offering constructive feedback and making accountability checks pleasant, and my *querida* co-writing companion and fellow shine theory advocate, Becca Howes-Mischel, for helping me complete this writing project and others while maintaining a good sense of humor, some time outdoors, and culinary fulfillment. I also want to thank the College of Arts & Letters for supporting two return trips to conduct fieldwork in 2014 and 2015, and the Department of Political Science for the Johnston Award to finalize this manuscript and begin the next project.

Finally, I want to thank my family, without whom this endeavor would have been impossible. My parents, grandmother, brothers and their families, and in-laws have all provided steadfast encouragement and love, and a healthy distraction when I needed to take a break. Cássio, my partner in life, love, and Brazil, your companionship, compassion, determination, and countless rounds of edits were essential to this project. I look forward to many more trips to Brazil together and cannot wait to share it all with our amazing Lucy Mae.

The Puzzle of Women's Underrepresentation in Brazil

...the underrepresentation of women is a persistent political fact of life in modern states, present across all types of institutional arrangements and cultures. It is one of the few generalizations that it is safe to make about the position of women (Lovenduski 2005, 45).

In 2010, Brazil elected its first woman president, joining Argentina, Chile, Costa Rica, and a handful of other nations in electing a female head of state. President Dilma Rousseff was reelected in 2014, in a contest that saw two other female contenders including Marina Silva, globally renowned environmentalist. But such prominent female leaders constitute noteworthy exceptions in a predominantly masculine formal political realm. And in 2016, the Brazilian Congress—one of the world's most male dominant legislatures—voted to impeach Rousseff. With just under ten percent women in its lower house of parliament, Brazil is ranked a lowly 154th of 193 countries, deviating from an impressive regional trend—seven Latin American democracies have over 30 percent women in their legislature (Inter-Parliamentary Union 2017).

Why do so few Brazilian women hold electoral office? This book explains women's limited presence in formal politics in Brazil, situating the pattern of underrepresentation within a broader "crisis of representation" undermining the quality of democracy in both recent and established democracies. It examines how the category and process of gender are embedded throughout political institutions, chronicling how gendered party structures, electoral rules, and voters interact to marginalize women and other traditional outsiders in Brazil's formal political sphere. In explicitly considering the intersection of gender and race, this book engages the political participation of white and non-white women, thus departing from the inadequate norm of universalizing the experiences of white women (Collins 2000; Crenshaw 1989, 1995; Young

1989).[1] It documents how Brazil's few female politicians have managed to defy the odds, and offers suggestions for mitigating the country's crisis of representation.

The book's major claim is that two important manifestations of that crisis—the weak institutionalization of parties and party systems and the underrepresentation of women and other marginalized populations (Jones 2010)—are related. It engages the issue of women's representation in Brazil (the third wave of democratization's most populous democracy) to explain how weakly institutionalized parties[2] undermine the representativeness of formal politics. It contends that weakly institutionalized parties are ill-equipped to provide the psychological, organizational, and material support necessary to mitigate the persistent gender gap in formal political power. In contrast, well-institutionalized parties operate as an organization, according to clearly defined rules of the game, and have at their disposal a host of material and human resources that they can marshal to cultivate, recruit, and support viable female candidacies.

The enduring political marginalization of women and minoritized groups despite widespread democratization has led to extensive discussions in the academic and policy worlds alike about the causes and consequences of women's underrepresentation. Yet the dilemma in Brazil confounds the conventional wisdom—a dearth of female candidates and deputies persists in spite of substantial socioeconomic progress, effective and dynamic women's movements, an electorate increasingly receptive to female politicians, and the 1998 implementation of a women's quota law stipulating that political parties reserve at least thirty percent of the spaces on their legislative candidate lists for women. Just 51 of Brazil's 513 federal deputies are female, with only four of those women identifying as Black.[3] While Brazil is certainly not unique in marginalizing women from formal politics, its level of underrepresentation is more pronounced than conventional wisdom would expect.

---

[1] When I employ the words "women" or "female," I am referring to the diverse experiences of the wide array of individuals that identify as women. Yet in recognition of the failure of many studies and policies targeting "women" to speak to women of color (Crenshaw 1995; Hughes 2011), where data permit I examine the often stark differences across white women and Afro-descendant women. As evidenced by the evolving ways in which the Brazilian census (un)sees racial identities, the question of data availability is itself interwoven into political projects to reproduce power and privilege and consolidate the nation-state (Reiter and Mitchell 2010).

[2] As developed further in Chapters 2 and 4, weakly institutionalized parties lack lasting societal ties, with limited "value infusion" (Janda 1980) and stability (Huntington 1968), have minimal organizational cohesiveness or "internal systemness" (Panebianco 1988), and are susceptible to personalist politics (Mainwaring 1999).

[3] To be elaborated below and further discussed in Chapter 7, racial identity in Brazil is complex and belies clear dichotomization (Bailey and Telles n.d.; Caldwell 2007; Loveman, Muniz, and Bailey 2012). Ten of the 51 women elected in 2014 self-identify as "parda" (brown) or "preta" (black), which government sources and activists often lump together as "negro" or "Afro-descendant." Yet when the racial binary is imposed, just 4 of those 10 Afro-descendant women consider themselves a part of the Black caucus.

This book explains the puzzle of women's extreme underrepresentation in Brazil. I discuss how the country's electoral rules disadvantage women and thwart the effectiveness of its gender quota, and then examine party characteristics that lend additional explanatory power, especially helpful for understanding the substantial variation in women's prospects across parties. I contend that it is the weakly institutionalized and male-dominant character of most Brazilian parties that has hindered women's political prospects and limited their pathways to power. I find that the intraparty competition in Brazil's candidate-centered elections and the preponderance of inchoate parties have maintained women's political marginalization, and conclude that to effectively promote women's participation, parties must have both the capacity to recruit and provide female political aspirants with essential psychological, organizational, and material support (forthcoming in well-institutionalized parties) and the will to do so (heralded by women in party leadership).

In this introductory chapter, I briefly contextualize the puzzle of women's underrepresentation in Brazil, and introduce the central research questions, research design, and data, and the relevance and contributions advanced herein. I then conclude by previewing the ensuing chapters.

THE WOMEN'S MOVEMENTS

The continued underrepresentation of women in Brazil is particularly puzzling given the strength and breadth of the country's women's movements and general presence of women throughout social movements. Women were active participants in the Amnesty and *Diretas-Já* (Direct Elections Now) movements of the 1970s and 1980s, and played a significant role throughout the (re)democratization process in Brazil (Alvarez 1990). Women also had a critical presence in the black movement, with Afro-descendant women forging autonomous black women's organizations throughout the country (Caldwell 2007; Carneiro 1999). The forceful and consequential presence of women in the Constitutional Assembly of 1987–88 led them to be considered one of "the most organized sector[s] of civil society" (Costa 2008; Macaulay 2006). Indeed, the *bancada feminina* (women's caucus) unified female politicians and activists across party lines, achieving approval for an impressive 80 percent of the proposals laid out in the "Carta das Mulheres aos Constituintes" (Women's Letter to the Members of the Constituent Assembly) (Pinto 1994).

Preparation for and follow-up to the United Nations Conference on Women in Beijing in 1995 led nearly 800 Brazilian women's organizations to coalesce under a "cohesive feminist platform" and advance the "Declaração das Mulheres Brasileiras à IV Conferência" (Declaration of Brazilian Women to the Fourth Conference) (Costa 2008). In recent years, activists have rallied around the National Plan of Policies for Women (PNPM), a comprehensive set of objectives and specific proposals for advancing women's rights. In 2007, with the participation of then President Lula, several members of his cabinet, and politicians and activists from throughout South America, 2,559 delegates elected from over 600 local and regional councils advanced the Second PNPM, which was subsequently approved by executive decree on March 5, 2008 (Special Secretariat for Policies for Women 2010).

The *bancada feminina* continues to unify female legislators, most recently using their "suprapartisan" orientation to influence debates over the political reform proposals under consideration (see Figure 1.1). Michel Temer, then president of the Chamber of Deputies and now acting president of Brazil, declared, "The *bancada feminina* is one of the most active and present in political activity and knows how to defend its causes, make a presence, and make demands" (Temer 2009, 3). In sum, women have enjoyed considerable success in both articulating and actualizing their demands, thus rendering quite conspicuous their absence from the highest echelons of political decision-making.

SOCIOECONOMIC PROGRESS

The near exclusion of Brazilian women from formal politics persists in spite of impressive progress on the fronts of education, literacy, and presence in the

FIGURE 1.1 The *Bancada Feminina* Mobilizing in Favor of Inclusive Political Reforms (2015)

workforce (Htun 2002). As of 2010, women are 59.8% of college graduates, have on average 1.1 more years of schooling than men, and represent 43.6% of the workforce and 45% of the three lowest tiers of federal government posts (Special Secretariat for Policies for Women 2010). Moreover, the Order of Attorneys of Brazil (OAB) indicates that 50.5% of registered attorneys are women. Men still drastically outnumber women in political office, however, comprising more than 10 times the number of federal representatives than women. As shown in Table 1.1, with just 10 percent women in its national congress, Brazil remains stymied as Latin America's most male-dominant legislature (Inter-Parliamentary Union 2017).[4]

FAVORABLE PUBLIC OPINION

Further confounding the extreme underrepresentation of women is the postulated support of the electorate. In recent public opinion polls, Brazilians have responded rather favorably to the prospect of female politicians.[5] A nationally representative survey conducted by the Brazilian Institute of Public Opinion and Statistics (Ibope) in February 2009[6] found that 94% of respondents would vote for a woman, 83% believed that "women in politics and other spaces can improve politics and these spaces," 75% agreed that "true democracy exists only with the presence of women in spaces of power," and 73% concurred that "the Brazilian population wins with the election of a greater number of women." When asked explicitly about the offices for which respondents would support female candidates, 66% of 2,002 respondents indicated they would vote for a woman for any office or federal deputy in particular. Levels of agreement to a subsequent question about hypothetical support for an Afro-Brazilian woman reached 80.2% (Brazilian Institute of Public Opinion and Statistics 2009).[7] So although machismo and racism are interwoven into Brazilian society, survey data demonstrate a postulated receptiveness to white and Afro-descendant female candidates among most Brazilians varying only slightly by respondent sex.

---

[4] The Inter-Parliamentary Union (IPU) data for Brazil tally the women currently serving as federal deputy, including those not initially elected but subsequently assuming a substitute role based on their list ranking. As such, the figure departs minimally from the database used for analysis throughout this book, which is based on electoral returns.

[5] This is not to negate the persistence of machismo in Brazil. Of 2,365 women and 1,181 men surveyed in a nationally representative sample, just 5% of women and men stated that machismo did not exist in Brazil, with 67% and 58%, respectively, indicating that machismo was extensive (Fundação Perseu Abramo 2010).

[6] It is important to note that these surveys were conducted prior to the emergence of Dilma Rousseff's candidacy for the presidency.

[7] Presuming Afro-descendant women are included in respondents' understanding of "woman" in the prior question, the higher level of agreement when asked explicitly about an Afro-descendant female candidate is suggestive of the social desirability bias likely at work in such survey questions (Streb et al. 2008).

TABLE 1.1 *Women's Parliamentary Presence in American Electoral Democracies (2017)*

Rank	Country	% Women in Lower House
2	Bolivia	53.1%
5	Nicaragua	45.7%
8	Mexico	42.6%
15	Argentina	38.9%
19	Ecuador	38.0%
27	Costa Rica	35.1%
37	El Salvador	32.1%
53	Peru	27.7%
58	Dominican Republic	26.8%
62	Canada	26.3%
101	United States	19.3%
105	Colombia	18.7%
107	Panama	18.3%
129	Chile	15.8%
134	Paraguay	13.8%
141	Guatemala	12.7%
154	Brazil	10.7%

Sources: Freedom House (2016); Inter-Parliamentary Union (2017)

Table 1.2 displays the percentage of respondents who, in the 2010–2014 wave of the World Values Survey (WVS), *strongly agreed* with the statement "men make better politicians than women," in several electoral democracies around the world (World Values Survey 1981–2014). It also includes 2017 data from the Inter-Parliamentary Union (IPU) on the percentage of women in the lower house of parliament for those 33 countries. As we can see in Table 1.2, public opinion on women in politics in Brazil suggests an electorate that is rather receptive to women politicians. Ranking 13th of 33 electoral democracies (5th of 8 in Latin America and tied with Germany), many countries exhibit far more prohibitive levels of bias against women than does Brazil. Clearly, public opinion toward women cannot explain the striking underrepresentation of women in Brazilian politics.

When asked about the particular gains a greater female presence would bring, 7 in 10 Brazilian respondents cited greater honesty, competence, administrative capacity, and commitment to voters, the very traits that

TABLE 1.2 *A Cross-National Glimpse at Voter Bias in Electoral Democracies*

Rank	Country	% Male Sup	% Wmn in Leg	Rank	Country	% Male Sup	% Wmn in Leg
1	Netherlands	1.4	36.0	18	Chile	8.3	15.8
2	Uruguay	2.3	20.2	19	Cyprus	9.7	17.9
3	Slovenia	2.5	36.7	20	South Korea	10.6	17.0
4	New Zealand	3.1	34.2	21	Ecuador	12.1	38.0
5	Sweden	3.3	43.6	22	Estonia	15.9	26.7
6	United States	3.4	19.3	23	Romania	16.3	20.7
7	Japan	3.7	9.5	24	South Africa	19.6	41.5
8	Peru	4.1	27.7	25	Ukraine	21.5	12.3
9	Spain	4.3	39.1	26	Georgia	25.5	16.0
10	Australia	4.9	28.7	27	Philippines	27.3	29.5
11	Colombia	5.4	18.7	28	India	30.7	11.8
12	Mexico	6.2	42.6	29	Turkey	32.0	14.6
13	Brazil	6.7	10.7	30	Pakistan	42.6	20.6
13	Germany	6.7	37.0	31	Ghana	44.3	12.7
15	Trinidad and Tobago	7.5	31.0	32	Tunisia	45.0	31.3
16	Argentina	8.0	38.9	33	Nigeria	46.6	5.6
16	Poland	8.0	28.0				

Notes: % Male Sup = % Strongly Agreeing with Male Political Superiority; %Wmn in Leg = % Women in Legislature.
Sources: Inter-Parliamentary Union (2017); World Values Survey (1981–2014); Freedom House (2016)

a majority of electors claimed to evaluate when choosing a candidate (Brazilian Institute of Public Opinion and Statistics 2009). Perhaps most striking is the finding that 78 percent of respondents agree (fully or in part) that it should be *mandatory* for *half* of all legislative candidates to be women (Brazilian Institute of Public Opinion and Statistics 2013). Moreover, in Brazil's 2010 and 2014 presidential elections, 66.2 and 64.5 percent of voters, respectively, cast a vote for a woman, leading to the election and reelection of Dilma Rousseff, Brazil's first female president.[8] Despite this propensity of the Brazilian electorate to support female candidates, most parties, as we shall see, have failed to stimulate and support their candidacies, leaving women woefully underrepresented.

---

[8] The two other female candidates contesting the presidency were two former *petistas*, Marina Silva (with the PV in 2010 and PSB in 2014) and Luciana Genro (with the PSOL in 2014).

ELECTORAL RULES

Many are quick to dismiss Brazil's underrepresentation of women as a result of its pairing of the gender quota with open-list proportional representation (OLPR). While the combination is far from ideal, as detailed in Chapter 3, other nations with similar quotas, electoral systems, and cultural contexts have made significantly greater progress. In order to understand the failure of the gender quota—and indeed, to understand the successes and shortcomings of any institution—we must consider how they interact with the sociopolitical contexts in which they are embedded. Electoral rules do not exist in a vacuum, with the party system and historical tendencies of parties therein being particularly salient (Kittilson 2013; Krook 2009; Lovenduski 1998, 2005). I illustrate the challenges posed by OLPR and related inadequacies of the quota in detail in Chapter 3, but below quickly preview the background and explanation of the quota's limitations.

Seeking to emulate Argentina's success with its groundbreaking gender quota,[9] and build on the international momentum surrounding women's empowerment resulting from the upcoming Beijing Conference on Women, deputies Marta Suplicy and Paulo Bernardo introduced a proposal to implement a gender quota in proportional elections.[10] As will be discussed further in Chapter 3, these deputies foresaw the difficulties inherent in enforcing a gender quota in Brazil's electoral context, and therefore proposed additional measures intended to facilitate its earnest implementation. Just two weeks after the close of the Beijing Conference, Brazil approved the law, but without the additional measures, resulting in a watered down version of the initial proposal (Araújo 1999; Marx, Borner, and Camionotti 2007; Suplicy 1996) and a typical instance of layered institutional change (Thelen 1999).

Thus, in contrast to the experiences of neighboring countries, including others with OLPR elections, Brazil's electoral quota law and subsequent revisions (9.100/1995, 9.504/1997, 12.034/2009) have been unable to mitigate the gender gap in political power (Araújo 2001a; Wylie and dos Santos 2016). The countries that have enjoyed the most success with women's electoral quotas are those with closed-list proportional representation systems, which allow the parties to establish the list ranking with consideration of the candidate quotas and to alternate candidates by sex (Tripp and Kang 2008).[11] In OLPR elections, because the electors rather than the parties decide the position of candidates on the lists, a party could advance a list with 30 percent female candidates and not elect a single woman. Yet as I discuss in Chapter 3, Brazil ranks the lowest in women's representation of all countries with OLPR voting.

---

[9] In 1991, women were 5.4% of the Argentine Chamber of Deputies; ten years after the full implementation of the quota, they had reached 29.2% (Marx, Borner, and Camionotti 2007).
[10] Interview with Senator Marta Suplicy, June 2015.
[11] There exists significant variation in the rules and enforcement of alternation.

While the structural flaws in the Brazilian quota law render it a poor fit for its electoral system, they are only part of the explanation of its spectacular failure to induce genuine change. Brazil ranks the lowest in women's representation of all countries with OLPR voting, and has the 6th lowest proportion of women legislators of the 77 countries with legislated gender quotas or reserved seats, indicating that other factors are clearly at play. I contend that Brazil's preponderance of weakly institutionalized parties—incentivized by its electoral rules—has instilled a norm of non-compliance,[12] facilitating an environment in which formal laws such as the quota are regularly flouted, with earnest party compliance[13] with the quota stipulations remaining the exception.[14] The failure of parties to reach the 30 percent threshold is certainly in part due to the language of the quota law, which until a 2009 "mini-reform" (12.034/2009), only required parties to *reserve* vacancies for women. But even with that institutional change mandating that parties actually *fill* 30% of their candidate lists with women[15]—leading to a 51% increase in the overall percentage of female contenders in the 2010 elections (up to 19.1% from 12.7% in 2006)—a mere 25.4% of parties complied with the strengthened quota.[16]

In 2014, just under half (48.6%) of state parties contesting the Chamber of Deputies elections advanced at least 30% female candidates, with *nearly a third of state parties (30.7%) not running a single female candidate* (see Table 1.3). While parties often use coalition partners to meet the quota target (dos Santos n.d.), in the end, just 56.7% of state coalitions met the 30% target. Tellingly, the percentage of coalition lists reaching 35% female candidates drops to 27.7% (Tribunal Superior Eleitoral 1994–2016). After more than a decade of parties neglecting what was essentially a toothless quota law, it had become entrenched

---

[12] To be elaborated in Chapter 2, the expectation of a norm of (non)compliance draws from the international organizations literature, which has found that states' internal institutional constraints (or lack thereof) affect their probability of (non)compliance with rarely enforced international laws (Dixon 1993; Simmons 1998).

[13] The notion of a norm of non-compliance speaks to violations of both the letter and the spirit of the law. Yet because the latter is difficult to measure systematically, in what follows, I treat quota compliance as formally meeting the legal target (i.e., post-2009 mini reform, party list comprising at least 30 percent women). That treatment is imperfect, since major parties may use smaller coalition partners' contributions to the coalition list to meet the quota (dos Santos n.d.).

[14] Across all state parties contesting the 1998–2010 Chamber of Deputies elections, the rate of quota compliance for Chamber of Deputies elections was 16.1%, ranging from 5.6% (PP) to 39.0% (PC do B). Beyond the PC do B, the most compliant parties (meeting the quota target more than 20% of the time) were small, uncompetitive leftist parties (PCO, PSTU).

[15] The mini-reform requires that 30% of the candidates actually advanced are women. Prior to the reform, the language stipulated that they reserve—but not fill—30% of candidate slots for women. The gender binary reinforcing law is characterized as "gender neutral," meaning candidate lists can have no more than 70% of "either sex."

[16] Despite credible threats of enforcement by the Tribunal Superior Eleitoral in Brasília (Agência de Notícias da Justiça Eleitoral 2010b; Coelho and Costa 2010), several regional electoral courts chose not to enforce the quota (e.g., Agência de Notícias da Justiça Eleitoral 2010a). For further discussion of the failure of this institutional reform, see Wylie and dos Santos (2016).

TABLE 1.3 *Proportion of State Parties Complying with 30 Percent Gender Quota, by Party (2014)*

Party	Proportion of State Parties Running 30%+ Women Candidates (2014)
LEFT	0.57 (0.50)
PCdoB	0.64 (0.49)
PCB	0.60 (0.51)
PCO	0.20 (0.45)
PDT	0.38 (0.50)
PPS	0.36 (0.49)
PSB	0.56 (0.51)
PSOL	0.70 (0.47)
PSTU	0.77 (0.43)
PT	0.56 (0.51)
PV	0.56 (0.51)
CENTER	0.56 (0.50)
PMDB	0.48 (0.51)
PSDB	0.64 (0.49)
RIGHT	0.45 (0.50)
DEM	0.41 (0.50)
PEN	0.40 (0.50)
PHS	0.44 (0.51)
PMN	0.64 (0.49)
PP	0.44 (0.51)
PPL	0.41 (0.50)
PR	0.41 (0.50)
PRB	0.48 (0.51)
PROS	0.44 (0.51)
PRP	0.40 (0.50)
PRTB	0.35 (0.49)
PSC	0.54 (0.51)
PSD	0.37 (0.49)
PSDC	0.30 (0.47)
PSL	0.67 (0.48)
PT do B	0.48 (0.51)
PTB	0.58 (0.50)
PTC	0.39 (0.50)
PTN	0.41 (0.50)
SD	0.38 (0.50)
TOTAL	0.49 (0.50)

Note: Standard deviation in parentheses

as yet another *"lei que não pega"* (law on paper only) (Wylie and dos Santos 2016), particularly among those inchoate parties lacking a norm of compliance.

In sum, although recent and significant accomplishments by women generate expectations to the contrary, the proportion of women elected to Brazil's lower house (Chamber of Deputies) remains near the global low, ranking 154th out of 193 countries, with its nearest neighbors being Samoa and Myanmar. As demonstrated in Table 1.1, this is in sharp contrast to the regional experience with women's representation in Congress, with seven Latin American democracies currently ranking in the top 40 and the entire region outranking Brazil (Inter-Parliamentary Union 2017).

Despite comprising a majority of the electorate for more than a decade[17] and considerable advancement in other spheres, Brazilian women remain severely underrepresented in all elected posts (see Table 1.4). Notably, women have attained their greatest presence—still less than 20 percent—in elections to the Senate, which have no candidate quota.[18] Given the aforementioned progress on women's rights in Brazil, *why does the dearth of female politicians persist? What are the obstacles that hinder women's political participation, and how have Brazil's few female politicians managed to defy the odds?*

THE ARGUMENT IN BRIEF

This book contends that the key to understanding women's persistent underrepresentation lies in the inchoate character of most Brazilian parties. It uses party institutionalization as a lens through which the interrelated deficiencies of Brazil's political system, particularly as they relate to women's representation, come into view. In what follows, I illustrate how parties have been resistant to the gender quota and therefore failed to transform women's substantial societal progress into political presence, and how Brazil's "entrepreneurial" electoral context (Morgenstern and Siavelis 2008) exacerbates a socialized gender gap in formal political ambition and maintains women's political marginalization. It advances an original multilevel database of the 27,653 candidacies to the Brazilian Chamber of Deputies and Senate from 1994 to 2014, finding no empirical support for explanations of women's (under) representation that focus on culture, development, and district magnitude, recasting the role of ideology as indirect, and advancing an argument that it is the interaction of party institutionalization and women in party leadership

---

[17] In December 2014, women were 52.07% of the electorate, up from 49.76% in October 1998 (Tribunal Superior Eleitoral 1994–2016).

[18] Brazil elects its senators in turns, with one-third elected in 2014 and two-thirds elected in 2010. Five of the 27 senators elected in 2014 are women (18.5%), and 13 of the 81 total senators currently serving are women (16.0%). The puzzle of women's relatively greater representation in the Senate is the subject of Chapter 5.

TABLE 1.4 *Percentage of Women among Candidates and Elected, by Office (1994–2016)*

State Elections	Governor		Senator		Federal Deputy		State Deputy	
	Candidates	Elected	Candidates	Elected	Candidates	Elected	Candidates	Elected
1994	9.7	3.7	7.3	7.4	6.2	6.2	7.2	7.8
1998	8.1	3.7	14.0	7.4	10.4	5.7	12.9	10.0
2002	9.9	7.4	11.9	14.8	11.4	8.2	14.7	12.7
2006	12.7	11.1	15.9	14.8	12.7	8.8	13.9	11.4
2010	11.0	7.4	13.3	14.8	19.1	8.8	20.9	13.0
2014	12.1	3.7	20.4	18.5	29.3	9.9	29.1	11.3

Local Elections	Mayor		Municipal Councilor	
	Candidates	Elected	Candidates	Elected
1996	5.3	5.5	10.9	11.2
2000	7.6	5.7	19.1	11.6
2004	9.5	7.4	22.1	12.7
2008	11.2	9.1	21.6	12.5
2012	13.4	11.8	31.9	13.3
2016	13.1	11.6	32.5	13.5

Source: Tribunal Superior Eleitoral (TSE) (1994–2016)

(which are more likely in leftist parties) that is most critical to women's electoral success in Brazil's Chamber of Deputies.

This study builds on the insights from the candidate-centric US case, where women's underrepresentation is best explained not by socioeconomic development, but rather by strong incumbency bias and the necessity for "self-starting nominees in a decentralized party system" (Studlar 2008, 65). Although the amorphous character of many Brazilian parties leads the Brazilianist literature to discount the theoretical relevance of parties for explaining electoral outcomes, this study brings parties to the center of the analysis and finds that parties play a crucial gatekeeping role through their (in)capacitation of female candidacies and are therefore essential actors in the political empowerment of women. I thus bridge the insights of the Brazilianist literature regarding the implications of Brazil's often inchoate parties for democracy, with findings from the women's representation literature heralding parties as the key gatekeepers of political power and party elites as one of the most foreboding obstacles confronting female political aspirants.

This book illuminates how the preponderance of inchoate parties has bounded[19] the profiles available to female political aspirants and draws upon case studies of women exemplifying three ideal types of electorally viable paths to power given the existing constraints—the *supermadre*, the *lutadora*, and the technocrat.[20] While Brazil's inchoate party system and candidate-centered electoral contests allow ambitious self-promoters to parlay their individual resources into electoral success, wage inequities and traditional gender norms render such resources out of reach for the vast majority of women in Brazil. Women and other outsiders confronting similar discrepancies in elections around the world have come to power by working their way up through the party ranks of institutionalized parties.

Yet this option remains rare in Brazil, where most successful female contenders have had to convert capital acquired in alternate spheres into the political capital necessary to thrive in the face of residual levels of *machista* voter bias in the Chamber of Deputies' candidate-centered context rife with

---

[19] *Bounded profiles* builds on the concept of bounded rationality, which political scientists have applied to qualify assumptions of rationality under utility maximization models and recognize constraints to comprehensive rationality (Jones 1999; Weyland 2006). As previewed below and explained in Chapter 6, the profiles of female political aspirants are bounded in the sense that the path to power of the typical male candidate is largely closed to women, with gendered party and district constraints interacting to channel women into particular profiles that can enable them to overcome those obstacles.

[20] As discussed at length in Chapter 6, the *supermadre*, or supermom, refers to a historically common profile of female politicians in Latin America (and beyond) that grounds women's presence in politics via their role as mothers, with their relationship to their constituents assuming a maternal orientation and their policy roles often confined to issues that conform to traditional gender norms (Chaney 1979, Franceschet et al. 2015; Schwindt-Bayer 2006). In contrast, the *lutadora*, or female fighter, deviates from such gender norms and often derives her political capital from activism in popular or syndical social movements.

intraparty competition. When these constraints are alleviated, and women contest elections in districts with negligible levels of voter bias against women, with the support of an institutionalized party with female leadership, women need not conform to the stipulated profiles, but are emboldened to pursue any path to power. The book concludes that to effectively enhance women's representation parties must have both the *capacity* to provide essential psychological, organizational, and material support on behalf of women (more forthcoming in institutionalized parties), and the *will* to do so (signaled by party leadership). This approach illuminates how structures and actors interact to affect women's representation.

This study also works to elaborate the effects of gender on representation as a multilevel structure, including "cultural beliefs and distributions of resources at the macro level, patterns of behavior at the interactional level, as well as roles and identities at the micro level," and as an ongoing process of expectations and consequences (Correll et al. 2007, 3; Beckwith 2005). In other words, it incorporates societal expectations deriving from traditional gender socialization and their effects on public opinion toward women in politics and the political ambitions of individual women with an explanation of how these expectations and the resultant male dominance in political party leadership have constrained women's viable paths to political power.

I find that the macro-level pattern of women's near exclusion from formal politics is the result of a series of micro-level social psychological processes that prevent most women from acquiring the requisite formula for success in Brazilian politics: (1) a psychological affinity for self-promotion and thus aptitude to be an entrepreneurial candidate who self-nominates, (2) political interest and knowledge and the ability to use this to ascend within the party organization, or as is more often the case, to thrive independently in the absence of any real party organization, and (3) individual political (or converted) capital essential in personalist politics. These factors, however, are neither unique nor universal to women, with the last two being applicable to any traditional outsider. Throughout the book and especially in Chapter 7, I examine differences in the obstacles confronted and pathways pursued by white and Afro-descendant[21] women, illustrating how individuals' lived realities and interactions with political institutions are simultaneously raced and gendered (Crenshaw 1995; Hawkesworth 2003). As the primary arbiters of political power, parties hold the key to enhancing the representation of traditionally marginalized groups because they can mitigate the effects of the compounding factors of exclusion, providing outsiders with the psychological, organizational, and material support they need to thrive in Brazil's entrepreneurial system.

---

[21] I use "Afro-descendant" to refer to Brazilians of African descent, which combines two census categories, *preta* (black) and *pardo* (brown). I use "Black" and "Afro-Brazilian" interchangeably to refer to individuals (/ entities) identifying as either *preta* or *pardo* and assuming *negritude* (blackness / black consciousness) (da Costa 2014; Telles 2004).

RELEVANCE

Mechanisms of exclusion/inclusion in democratic decision-making processes are inherently important for political scientists and constituents alike. A report card on women's representation in the Americas reminds us that:

[i]t is important for women to be represented at all levels of the political spectrum and the decision-making process and we know why: because women's political rights are fundamental in any democratic framework, because democracy isn't complete without us, and because experience shows that women at high levels are more likely to bring changes and policies that improve the situation for other women (Inter-American Dialogue 2008, 2).

This sentiment is echoed in survey data from Schwindt-Bayer, who found that women legislators were more likely than male legislators to "place special priority on women" and women's groups, with a legislator's gender influencing the way they view organized constituency groups and their support for issues related to women's equality and family and children (but not education or health) (2010, 67–81). With more women in legislatures, including women of color, these voices and issues are more likely to be represented. As Lovenduski and Norris (1993), Phillips (1995), and others have asserted, truly democratic representation entails both a "politics of ideas" (substantive representation) and a "politics of presence" (descriptive representation).

The full inclusion of women in formal decision-making processes is essential for truly representative democracies because female politicians bring the voice and often the interests of women to the legislative agenda. Empirical analysis has also suggested that the increase of women's presence in politics is partially responsible for enhancing citizens' satisfaction with democracy (Schwindt-Bayer 2010). With 74 percent of respondents across Brazil agreeing that "true democracy exists only with the presence of more women in spaces of power and decision-making" (Brazilian Institute of Public Opinion and Statistics 2013), and only 41 percent of respondents in a 2014 survey reporting that they are satisfied with Brazilian democracy (LAPOP n.d.), the representativeness of government and resultant quality of democracy bear utmost significance.[22]

In addition to broader theoretical implications regarding representation, satisfaction with democracy, institutional change, and the interaction of structure and agency, this book bears substantive implications for the lives of Brazilians. A startling 4 in 10 Brazilian women have been victims of domestic violence (Brazilian Institute of Geography and Statistics 2009). Six out of 10 Brazilians know some woman who was a victim of domestic violence, with machismo being the factor most commonly pointed to by respondents (46%) as contributing to this violence (Avon Institute/Ipsos 2011). While only 9.7% of

[22] I thank the Latin American Public Opinion Project (LAPOP) and its major supporters (the United States Agency for International Development, the UN Development Program, the Inter-American Development Bank, and Vanderbilt University) for making the data available.

male homicides occurred in a domestic residence, 28.4% of female homicides occurred in the home (Desidério 2011; Waiselfisz 2012). Every single day, *Machismo Mata* (2012) reports at least one and usually several new case(s) of a Brazilian woman being murdered—most often stabbed, shot, or strangled—by her male partner (http://machismomata.wordpress.com/). With 4,297 female homicides in 2010, or 4.4 per 100,000 women, Brazil is the 7th of 84 nations ranked by rate of female homicides (Waiselfisz 2012). In five years, the "180" hotline for domestic violence against women—Central de Atendimento à Mulher—received nearly two million calls. In 72% of the cases of women reporting abuse, they are victimized by their husband (Desidério 2011).

The 180 hotline and the pioneering Lei Maria de Penha,[23] which protects victims of domestic violence, were the fruit of collaboration among the women's caucus of the 2003–2007 Congress. These are the kind of laws and changes in women's lives that increased women's political empowerment can bring. As the National Congress debates how to address the violence disproportionately plaguing Afro-descendant youth—77 percent of youth homicide victims are Afro-descendant, with two young Afro-Brazilians killed every single hour (Borges 2015)—one cannot help but wonder how the discussion would differ if the legislators looked more like Brazil. With 72 percent of the seats in the so-called "casa do povo" (house of the people) occupied by white men, in a country that has a female and Afro-descendant majority, enhancing the political participation of women and Afro-descendants is important in its own right for furthering democratic representativeness. And by improving and perhaps even saving the lives of ordinary citizens, it also wields an immeasurable practical value.

CONTRIBUTIONS AND SCOPE CONDITIONS

In addition to posing an interesting empirical puzzle, the Brazilian case proffers several under-theorized and untested dimensions to the research agenda on politics and gender. Despite acknowledgement of the methodological and substantive implications of a "Western" country bias for research on women's representation (e.g., Salmond 2006), the bulk of the literature is either based exclusively on Western Europe and the US or simply applies expectations developed in the advanced-industrial context. The drive to understand women's representation outside the advanced-industrial context is, therefore, a principal enterprise of this research.

A related limitation of the women's representation literature, derived primarily from Western Europe and the US, is the general assumption of institutionalization of party systems. As demonstrated in the Brazilianist literature on electoral institutions and career paths, the weakly

---

[23] A law implemented in September 2006 that raised the legal penalties for cases of domestic violence.

institutionalized character of the Brazilian party system renders many of the traditional assumptions (e.g., reelection, party discipline) tenuous, often warranting important theoretical revisions. I build on these Brazilianist insights regarding the critical importance of party institutionalization but extend the domain of the literature, which in studying congresses that have remained vastly masculine, has depended upon male-dominant samples and largely neglected gender (e.g., Ames 2001; Mainwaring 1995, 1999; Samuels 2003, 2008).

In introducing women and gender into the analysis of Brazilian electoral and party systems, this book enhances our understanding of the role of parties in open-list elections. Although parties have indeed proven less important for men possessing independent political (or converted) capital, the negation of the party gatekeeping role simply does not hold for actual outsider candidates. This finding could only be uncovered by bringing gender (and/or race) into the analysis. Moreover, as the literature itself acknowledges, variation exists among Brazilian parties (Mainwaring 1999; Morgenstern and Vázquez-D'Elía 2007; Samuels 1999), with the Workers' Party (PT) often the lone cited exception to the country's pattern of weak party institutionalization. This book capitalizes on rich interparty variation within Brazil to illuminate the critical role of parties in mediating the effects of electoral rules and enhancing the political representation of women.

Another contribution offered in this book is one of the few *individual candidate-level* quantitative analyses of the conditions under which women can acquire political power.[24] The country-level aggregation prevalent in the dominant cross-national approach potentially obscures the relationship between electoral success and the factors that drive it,[25] especially in candidate-centered elections. Moreover, using aggregate-level findings to infer effects on individuals is to commit an ecological fallacy (King, Keohane, and Verba 1994). Rather, if we are to understand the effects of voters, electoral rules, and parties on women's electoral prospects, we must test them at the candidate level.

Although the country context remains constant, I use an explicitly comparative lens to assess the variance in the relationships between candidate electoral performance and several multilevel characteristics over states, electoral rules, and parties. In an article on the state of the art of gender and politics, Childs and Krook (2006) argue that future work must proceed from a micro-level approach to elaborate the causal linkages in our theories. Childs and Krook push gender and politics scholars to progress beyond oversimplifying assumptions regarding female politicians and instead to

---

[24] Exceptions include Rainbow Murray's work (2008) on candidate performance in France and Melody Crowder-Meyer et al.'s study (2015) on municipal elections in California.

[25] A recent advance on this front has emerged from the Comparative Study of Electoral Systems with its groundbreaking cross-national study using multilevel analysis to embed individual voters in their country-level contexts (Dalton and Anderson 2011).

disaggregate women (2006) and acknowledge and analyze the diversity of women (Avelar 2001; Celis et al. 2013). Accordingly, this book also allows for heterogeneity among women, acknowledging differences across racial identities and analyzing the variation in individual characteristics and campaigns of Brazil's female contenders. Rather than assuming that women represent a homogenous group and pursue a single path to power, I examine the (albeit circumscribed) range of profiles of women in Brazilian politics and the individual-, party-, and district-level characteristics that comprise these profiles, explaining how parties have interacted with voters and electoral rules to limit women's paths to power, and how the structure and process of gender are intertwined throughout those interactions. I work to consider how gender manifests at various levels, including traditional gender norms regarding women's aptitude for politics and the issue areas with which women should engage, structural disadvantages, voter and party biases, and the perceptions and confidence of female political aspirants themselves.

This study aims to fulfill these goals of the literature with a contextually embedded individual-level theory of women's representation outside the standard US/Western European setting. I push beyond oversimplified and untested explanations of how women attain elected office in Brazil that focus merely on family connections and/or ties with civil society and instead specify precisely and provide empirical evidence for whether and how several individual-, party-, and district-level characteristics interact to illustrate how women, as individuals, are elected. This work thus illuminates how female political aspirants navigate Brazil's weakly institutionalized party system through an analysis of the interaction of the individual-, party-, and district-level characteristics associated with successful electoral strategies of Brazil's female politicians, thereby exploring the conditions under which women can acquire political power.

The book's general theoretical claim—that parties are the central arbiters of women's descriptive representation and must have both the *will* and *capacity* to recruit and support viable female candidates—is broadly applicable beyond Brazil. The claim resonates with the gender politics literature demonstrating the pivotal role of parties in mediating political power (Kittilson 2006, 2013; Verge and Claveria 2016; Verge and de la Fuente 2014). Yet it departs from conventional wisdom in the Brazilianist literature, which has discounted the role of parties for understanding candidate selection and election in "entrepreneurial" electoral contexts like Brazil (Morgenstern and Siavelis 2008; Samuels 2008; Schedler 1995). In integrating those literatures on gender politics and Brazilian political institutions, the analysis centers gender and reveals the salience of parties. It thus extends the domain of the argument that parties are the central gatekeeper of political power to encompass the entrepreneurial context (Morgenstern and Siavelis 2008). The book's integrative approach also offers important insights about party institutionalization, a common theme in studies of

Brazil's political institutions (e.g., Mainwaring 1999) that is rarely treated in the gender politics literature.

That emphasis on party institutionalization constitutes the book's more specific theoretical claim that party will and capacity are substantiated by women in party leadership and party institutionalization, respectively. Although the book only tests that interactive claim within a weakly institutionalized party system, research from Guadagnini (1993), Waylen (2000), and Kittilson (2006) about the gendered implications of party (system) institutionalization in Argentina, Chile, and Western Europe suggests its generalizability. In Waylen's analysis of gender and parties in Argentina and Chile, she explains that "women activists both inside and outside the parties can exert pressure more effectively on an institutionalized party system than on a weak party system. In an institutionalized party system it is clearer where the pressure points are and any changes to the rules can be enforced more easily" (2000, 790). Kittilson (2006) corroborates that claim about enforceability and further articulates the implications of party institutionalization for outsiders' abilities to ascend the party ranks. And Guadagnini's study of Italian parties illustrates how institutionalized parties are more conducive to "less 'advantaged' groups and individuals, like women, who possess fewer external resources" (Guadagnini 1993, 181).

This book builds on those insights to demonstrate how party institutionalization facilitates quota compliance and women's involvement, and yields opportunities for candidate capacity-building and material party resources. I also incorporate findings from Hinojosa's (2012) study of candidate selection in Latin America, grounded in case studies of Chile and Mexico, to explain the gendered implications of party institutionalization for candidate selection. Inchoate parties lack a recruitment network and require self-nomination, which upholds a constructed gender gap in formal political ambition and fabricates a robust psychological disincentive to participate. Finally, studies based on Europe, Japan, and Latin America (Ellis 2002; Escobar-Lemmon and Taylor-Robinson 2008; Valdini 2012, 2013a) suggest that programmatic campaigns, which are more likely in institutionalized parties, may facilitate women's participation by minimizing the salience of gender discrimination and by incentivizing a more collaborativist campaign ethic.

As discussed in Chapters 5 and 7, which evaluate the scope conditions of my central claim about party institutionalization and female leadership, there are two apparent caveats to the argument. First, as discussed and then illustrated empirically in Chapter 5, the salience of party institutionalization is heightened in electoral contexts of intraparty competition. When electoral rules incentivize intraparty competition, as is the case in Brazil's open-list PR elections for the Chamber of Deputies, parties that are both well-institutionalized and have women in leadership are best positioned to help female contenders navigate the constraints of a hypercompetitive electoral context. Such parties are most likely to offer female political aspirants critical psychological, organizational, and material support. In contrast, when electoral rules incentivize unified party support as they do in Brazil's Federal Senate (and in closed-list PR elections, to a somewhat lesser extent), party institutionalization loses significance for predicting women's electoral success. A mini-case study of Peru in Chapter 8 complements that finding and further suggests that when electoral rules mitigate incentives for intraparty competition, party institutionalization loses salience for women's representation. Another caveat to the generalizability of the book's central claim emerges from Chapter 7, which offers suggestive evidence that the apparent benefit of party institutionalization for women's electoral prospects in Chamber of Deputies elections may not extend to Afro-descendant female candidates.

The analyses in Chapters 5, 7, and 8 indicate that the findings on the significance of the presence of women in party leadership for predicting women's electoral fortunes are robust. In contrast to the above stated caveats about party institutionalization, the effect of women in party leadership does hold for female candidates to the Brazilian Senate and Afro-descendant female candidates to the Brazilian Chamber of Deputies, and may also carry explanatory weight in Peru's legislative elections, thus corroborating claims in the gender politics literature about the key role of women party leaders (Kittilson 2006). This book contributes to our ongoing discussion about critical mass, critical acts, and critical actors (Beckwith 2007; Beckwith and Cowell-Meyers 2007; Childs and Krook 2006, 2008, 2009; Childs and Lovenduski 2013; Dahlerup 2006a; Krook 2015b), offering empirical evidence for the significance of women's presence among party elite while documenting precise mechanisms constituting that positive relationship with an emphasis on the critical acts performed by female party leaders.

Finally, this book offers empirical evidence from an understudied case to support the broad claim of the feminist institutionalist literature that institutions and institutional change are fundamentally gendered (e.g., Krook and Mackay 2011; Mackay 2014; Mackay et al. 2010; Mackay and Waylen 2014). Chapter 3 draws on Brazil's experience with the gender quota law to illustrate how and why formal institutional reforms are often insufficient to induce meaningful change, particularly in the context of weak institutions. Building on that insight and the central role of parties in mediating electoral rules, this book chronicles the gendered character and implications of party leadership and institutionalization. While the scope conditions of this book's central argument—that women's extreme underrepresentation in Brazil is explained by its plethora of weakly institutionalized, male dominant parties—may be limited to electoral contexts with intraparty competition, that claim is in dialogue with broader theoretical expectations about gendered institutions, the gatekeeping role of parties, the gendered implications of party institutionalization, and the importance of women in party leadership.

RESEARCH DESIGN AND DATA

This research is expressly mixed-method, drawing on cross-national aggregate-level data, survey data, an original database of several individual, party, and district characteristics of all 27,653 candidacies to the Chamber of Deputies and Senate (1994–2014), primary source documentary research, and over 100 in-depth interviews with female politicians, candidates, party officials, bureaucrats, activists, and experts in eleven states throughout Brazil's five regions. I also accompanied a female candidate for local office[26] on the campaign trail and observed a state party convention in Bahia and several meetings of the *bancada feminina* in Brasília.

I overcome a significant limitation of most individual-level research on representation by broadening the universe of observations analyzed to include all candidates. We cannot speak confidently about what it takes to win by focusing merely on the winners, but must also consider the losers. Similarly, if we wish to comprehend the effects of candidate gender on electoral prospects, we must consider women and men. The database comprises all valid candidates to the Brazilian Congress in the last six election cycles (1994–2014). A common approach to individual-level data in the extant literature is to analyze a subset of the data, such as elected legislators or candidates from the major parties. Instead, I analyze all 27,653 cases of candidacy to the Brazilian Congress from 1994 to 2014. I also incorporate case studies of the pathways to power pursued by Brazil's few female politicians.

In sum, this study engages the central research questions—what are the barriers preventing women's substantial societal gains from parlaying into greater political presence, and how have Brazil's few female politicians managed to overcome these obstacles—by advancing an array of quantitative and qualitative data. I use those data to explore variation in the electoral performance of candidates across districts, electoral rules, parties, sex, racial identity, and women, thus illuminating how state, electoral, and party contexts can interact to mediate the effects of gender (and racial identity) on electoral outcomes.

INTERVIEW SELECTION

I selected my interviews with failed and successful female candidates to ensure representation from the major parties (PFL, PMDB, PP, PSDB, PT) and the PC do B and in each of the five regions. I interviewed party officials, most often the Women's Secretary and/or Secretary of Organization, in these six parties in six states (Bahia, Maranhão, Pará, Rio de Janeiro, Rio Grande do Sul, and São Paulo) and the Federal District. I also interviewed scholars of gender politics

---

[26] Councilwoman Vânia Galvão, Municipal President of the PT in Salvador da Bahia.

and activists in the women's movement in each of the five regions to ascertain local historical dynamics regarding women's participation in informal and formal politics. Finally, I interviewed federal-, state-, and municipal-level bureaucrats in the women-specific secretariats in Brasília, Alagoas, Fortaleza (municipal), Pará, Pernambuco, Rio de Janeiro (municipal), Rio Grande do Norte, Rio Grande do Sul, Salvador (municipal), and São Paulo. The first wave of 73 interviews were conducted from September 2008 to July 2009, with subsequent waves conducted in July 2010, April–May 2012, August 2014, and May–June 2015.

ORGANIZATION OF THE BOOK

Chapter 2 reviews the insights and limitations of the extant explanations of women's representation for understanding the obstacles confronting female political aspirants in Brazil. It then maps out the theoretical argument advanced in this book, which contends that two important challenges to Latin American democracies—the underrepresentation of marginalized groups and the weak institutionalization of parties and party systems—are related. I explain how Brazil's weakly institutionalized parties undermine women's representation. First, a lack of clearly defined rules of the game makes it difficult for outsiders to ascend the party ranks. Such limited transparency also fosters a norm of non-compliance with internal and external laws, such as the quota. Second, in the absence of an effective party recruitment network, candidates must self-select, with political entrepreneurs being the norm. A resilient constructed gender gap in formal political ambition means that women are far less likely than men to self-select. Weak party organizations are also unable to offer opportunities for capacity-building, whether through internal elections, political training, or mobilizational events, which deprives outsider candidates of the chance to develop the requisite political skillset. Finally, in weakly institutionalized parties, personalist politics dominate and programmatic appeals are rare. Due to wage inequities and traditional gender norms, women generally lack the personal political capital—accrued by individual status, wealth, and connections—necessary to sustain a candidate-centered campaign, and also tend to eschew individualistic enterprises in favor of more collective endeavors.

Together, those manifestations of inchoate parties undermine the electoral prospects of women by leaving intact a constructed gender gap in political ambition and favoring those with accumulated personal political capital. Given the paucity of women in Brazilian politics (see Table 1.4 above), I argue that parties must actively intervene to enhance women's political participation. Their *capacity* to do so effectively, however, is constrained by their *level of institutionalization*, with weakly institutionalized parties being ill-equipped to provide women with the requisite psychological, organizational, and material support for confronting Brazil's entrepreneurial system. I contend that this capacity of parties to promote women's participation is affected by their *will* to do so, with parties that incorporate *women in their party leadership* being the most likely to mobilize resources on behalf of women. Often a sin of omission rather than commission, when party leadership lacks a critical mass of female voices it will likely lack consciousness of the need and mechanisms for leveling the playing field for women. An explicitly gendered frame of reference, whereby we consider the implications of and for gender in structures and processes (Beckwith 2005; Lovenduski 1998) must be introduced[27]—and women leaders are far more likely than male leaders to show the initiative and know how to do so.

Figure 1.2 depicts how party capacity and party will interact, and the variation among parties within Brazil. It previews the national averages across a party's state-level organizations[28] over the 1998–2010 elections to the Chamber of Deputies on the central party characteristics of interest, illustrating the range within Brazil as well as the extent of the obstacles confronted by female contenders, with half of the parties having neither the capacity nor the will to support women, and only three of the 28 parties enjoying both, on average. Table 1.5 displays the percentage of national party leaders, Chamber of Deputies candidates, and elected federal deputies (2014) that are women, by party and ideology.

By acknowledging such interparty variation in key party characteristics and women's electoral prospects, I unpack the mechanisms substantiating leftist parties' apparent superiority in electing women. Leftist parties have, through their greater tendency to be institutionalized and to incorporate women in party leadership, proven more capable and willing to actively promote women's participation. This finding has important implications for the future of women's empowerment in Brazil, because the institutionalization of parties and inclusion of women in their decision-making structures are universal goals within the reach of leftist and non-leftist parties alike.

In Chapter 3, I discuss the successes and failures of the Brazilian gender quota, asserting that there are limitations to formal institutional fixes in the context of weak institutions. Although many observers are quick to attribute its inadequacies to the open-list electoral context, I reveal that this is only part of the explanation. I explain why the open-list system has been expected to disadvantage women and its incompatibility with candidate quotas, and explore the experiences with women's representation in the other nations

---

[27] A similar conclusion has finally been reached in the development community, where gender is now an explicit consideration for budgeting and other policy decisions. For more on this, see Quinn (2009) and UN Women's Gender Responsive Budgeting website (www.gender-budgets .org).

[28] This is intended solely as a preview, with the national averages obscuring state-level variation (see Appendix 4.2).

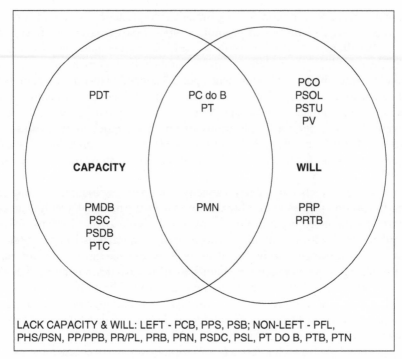

FIGURE 1.2 Interparty Variation among Brazilian Parties' Capacity for and Will to Support Female Candidates, National Level (by Ideology)

with candidate-based proportional representation (hereafter, "preferential") voting. I then review the literature on quotas as a fast-track for women's representation. Next, I discuss Brazil's process of quota implementation and examine recent mobilization by various organs of the women's movement for greater female presence in politics. I draw on accounts of the quota negotiations to explain how the finished product was a diluted version of the initial proposal, and discuss why this quota—poorly implemented and weakly enforced—has been unable to enhance women's representation, even after attempts to reform it.

Chapter 4 employs a multilevel model of the electoral performance of candidates to the Chamber of Deputies (1994–2010) to explore variation across states and parties. I review the obstacles confronted by women, introduce my party institutionalization index, and elucidate the conditions hindering/hastening female candidate success. The findings demonstrate that the traditional explanations of women's underrepresentation emphasizing district modernization and magnitude do not hold in Brazil. While non-negligible levels of voter bias against women exist, and are predicted by district development, such bias has not depressed the vote share of female

TABLE 1.5 *Interparty Variation among Brazilian Parties' Inclusion of Women in Party Leadership and Chamber of Deputies Elections, National Level (2014)*

Party	National Executive Committee		Women Candidates (%)	Women Elected (%)
	Members	Women (%)		
LEFT				
PCdoB	23	5 (21.7%)	27 (36.0%)	4 (40.0%)
PDT	22	4 (18.1%)	81 (27.5%)	1 (5.0%)
PPS	31	9 (29.0%)	34 (28.6%)	2 (20.0%)
PSB	38	7 (18.4%)	111 (29.8%)	5 (14.7%)
PT	21	9 (42.8%)	105 (28.8%)	9 (13.2%)
PV	50	11 (22.0%)	80 (28.8%)	1 (12.5%)
NON-LEFT				
DEM	48	3 (6.3%)	38 (24.7%)	1 (4.8%)
PMDB	32	3 (9.4%)	103 (30.2%)	7 (10.8%)
PMN	17	5 (29.4%)	47 (32.9%)	1 (33.0%)
PP	120	11 (9.2%)	47 (29.0%)	2 (5.3%)
PR	23	3 (13.0%)	51 (28.0%)	4 (11.8%)
PRB	7	0 (0.0%)	76 (31.4%)	2 (9.5%)
PSC	19	3 (15.7%)	46 (28.8%)	2 (15.4%)
PSDB	39	6 (15.4%)	100 (33.8%)	5 (9.3%)
PT do B	17	3 (17.6%)	61 (28.5%)	0 (0.0%)
PTB	99	24 (24.2%)	67 (27.6%)	1 (4.5%)
PTC	14	1 (7.1%)	46 (25.8%)	1 (50.0%)
PTN	16	4 (25.0%)	35 (31.8%)	2 (50.0%)

Note: Values in parentheses represent the proportion of the party's candidates and elected that are women

candidates. Moreover, women have not performed better in districts or parties with a greater seat share.

Instead, party institutionalization and the presence of women in party leadership explain variation in women's electoral performance in Brazil. I find the role of party ideology to be indirect; while running with a leftist party is neither a necessary nor sufficient condition for women's electoral success, leftist parties are more likely than non-leftist parties to be institutionalized and incorporate women into party leadership, which in turn leads such parties to mobilize resources on behalf of women. I then use the illustrative case of the Workers' Party (PT) to chronicle how ideology, party institutionalization, and women in party leadership have interacted to enhance women's electoral prospects, and discuss the challenges that remain for the PT and other parties, and the inroads accomplished by the Communist Party of Brazil (PC do B). The most striking and unique contribution of the chapter is the finding that party matters in Brazilian elections.

In Chapter 5, I compare women's electoral performance across the Chamber of Deputies and Senate, using the variation in electoral rules within Brazil as a natural laboratory to explore the effects of electoral rules on women's electoral prospects while holding constant numerous potentially confounding factors. While the more prestigious Senate poses a higher electoral hurdle, low-magnitude plurality elections with restricted ballot access generate significantly greater incentives for party support than do the Chamber's high-magnitude OLPR elections. I demonstrate that women have consistently achieved proportionately greater electoral successes in the Senate since 1994 because its electoral rules incentivize unified party support, which when mobilized by women in party leadership provides a powerful boost to female candidates.

The empirical evidence supports an indirect rather than direct effect for electoral rules. While an analysis of the direct effects of plurality elections, low district magnitude, and no candidate quota would expect those conditions to undermine women's electoral prospects, a broader consideration that accounts for how those rules are mediated by political parties demonstrates their relative favorability for female contenders. The distinct electoral rules across the chambers yield varying incentives for party support and intraparty competition, with the consequences of those incentives for female candidates contingent upon party institutionalization in the Chamber, and women in party leadership in both houses. When compared to the intense climate of intraparty competition incentivized by the electoral rules of the Chamber of Deputies, it is no surprise that female candidates running in parties with a critical mass of women leaders have performed better in the Senate, where the electoral rules incentivize unified party support.[29]

Drawing on the findings of Chapters 4 and 5, Chapter 6 explains how Brazil's few female deputies have been able to attain election in the midst of such intraparty competition, weakly institutionalized parties, unsupportive party elites, and persistent traditional gender norms. I contend that the statistical non-significance of the traditional explanatory factors for women's representation in models of women's electoral prospects does not mean that obstacles such as *machista* voter bias and electoral arrangements do not exist. Rather, (some) women have crafted profiles enabling them to thrive in inhospitable contexts. Alternate profiles are necessary because the traditional path pursued by most

---

[29] As I discuss in Chapter 5, while female party leaders in the traditional oligarchic parties (PFL/DEM) are more likely to mobilize such unified party support in the Senate elections on behalf of women candidates running with familial capital (wives and daughters), women elected with the PSDB are more likely to have converted technocratic capital, and women elected from the PT most often worked their way through the party ranks. Those three parties represent 73 percent of the women elected to the Senate.

successful white male politicians in Brazil—the consummate insider, with status, wealth, and connections—is closed to most women by wage inequities and traditional gender norms.

Chapter 6 uses the cross-national literature and descriptive data from Brazil to delineate women-friendly and women-adverse parties and districts, and the profiles that have enabled women to thrive in each of those contexts. Exemplified with case studies, the chapter explains how the characteristics of the *supermadre*, the *lutadora*, and the technocrat have afforded women electoral success despite the obstacles. In sum, I explore how the preponderance of inchoate, male-dominated parties and persistence of traditional gender norms have bounded the profiles available to women, and explain how the strengthening of parties can open up space to female political aspirants and in turn enhance both the accountability and representativeness of Brazilian democracy. I also illuminate how women have employed alternate spaces to acquire political capital and consider the role played by those experiences in developing their political aspirations and campaign strategies.

Chapter 7 expands upon the insights developed throughout the book to evaluate sociopolitical dimensions of the intersections of gender with race in Brazil, which since 2010 has had an Afro-descendant majority. It engages Brazilian critical race scholars to describe the construction of race, and assesses the growing availability of individual data disaggregated by sex and race, including, as of 2014, candidate-level data. Drawing on socioeconomic data, electoral returns, party characteristics, and interviews, the chapter illustrates the causes and consequences of the marginalization of Afro-descendant women. Descriptive statistics from the 2014 Chamber of Deputies elections highlight significant differences between the electoral prospects of Afro-descendant women and those of Afro-descendant men and white women and men. Multivariate findings reveal that even after controlling for traditional indicators of candidate quality, the race and gender of Afro-descendant women candidates exercise a statistically significant negative effect on their vote share. The chapter demonstrates the importance of an intersectional approach for understanding and addressing underrepresentation.

The concluding chapter reviews the core findings of the book, and employs analytical insights yielded to engage broad theoretical debates about democratic representation, the quality of democracy, the role of parties, and institutional change amidst gendered institutions. I examine the generalizability of the book's core argument with a mini-case study of women's representation in Peru, using the representation of traditional outsiders as a lens for understanding the role of parties and processes of institutional change and reproduction in and beyond the Brazilian context.

I draw on my findings and comparative perspectives to outline strategies for enhancing the representation of women and Afro-descendants in Brazil, and consider the prospects for political reforms that would entail broad implementation of such strategies. I conclude that reforms that strengthen parties while incentivizing the promotion of women's participation within parties offer the greatest potential for mitigating Brazil's crisis of representation, situating once more the goals of the women's movement within the broader democratic reform agenda.

I make explicit my point of departure, which is an understanding of democracy that entails both descriptive and substantive representation. Rather than appointing a few hundred elite white men to represent the interests of a population that is 51% female and 52% Afro-descendant, descriptive representation requires that representatives loosely mirror their constituents in demographic characteristics. In accordance with this vision of democratic governance, a legislature that is 90% male cannot adequately represent a majority female electorate. The same holds for race and ethnicity, religion, income, and educational background. In other words, representatives can best represent their constituents' interests when they themselves share those interests (Mansbridge 1999). This is, however, an incomplete conception of democracy, with substantive representation also playing an important role.

The chapter considers how institutions are gendered and can shape the quality of a democracy—both its representativeness and accountability, and contemplates the viability of institutional engineering in the context of formally weak but robustly gendered institutions. I close by reviewing avenues for future research.

Brazil's "crisis of representation"—in part manifested by weakly institutionalized parties and the underrepresentation of marginalized groups— can be mitigated by reforms that strengthen parties and incentivize their active promotion of women's political participation. Thus the goals of the women's movement and the broader movement for democratic reforms coincide once more. This book endeavors to elucidate the conditions that realize the goal of increased representativeness. As outlined in the 1995 Beijing Conference and reiterated in the Millennium Development Goals, the equalization of opportunities for women to reach the highest nodes of decision-making is a critical next step in the ongoing processes of democratization and development in Latin America and beyond.

2

Willing and Able: Party Institutionalization, Party Leadership, and Women's Representation

> If there is a single conclusion to be drawn from our account of the political representation of women, it is that their exclusion from politics is ubiquitous, operated through layer upon layer of established male dominated institutions (not least political parties) that are insulated by layer upon layer of formal and informal rules of exclusion.
>
> (Childs and Lovenduski 2013, 507)

The lingering underrepresentation of women in Brazil despite having the region's strongest women's movement (Alvarez 1990; Costa 2008), substantial socioeconomic progress (Special Secretariat for Policies for Women 2010), an increasingly receptive electorate (Brazilian Institute of Public Opinion and Statistics 2013), and two decades of experience with a gender quota for proportional elections poses an important challenge to Brazilian democracy. Not only does women's political presence remain woefully scarce even in the "representative" chamber of congress (Chamber of Deputies), but institutional remedies have thus far proven insufficient mechanisms for altering the predominantly masculine political landscape. I argue this failure results from the weak institutionalization of most Brazilian parties—itself a shortcoming confronting many third-wave democracies—and contend that the preponderance of inchoate parties has fostered a climate in which decisions on leadership and candidate selection lack transparency and the expectations of compliance with formal rules such as the gender quota are limited. Weakly institutionalized parties are also ill-equipped to level the playing field for female political aspirants because they lack clearly defined rules of the game for ascension within the party, rely on self-nomination, are unable to provide critical capacity-building opportunities, and suffer from a deficit of programmatic politics. Moreover, Brazilian party organizations are often dominated by men, with the near exclusion of women from leadership structures by many parties resulting in decision-making processes on candidate selection and support that are, at best, gender negligent.

The focus on parties as the key arbiters of women's political representation in Brazil offers superior explanatory power than several of the traditional explanations of women's (under)representation, which have emphasized economic development and culture (Inglehart and Norris 2003),[1] electoral systems (Darcy, Welch, and Clark 1994; Duverger 1955; Kenworthy and Malami 1999; Matland 1993; Moser 2001a; Rule and Zimmerman 1994), and the strength of leftist parties (Duverger 1955; Studlar and McAllister 1991). The following discussion considers the explanatory capacity of voter bias, electoral institutions, and strength of leftist parties for the Brazilian case, and then introduces the book's central claim—that weak party institutionalization and male domination of party leadership interact to sustain women's political exclusion, anchoring the theoretical contributions within a gendered institutions framework.

VOTER BIAS

Some of Brazil's most prominent female politicians hail from less developed, electorally smaller states; the country's recent presidential challenger candidate, Marina Silva, is a former environment minister and deputy and senator from the small Amazonian state of Acre. And of the six women who earned the honor of being the most voted candidate in her state in the 2014 Chamber of Deputies elections, five were from less developed states (under the national average), four were from states electing just 8 to 10 deputies (district magnitude ranges from 8 to 70), two were from smaller parties, and four were from non-leftist parties (Tribunal Superior Eleitoral 1994–2016).

Their relative success exceeds expectations derived from conventional wisdom, which considers voter bias to be the most formidable impediment to women's representation due to the glacial velocity of changes in cultural attitudes (Inter-Parliamentary Union 2000). Cross-national analyses have found *national gender ideology*—the extent to which the national sociopolitical climate is receptive to female politicians—to be a key predictor of women's overall legislative presence (Paxton and Kunovich 2003, 93). Indeed, the correlation between the 2010–14 World Values Survey (WVS) data ($N=56$) on perceived male political superiority and percent of women legislators (including the 33 countries displayed in Table 1.2 and 22 countries categorized as "not free" by the Freedom House) is negative (-0.42) and statistically significant, with voter bias alone accounting for 18 percent of the variation in women's representation (Freedom House 2016; Inter-

---

[1] Other renditions of the cultural argument look to structural manifestations of economic changes, such as women's workforce presence (Salmond 2006) and the welfare state (Rosenbluth, Salmond, and Thies 2006).

Parliamentary Union 2017; World Values Survey 1981–2014). Yet there is an apparent mismatch in Brazil, where relatively moderate levels of intense bias against women persist alongside a drastic underrepresentation of women (see Table 1.2).

While gendered expectations for the appropriate division of labor in public and private spheres have long dictated differential societal and political latitude afforded to women and men, scholars rooted in modernization theory assert that economic development will usher in gender egalitarian norms (Inglehart and Norris 2003, 8). According to the modernization approach, less developed contexts should therefore prove less favorable for women's representation, with more resistance among voters to the idea of women in politics and fewer opportunities for women to acquire sociopolitical capital. But cross-national evidence suggests that the modernization argument has lost ground with the diffusion of gender quotas (Tremblay 2012); seven of the top ten countries on the IPU's ranking of women's representation are in the global South, with Rwanda and Bolivia in the top two positions (Inter-Parliamentary Union 2017).

The Brazilian case offers additional reasons to question the explanatory capacity of the modernization approach. With a national-level Human Development Index (HDI) of 0.754, Brazil is ranked 79 of 188 countries, far higher than its IPU ranking of 154 (Inter-Parliamentary Union 2017; United Nations Human Development Report 2016). Subnational variation also lends support to skeptics of modernization theory; in Brazil's least developed region, the northeast, just 4.1% of respondents in a regionally representative 2010 survey strongly agreed with a statement of male political superiority, compared to 3.7% in the country's more developed southeastern region (Center for Studies and Advisory Services 2010). And as stated above, five of the six female "vote champions" in the 2014 elections were elected in less developed states.

In sum, explanations of women's electoral prospects that are driven by voter bias and economic development may not carry much weight in Brazil. First, the extant literature has drawn largely on aggregate-level evidence to substantiate its claims, a relationship that does not necessarily apply to the individual level. Moreover, while hostility to women in politics in Brazil persists, it is relatively moderate (See Table 1.2), even in the country's less developed regions. Finally, public opinion polls, the election and reelection of Dilma Rousseff, and the strong performance by several female candidates in recent legislative elections demonstrate substantial postulated support for women in politics throughout the country.

ELECTORAL INSTITUTIONS

Another prevalent explanation for women's (under)representation emphasizes the primacy of electoral rules. From discussions of gender quotas (Dahlerup 2006b; Franceschet, Krook, and Piscopo 2012; Krook 2009; Tremblay 2012;

Tripp and Kang 2008) and the relative benefits of proportional representation (PR) or plurality elections (Htun and Jones 2002; Matland 1993; Matland and Studlar 1996; Matland and Taylor 1997; Moser 2001a; Rule and Zimmerman 1994; Salmond, 2006), to analyses of how those factors interact (Jones 2009; Krook 2009; Piatti-Crocker, Schmidt, and Araújo 2017; Schmidt 2009; Schwindt-Bayer 2010; Tremblay 2012), the emphasis on electoral institutions so prevalent in contemporary political science (i.e., Cox 1997; Iversen and Soskice 2006; Peters 2005; Weingast and Shepsle 1995) is echoed in studies of women's representation.

A resolute consensus of the literature on women's representation and electoral systems is that the elections most conducive to women's representation are those conducted under closed-list PR rules with enforced gender quotas that include placement mandates (Ballington and Karam 2005; Htun and Jones 2002; Krook 2009; Moser 2001a; Tremblay 2008, Tripp and Kang 2008). In 2011, among 86 countries considered "free" by Freedom House, the average proportion of women legislators in countries with PR systems was 24.2 percent, more than twice that of plurality/majoritarian systems (11.1%) (Tremblay 2012, 7).

The most prominent explanation for PR's demonstrated superiority in electing women is the higher district magnitudes, or seats available per district, in PR elections. The higher district magnitudes of PR elections enhance proportionality by definition (Duverger 1954; Lijphart 1994; Taagepera and Shugart 1989), and by reducing the threshold required to gain a seat, also increase the viability of outsider candidacies unlikely to command a plurality of votes (Moser and Scheiner 2012; Schwindt-Bayer 2010). Moreover, by virtue of the multiple seats available per district, large district magnitudes facilitate "ticket balancing," whereby parties can reach out to particular constituencies (including women), promoting equity while maintaining party peace (Matland 1993; Matland 2005; Matland and Taylor 1997; Salmond 2006). Finally, single-member district (SMD) systems foster an incumbency advantage, while higher district magnitude elections tend to have a higher rate of turnover (Moser and Scheiner 2012; Schwindt-Bayer 2010), itself conducive to women candidates in electoral systems currently dominated by male incumbents.

Extremely high district magnitudes, however, are associated with a proliferation of parties, which often splits the seat share across parties, resulting in low effective magnitudes for each party. Party magnitude, or "the number of seats a party has (wins) in a district" (Matland 1993, 742), has thus been used as an alternative institutional variable explaining the positive correlation found between PR and women's representation (but see Jones 2009; Schmidt 2009). If parties win more seats, they are able to delve deeper into their candidate lists when allocating seats. In the context of closed-list elections with no placement mandates, this will help women since parties (unless mandated otherwise) tend to cluster female candidates at the bottom of their lists (Htun and Jones 2002; Moser and Scheiner 2012; Schwindt-Bayer 2010).

By enabling the use of placement mandates, PR's multimember elections also facilitate the mechanics of quotas (Htun and Jones 2002; Tremblay 2012). Placement mandates, which are unfeasible in SMD elections,[2] overcome the party tendency to place female contenders in unelectable list positions in closed-list elections (Htun and Jones 2002; Moser and Scheiner 2012; Schwindt-Bayer 2010). Resistance to quotas may also be more likely in the context of SMD rules, where the introduction of outsider candidates necessarily displaces traditional power holders. Again, the availability of multiple seats in PR elections is expected to enhance women's representation; when nominations are a scarce resource, the introduction of a quota is more likely to generate opposition from other contenders. As mentioned above and discussed at length in Chapter 3, Brazil's quota law does not work well in its high magnitude OLPR elections, which incentivize a vast quantity of candidates (5,866 in 2014), effectively precluding the regular distribution of lists of candidates to voters; lists are available in newspapers and online, but are alphabetized and so placement mandates do not offer the same appeal as they would in contests where the pre-election list ordering weighs more heavily (i.e., closed- or flexible-list elections).

Brazil's high district magnitude PR elections (8 to 70) have not, however, translated into significant gains for women. Looking to the 2014 elections, we see that the average proportion of women elected in the 11 states with a district magnitude of 8 (17.1%) was nearly double the average for the 11 states with the largest district magnitudes (8.7%). Moreover, as mentioned above, four of Brazil's six women "vote champions" in 2014 won in electorally smaller states. But as discussed by Matland (1993) and evidenced by Brazil's 35 political parties—28 of which won seats the 2014 Chamber of Deputies elections—high district magnitudes lead to a proliferation of parties. The 2014 elections also offer variation on party magnitude, with an average among winning parties of 1.8 (0.7 overall) and a high of 14 (PSDB in São Paulo). Yet the majority of deputies—50% of men and 67% of women—won election for parties with a party magnitude of 1–2. And neither district nor party magnitude is correlated with a state party's proportion of women candidates or elected (Tribunal Superior Eleitoral 1994–2016). Descriptive data on both district and party magnitude thus suggest those electoral system characteristics cannot explain the Brazilian case.

---

[2] Several parties (e.g., Canada's Liberal Party), however, implement the equivalent of placement mandates in SMD elections, mandating that their candidates for a certain percentage of "safe seats" are female. This stands in contrast to the common practice of parties that, seeking to merely gesture to gender equality, advance women candidates as "party standard bearers" or sacrificial lambs in contests the party has little to no chance of winning (Thomas and Bodet 2013).

A critical feature of most PR systems, but in fact contingent upon the ballot structure and party characteristics, is the tendency of (closed-list) PR elections toward party-centered competition. In the vast majority of countries with PR elections, closed-list rules dictate that voters cast their ballot for a party rather than a candidate (Schmidt 2009). In such a system, party reputation and platforms are more salient in the elector's vote choice than are the relationships personalized by clientelism, pork-barrel politics, and/or "identifier characteristics" that permeate candidate-centered elections (Valdini 2013a). Open-list variants of PR elections, however, significantly heighten the incentives to cultivate a personal vote (Carey and Shugart 1995; Thames and Williams 2010; Valdini 2013a) and are thus typically candidate- rather than party-centered; as developed further below, candidate-centered competition may disincentivize women's participation.

Closed-list PR's party-centered elections can also enhance women's representation through the mechanism of candidate selection. Whereas candidate-centered elections (whether majoritarian, plurality, or OLPR) often result in decentralized and inclusive candidate selection processes such as primaries, in closed-list PR elections the selectorate—the actors responsible for selecting candidates—is more likely to be centralized and exclusive (Hazan and Rahat 2006; Rahat and Hazan 2001). A centralized selectorate allows national party leaders to circumvent predominantly male "local power monopolies," freeing them to nominate outsiders such as women (Hinojosa 2009, 2012). While this does not guarantee that national party leaders will promote women's candidacies, they are more likely to select candidates that will benefit the party's overall fortunes and image, while local power monopolies tend to focus on preserving their own power (Hinojosa 2009, 2012). And as discussed below, due to a socialized gender gap in formal political ambition, women are significantly less likely to self-nominate than are men. When external rather than self-nomination is the norm, the effects of this gender gap are attenuated (Fox and Lawless 2004; Hinojosa 2009, 2012; Lawless and Fox 2005, 2010).

The simple dichotomization of electoral systems between majoritarian/ plurality and PR thus overlooks important variations in ballot structure and beyond. Accordingly, many recent studies have explored how certain characteristics (rather than categorizations) of electoral systems affect women's representation (Jones 2009; Krook 2009; Schmidt 2009, 2017; Thames and Williams 2010), with others emphasizing how the parties designing and mediating electoral rules may hasten/hinder women's political participation (Caul 1999; Childs 2013; Davidson-Schmich 2010; Kittilson 2006; Krook 2010a; Luhiste 2015; Verge and de la Fuente 2014).

POLITICAL PARTIES

As stated by Verge and de la Fuente, "despite playing a key role in the production and reproduction of gender effects in politics, political parties are the 'missing variable' in women and politics research" (2014, 68). This study responds to their call and joins the growing body of work emphasizing political parties, arguing that parties hold the key to understanding women's political marginalization in Brazil. I first survey conventional party-based explanations for women's representation focusing on ideology and the proportion of women in party leadership, and then explain how those characteristics interact with party institutionalization to condition women's electoral prospects in Brazil, embedding that theoretical contribution within the burgeoning literature on gendered institutions.

The left's historical emphasis on social equality—a stance hypothesized to be conducive to gender egalitarianism—generates the expectation that parties that lean left are more hospitable to women politicians (e.g., Duverger 1955). Yet much like voter bias, evidence linking ideology and women in party leadership to women's representation has almost exclusively been tested at the aggregate or party level rather than candidate level. Cross-national analyses upholding the influence of ideology (on overall proportions of women in parliaments) usually operationalize the concept as the strength of leftist parties based on the executive presence and/or proportion of seats in the lower house of congress held by leftist parties (Caul 1999; Kenworthy and Malami 1999; Kittilson 2006; Krook 2010b; Norris 1987; Reynolds 1999; Rule 1987; Schmidt 2009; Tripp and Kang 2008). The relationship appears not to hold in Brazil, where in the wake of the 2014 elections, leftist parties held 30.8% of congressional seats, the presidency, and 11 of 27 governorships (40.7%), yet women comprised less than 10% of the Congress (Chamber of Deputies 2015; Federal Senate 2015; Tribunal Superior Eleitoral 1994–2016).

Do the mechanisms connecting a country's tendency to elect a large share of leftists with the overall proportion of women legislators operate at the individual level? Countries with an affinity for leftist parties may have greater support for welfare state policies, which has been shown to enable women to enter the paid workforce—especially the public sector—and thus change working women's political interests sufficiently to induce an ideological gender gap, which in turn incentivizes electorally motivated parties to respond by competing for women's votes by augmenting their female parliamentary presence (Rosenbluth, Salmond, and Thies 2006). While it is not immediately clear how such logic would apply to the individual candidate running in a leftist party, we have historically seen a disproportionate representation of leftists among elected women in Brazil and elsewhere (Avelar 2001). Does this mean that women are electorally advantaged in leftist parties? If so, why? Must female contenders then run with a leftist party to have a shot at election? The fact that 28 of 51 women who won seats in the 2014 Chamber of Deputies elections did so in non-leftist parties (55%) suggests otherwise. May the salience of ideology's effect have declined via a "contagion from the left" effect, whereby the promotion of female candidates by (small) leftist parties drives all rational and competitive parties to advance female candidacies

(Matland and Studlar 1996; but see Kenny and Verge 2015)? The hypotheses must be assessed at the candidate level to discern their effects on individual women.

A few studies of women's representation have also looked to the role of women in national party leadership in promoting women's political participation (Caul 1999; Kittilson 2006; Kunovich and Paxton 2005). Female party leaders are able to "let the ladder down" to other women, using their position to convince traditionally male party leaders of the electoral utility of recruiting and training female candidates, and can also pressure for the adoption of internal gender quotas (Kittilson 2006; Kunovich and Paxton 2005).

This possibility becomes more likely as women approach a critical mass, conventionally deemed somewhere between 20 and 30 percent, and thus progress beyond the constraints of mere "token" status (Childs and Krook 2008; Kittilson 2006; Matland 1998). Childs and Krook trace the application of critical mass theory (Schelling 1978) to gendered dynamics to Kanter (1977), which subsequently spawned its use as a lens to explain why incremental increases in women's legislative presence have often not ushered in drastic changes in the substantive representation of women (e.g., Dahlerup 1988).

In a study of corporate men and women, Kanter finds that until minority groups reach at least "tilted" status—of a ratio around 65:35, the "dominants" (or majority, which in her case, are men) "control the group and its culture" while the minorities (women) confront "performance pressures ..., token isolation, which forces them to remain an outsider or become an insider by being a 'woman-prejudiced-against-women ..., and role entrapment, which obliges them to choose between alternative female stereotypes" (Kanter 1977, 966, cited in Childs and Krook 2008, 727). As their presence approximates titled status, members of the minority group can form alliances to diminish pressures and isolation, and are also increasingly free to differentiate themselves. Dahlerup applies Kanter's approach to the study of women in politics, concluding that "critical acts" are key, and what is "most significant is the willingness and ability of the minority to mobilize the resources of the organization or institutions to improve the situation for themselves and the whole minority group" (1988, 296, cited in Studlar and McAllister 2003, 236).

Although evidence that a critical mass of women legislators facilitates women-friendly policies or the election of more women remains mixed (Beckwith 2007; Beckwith and Cowell-Meyers 2007; Childs and Krook 2008; Studlar and McAllister 2003), as articulated by Beckwith (2007, 31), the critical mass argument may gain utility when tests operationalize the concept at the party level. Indeed, Kittilson (2006) finds strong support that a critical mass of women in national party leadership structures enhances women's representation. Leveraging Tarrow and McAdam's insights on political opportunity structures, Kittilson contends that "the addition of women to the subset of party elites may introduce a new perspective on the utility of women's votes," with women leaders introducing "new frames of meaning" for women's groups' demands for greater representation (2006, 26). Women in party leadership can thus provide a new outlook that convinces male leaders of the electoral value of promoting women's participation.

While women acting on behalf of women is not guaranteed (Htun and Power 2006), at a minimum, the inclusion of women in party leadership structures helps them to "stop functioning exclusively as masculine clubs" (Godinho 1996, 155), in turn facilitating the conquest of space for the voice of women at the decision-making table rather than ghettoizing them in women's sections as has long been the norm in parties around the world (Roza, Llanos, and Garzón de la Roza 2010). Indeed, women staffers in the Obama White House realized their collective strength despite being outnumbered (most top aides were male) by adopting a strategy of "amplification," repeating and crediting each other's ideas to amplify women's voices and enhance their impact on the president's decision-making. That strategy is reflective of the possibilities facilitated by a critical mass of female leaders; as White House senior adviser Valerie Jarrett herself explicitly stated, "I think having a critical mass makes a difference" (Eilperin 2016). Incorporating women in party leadership can itself capacitate women for high-level electoral campaigns, with service in party leadership often considered a "necessary apprenticeship" (Henig and Henig 2001, 48, cited in Kunovich and Paxton 2005, 521) for political aspirants.

Although the argument has yet to be empirically tested at the candidate level, women politicians do believe that the presence of women in party leadership is beneficial (Inter-Parliamentary Union 2000). Indeed, cross-national findings (aggregated across parties) suggest that women running in candidate-centered campaigns are bolstered by the presence of women in party leadership. This is because female party leaders have access to and are able to distribute material and institutional support to women candidates (Kunovich and Paxton 2005, 538), an argument I develop further below and test in subsequent chapters.

As of 2014, the mean proportion of women on the NECs of Brazil's 28 parties with seats in the Chamber of Deputies was 17.7 percent.[3] This average conceals significant variation across parties, with several parties including no women in their national leadership structures and even variation within the left, with the PT and PSB[4] respectively having 39% and 18% women in their national decision-making structures. While Brazil fares moderately on all of the obstacles discussed above, ranking 13th of 33 electoral democracies in terms of perceived male political superiority, having high magnitude (but open-list) PR elections with a gender quota (only recently enforced), and

[3] Calculated by the author using data from party websites and the Tribunal Superior Eleitoral (1994–2016). The Inter-American Development Bank's Gender and Political Parties in Latin America Initiative (GEPPAL) maintains regional data at the party level, gathered in 2009 and updated 2011–2012.

[4] The Brazilian Socialist Party (PSB) is a center-leftist party founded in 1947 and reestablished in 1985.

leftist parties holding 30.8% of congressional seats, its poor incorporation of women in party NECs is far more proportionate to its exceedingly low level of women in Congress. Although the other obstacles certainly persist at non-negligible levels, with 28.4% Brazilians expressing some skepticism of women's capacity for the political realm (6.7% strongly agree and 21.7% agree), and a quota that constitutes a far from ideal fit for open-list electoral rules, Brazil's middling status on these factors—with numerous countries faring much worse on these fronts, including those with significantly higher levels of women in parliament—simply cannot explain its severe underrepresentation of women in Congress. The expectation that incorporating women into party decision-making structures will facilitate increases in women's legislative representation, however, appears quite plausible. I consider how each of the abovementioned obstacles affects individual women's electoral prospects in the analyses ahead, first anchoring them within a gendered institutions framework.

GENDERED INSTITUTIONS

By revealing and explaining the differential effects of male-designed but allegedly "neutral" political institutions on men and women, feminist political science and sociology has made major inroads into the study of power, a profoundly gendered phenomenon (Acker 1990, 1992; Duerst-Lahti and Kelly 1995; Kenney 1996; Lovenduski 1998). Preeminent feminist political scientist, Joni Lovenduski offers a pointed critique of the extant parties' literature:

That the institutional sexism of the parties is apparently invisible to mainstream analysts of their ideologies and organizations is a major failing. The vast political science of party politics pays little attention to the effects of gender. Yet gender effects are present in both their ideologies and structures. ... Thus any study of political parties that fails to take account of gender effects will be inadequate. (Lovenduski 2005, 59)

More than two decades after Joan Acker (1990, 1992) and others offered their seminal contributions documenting the ways in which "universal" or "neutral" institutions are in fact highly gendered and have the effect of naturalizing power and leadership as masculine (Duerst-Lahti and Kelly 1995; Kenney 1996; Young 1989), much of mainstream political science remains gender blind. An emergent approach called *feminist institutionalism*, which combines feminist political science with new institutionalism, is poised to fill the gap (Campbell and Childs 2014; Krook and Mackay 2011).[5] The feminist

---

[5] The feminist institutionalism approach emerged through collaborative endeavors of the Feminism and Institutionalism International Network (FIIN), established in 2006. It "synthesizes insights from institutionalist theory and institutionally-focused feminist political science. *See* www .femfiin.com" (Mackay, Armitage, and Malley 2014, 93).

institutionalist approach builds on feminist analyses of gendered institutions, acknowledging political institutions as "sites of gendered power relations" that structure the expectations and opportunities afforded men and women (Mackay and Waylen 2014, 659). The framework helps to explain the gendered causes and consequences of the design, implementation, change, and continuity in formal and informal rules of the game (Kenny 2013, 2014; Mackay, Kenny, and Chappell 2010; Waylen 2017). "Political institutions are in a very real sense constructed on the basis of women's exclusion" (Kenney 1996, 462), and the gendered institutions and feminist institutionalist approaches illuminate the mechanisms that sustain that exclusion.

This book applies the gendered institutions framework to explain how Brazilian party politics contribute to women's underrepresentation. I demonstrate the gendered consequences of a preponderance of weakly institutionalized, male-dominant parties, and discuss the implications for the quality of Brazilian democracy. Responding to Miki Caul Kittilson's recent call, "The most promising new research highlights a web of gendered structures and institutions within parties. Attention to the gendered and dynamic nature of opportunities within parties is key to advancing research on gender and party politics" (Kittilson 2013, 536), this book centers the analysis on political parties, bridging mainstream discussions of party organization and institutionalization with feminist scholarship on gendered institutions to illuminate how weakly institutionalized, male-led parties feed a crisis of representation in Brazil.

PARTY INSTITUTIONALIZATION

For decades the significance of party (system) institutionalization for democratic governance has been a stalwart in the political science literature (Arter and Kestilä-Kekkonen 2014; Booth and Robbins 2010; Jones 2005, 2007, 2012; Mainwaring 1999; Mainwaring and Scully 1995; Schedler 1995; Shugart and Mainwaring 1997). Under-institutionalized parties—which lack "value-infusion" (Janda 1980) and stability (Huntington 1968) or "internal systemness" (Panebianco 1988)—have been shown to hinder identifiability, accountability, and programmatic appeals. Such tendencies are conducive to anti-system politics, and often result in a Wild-West style politics where each politician is on her own and collective party organizations are elusive.

But while the general issue of party institutionalization has enjoyed a rather salient position within the literature, surprisingly little has been said about its implications for the representation of women and minorities (but see Guadagnini 1993, Kittilson 2006, and Moser and Scheiner 2012).[6]

---

[6] I discuss Marila Guadagnini (1993) and Miki Caul Kittilson's (Caul 1999; Kittilson 2006) arguments from their studies of the Italian party system and Western European parties, respectively, below. Moser and Scheiner find that the condition of weakly institutionalized parties

This research then helps to fill this void, explaining the gendered consequences of party institutionalization, with explicit consideration given to how racial identity mediates those effects. In particular, I contend that the prevalence of weakly institutionalized parties in Brazil has undermined representativeness in four ways. (1) The absence of a norm of compliance has facilitated an environment in which internal and external formal laws are flouted, providing no clear means for ascension through the party, making it difficult for outsiders to gain entry, while also limiting the reach of the gender quota. (2) By emphasizing self-nomination it exacerbates the socialized gender gap in formal political ambition. (3) Amorphous party organizations are ill-equipped to provide critical capacity-building opportunities for women and other outsiders. (4) The rarity of programmatic appeals and dominance of personalist politics favor those with personal political and financial capital, which—due to raced-gendered wage inequities, traditional gender norms, and the still vastly white, masculine character of Brazilian electoral politics—tend to be white men. I develop and substantiate each of these points below.

"Lei Que Não Pega": A Norm of Non-Compliance

The inchoate character of the Brazilian party system has facilitated an environment in which formal rules remain nominal and informal norms and practices carry the day. A clear understanding of the rules of the game and expectation that those rules will be followed is less likely in weakly institutionalized parties because the few leaders that dominate such parties often operate beyond the bounds of formal rules. When outsiders cannot "anticipate the criteria" for ascending in the party organization, their path to a viable candidacy is obscured (Caul 1999, 81; Czudnowski 1975; Kittilson 2006, 29; Sacchet 2007). In contrast, when "formal institutions are transparent to all aspirants, they are not limited to those already on the inside. Where and when women and men can similarly discern these institutions, women's opportunities for advancement are enhanced (Lovenduski and Norris 1993)" (Kittilson 2013, 543).

As revealed by Guarnieri, although the formal rules of most Brazilian party statutes regarding candidate selection dictate hierarchical participation through conventions in a clear, predictable way, parties routinely abuse a provisional commissions mechanism (formally, intended for instances of limited party members) that enables domineering leaders to dissolve municipal or state directorates, and thus avoid the constraints of lower-level conventions or delegations and nominate whomever they want

---

negates the expected negative effects of single member district (SMD) systems relative to proportional representation systems due to the absence of SMD's usual mechanical effect of constraining the number of parties (2012).

(Guarnieri 2011).[7] Guarnieri offers compelling empirical evidence demonstrating the disproportionate use of the provisional commissions mechanism across all major parties, finding it especially heightened among those he characterizes as "weakly organized/monocratic" (Guarnieri 2011). His analysis demonstrates that the absence of strong party organizations substantially undermines the ability of outsiders to "anticipate the criteria" for ascending the ranks, as well as the substantial interparty and intraparty variation in Brazil.

Such a norm of (non-)compliance with internal party statutes may carry over into other realms, with party leaders accustomed to being held accountable to internal rules of the game more likely to comply with external rules such as the gender quota, in spite of its (until recently) weak enforcement. Indeed, studies from the international organizations literature have documented the greater likelihood of rule-bound states to comply with rarely enforced international agreements due to a norm of compliance entrenched in such states. "Political leaders accustomed to constitutional constraints on their power in a domestic context are more likely to accept principled legal limits on their international behavior; therefore, governments with strong constitutional traditions, particularly those in which intragovernmental relations are rule governed, are more likely to accept rule-based constraints on their international behavior" (Simmons 1998, 83–84).

I draw on the norm of compliance instilled by transparent and universal internal rules of the game and insights from the literature on gendered institutions to explain the significant variation across Brazilian parties in their responsiveness to the quota provisions. This yields superior analytical leverage than does the emphasis on the quota law's poor fit for the OLPR system and its only recent enforcement, which while certainly inhibiting its effectiveness, cannot explain variation across parties confronting the same Electoral Law. For Brazil's inchoate parties, the gender quota persists as a "lei que não pega" (roughly, "law on paper only") in spite of the 2009 mini-reform emboldening enforcement efforts (Wylie and dos Santos 2016). As mentioned above, only a quarter of state parties participating in the 2010 Chamber of Deputies elections met the 30 percent target for female candidacies. By 2014, most state parties still failed to comply with the reinforced quota law; nearly a third (30.7 percent) did not run a single female candidate (Wylie, Marcelino, and dos Santos 2015). The vast disregard of the quota in spite of the mini-reform

---

[7] Municipal conventions elect state conventional delegates and choose municipal directorates that in turn choose the municipal executive commission (which selects municipal candidates), with the process repeated at state and national levels. The executive commissions typically present an already composed candidate list (*chapa única*) at the conventions, with the expectation that they will be summarily approved (Braga 2008; Guarnieri 2011). The PT is somewhat different, which as of 2001, has direct membership elections for its party leadership through the Process of Direct Elections (PED) (Hunter 2010).

strengthening it and credible threats of enforcement is reflective of the abundance of weakly institutionalized parties.

I argue that weakly institutionalized parties are unlikely to comply with the quota because they—rather than existing as an organization in their own right operating under transparent rules of the game—suffer from a norm of non-compliance, dominated by a few leaders who function with impunity in decision-making. The dominant leaders of such parties often abuse the provisional commissions mechanism, allowing them to circumvent compliance with other party statutes, which in effect "permits the more absolute control over the formation of (party) lists" (Guarnieri 2011, 241). Indeed, a simple logistic analysis of state party compliance with the quota from 1998–2010 demonstrates that a one-unit increase in party institutionalization increases a state party's odds of quota compliance by 25.2 percent (see Appendix 4.3).[8]

Moreover, even in the few instances where Brazilian parties have complied with the gender quota, the quota's intended result has not been met. That is because party leaders often do not confront their deficit of female contenders until the last moment, at which point they fill the slots reserved for women with *candidatas laranjas*[9] (phantom candidacies/sacrificial lambs) with no intention of supporting their candidacies. The 2010 elections—the first after the 2009 mini-reform strengthened the quota—saw a striking number of apparent *candidatas laranjas*, with an average of 39.5 percent of female candidates earning less than one percent of the minimum vote acquired by a winning candidate in their state. For male candidates, this average was less than half that, at 16.6 percent. With 21 of 27 states having significantly more *candidatas laranjas* in 2010 than in 2006, I contend that the preponderance of female *laranjas* in 2010 constitutes an observable implication of the elite resistance to the reformed quota law.

So while a 2009 mini-reform enabled greater enforcement of the formal quota law, the decade-long disregard for the quota by Brazil's often inchoate and male-run parties was entrenched. Nearly 80 percent of women surveyed in a 2009 poll had never even heard of the gender quota more than a decade after its implementation (Brazilian Institute of Public Opinion and Statistics 2009), suggesting that for the majority of parties and electors, the law existed only in the books, or "para ingles ver,"[10] with no real intention of earnest or even formal

---

[8] This is calculated applying a new party institutionalization index (PII), introduced in Chapter 4.

[9] According to a Brazilian etymologist from the University of São Paulo, using the term *laranja* (orange) to describe a figurehead or pawn is thought to have emerged in the 1970s, with two potential origins: (1) the juice of the orange is extracted, leaving only the tasteless remains behind, and (2) people in countries prohibiting the public consumption of alcohol injected their booze in an orange to avoid getting caught (Perissé 2010).

[10] "For the English to see," meaning a law existing on paper only. The Brazilian idiom references the country's 1831 law declaring free any Africans arriving in Brazilian ports, which was

compliance. As discussed at length in Chapter 3, the emphasis of Brazil's gender quota on the formal rules of candidate selection leaves much to be desired.

In the Brazilian case, such formal electoral rules have long gone unheeded with local bosses often calling the shots.[11] Aspiring candidates cozy up to mayors and governors to gain entry and access to resources (Samuels 2003), with the coveted *dobradinha* (an alliance between candidates running concurrently, displayed prominently in electoral propaganda materials and events) serving as visual evidence to this practice. For most parties, decisions are made within an exclusive realm of state party elites rather than according to clearly defined rules of the game, with the leadership simply presenting candidate lists at state party conventions. Party leaders in inchoate parties dominate decision-making, acting with impunity at the cost of transparency and accountability.[12] For the few more institutionalized parties, party delegates propose and vote on individual candidates or slates of candidates at local or state meetings (Braga 2008). Such parties will be more compelled to comply with the gender quota than will parties in which formal rules are regularly flouted.

Finally, as developed further in the following point, recent work on candidate selection in Latin America contends that exclusive, centralized candidate selection processes facilitate the nomination and election of women, while decentralized processes (as is the case throughout Brazil; Samuels 2008) undermine women's prospects for inclusion due to the influence of "local power monopolies" generally dominated by men (Hinojosa 2009, 2012). In sum, Brazil's electoral infrastructure and a widespread lack of transparency and associated norm of non-compliance have gendered effects; in limiting women's ability to anticipate the criteria for selection and deterring all efforts at leveling candidate selection processes, the country's gender quota has been effectively nullified.

Self-Nomination and the Gender Gap in Political Ambition

In the weakly institutionalized context where "political parties have limited resources, internal processes are unpredictable, and individual party leaders dominate the parties, with the party as an institution weak to nonexistent"

---

promulgated as a symbolic act to appease the British, who had prohibited the slave trade in 1807 (Bethell and Carvalho 1985, 696).

[11] Guadagnini paints a similar portrait in her analysis of the Italian party system. "Although the various parties have developed formal rules governing the selection of candidates ... in fact candidate selection has been a prerogative of top party leaders. Furthermore ... mere inclusion on a party's list of candidates is not highly significant as it does not mean that an individual's candidacy has the real support of his or her party" (1993, 183).

[12] Hicken and Kuhonta's volume on party systems in Asia similarly claims, "Where parties are weakly institutionalized, they tend to be thinly organized temporary alliances of convenience and are often extensions of or subservient to powerful party leaders" (2014, 309).

(Jones 2005, 12), self- rather than external nomination is the norm. Such an "entrepreneurial" (Morgenstern and Siavelis 2008) system has led many to conclude that "parties do not perform even minimum functions of gatekeeping" with "routes to power" deemed "open for easy ascent" (Schedler 1995, 18; Samuels 2008); entrepreneurial systems have, however, proven daunting for women and other marginalized groups. Morgenstern and Siavelis's authoritative volume on candidate selection in Latin America characterizes Brazil as conducive to the "entrepreneur" ideal type of legislator due to its high-magnitude open-list elections, federal structure, weak legislative parties, localized and exclusive candidate selection, reliance on self-selection, inchoate party organizations, and campaigns financed privately, rather than by parties (2008, 18).

The authors assert that those variables converge to make parties "unnecessary for entrepreneurs to succeed in getting on the ballot and being elected" (Morgenstern and Siavelis 2008, 23). But while a weakly institutionalized party system may facilitate partisan outsiders' entry due to the diminished ballot control of party leaders in such systems (Mainwaring 1999), those "outsiders" gain entry by converting their economic and/or social capital into political capital (Bourdieu 1986). So although the notion that the electoral context constitutes "nonregulated markets" open to all (Schedler 1995, 18) is formally true, the reality brought into focus through a gendered analysis is that open or "entrepreneurial" systems tend to reproduce societal inequities and maintain patterns of marginalization. If party leaders do not actively recruit women, female political aspirants will be hesitant to confront this elitist system. As professional career paths become increasingly viable alternatives for women, who comprise 46 percent of the economically active workforce (Brazilian Institute of Geography and Statistics 2010),[13] and Brazil's political system remains executive-dominant, women may understandably be hesitant to seek election to a position they perceive as corrupt and ineffective (LAPOP n.d.).[14]

[13] It is not my intention, however, to gloss over the fact that women continue to confront foreboding obstacles in the workforce, where they receive less pay for equal work (Brazilian Institute of Geography and Statistics 2010), have to wait longer to get promoted (Institute for Applied Economic Research 2010b), and remain disproportionately absent from leadership positions, with less than 14% of the leadership positions in Brazil's top 500 businesses being women. These figures are even less favorable for Afro-descendant women, with recent data revealing the intersecting sources of oppression; on average, white women and Afro-descendant women earn 69.1% and 39.5% of what white men earn (Institute for Applied Economic Research 2014).

[14] LAPOP data from 2008 and 2010 surveys suggest that women have significantly lower levels of agreement that the federal government is fighting government corruption, confidence in political institutions, and satisfaction with Brazilian democracy than do men. Notably, in the 2014 wave of LAPOP, those gendered differences had disappeared or reversed (LAPOP n.d.). Jalalzai and dos Santos (2015) argue that President Rousseff's presence has furthered symbolic representation of women in Brazil, which they posit may be responsible for the suggested trend (personal communication with authors). Yet as discussed below, gendered differences in political interest persist.

The socialized gender gap in formal 'political ambition,' or the expressed desire to seek political office, intensifies the marginalization of outsiders (Lawless and Fox 2005, 2010; Schlesinger 1966). Through socially constructed gender roles and norms, women have long been dissuaded from entering the public sphere, particularly at the national level. Three manifestations of traditional gender socialization identified by Lawless and Fox, the leading authorities on gender and political ambition in the United States, are instructive. Traditional gender socialization, along with disenchantment with the corrupt and ineffective state of politics, inherent risk and uncertain reward of seeking office, and increasing opportunities in the professional realm, comprise part of an interconnected web of gendered factors dissuading women from entering the formal political sphere. First, traditional family role orientations mean that most women shoulder the burden of unpaid domestic responsibilities, constituting a "second shift" on average equal to 26.6 hours each week (Hochschild and Machung 1989; Institute for Applied Economic Research 2012).[15] For the vast majority of women, party activism and high-level electoral office would entail a "triple shift."

Political party meetings are often held at night, which due to gendered ideas about appropriate societal roles, poses a disadvantage to women because they are expected to be home with their family. *Marianismo* (the counterpart to machismo) idealizes women as "semi-divine, morally superior and spiritually stronger than men" (Stevens 1973, 62) and in addition to sustaining traditionally gendered family obligations, can make it less acceptable for women to leave the house at night to attend party meetings. As discussed in detail in Chapters 4 and 6, the women I interviewed frequently cited the incompatibility of party meeting times and locations with their familial commitments. Moreover, elected federal deputies divide their time among their home district and Brasília,[16] spending Monday to Thursday afternoons in the Congress and the extended weekend at home. As discussed above and corroborated in interviews, that schedule poses significant constraints to

---

[15] Although the vast socioeconomic inequalities within Brazil have made domestic labor an affordable commodity for even the middle class, most women nonetheless endure time constraints on the basis of traditional gender norms. Income has no relationship to the number of hours men dedicate to domestic chores, and 76.6% of women earning more than eight times the minimum wage and 93% of women earning less than the minimum wage spend on average 25.2 hours a week on domestic chores, constituting a second shift for most women (Institute for Applied Economic Research 2011, 37). It is critical to recognize that paid household help is disproportionately served by Afro-descendant women, 21.8% of whom are employed in domestic labor (compared to 12.6% of white women). Afro-descendant domestic workers are also far less likely to have formal employment and its associated protections, and therefore receive less pay than white domestic workers (Institute for Applied Economic Research 2011, 29).

[16] Poor road conditions and Brazil's vast geographic terrain add to the logistical difficulties of the commuter schedule—deputies from many states in the Amazon region have to travel five hours by plane(s) to reach Brasília.

women, who remain largely accountable for household responsibilities. Former Minister of the Special Secretariat for Policies for Women, Eleonora Menicucci, stated, "Women enter politics, but they have a world that goes with them: the house, their kids ... so they enter politics either when they are single, or when their kids have already left the house" (Quoted in Grayley 2012). The fact that 72 and 81 percent of male Chamber candidates and elected deputies, respectively, are married, but only 56 and 61 percent[17] of female Chamber candidates and elected deputies are married lends support to Minister Menicucci's claim.

Second, the vastly white, male dominant character of Brazil's political institutions[18] entrenches a masculinized ethos of politics that privileges masculinity, devalues femininity, and normalizes white, male power. This not only discourages women from getting involved in politics, but also maintains a set of rules and norms that was designed by and for white men (Duerst-Lahti and Kelly 1995; Kenney 1996; Lovenduski 2005; Young 1989). An extensive literature on institutional change suggests that those in power formulate institutions to preserve their own position (North 1990; Thelen 1999), and Brazil's predominantly white, male politicians are by no means exempt from that tendency (Gatto 2016).

As illustrated in Chapter 6, some women have managed to overcome such gendered constraints by conforming to traditional gender roles, working with their party, or, as is the case with former President Rousseff, converting their expertise from the professional world into political capital. Yet, like many women politicians, Rousseff was initially encouraged to embark upon electoral politics and run for the presidency by a male party leader, former President Lula, who had appointed her to serve as Minister of Mines and Energy and Chief of Staff. Even Brazilian women with great personal ambition often espouse a disdain for electoral politics and are hesitant to enter an arena which they perceive to be not only vastly male dominant, but also extremely corrupt and ineffective.

Indeed, nearly all of the female politicians I interviewed, questioned, and studied have cited external encouragement rather than some internal affinity for electoral politics in their decision to run for office. As articulated by Susan Carroll and Kira Sanbonmatsu in their recent study of US state legislators, "a traditional model of ambition, in which candidacy is self-initiated, offers a less adequate account of how women reach office than of how men do so" (2013, 42). Women's decisions to run are rarely made independently or autonomously, but rather, represent "relationally embedded decisions," whereby women take

---

[17] These differences are calculated using candidate data from 1994–2014, and are statistically significant at the $p < 0.001$ level.

[18] The few recent prominent exceptions such as President Dilma Rousseff belie the widespread pattern of exclusion of women from high-level office demonstrated in Table 1.4.

into consideration the "beliefs and reactions, both real and perceived, of other(s)" (2013, 45).

Lawless and Fox's final point about traditional gender socialization speaks to the resilient gendered psyche, "a deeply embedded imprint that propels men into politics, but relegates women to the electoral arena's periphery," which is instilled and sustained by traditional gender role expectations and the masculinized ethos of politics (2005, 10–11). Despite economic development and cultural progress, from an early age girls continue to be socialized as caregivers rather than leaders. The internalized results of this traditional gender socialization are manifest, with pervasive gender gaps in political interest, political knowledge, and political efficacy identified in the US case (Moore 2005). In the 2014 Latin American Public Opinion Project (LAPOP) surveys, Brazilian women reported significantly lesser levels of political interest than did men, with 6.4% and 9.4% of women and men, respectively, saying they were very interested in politics, and 40.1% of women and 33.0% of men indicating no interest (LAPOP n.d.). Experimental and observational evidence demonstrate that self-promoting behavior enhances public perception of one's competence, yet women are penalized for self-promotion while men are rewarded for it (Correll, Thébaud, and Benard 2007; Rudman 1998). By "violat(ing) prescriptive stereotypes" of femininity, self-promoting or assertive women "are derogated as interpersonally hostile ... (and) personally disliked" (Correll et al. 2007, 7).

> Women, in essence, tend not to be socialized to possess the qualities the modern political arena demands of its candidates and elected officials. Whereas men are taught to be confident, assertive, and self-promoting, cultural attitudes toward women as political leaders, expectations of women's family roles, and the overarching male exclusiveness of most political institutions leave an imprint suggesting to women that it is often inappropriate to possess these characteristics. (Lawless and Fox 2005, 11)

Although I unfortunately do not yet have access to such experimental or extensive survey data in Brazil, the empirical evidence cited above, interviews discussed in Chapters 4 and 6, the gendered treatment of women in the media (Finamore and Carvalho 2006; Miguel and Biroli 2009, 2011; Paiva 2008), and my own observations of the double binds confronted by President Rousseff in her 2010 campaign[19] give me no reason to suspect that such traditional gender roles would be more egalitarian in Brazil than they would in the US case discussed in Lawless and Fox (2005, 2010), Carroll and Sanbonmatsu (2013), Correll et al. (2007), Moore (2005), and Rudman (1998).

---

[19] I surveyed media coverage of President Rousseff's campaign for an expert survey solicited for Murray and Piscopo's manuscript on the double bind confronted by women in executive elections. The "double binds" are lose–lose scenarios in which women are at once penalized for being too feminine and too masculine, are considered either too young or too old, or too connected or too independent, and are often criticized for a lack of experience when attempting to emphasize their novelty (Murray 2010; Murray and Piscopo n.d.).

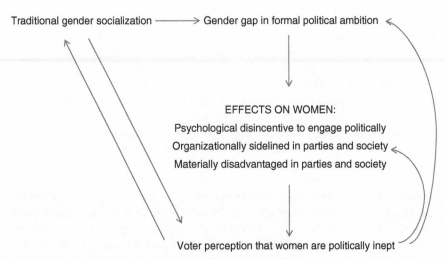

FIGURE 2.1 Voters, Parties, and Women's Representation

Figure 2.1 maps the gendered processes and structures conceptually, demonstrating the interacting effects of traditional gender socialization on individual women's formal political ambition, public opinion of women in politics, and the structural disadvantages confronted by white and Afro-descendant women in parties and society. The outcome of these gendered-raced processes and structures is a resilient gender gap in formal political ambition.

The problems of the formal ambition gender gap are compounding, with women more likely than men to doubt their qualifications for office and less likely to be encouraged to run (Fox and Lawless 2004). Hinojosa confirmed those findings in her study of gender and candidate selection in Chile and Mexico, concluding that while men were open about their political ambition, women would defer to the party, stating that they would do "whatever the party asks of me" (2009, 389). In concordance with the literature on the US, Hinojosa found that women were less likely than men to espouse political ambition, with the constructed gender norms regarding women's appropriate societal roles remaining a powerful psychological constraint on their ambition (2009, 2012). Building on those findings and the parallels with those cases illustrated above, I expect that similar dynamics operate in Brazil and argue that women's hesitance to self-nominate coupled with the entrepreneurial character of Brazilian elections renders active party recruitment essential for their meaningful inclusion in formal politics.

Amorphous Party Organizations

Weakly institutionalized parties are also characterized by amorphous party organizations that provide few opportunities for less experienced political aspirants to ascend the ranks and hone their political capital. Such parties—in addition to eschewing a universal set of rules and thus negating the ability of women and other outsiders to "anticipate the criteria" for candidate selection and to hold leaders accountable to those rules (Caul 1999, 81; Kittilson 2006, 29) as discussed above—are ill-equipped to recruit and develop viable female candidacies. Often a one-man show rather than a cohesive organization, inchoate parties may have few internal leadership positions, are dominated by a small and unchanging cadre of party elite, offer little in the way of programmatic training, and exist as a mere electoral vehicle with inadequate mobilizational activities.

In contrast, an institutionalized party is more likely to facilitate training opportunities and other mechanisms for capacity-building. The availability of capacity-building opportunities may help all candidates, but is not gender-neutral. Studies suggest that women are in general more risk averse than men (Eckel and Grossman 2008; Schubert 2006) and therefore unlikely to throw their hat in the ring without the requisite preparation. An observable implication of that tendency is that women candidates are in general much more qualified than male candidates (Anzia and Berry 2011). Opportunities for capacity-building thus not only provide organizational support by enabling women to acquire the requisite toolkit, but they also instill a powerful psychological effect, boosting women's political ambition.

Chapter 4 elaborates further on the capacity-building opportunities offered in institutionalized parties—with a strong organization, programmatic platforms, and material and human resources, but a quick preview of the Communist Party of Brazil (PC do B) is illustrative. The PC do B regularly offers multiday courses in "political formation" or training through its National School of Formation (ENF), where party members take several levels of courses on philosophy, class and the state, economics, socialism, and the party, and are certified at advanced levels only after they submit a monograph or article with themes and bibliography to be approved by senior party members (PC do B 2010). The ENF works with state party organizations to offer "local courses that help in the training and realization of candidates" (PC do B 2010). This reality sharply contrasts with the entrepreneurial candidate setting painted in Morgenstern and Siavelis (2008) and Samuels (2008), which while capturing the overall patterns of Brazilian politics, gloss over significant variation across the parties. By providing women and other outsiders with opportunities to acquire the requisite toolkit, a strong party organization can level the playing field for these contenders while also enhancing their confidence, thus preparing them for the difficult path to elected office.

Personalist Politics

As demonstrated by Ames (2001) and others, weakly institutionalized parties are particularly susceptible to personalist politics. Such parties are fleeting, have weak societal roots, and due to weak party discipline and shifting loyalties within constituencies, coalitions, and ideologies, party switching is rampant (Ames 2001; Mainwaring 1999; Nicolau 2006). True outsiders will often lack the personal appeal necessary to thrive in such a system (Guadagnini 1993). Institutionalized parties are more conducive to "less 'advantaged' groups and individuals, like women, who possess fewer external resources" (Guadagnini 1993, 181). In contrast, personalist competition advantages those with accumulated personal political capital, "all those resources based on status (social position, professional career etc.) and/or on strong external group support and/or on a political career through which an individual can develop an extensive electoral base ... [as well as] the capacity to channel funds from the business community and other powerful interests to the party leadership" (Guadagnini 1993, 181).

The personalist politics that dominate weakly institutionalized parties result in candidate-centered elections that require a contender to distinguish herself from her co-partisans, thus necessitating an inflated campaign budget. Tellingly, the correlation between both the self- and corporate-financed proportion of candidate campaign contributions and party institutionalization is negative and statistically significant. That suggests that candidates in weakly institutionalized parties were compelled to either seek funding from corporate donors, or finance their own campaign. In the 2010 elections to the Chamber of Deputies, campaign contributions to winning candidates averaged over R$1.1 million (more than US$600,000), with campaign finance being one of the strongest predictors of an individual candidate's chance of success (Samuels 2001a, 2001b; author calculations).

Given Brazil's pervasive raced-gendered wage inequities (Institute for Applied Economic Research 2014),[20] with men earning 30 percent more than women of the same age and education level (Downie and Llana 2009), such expensive campaigns further disadvantage women and minoritized groups while favoring incumbents and others with established material capital. Personal wealth allows candidates to self-finance their costly campaigns and also affords status and access to business elites and corporate donations. While winning candidates to the Chamber of Deputies (1994–2010) drew on average 47.9% of their campaign budgets from corporations, female deputies tended to raise significantly less from corporate donors (39.4%) than did male deputies (48.6%). Overall, women candidates received only 14.6% of their funds from

---

[20] The average monthly salary for white men and women, respectively, in 2014 was R$2393.12 and R$1654.12. For Afro-descendant men and women, it was R$1374.49 and R$945.92 (Institute for Applied Economic Research 2014).

corporations, compared to 24.8% for male candidates. The average campaign contributions of female candidates was R$225,575 (R$834,621 for elected), while male candidates averaged R$347,400 (R$997,389 for elected). In sum, the necessity of personal wealth and/or access to corporate donors in weakly institutionalized parties disadvantages most women and other outsiders.

The emphasis on programmatic politics in institutionalized parties, however, allows women to focus the campaign on their policy positions rather than their individual characteristics. In addition to being more palatable to female political aspirants, who in general eschew the combative climate of personalist campaigns (Ellis 2002; Escobar-Lemmon and Taylor-Robinson 2008, 350), emphasizing programmatic policy appeals may enhance women's electoral prospects in two ways. First, it allows for a more collective campaign, where party militants rather than material resources driven by personal wealth or political capital fire up the base, and parties shoulder more of the financial burden. Indeed, the correlation of the proportion of candidate campaign contributions from parties and party institutionalization is positive and statistically significant. Second, as discussed in Chapter 3, ideas-based campaigns may diminish the elector's reliance on gender (and racial) stereotypes to evaluate the candidate (Valdini 2013a).

The Gendered Effects of Party Institutionalization: The Argument in Brief

The debilitating effects of weakly institutionalized parties for women's electoral prospects are compounding. Not only are such parties apathetic in complying with the spirit or even the letter of the quota law, but the necessity to self-nominate upholds the constructed gender gap in formal political ambition, fabricating a robust psychological disincentive to participate. Amorphous party organizations sustain that disincentive by inhibiting the development of political skillsets and organizational support, essentially leaving women (and others) to survive on their own devices. The prevalence of personalist politics and prioritization of personal political and financial capital then exacerbates inchoate parties' inability to develop capacity-building opportunities for women and other outsiders.

In contrast, as displayed in Table 2.1, institutionalized parties provide a more hospitable environment for outsiders as they are more likely to actively recruit candidates, have clear internal rules, offer opportunities for political training, emphasize programmatic politics, and have and distribute material party resources. These benefits bolster female candidates, both in the eyes of voters, and in candidates' own self-perceptions. Nevertheless, I argue that the prospective psychological, organizational, and material support effectuated by party institutionalization is conditioned by the presence of party leadership that is willing to mobilize that potential in the name of actively promoting women's participation. Thus, a given party's level of institutionalization

TABLE 2.1 *The Gendered Effects of Party Institutionalization*

Capacity—Party Institutionalization	Weakly Institutionalized	Well-Institutionalized
(1) * Norm of compliance	No transparent rules for candidate selection and ascending party ranks, no expectation of quota compliance with "good ole boy" network prominent in leadership and candidate selection	Clear and universal rules for leadership and candidate selection, outsiders can anticipate the criteria for ascension and there is an expectation of quota compliance
(2) * Nomination	Self-nomination exacerbates gender gap in political ambition	External nomination, active recruitment mitigates gender gap in political ambition
(3) * Organizational strength	Insufficient organizational strength (human/material resources) to offer capacity-building opportunities	Training opportunities offer chance to acquire requisite toolkit, enhances confidence and perceived viability
(4) Personalist/ Programmatic	Personalist politics favors those with accumulated personal political and financial capital	Programmatic politics favors more collective campaigning, minimizes prospect of gender and racial stereotyping by electorate

* Will—Contingent upon women-friendly leadership promoting these opportunities for women.

influences its *capacity* to support women, but its *will* to do so is driven primarily by the party leadership's willingness to champion women's involvement (see Figure 1.2).

IDEOLOGY, PARTY LEADERSHIP, AND THE "WOMEN-FRIENDLINESS" OF PARTIES

Most explanations of the "women-friendliness" of parties center on ideology, with some expecting its declining salience (Matland and Studlar 1996). I build on the latter expectation, arguing that any remaining observed effects of ideology on women's electoral prospects are indirect. I contend that the mechanisms substantiating leftist parties' apparent superiority in accommodating women's demands operate through their greater propensity to: (1) be institutionalized, which grants them the capacity to support women, and (2) to have a strong female presence in their top decision-making bodies, which enhances their will to support women. I expect those two tendencies to hold for leftist parties across a variety of electoral contexts, and use the Brazilian case to test them and their implications for women empirically in Chapter 4.

Drawing on prior studies of OECD democracies that have demonstrated that "women's presence among the party leadership is the single most important mechanism for initiating women's gains in parliament" (Kittilson 2006, 37), this book's central claim is that Brazil's most women-friendly parties are those that are well-institutionalized and have a critical mass of women in top party decision-making structures. In male-dominant parties, women are typically ghettoized into women's sections often denied any say in important party decisions. Such parties call upon their women's sections to mobilize women in the electorate with the sole intent of rallying support for the campaigns of male candidates (Llanos and Sample 2008; Roza et al. 2010, 9–10). In contrast, parties with a substantial female presence in party leadership afford women a space at the decision-making table. That access increases the likelihood that women can amplify each other's voices and thus have real influence within party decision-making structures, which in turn enables them to "let the ladder down" to female political aspirants (Godinho 1998; Kittilson 2006; but see Verge and Claveria 2016).

As mapped conceptually in Figure 2.2, when women occupy leadership positions in institutionalized parties, they can hold parties accountable to

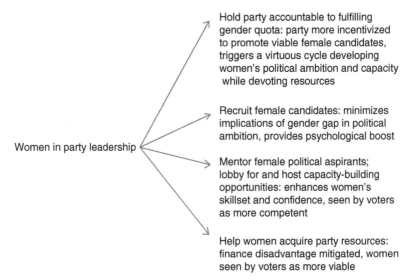

FIGURE 2.2 The Gendered Effects of Women in Leadership of Institutionalized Parties.

the quota provisions, recruit and train female candidates, and mobilize party resources on behalf of female aspirants and their campaigns. Indeed, a simple logistic analysis of party compliance with the quota demonstrates that state parties with a critical mass of women in their leadership are 76.2 percent more likely than those without a critical mass of women leaders to comply with the quota (see Appendix 4.3).[21] As summarized by expert José Eustáquio Diniz Alves, "The more women in party directorates, the more support to women to run for office. The parties that have women in their party leadership are able to elect more women" (quoted in Agência Patrícia Galvão 2011). A critical mass of women leaders in institutionalized parties enables them to carry out a range of "critical acts" (Dahlerup 1988), portrayed in Figure 2.2.

Under historical conditions of inclusion, women in leftist parties are more likely to have developed critical organizing experience and thus able to ascend through the party ranks. In many non-leftist parties, women have only recently been prioritized with the quota reforms and evolving electorate preferences. This means that while there are almost as many female candidates in non-leftist parties as in leftist parties, women in non-leftist parties are less likely to have reached leadership ranks. In short, there is a certain degree of path dependence, with leftist parties traditionally more conducive to women's participation than non-leftist parties. But despite the tendency of leftist parties to be sympathetic to issues of equality and positive discrimination measures, I contend that leftist ideology per se is an insufficient condition for the effective promotion of women's participation. Rather, institutionalized parties must incorporate women in party decision-making, thereby enhancing the prospect that the ideals of equality espoused but often relegated to the realm of the theoretical in leftist parties will be realized.

Analyzing rich variation across Brazilian state party organizations, this book explores the gendered effects of party institutionalization and women's presence in party leadership, examining how those party characteristics interact to explain variation in women's electoral prospects across Brazil. As demonstrated in the analyses that follow, parties must have *both the capacity* (institutionalization) to promote women's political participation and the *will* (women in party leadership) to do so.

---

[21] And notably, a simple logistic regression of state parties (1998–2010) suggests that a party's ideology does *not* predict its odds of complying with the gender quota.

3

Brazil's Quota Law and the Challenges of Institutional Change Amidst Weak and Gendered Institutions[*]

> The candidate quota ... proved insufficient to overcome the true blockade faced by the women in the quest to occupy participatory spaces in the political world.
> (Senator Vanessa Grazziotin, Deputy Dâmina Pereira, and Deputy Elcione Barbalho in Senado Federal 2015).

> The quotas have never been a threat to men's power in politics.
> (Celi Pinto, quoted in Moura 2014).

Countries around the world have achieved considerable gains in women's representation through the implementation of gender quotas (Krook 2009; Piatti-Crocker, Schmidt, and Araújo 2017; Tripp and Kang 2008). Whether through reserved seats, legislated candidate quotas, or voluntary party quotas, such mechanisms have contributed to leveling the playing field between male and female contenders in the heretofore pervasively masculine political realm. The results, however, have not been uniformly positive. In several cases there have been instances of elite resistance and backlash, leading to a circumvention of the intended results of the quota (Franceschet, Krook, and Piscopo 2012; Krook 2015a, 2015b).[1] Moreover, as will be explored below, not all electoral and party systems have proven conducive to the use of quotas.

This chapter contends that Brazil's *Lei de Cotas* has been substantially undermined not only by the country's open-list electoral context, but also by its abundance of inchoate and male-dominant parties. I start with a brief explanation of Brazil's electoral and party systems that establishes for the reader a baseline understanding of Brazilian elections. I then present electoral systems as a competing argument for women's limited descriptive representation in Brazil, and discuss the hypothesized effects of the electoral system on women's representation. The analysis draws on cross-national

---

[*] Segments of this chapter appear in Wylie and dos Santos (2016).
[1] In Bolivia for example, (predominately male) party elites actually tweaked the names of candidates to feign compliance with their electoral quota (Costa Benavides 2003).

experiences under the condition of preferential (candidate-based list) voting to explain the gendered effects of open-list and other preferential electoral systems,[2] and how they may disadvantage female contenders. This is followed by a brief discussion of the role of women in contemporary Brazilian politics. Next, I review the literature on gender quotas and the global campaign to fast-track women's representation through quotas, and discuss the process of quota design, implementation, and reform in Brazil. Building on those discussions, I advance an alternative argument to the conventional singular (and often disembodied) focus on electoral systems, instead explaining how Brazil's electoral context is shaped by both the electoral and party systems, with gendered implications for the quota law. I conclude that because electoral rules do not exist in a vacuum, formal institutional fixes to electoral systems must be paired with reforms that explicitly target the informal practices of party elites.

Driven by select success stories widely trumpeted by international organizations and pressures to appear "modern" and inclusive, the use of quotas to enhance women's representation has diffused around the world (Dahlerup 2006b), reaching countries from Rwanda (ranked 1st worldwide, with 61.3% women in the lower house) to Afghanistan (ranked 53rd with 27.7% women in the lower house) (Inter-Parliamentary Union 2017). Since closed-list proportional representation elections greatly facilitate the mechanics of candidate quotas (Htun and Jones 2002), many analyses hastily dismiss quotas in open-list proportional representation (OLPR) elections such as those in Brazil and move on.[3] As a result, knowledge of the effects of quotas on women's representation in preferential voting systems in general and OLPR in particular remains limited (but see Piatti-Crocker, Schmidt, and Araújo 2017). Discussions of the effects of party systems on the functioning of quotas are even more elusive.[4]

If quotas are to be promoted as mechanisms to achieve equality in legislative representation, we must broaden our understanding of their interactions with the electoral and party systems in which they are embedded (Krook and Zetterberg 2014). This chapter contributes to that mission, responding to Mona Lena Krook's call—"Ideally, future work will focus on analyzing single cases and situating them in relation to other quota campaigns" (2009, 226)—and thus enhancing our comprehension of how quotas may be successfully employed to empower marginalized groups. It also reveals that while the

---

[2] Examples of preferential voting systems are open-list PR, flexible formats, single transferable vote, and the single non-transferable vote (Schmidt 2009).

[3] Brazilian political scientist Clara Araújo (1999, 2001a, 2001b, 2005, 2017) has been a pioneer in research on the Brazilian quota, but much work remains.

[4] A noteworthy exception is Mona Lena Krook's recent study, which examines how systemic (electoral and party systems), practical, and normative institutions are gendered, can hinder women's representation, and can be ameliorated by reserved seats, party quotas, and legislative quotas, respectively (2009).

Brazilian quota law is certainly limited in scope by the open-list format of its proportional elections, that feature cannot fully account for its striking failure to induce real change in the tendencies by many parties to marginalize women, nor can it explain the variation among parties. Rather, a key component of the explanation for why the quota has failed rests in the inchoate and male-dominant character of most Brazilian parties, for which the quota law remains a *lei que não pega* (law on paper only) and where, in the absence of effective party organizations, candidate recruitment and support are driven by the whims of domineering personalist party leaders. This conclusion has fundamental implications for reform efforts, which must work to strengthen parties if they are to achieve significant advances in the representation of women and other marginalized groups.

BRAZIL'S ELECTORAL CONTEXT

The Brazilian legislature is bicameral, with an upper house (Senate) and lower house (Chamber of Deputies) comprising 81 and 513 members, respectively. Elections to the Chamber of Deputies are held every four years, concurrently with presidential, gubernatorial, senatorial, and state legislative assembly elections. Each of Brazil's 27 districts elects multiple statewide representatives to the Chamber of Deputies, with a minimum of 8 and a maximum of 70. Those floor and ceiling limits on the number of representatives per district, or "district magnitude," induce a high degree of malapportionment, with the most populous state, São Paulo, having more than ten times more inhabitants per deputy than the least populous state, Roraíma (Brazilian Institute of Geography and Statistics 2010).

Voters cast a single vote for federal deputy, and while they can vote either for a party (*voto de legenda*) or a candidate, 91.9% of valid votes[5] cast in the 2014 Chamber of Deputies elections were for a candidate (21.7% of *legenda* votes were for the governing Workers' Party [PT] alone).[6] Coalitions across Brazil's 35 registered political parties are common, and often afford political influence to smaller parties in spite of an electoral threshold. Seats to the Chamber of Deputies are allocated using the Hare method to calculate the electoral quotient threshold—the minimum votes a party/coalition list must collectively earn to gain a seat—with each list that meets that threshold granted one seat per electoral quotient it collectively earns; the d'Hondt highest averages method is then used to distribute remaining seats (Carvalho 2006; Lamounier and Amorim Neto 2005).

Seats are subsequently divvied up among each party/coalition list according to each candidate's preference votes. For example, if a candidate attains the

---

[5] The "valid votes" total used in electoral calculations excludes blank and null ballots (as of 1998) (Tribunal Superior Eleitoral 1994–2016).

[6] Calculated by the author (Tribunal Superior Eleitoral 1994–2016).

third highest quantity of votes in her coalition, but the coalition only wins enough total votes (equal to the sum of its candidates' preference votes and the member parties' *legenda* votes) for two seats, that candidate is not elected[7] but remains the highest ranked substitute (*suplente*). Substitutes are called upon when elected members leave office before their term is up. It is quite common for federal deputies to contest the mayoral post, with municipal elections staggered by two years with presidential, gubernatorial, and federal and state legislative elections. From 1996–2016, on average 4 senators and 92 federal deputies ran for mayor or vice-mayor. Of the five senators and 87 federal deputies in the 54th Congress (2011–2014) who ran for mayor in the 2012 elections, 25 were ultimately successful (Congresso em Foco 2012; DIAP 2016). This practice means that substitutes often reach office, with the 54th Congress (2011–2014) including 158 substitutes who were called to serve as federal deputies.[8]

Brazilian elections—even for the proportional contests—are largely candidate-centered affairs. This is a by-product of the OLPR system used in elections for federal and state deputy and municipal councilor, with electors casting their votes for candidates rather than for parties (as is the case in closed-list PR elections).[9] The open-list format incentivizes fellow partisans to compete amongst themselves (Ames 2001; Carey and Shugart 1995; Nicolau 2006; Nicolau and Schmitt 1995), leading to extremely expensive candidate-centered campaigns as candidates spend to lend visibility to their individual campaign (Samuels 2001a, 2001b). The name and number of candidates rather than the party label often figure most prominently. In the (usually electronic) voting booth, electors are not presented with a list of candidates but instead must recall and key in the four-digit number of their candidate for federal deputy.[10] The first two digits are the party number, with the second two indicating the candidate.

Electoral campaigns distribute flyers (*"santinhos"*) as guides for electors to bring into the voting booth with the numbers and images of candidates figuring prominently. Candidates scramble for the most desirable (easy to remember) number, with incumbents entitled to their number from prior campaigns and newcomers left to pick among the remaining available numbers. Throughout the 45-day[11] campaign season, candidates contract drivers to circulate their

---

[7] The 2015 mini-reform (13.165/2015) stipulates that candidates earning at least 10 percent of the electoral quotient will be elected, provided their party/coalition list collectively meets the electoral quotient.

[8] Calculated by author using data from the Chamber of Deputies website (www2.camara.gov.br).

[9] As mentioned above, the *voto de legenda* option is infrequently exercised.

[10] Candidates for president and governor run under the two-digit party number, senatorial candidates have a three-digit number, and state legislative assembly candidates have a five-digit number. Electors must recall all of those numbers, or as is common, bring in *santinhos* (a cheat sheet of sorts), to reference as they key the numbers into the electronic voting machine.

[11] Prior to the latest mini-reform (13.165/2015), campaigns were 90 days.

districts in cars with external speakers blasting jingles that pound home their number for constituents.

Until the 2015 mini-reform (13.165/2015), campaigns were privately financed by donations from individuals and corporations, with an increasing share of revenues coming from parties. In the 2010 Chamber of Deputies elections, on average 16.1 percent and 43.5 percent of reported candidate funds came from corporations and party organizations, respectively. The campaigns are extremely expensive; the average contributions for winning candidates in 2014 reached R$1.4 million (over half a million dollars), with 35.3 percent on average coming from corporations.[12] The 2015 mini-reform imposed a ceiling for campaign spending and banned corporate funds, corresponding with a Supreme Court decision that corporate donations to the campaigns of candidates and parties were unconstitutional (*Notícias STF* 2015). The 2016 municipal elections were thus held with no (declared) corporate contributions and a ceiling for campaign spending, leading to a substantial drop in costs; candidates and parties spent over R$6 million in the 2012 elections, and less than R$3.5 million in the 2016 elections (Tribunal Regional Eleitoral de Alagoas 2017). As discussed further in Chapter 8, parliamentarians anticipate difficulties in cutting their costs for the upcoming 2018 state and federal elections and are scurrying to establish a public fund that can substitute the corporate revenue (Senado Notícias 2017).

Campaigns are indeed costly, with candidates spending a significant portion of their budgets traveling the large distances usually required to run a statewide campaign. For example, Amazonas (Brazil's largest state) is more than double the size of Texas at 1.5 million square kilometers, without the benefit of a well-maintained highway system. The production of campaign publicity materials (flyers, banners, stickers, etc.) often consumes the bulk of candidate budgets (Speck and Mancuso 2015).

While candidates are also responsible for paying to produce their media advertisements, which can be quite expensive, the federal government actually allocates free television and radio air time to each party, with purchased air time being strictly forbidden and even "earned" media being highly regulated during the campaign season.[13] Negative campaigning—including parodies or other sketches by media outlets ridiculing particular politicians—is also illegal. For recent elections to the Chamber of Deputies, a 25-minute segment (split across the statewide district's candidates) was broadcast twice a day, three days a week (Tuesday/Thursday/Saturday), on all open (non-cable) television channels and radio stations for the 90-day

---

[12] Among all candidates in the 2014 Chamber of Deputies elections, the average campaign expenditures were R$247,476 (about US$100,000), with 22.8 percent coming from corporate sources.

[13] If the Tribunal Superior Eleitoral (TSE) deems a media outlet to have non-equitable coverage of candidates, fines are assessed.

campaign season in the form of *Horário Gratuito de Propaganda Eleitoral* (HGPE, Free Hour of Electoral Propaganda), and also in off-years for party building in the form of *Horário Gratuito de Propaganda Partidária* (HGPP, Free Hour of Party Propaganda). The 2015 mini-reform limited the campaign season to 45 days and cut the HGPE time from 60 to 50 minutes daily for 35 days (instead of 45 days), reducing the allotment for candidates to the Chamber of Deputies to 12.5-minute segments, which are broadcast twice daily (*Lei Eleitoral* 13.165/2015, Article 47). The federal government has allocated this time in part (one-third) equally among parties and coalitions[14] and in part (two-thirds) in proportion to the size of their congressional presence (*Lei Eleitoral* 9.504/1997, Article 47).[15] How parties subsequently divvy up the HGPE time among candidates has historically been at their discretion, although mandates for equitable distribution of HGPE and HGPP time are the subject of proposed political reforms.

As predicted by Duverger's Law, the mechanical and psychological effects of Brazil's proportional representation electoral system have resulted in a plethora of parties, with 35 currently registered and an effective number of parties at the legislative level (ENPP) of 13.22 in 2014 (Gallagher 2015; Tribunal Superior Eleitoral 1994–2016). It is important to note, however, that over a third of the seats in the Chamber of Deputies and the majority of the Senate seats are currently held by the top three parties (PT, PMDB, PSDB), with the PT and PSDB winning six of the seven presidential elections held since the country's return to democracy.

The PMDB, or Brazilian Democratic Movement Party, is a catch-all party that emerged from the Brazilian Democratic Movement (MDB), the only sanctioned opposition party for most of the 1964–1985 military regime. Although the PMDB has not run its own viable presidential candidate since it won the (indirect) 1985 election, it remains a highly sought-after coalition partner that has alternately supported the rival parties, the PSDB and the PT. The PMDB is the party of former President Rousseff's vice-president, Michel Temer, who is currently the acting president. As a big tent party, the PMDB faces significant internal divisions, but has hopes to run its own presidential candidate in the 2018 elections (Carta Capital 2015, July 15).

The Brazilian Social Democracy Party (PSDB) was originally a center-left off-shoot of the PMDB, but since its 1988 founding has drifted rightward and become known for its support of neoliberal economic policies and technocratic directives, in addition to administrative decentralization and anti-corruption efforts. The PSDB's most prominent politician is the widely

[14] To qualify, parties/coalitions must currently have representation in the Chamber of Deputies.
[15] The 2015 mini-reform altered the allocation method to 10 percent equitable distribution to all parties/coalitions contesting the election, with the remaining 90 percent distributed in proportion to the party's representation in the Chamber of Deputies. In the case of coalitions, that 90 percent figure is calculated for majoritarian elections based on the seat share of the top six parties of the coalition, and for proportional elections based on the seat share of all parties in the coalition (13.165/2015).

respected social scientist and popular former president, Fernando Henrique Cardoso (1995–2001), who is credited with stabilizing Brazil's fiscal and political systems after rampant hyperinflation and the impeachment process of former president Fernando Collor de Melo (1990–1992). Many of its standard bearers have been tainted by the ongoing corruption probe, notably including former presidential candidate, Aécio Neves (Garcia 2017; Oliveira and Netto 2017).

Finally, the Workers' Party (PT) is "Latin America's largest, most organized and arguably most innovative left party" (Hunter 2010, 2). Founded in 1980 by São Paulo union leaders, liberation theologists, and leftist intellectuals and artists, the PT was pivotal in mobilizing the citizenry on a grassroots rather than corporatist basis and bringing democracy back to Brazil (Hunter 2010; Keck 1995; Meneguello 1989). The PT was seemingly in perpetual opposition until Luíz Inácio Lula da Silva (Lula) finally won his fourth bid for the presidency in 2002. The PT subsequently grew tremendously and retained the presidency from 2002 to 2016, with Lula's former chief of staff, Dilma Rousseff, gaining election in 2010 and reelection in 2014, and then being impeached in 2016 in a controversial move characterized by some as a parliamentary coup (e.g., Santos and Guarnieri 2016).

One of the most defining characteristics of Brazil's party system stems from its open-list variant of proportional representation legislative elections. The OLPR system formally diminishes the ballot control of party leaders, with candidates' rank order on lists and thus prospects for a seat determined not by the party leader but by candidate vote share. Until 2002, the *candidato nato*, or "birthright candidate," provision actually guaranteed incumbents a place on the party list, even if they had switched parties since first gaining election. This can result in weakened party discipline and undermine the significance of party labels for constituents. While a voluminous debate exists over the end product of the Brazilian party system, with Figueiredo and Limongi being the most prolific advocates of the view that presidential power and intra-legislative mechanisms induce party discipline and cohesion in spite of OLPR (1995, 2000), "there is much less debate over the (anti-party) incentives of the electoral rules" (Desposato 2006, 7–8).

The diminished ballot control by party leaders, the prevalence of candidate rather than party voting by electors, and the intraparty competition those factors induce led Carey and Shugart to characterize Brazilian elections as having a high degree of personalization (1995). Moreover, under the condition of intraparty competition, evidence suggests that the incentive to cultivate a personal vote increases with district magnitude (Carey and Shugart 1995; Shugart, Valdini, and Suominen 2005).[16] This is because candidates must

---

[16] Interestingly, the authors found district magnitude to be negatively correlated with the likelihood of a personal vote for systems without intraparty competition (Shugart, Valdini, and Suominen 2005; Valdini 2013a).

differentiate themselves from the mass of candidates running in their party and others.

As demonstrated in the US and comparative literatures, the personal vote—"that portion of a candidate's electoral support which originates in his or her personal qualities, qualifications, activities, and record" (Cain, Ferejohn, and Fiorina 1987, 9)—reifies the "electoral connection" (Mayhew 1974), incumbency, and personal wealth (Ames 1995; Carey and Shugart 1995). In such a system, candidates may also successfully use "identifier characteristics" indicating their societal grouping to distinguish themselves (Shugart, Valdini, and Suominen 2005). While voters often use party label as a heuristic, or information shortcut, in their decision-making calculus, voters may also employ such candidate traits, with "the sex of a candidate [being] one of the 'cheapest' bits of information to gather" (Valdini 2013a, 80).

That is particularly likely in Brazil's highly competitive OLPR elections, where a staggering number of candidates competing for the elector's single vote render party label of dubious value. Several iterations of Brazil's Electoral Law (including 4.737/1965, 6.990/1982, 7.454/1985, 9.100/1995, and 9.504/1997) allow each party to advance *excess candidacies* that exceed the number of available seats in a district in proportional elections (Lamounier and Amorim Neto 2005).[17] In the 2014 Chamber of Deputies elections, the average number of candidates across Brazil's 27 statewide districts was 217, with more than 1200 contesting São Paulo's 70 seats including 81 candidates from the *Partido Verde* (Green Party—PV) alone (three were elected). Amidst a sea of candidates (over 11 per seat, reaching 17.7–18.8 per seat in São Paulo

---

[17] Electoral law going back to 1965 permits each party excess candidacies, in total equal to 133% of available seats in districts with 30 seats or less (4.737/1965). In 1976, the provision was extended to 300% for municipal legislatures (6.324/1976). By 1982, the provision appears to have applied to all districts regardless of size, allowing 133% in the Chamber of Deputies elections, 150% in the state Legislative Assembly elections, and 300% in elections to the municipal legislature (6.990/1982). In 1985, the excess candidacies provision for the Chamber of Deputies elections was extended to 150% of available seats. The provision was lifted for the 1994 elections (Lamounier and Amorim Neto 2005); in the 1994 Chamber of Deputies elections (the first year for which we have candidate-level data), just four state parties advanced excess candidacies. In 1995, the provision was reintroduced at 120% for municipal legislatures, with several exceptions based on a party's delegation in the Chamber of Deputies that would allow more excess candidacies for larger parties (9.100/1995). From 1997 to 2015, the law allowed each party or coalition to advance total candidacies equal to 150 or 200 percent, respectively, of available seats in proportional elections; for elections to the Chamber of Deputies and state Legislative Assemblies, smaller states (less than 20 seats in the Chamber of Deputies) allowed each party or coalition to advance total candidacies equal to 200 or 300 percent, respectively, of available seats (9.504/1997). A 2015 reform removed the additional excess candidacies allowance for coalitions (now both single party and multiparty lists are allotted excess candidacies equivalent to 150% of available seats) and reduced the state size threshold from 20 to 12 Chamber of Deputies seats (party/coalition lists in states with district magnitude less than 12 are permitted 200%) (13.165/2015). By 1998, the norm of advancing excess candidacies was institutionalized (Araújo 1999; Tribunal Superior Eleitoral 1994–2016).

and Rio de Janeiro), it is typically those with personal connections and wealth that rise to the top.

WOMEN AND THE PERSONAL VOTE

Recent studies find that the personalization of elections often has a negative effect on women's representation (Thames and Williams 2010; Valdini 2013a). As discussed in Chapter 2, personalist elections and parties benefit individuals with accumulated personal capital, which given gendered and raced wage inequities, tends to be white men. In Brazil's OLPR system, where preference and party label votes pool to the coalition/party for the inter-list allocation of seats, and preference votes determine the intra-list allocation of seats, the votes won by most candidates are in the end effectively redistributed to the list's top performing candidates. "In this game, those with the most votes in each party win, which the majority of times, means white men with more resources and control of the party machine" (Congresso em Foco 2014, 17).

Interestingly, earlier scholarship—based primarily in Western European countries—had anticipated a positive effect of preferential voting on women's representation, presuming party elites to harbor more bias against women than would the electorate (Darcy, Welch, and Clark 1994; Rule and Zimmerman 1994). Valdini explains the discrepancy by demonstrating that the personal vote has a conditional effect on women that is contingent upon (even moderate levels of) voter bias against women (2013a). In countries where voter bias is nearly absent, the personal vote does not have a significant effect on the overall proportion of women elected, a finding she expected would also apply to individual women's electoral prospects.[18]

To be precise, Valdini finds that when the percent of World Values Survey (WVS) respondents in a country agreeing with the statement "men make better politicians than women" is very low (one standard deviation below the mean of 22), the marginal effect of the personal vote on women in the legislature is not statistically different from zero. As more and more respondents strongly agree with this statement, the effect becomes increasingly negative (Valdini 2013a). With 28.2% of Brazilian respondents in the 2014 wave of the LAPOP survey agreeing with that statement, it is plausible that the personal vote[19] is exercising a negative effect on women's representation in Brazil (LAPOP n.d.; World Values Survey 1981–2014).

Yet as demonstrated in Table 3.1, if the electoral disadvantage for women posed by the incentive to cultivate a personal vote is conditioned by voter bias, the severity of women's underrepresentation in Brazil seems excessive given relatively moderate levels of bias against women. Even countries with

---

[18] Personal communication with Valdini, April 30, 2011.

[19] Valdini applies Carey and Shugart's 0–6 cumulative scale measuring the personal vote, which rates (0–2) ballot composition, vote pooling, and the number/level of votes (1995).

TABLE 3.1 *Preferential Elections, Voter Bias, and Women's Representation*

Quota Type and Country	% Women in Lower House	Bias against Women (% Agreeing)
Legislated and Party Quotas		
Brazil	10.7	28.2
Dominican Republic**	26.8	43.3
Ecuador	38.0	26.9
El Salvador**	32.1	24.8
Greece	18.3	—
Honduras**	25.8	29.6
Peru	27.7	19.9
Poland	28.0	36.2
Legislated Quotas		
Colombia	18.7	28.5
Indonesia*	19.8	61.0
Panama**	18.3	36.7
Party Quotas* **		
Chile	15.8	28.2
(PDC, PPD, PS)	16.0	
Cyprus	17.9	36.1
(DISY, EDEK)	19.0	
Luxembourg	28.3	—
(CSV, The Left, LSAP, Greens)	29.5	
Switzerland*	32.5	14.9
(Socialist Party)	58.1	
No Quotas		
Finland*	42.0	19.1
Latvia	16.0	—
Liechtenstein	12.0	—
San Marino	26.7	—

Notes: * World Values Survey (1981–2014); ** AmericasBarometer (Latin American Public Opinion Project, years 2008, 2012, 2014); *** Includes women's representation nationally and among the parties with quotas.
Sources: Género y Partidos Políticos en América Latina (n.d.); Inter-Parliamentary Union (2017); Quota Project (2017); Schmidt (2009); World Values Survey (1981–2014); Personal communication with Matthew Shugart; www.camara.cl/camara/diputados.aspx#tab.

comparable and higher levels of bias among voters outperform Brazil in terms of women's legislative presence (Inter-Parliamentary Union 2017; LAPOP n.d.; World Values Survey 1981–2014). In a 2010 nationwide survey, 81.0–83.8 percent of respondents disagreed or strongly disagreed with similar statements regarding perceived male political superiority, with only 4.1–4.7 percent strongly agreeing (and an additional 12.1–14.3 percent agreeing) (Center of Studies and Public Opinion 2010).

Moreover, Colombia, Dominican Republic, Ecuador, El Salvador, Greece, Honduras, Indonesia, Peru, and Poland have all had significantly greater success combining legislated gender quotas with preferential voting than has Brazil, which ranks lowest among all countries employing preferential elections, including those with no quota mandates (see Table 3.1). In sum, while Brazil's OLPR electoral system does pose a disadvantage to women, it cannot fully account for their near exclusion from political decision-making, nor can it explain interstate and interparty variation within Brazil. To understand the gendered consequences of Brazil electoral institutions, it is critical to consider how political parties mediate electoral rules, and how formal and informal rules interact to affect women's electoral prospects. First, I contextualize that discussion with a brief history of women's participation in Brazilian politics.

WOMEN AND POLITICS IN BRAZIL

As discussed in Chapter 1, the extreme underrepresentation of women persists in spite of the strength and breadth of the women's movement, their vast participation in informal politics and among the party rank-and-file, and significant societal progress. Since gaining the right to vote by Getúlio Vargas' presidential decree in 1932—itself the result of a prolonged battle for women's suffrage—women's political progress in Brazil has been gradual (see Table 3.2). Vargas' authoritarian *Estado Novo* phase (1937–1945) and the 1964–1985

TABLE 3.2 *Women's Representation in the Chamber of Deputies (1932–2014)*

Year	Candidates	Elected	Year	Candidates	Elected
1932	1	1	1978	—	4
1935	—	2	1982	58	8
1946	18	0	1986	166	26
1950	9	1	1990	229	29
1954	13	3	1994	185	32
1958	8	2	1998	348	29
1962	9	2	2002	480	42
1965	13	6	2006	627	45
1970	4	1	2010	929	45
1974	4	1	2014	1723	51

Source: Avelar (2001); CFEMEA; Tribunal Superior Eleitoral (1994–2016)

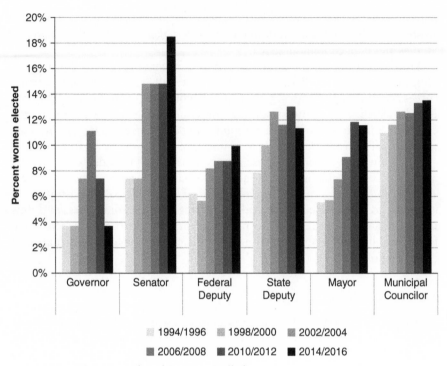

FIGURE 3.1 Women's Political Progress Stalled

military regime posed setbacks to this crawling progress. While a handful of women did serve during the period of military rule, it was mostly as surrogates for their husbands or male relatives who had been imprisoned, exiled, or otherwise declared ineligible through the infamous Institutional Act Number 1, in what was a largely ceremonial congress (Avelar 2001). Throughout this period, women remained economically and politically marginalized. As late as 1988, 78 percent of working women were employed in the lowest sectors, earning only 60 percent of that earned by men (Institute for Applied Economic Research 1988, cited in Avelar 2001).

Nevertheless, women mobilized in great numbers in the Amnesty and *Diretas Já* (Direct Elections Now) movements of the 1970s and 1980s, helping to re-democratize Brazil (Alvarez 1990). Their activism propelled women's engagement in formal politics and in 1986, 26 women were elected to the Constitutional Assembly. The so-called *lobby do batom* (lipstick lobby) of the Constitutional Assembly achieved impressive results and revitalized women's insertion into the formal political realm. In the second election to occur since the implementation of the gender quota, the 2002 elections saw another increase in women's political presence. It has since, however, more or less plateaued across elected offices (see Figure 3.1).

TABLE 3.3 *Women in Brazilian Politics*

Elected office	% Women (2015)	Appointed post in bureaucracy	% Women (2009)
Governor	3.7	Federal Minister (2015)	13.2
Senator	16.0	State Secretary	16.5
Federal Deputy	9.8	Municipal Secretary (capitals)	19.9
State Deputy	12.9	Municipal Secretary	8.0
Mayor	11.0		
Municipal Councilor	13.4		

To clarify the pervasively masculine character of Brazilian politics, a few points regarding the incumbency advantage and the revolving door are in order. Although the abovementioned *candidato nato* (birthright candidate) provision no longer exists, and rates of renewal are higher in the Brazilian Congress (an average of 46.2 percent from 1994 to 2010) than that of many countries allowing reelection, incumbency remains the key predictor of electoral success. Even after controlling for several candidate (sex, education, occupation, marital status, campaign finance), party (ideology, party magnitude, women on NEC), and district (Human Development Index) characteristics, incumbents were 5–10 times more likely to win election than non-incumbents in the 1994–2010 Chamber of Deputies elections.

Moreover, this renewal, or "oxygenation" as it has been called in Brazil, has itself historically occurred among the politically savvy, with it "difficult (for an aspirant) to reach the parliament without having had some type of political experience" (Santos 2000, 105). While Samuels' (2003) work on political ambition in the context of Brazilian federalism demonstrates that most politicians in Brazil do not seek a legislative career (using it instead as a springboard to subnational offices), it is also true that there is essentially a revolving door linking elected and appointed positions, with many politicians returning to the Congress after serving as mayor, governor, or even president. Of the federal deputies serving from 1987 to 1999, 19.8 and 72.3 percent (respectively) had already won executive and legislative elections in prior years, with 39.1% having been previously appointed to the bureaucracy (30.5% in the primary post) (Santos 2000, 102–104).

Yet, such a "political trajectory" has proven the least accessible to women (Álvares 2004). In short, the widespread claim of permeability of Brazil's Chamber of Deputies rings hollow for those without some kind of prior political experience. As shown in Table 3.3, women comprise a meager 3.7–19.9 percent of all bureaucratic and elected posts (other than the presidency) (Special Secretariat for Policies for Women 2010), constituting a "vicious cycle" of exclusion that is difficult to break (Pinheiro 2007, 83). The incapacity and/or unwillingness of most Brazilian parties to promote women's participation have essentially closed the traditional party-based trajectory to women. As will be discussed in Chapter 6, most of Brazil's few female politicians have managed to break the cycle of exclusion by toting traditional gender norms, inheriting familial political capital, or converting capital acquired through their experiences outside of formal politics into the requisite political capital.

An explanation of the limitations of Brazil's quota requires a brief survey of the international discourse and widespread push for the use of quotas to remedy gender inequities, followed by a discussion of the processes of quota design, implementation, and reform in the Brazilian case.

FAST-TRACKING WOMEN'S REPRESENTATION

Confronting the generally glacial pace of cultural changes, many nations have looked to quotas and other institutional reforms as promising mechanisms for fast-tracking the political participation of marginalized groups. Indeed, the more than 100 countries that have implemented gender quotas have achieved marked results in enhancing the representation of women, with cross-national studies finding quotas to be the single greatest explanatory factor of women's representation (Tripp and Kang 2008).[20] At least 20 countries employ minority quotas, but cross-national evidence suggest those do more to benefit minority men than women (Hughes 2008, 2011). As illustrated by the Brazilian case, given variation in the design and enforcement of quotas and the nuances of the electoral and party systems in which they are embedded, such institutional remedies have in many countries proven insufficient agents for enhancing women's representation.[21]

The Platform for Action agreed upon at the Fourth UN World Conference on Women in Beijing in 1995 shifted the discourse on women and politics toward targeting mechanisms of exclusion and affirmed the goal of women's equitable decision-making power, recommending the use of positive affirmative action to

---

[20] With a sample of 153 countries (77 with a quota), Tripp and Kang found the effect of gender quotas to be positive and statistically significant. Constructing a baseline model (setting other common explanatory factors to their mean), they find that the addition of a quota raises the percentage of women elected from 9.3 to 16.1, a jump of more than 70 percent (2008, 351).

[21] Furthermore, recent studies have shown the insufficiency of quota laws in achieving meaningful substantive representation ("politics of ideas," Phillips 1995), due not only to the possibility of unintended consequence of such laws limiting their benefactors' credibility and policymaking latitude (Franceschet and Piscopo 2008), but also to the heterogeneity of these groups and their interests (Franceschet, Krook, and Piscopo 2012) and the gendered institutional context in which policymaking takes place (Beckwith 2007; Beckwith and Cowell-Meyers 2007; Piscopo 2014). This study, however, is limited to explaining the conditions under which women get elected.

achieve equality (Dahlerup 2006b, 4). Women's movements leveraged this discourse to confer legitimacy to still controversial quota measures, with international organizations such as the UN, the International Institute for Democracy and Electoral Assistance (International IDEA), and the Inter-Parliamentary Union (IPU) playing an active role in promoting quotas (Dahlerup 2006b; International IDEA 2015; Inter-Parliamentary Union 2000).

In 1992, the IPU issued a strong resolution emboldening the drive for equitable representation, "The concept of democracy will only assume true and dynamic significance when political policies and national legislation are decided upon jointly by men and women with equitable regard for the interests and aptitudes of both halves of the population" (Inter-Parliamentary Union 1994; Pintat 1998). The Beijing Platform subsequently asserted that "without the active participation of women and incorporation of women's perspective(s) at all levels of decision-making, the goals of equality, development and peace cannot be achieved" (Fourth UN World Conference on Women 1995, Article 181). In sum, by the mid-1990s, the goal of women's empowerment had gained tremendous visibility, with quotas becoming the go-to solution to remedy their persistent exclusion from political power in many parts of the world (Dahlerup 2006b).

With 16 of 18 Latin American democracies adopting legislated gender quotas, it is considered the leading region in the drive to fast-track women's representation through quotas.[22] Eager to differentiate themselves from military regimes and accrue both domestic and external legitimacy, post-dictatorial governments have espoused a rhetoric of "good governance," a discourse often associated with equality and rights for marginalized groups (Araújo and Garcia 2006). The story of Argentina's impressive success was widely trumpeted—just four years after introducing the quota in 1991, the Argentine Chamber of Deputies saw a fivefold increase in women's legislative presence. Referred to as the "Argentina 'contagion effect,' " countries across the region (and beyond) implemented party and legislative quotas in the late 1990s (Araújo and Garcia 2006; Marx, Borner, and Camionotti 2007; Piatti-Crocker et al. 2017).

BRAZIL'S LEI DE COTAS

The use of gender quotas in Brazil was initiated by the PT, which in 1991 instituted a requirement that party directorates must at minimum comprise 30 percent women. In 1993, the Unified Workers' Central (CUT), the country's largest union, followed suit. Although discussions of the successes of these measures as well as the Argentine quota appeared in reports from meetings of

---

[22] Venezuela's 1997 gender quota was declared unconstitutional in 2000, reducing the number to 15. Of the two remaining countries, Chile recently approved a quota that should soon be implemented (pending judicial approval), and Guatemala has voluntary party quotas.

the women's movement in preparation for the 1995 Beijing Conference, along with recommendations for positive actions to achieve gender equality in decision-making spheres, much of the women's movement appears to have tiptoed around any explicit reference to legislated gender quotas (Araújo 1999).

Instead, it was PT Deputies Marta Suplicy and Paulo Bernardo who first introduced the proposal to amend the electoral law to require parties to advance female candidacies. In preparation for the pivotal 1995 Beijing Conference, Marta Suplicy (then federal deputy, currently senator) had attended two conferences, one in Brussels of the European Union, and one soon thereafter in São Paulo of Latin American and Caribbean women legislators where the groundbreaking experiences with voluntary party and legislated candidate quotas in Scandinavian countries and Argentina, respectively, were discussed. A few weeks after the São Paulo conference, building on Argentina's success and the international attention surrounding women's empowerment resulting from the upcoming Beijing Conference, she and Deputy Bernardo proposed the gender quota (Suplicy 1996).

With a surprising lack of publicized debate throughout the process (Araújo 1999, 117), several qualifications of the proposed quota law emerged.[23] The final product not only saw a reduction in the target from 30 to 20 percent, but also an application of the target to the candidacies allowed rather than seats available (9.100/1995). As several iterations of Brazil's Electoral Law (including 4.737/1965, 6.990/1982, 7.454/1985, 9.100/1995, 9.504/1997, and 13.165/2015) allow each party to advance *excess candidacies* that exceed the number of available seats in a district in proportional elections, applying the quota target to permitted candidacies entailed a substantial dilution of its effect. In popular memory, the excess candidacies provision was introduced alongside the quota (Araújo 1999; Suplicy 1996); actually, it was *re*introduced with the quota (9.100/1995), having been lifted temporarily for the 1994 elections (Lamounier and Amorim Neto 2005). Although the quota target was raised back to 30 percent prior to the 1998 Chamber of Deputies and state Legislative Assemblies elections, it remained applicable to candidacies allowed, equal to 150 percent of available seats, with greater allowances for coalitions and lists in smaller states (9.504/1997).

The lack of vocal opposition to the gender quota's initial approval is illustrative of its limited anticipated effects. It also stands in stark contrast to the experience with racial quotas for admission to public universities, which has garnered intense and well-organized opposition (Johnson and Heringer 2015; Roza 2009). Former Deputy, Senator, and Minister Emília Fernandes said the

---

[23] Among the provisions excluded from the approved version were proposals to require each candidate's sex be listed on ballots/electronic voting machines, greater female presence in HGPE, and a publicity campaign divulging the existence of the quota. The TSE did, however, require candidates to list their sex upon registering their candidacy (Araújo, 1999, 116).

bancada feminina knew then that the quota law was "completely insufficient," but it was all they could get through.[24] In practice, the compromise ensured that the number of vacancies available for men was not reduced, therefore sustaining general support for the measure (Fêmea 2006a). For example, in the 1994 elections, each party/coalition list in a state with a district magnitude of eight could include eight candidates. Instead of the quota requiring that (of those eight) no more than five were men, the increase allows each party to advance 12 candidates (thus still allowing each party to advance eight male candidates). As demonstrated by Baldez, the adoption of functioning gender quota laws by male-dominated institutions is surprising largely because it entails male politicians ceding their power to women (Baldez 2004).[25] Yet quota negotiations, and institutional change more broadly, are often undertaken in ways that minimize their actual impact on those in power (Gatto 2016).

While the compromised process of quota adoption in Brazil did enable its swift approval, the result was a diluted quota, with no real prospect for broad displacement (Suplicy 1996; Wylie and dos Santos 2016). With so many vacancies, parties need not fill their lists to be competitive and are therefore not incentivized to fill the quota.[26] In the end, the candidacies most lacking are female candidacies, with parties rarely coming close to meeting the quota. For example, in the 2014 elections to the Chamber of Deputies, the electoral rules allowed 10,809 candidacies (for 513 seats!), but there were "only" 5,866 candidates (54.3 percent of the available spots), 29.4 percent of these women.[27] Moreover, such a large number of candidates drives up campaign budgets by requiring that candidates spend more to differentiate themselves from their co-partisans. Given raced and gendered patterns of access to financial resources in general and campaign finance in particular (discussed above and in Chapters 4 and 7), that factor further disadvantages most contenders from traditionally marginalized groups.

Moreover, the effects of the Brazilian quota are inherently limited given open-list PR elections, where a party could advance 30 percent women candidates and still elect an exclusively male delegation. Closed-list PR elections with placement mandates almost guarantee that candidate quotas will deliver results. Placement mandates, which require parties to present a pre-ordered list of candidates that alternates candidates by sex in accordance with the quota target, stipulate that party leaders put women in electable positions.[28] For example, for a quota of 30 percent, every third candidate must be female. That inhibits the tendency of party leaders to cluster female candidacies at the bottom of their lists. But in the

---

[24] Interview with Deputy Emília Fernandes, April 2009.

[25] Baldez cites an illustrative quote from a Uruguayan legislator in a debate on gender quotas, "We're talking about giving up positions of power here, and nobody likes to give up power" (quoted in Baldez 2004, 232).

[26] Interview with Former Deputy Judge Denise Frossard, June 2009.

[27] Calculated by the author using data from the Tribunal Superior Eleitoral (1994–2016), following Samuels (2008).

[28] There exists significant variation in the rules and enforcement of alternation.

Brazilian case, where candidate ordering on the pre-electoral list is irrelevant for electoral outcome, placement mandates are inapplicable.[29]

The top-down implementation of the *Lei de Cotas* driven by the Argentine experience and the hype surrounding the Beijing Conference resulted in a process that was not only a poor fit for the Brazilian system, but also not organic, lacking broad participation from the women's movement (Araújo 1999). Many feminists viewed quotas with reservation due to their emphasis on difference, quantification, and the potential to set a ceiling, and no consensus emerged. In the final reports and statements of the women's movement leading up to the Beijing Conference, quotas were not mentioned; rather, the women's movement emphasized pushing parties directly to incentivize women's participation in party life and as candidates and in particular, to promote political capacity-building opportunities for women (Araújo 1999). As recently as 2009, more than a decade after its implementation, less than a quarter of respondents in a national survey had even heard of the quota law (Brazilian Institute of Public Opinion and Statistics 2009). It is therefore no surprise that the generic quota, a product of diffusion from the Argentine success, has not materialized results in Brazil's quite different open-list PR elections.

While the above narrative provides part of the explanation for the failure of the quota, it is not the entire story. Brazil ranks the 6th lowest in terms of women legislators of the 77 countries with legislated quotas or reserved seats, and other countries have attained considerably greater success combining OLPR and quotas (Inter-Parliamentary Union 2017; Quota Project 2017; see Table 3.1).[30] Moreover, some parties have achieved significantly greater results than others. In sum, the mechanics of OLPR elections are part of the problem, but we must also consider the context in which those rules are embedded. The following discussions on the limited results of the quota and its recent mini-reform demonstrate the insufficiency of an exclusive focus on changing the formal rules; rules do not exist in a vacuum, and adequate consideration must be given to the interactions between electoral rules, parties, and voters.

PARTIES AND THE (REFORMED) LEI DE COTAS

As North argues, formal institutional change that "ignores the deep-seated cultural inheritance that underlies many informal constraints" will often fall short of producing a new equilibrium; even in the instance of a "wholesale

---

[29] Recall the discussion from Chapter 2, which explains the question of list placement in general and in Brazil.

[30] Two of the five countries that have legislated quotas or reserved seats and rank below Brazil on the IPU ranking of women's representation have low quota targets (10 percent in Samoa and Solomon Islands). Essentially, only the Democratic Republic of the Congo, Haiti, and Swaziland fare worse than Brazil in terms of quota performance (Quota Project 2017).

change in the formal rules ... there will be many informal constraints that have great survival tenacity" (1990, 91). Consistent with accounts of layered institutional change (Thelen 1999) and gendered institutions (Krook and Mackay 2011), male politicians voting to implement the quota sought rationally to accommodate demands for change and greater inclusion while maintaining their own power, which would have necessarily been diluted by an effective gender quota (Fêmea 2006a; Gatto 2016).[31] As will be substantiated in the ensuing chapters, electoral rules are endogenous to power structures themselves, and despite the focus of the electoral systems literature, such rules rarely exercise a direct and unmediated effect on outcomes. "Quotas per se do not fully level the political playing field: they are introduced in gendered political environments" that often disempower women, undermining their chances at selection and election as well as their authority in office (Krook 2015b, 185).

Araújo explains that debate against the quota was so limited because there was a complicit understanding that "quotas would not alter the political engineering of the process of political composition of candidacies and of competition" (1999, 129). A clear instance of layered institutional change (Thelen 1999), the quota was summarily diluted and pushed through with no expectation that it would actually change the power structures in place. Indeed, Deputy Jandira Feghali stated that while it was politically incorrect for a politician to position himself against the gender quota, "they also knew deep down that it (the quota) did not have the power to alter this structure, such that nothing passed that signified concrete support" (quoted in Araújo 1999, 125). Given that mere inclusion on the electoral list was secondary to "the weight of subsequent arrangements that are necessary to turn a candidacy potentially electable," the potential of the quota to fundamentally alter power structures through the incorporation of new voices into the political decision-making process was inherently limited (Araújo 1999, 129). As stated by Deputy Luiza Erundina, the quota law "has had almost no efficacy, it was merely a formal achievement" (quoted in Agência Câmara de Notícias 2011a).

In sum, an excessive emphasis on formal structures is inappropriate. "Many studies have focused on the formal recruitment process as set out in legal regulations, constitutional conventions and formal party rules. These studies often assume that the formal processes determine the outcome. The obvious weakness of this approach is that formal rules may have little bearing on informal practices" (Norris 1997, 9). As I make clear in the following discussion of the inability of even the emboldened quota to compel party

---

[31] "The political parties—institutions notoriously masculine in terms of their leadership, functioning, and priorities—were able to make it such that the minimum of 20 percent was not defined as obligatory in the legislation, and that the number of spaces on the electoral list was increased ... so that the number of spaces available for male candidates did not diminish" (Fêmea 2006a).

leaders to comply, comprehensive reform efforts must target both formal and informal constraints in order to induce party change.

In the wake of international women's day in 2009 with heightened pressure from the *bancada feminina* (women's caucus) and women's movement stalwarts such as the Feminist Center for Studies and Advisory Services (CFEMEA), President Lula's Special Secretariat for Policies for Women (SPM) formed a Tripartite Commission (with representatives from the executive and legislative branches as well as from civil society) to deliberate and propose changes to the Electoral Law that would enhance women's participation in formal politics. According to then Minister Nilcéa Freire of the SPM, the Commission's approach was to ratchet up support for proposals that had already made their way to Congress, thereby facilitating their quick adoption.

One such measure is Deputy Luiza Erundina's 2002 proposal (6.216/2002) requiring parties to devote: (1) 30% of their federally allocated funds for party organization to the promotion of women's participation, and (2) 30% of their publicly funded television and radio propaganda time to women. Although a government that espouses a rhetoric of equality[32] should in theory not object to directing federally funded party resources to effectuate such equality, debates with Chamber leadership ensued in the Commission deliberations[33] and the approved version entailed only a fraction of these requirements. Other proposals of the women's movement considered by the Commission included public financing of electoral campaigns and the adoption of closed-lists with placement mandates,[34] which would respectively level the playing field for outsider candidates, and strengthen Brazil's notoriously inchoate parties while allowing for a strict implementation of the gender quota.

Despite the broad toolkit of possibilities advocated by the *bancada feminina* and women's organizations in the Tripartite Commission, the accomplishments of the subsequent mini-reform (12.034/2009) were more limited. The approved measures directly affecting women include: (1) changes in the language of the quota law from "reserve" to "fill" a minimum of 30% and maximum of 70% of candidacies per party list with candidates of each sex[35] (Article 10), (2) a minimum of 5% of federally

---

[32] On March 5, 2008, President Lula approved by executive decree the Second National Plan of Policies for Women, a comprehensive plan of objectives and specific proposals for advancing women's rights (Special Secretariat for Policies for Women).

[33] Personal communication with civil society and *bancada feminina* representatives to the Commission.

[34] Comissão Tripartite irá Rever a Lei Eleitora [Tripartite Commission to Reform the Electoral Law], March 30, 2009; Alerta Feminista dos Movimentos de Mulheres que Assinam a Plataforma dos Movimentos Sociais pela Reforma do Sistema Político [Feminist Alert of Women's Movements that Signed the Social Movements' Platform for Reform of the Political System], October 31, 2008.

[35] The gender binary reinforcing law is characterized as "gender neutral," meaning candidate lists can have no more than 70 percent of "either sex."

allocated party organization funds devoted to the promotion of women's participation (Article 44), and (3) a dedicated 10% of each party's publicly funded television and radio time (in non-election years) to women (Article 45). Importantly, these changes come with enforceable sanctions, perhaps the most noteworthy achievement of the mini-reform.

Despite the impressive convergence of attention to women's underrepresentation and the ensuing concrete policy proposals and actual changes to the institutions perceived to be undermining women's participation, the immediate results were minimal. Although significantly more women threw their hat in the ring in the 2010 elections, the outcome was stagnation, with a Chamber of Deputies with exactly the same number of women that it had in the prior legislature, for a meager total of 8.8 percent. And although the 2014 elections saw additional increases in female candidacies, the end result remains meager, with a 1.1 percentage point gain in the Chamber of Deputies (see Table 1.4). As argued above, formal institutional mechanisms are often insufficient for alleviating (gender) inequality in the context of weak and gendered institutions (Krook and Mackay 2011).

The often mere formality of the written rules of the game among Brazil's weakly institutionalized parties becomes evident when considering the enforcement of the 2009 mini-reform to the gender quota (12.034/2009). In a 6–1 vote on August 12, 2010 by the Supreme Electoral Court (Tribunal Superior Eleitoral [TSE]), the ministers ruled that "30% women is law" and lists that did not comply with the recently revised electoral law would have to increase the number of female candidates, decrease the number of male candidates, or have the list rejected, with "exceptional" justifications being granted only by the electoral court (Abreu 2011; Coelho and Costa 2010).

The decision was widely praised by scholars, activists, and politicians sympathetic to women's representation, with Sônia Malheiros Miguel, Undersecretary of Institutional Articulation for the Minister of the Special Secretariat for Policies for Women, proclaiming "The decision of the TSE is historic, because it signifies recognition by the highest electoral court in Brazil of the necessity for this country to overcome this embarrassing democratic deficit, ensuring a more equitable participation of Brazilian women in the political process." After all, as stated by demographer and Professor for the Brazilian Institute of Geography and Statistics (IBGE) Dr. José Eustáquio Diniz Alvez, "The decision of the TSE to require compliance with Law 12.034, of the 29th of September of 2009, must be doubly celebrated, because the Law is meant to be complied with and the country cannot condone this culture of '*Lei que não pega*' ('Law on paper only')" (quoted in Agência Patrícia Galvão 2010).

But under pressure from political parties, regional electoral officials varied widely in their enforcement of the quota in the 2010 legislative elections (e.g., Agência de Notícias da Justiça Eleitoral 2010a), and in the end, less than 18% of the party/coalition lists met the 30% quota (Diário do Grande ABC 2010). Of the 607 state parties contesting the 2010 Chamber of Deputies elections,

44.2% *did not run a single female candidate* (Tribunal Superior Eleitoral 1994–2016). Nearly twenty years after the quota's adoption, the 2014 elections saw the first earnest enforcement of the 30% target for candidacies to the Chamber of Deputies and state legislative assemblies. Nevertheless, just under half (48.6%) of 768 state parties contesting the Chamber of Deputies elections advanced at least 30% female candidates, *with nearly a third of state parties (30.7%) still failing to run a single female candidate.* While parties often use coalition partners to meet the quota target (dos Santos 2012), in the end, just 56.7% of state coalition/party lists met the 30% target. Tellingly, the percentage of lists reaching 35% female candidates drops to 27.7% (Tribunal Superior Eleitoral 1994–2016). In spite of the reformed quota and now credible threats of enforcement, the *"lei que não pega"* culture among party elites of Brazil's inchoate and male dominant parties persists unscathed (Wylie and dos Santos 2016).

MIXED RESULTS

The 2010 elections delivered mixed results. In addition to the election of Brazil's first female president (with Dilma Rousseff winning 56 percent of the vote in the second round) a female candidate was the top vote earner in seven of the 27 statewide districts in the Chamber of Deputies elections. Nevertheless, the percentage of female deputies remained the same, and there was a drastic increase in the proportion of extremely unviable candidacies among women, reeking of a widespread offering of *candidatas laranjas* (phantom candidacies and sacrificial lambs)[36] by parties seeking to make a minimal but empty gesture at the reformed gender quota law (Wylie 2011; Wylie, Marcelino, and dos Santos 2015). Minister of the Special Secretariat for Policies for Women, Eleonora Menicucci, stated "The political parties are not interested in complying with the (quota) legislation. The law is as follows for every party: it must have at least 30% (candidates) of each sex. So if it has 70% men, it has to have 30% women, but the parties do not respect it. At all. Party resources for women are few and far between" (Quoted in Grayley 2012). Looking just to party funds (which, along with campaign materials, production assistance for the HGPE spots, and support from the party's gubernatorial campaign, constitute valuable party resources for a campaign), we see that in 2010, among the top 14 parties, national directorates devoted only 8% of their

---

[36] *"Candidatas laranjas"* are essentially ghost candidates whose names are submitted to the electoral officials, but do not run a serious campaign. As discussed at length in a paper by Wylie, Marcelino, and dos Santos (2015), parties' nominal compliance with the quota is the most influential source of the multitude of (mostly female) *laranjas* in recent elections. Other motives include a provision that gives government employees that are running for electoral office three months of unpaid leave, and long-term strategic decisions by *laranjas* who campaign instead for the party's *puxadores de voto* with the understanding that the party will compensate their team efforts by supporting a subsequent viable campaign by the *laranja*.

party funds to the campaigns of women, who represented 19.7% of the total candidates. The PSDB, which advanced 20.4% female candidates, dedicated less than 2% of its funds to women candidacies (Mendonça and Navarro 2012).

The 2014 elections yielded another significant boost in female candidates (29.4%) that materialized disappointing results. As the first federal elections in which the 20-year-old quota mandates were broadly enforced, amidst an entrenched informal institution of quota neglect and an abundance of inchoate, male-dominant party organizations, many parties scrambled to find female candidates at the last minute. The numbers of apparent *laranjas* again increased substantially—based on a metric developed in Wylie et al. (2015), we see that nearly half of the female candidates[37] (and just 13.5% of male candidates) ostensibly seeking a seat in the Chamber of Deputies were *laranjas* (Barba 2014; Furlan 2014; Lima 2014; Magalhães 2015; Paes 2014; Wylie et al. 2015). In elections to the state legislative assemblies, there was actually a decrease in the proportion of women elected (see Table 1.4). The poor performance of female candidates was not universal, however, with six female candidates to the Chamber of Deputies winning the highest vote total in their state, 18.5% of the one third of Senate seats being contested going to women, and Marina Silva competing closely with President Dilma Rousseff in her ultimately successful bid for reelection. The PT elected nine women to the Chamber of Deputies, including four Afro-descendant women, and nearly half of the PC do B's 10-member delegation is female, most of whom identify as Afro-descendant (Tribunal Superior Eleitoral 1994–2016).

The following Chapter 4 delves into such variation across and within candidate sex, states, and parties in the Chamber of Deputies elections and how that variation can explain women's electoral prospects. I find that female candidates are indeed electorally disadvantaged, but that party-level factors can ameliorate this disadvantage. Then, in Chapter 5, I compare women's electoral prospects in concurrent elections to the Chamber of Deputies and the Senate. By providing institutional variation while maintaining many other factors under consideration constant, the controlled comparison analysis sheds light on the difficulties faced by women in Brazil's OLPR elections, where incentives for intraparty competition often leave female candidates un-prioritized and lacking the necessary structure to wage a successful campaign, and how party support can overcome those obstacles. When electoral rules incentivize party support, as in the Senate, its effect is amplified, with women running in parties that are institutionalized and incorporate women in party leadership being particularly well-equipped for electoral success.

---

[37] To be discussed more explicitly in Chapter 7, the proportion of *laranjas* among female candidates was 18% higher among Afro-descendant women (53.0%) than white women (44.8%). Interestingly, among male candidates, the rate of *laranjas* among those identifying as black/*preto* (19.3%) was 70% higher than the rate for white men (11.4%).

4

Overcoming Gendered Obstacles: Voters, Electoral Rules, and Parties

> ... the parties have not undertaken the challenge to stimulate and contribute substantively to the increased political participation of women. They are masculine institutions whose functioning and structure make female participation difficult. It is necessary to democratize the party life and structures.
>
> (Fêmea 2004, 5)

Conventional wisdom rooted in gender-blind readings of the formal rules of the game dismisses the gatekeeping role for parties in an entrepreneurial context like Brazil's. Yet this chapter offers empirical evidence demonstrating that parties, or more precisely, weak party institutionalization and unsupportive party leadership—manifested as an absence of critical psychological, organizational, and material support—remain the central barrier to women's representation in Brazil. The successful incorporation of women in Brazilian politics has been contingent not on the development levels or electoral size of districts, but rather on the effective commitment of parties to the promotion of women's political participation. Thus, the amorphous character of many Brazilian parties does not preclude their theoretical and empirical relevance for explaining electoral outcomes. This research brings parties to the center of the analysis, interrogating their gendered character and exploiting significant interparty variation to reveal that the key to enhancing women's political representation in Brazil is the inclusion and championing of women by party leadership in institutionalized parties.

The parties that have proven women-friendly have tended to be leftist due to their typically more comprehensive infrastructure (Toole 2003) and historical rhetorical emphasis on egalitarianism (Duverger 1955). Yet rather than leftist ideology per se, the most salient factors for predicting women's electoral prospects are the party structure and critical acts performed by women in party leadership. This is especially true given the postulated support for female candidates in the electorate, and the recently emboldened gender quota, with all parties standing to gain from the effective promotion of strong female candidacies. As such, leftist and non-leftist parties alike can mitigate the severe gender gap in women's legislative presence by institutionalizing their party and including women in their party leadership, conditions under which, as the following analysis demonstrates, women's electoral prospects are heightened.

Electoral institutions are fundamental for understanding political power and representation because they can either reproduce or mitigate societal inequities. Yet such rules do not act in a vacuum, but are endogenous to the historical and cultural contexts in which they are embedded. Moreover, the effects of electoral rules are mediated by political parties. Indeed, there is a growing consensus that electoral institutions are best understood through an integrative approach that explicitly considers how voters, electoral rules, and political parties interact to affect representation. In what follows, I apply that approach to understand how Brazil's few female politicians have managed to overcome the obstacles and attain elected office.

I subject the central explanations for the underrepresentation of women to empirical testing at the candidate level, in a context that is recently (re)democratized, has OLPR elections, and a still inadequately institutionalized party system replete with a range of institutionalization among parties, ranging from inchoate to fully institutionalized. I leverage extensive quantitative and qualitative data to assess the explanatory capacity of the principal explanations in contexts that extend beyond the traditional approach. While conventional wisdom considers voters (*machista* attitudes) and electoral rules (district and party magnitude) to be significant barriers undermining women's representation, this research finds that those factors do not predict variation in women's electoral performance in Brazil. Moreover, lesser levels of voter bias against women have not correlated with increases in female candidates or deputies. Instead, I find that parties (the "good ole boys' club") play a crucial gatekeeping role through their (in) capacitation of female candidacies and are therefore essential actors in the political representation of women. The chapter concludes with a discussion of findings, how the electoral rules of the Chamber of Deputies amplify the importance of party institutionalization for women (demonstrated in Chapter 5), and the lingering variation to be explained (the subject of Chapter 6).

VOTERS: MACHISTA BIAS

Aggregate cross-national evidence finds *national gender ideology*, or societal attitudes about women's sociopolitical roles, to be a key predictor of women's overall representation (Paxton and Kunovich 2003, 93). Modernization-based explanations root such attitudes (and others) in economic development, asserting that as societies develop economically, the rates of educational attainment, literacy, and workforce presence of women increase, leading invariably to a shift from traditional societal values to modern values, and thus significant attitudinal change toward more progressive conceptions of gender equality (Inglehart and Norris 2003). In Brazil, regional socioeconomic inequality results in ample variation in development levels across the country, with Human Development Index (HDI) equivalents ranging from Botswana (Alagoas) to Andorra (Distrito Federal) (Banco Central 2009; United Nations Human Development Report 2009, 2010, United Nations Development Program 2013). Can modernization-based explanations predict female candidates' electoral prospects in Brazil? Are voters across Brazil equally likely to support women in politics, both hypothetically and at the polls?

The Latin American Public Opinion Project survey data reveal considerable interstate variation in respondents' perceptions of the political aptitude of women (LAPOP n.d.). The variation in public opinion may have important implications for women's electoral prospects, with women in states with more favorable perceptions of female candidates likely to fare better electorally than women in states with negative perceptions of female candidates. Can the modernization hypothesis explain such interstate variability? If so, the least developed states would harbor more negative perceptions of female candidates than would the more developed states, leading female candidates to enjoy their greatest electoral prospects in the latter.

Figure 4.1 maps those 2014 LAPOP data on negative perceptions of women in politics and the United Nations Development Program (PNUD)'s calculations for municipally-based state-level values of the HDI (United Nations Development Program 2013, 2014; LAPOP n.d.). It suggests a plausible bivariate relationship between voter bias and district development, with many of the larger circles (indicating that respondents in the state expressing bias against women in politics exceeded the national average) clustered in the lesser developed Northeast, and the southern and southeastern states having mostly small circles. A simple logistic regression with only two dichotomized predictors—one for respondent sex, and one for whether the respondent lives in a state with an HDI above the national mean—suggests that the odds of a respondent in a more developed state (compared to one in a less developed state) agreeing or strongly agreeing that men are better politicians are 0.55 to 1. Yet, as demonstrated in Figure 4.1, there are some noteworthy outliers. In the most developed district, the nation's capital, a striking 38.9% of respondents either agreed or strongly agreed with the statement. Respondents in the least developed state, Alagoas (16.7%), exhibited levels of machista voter bias well below the national mean (24.7%). In any case, limitations in the reach of the LAPOP survey, which was not designed to be representative at the state level, preclude conclusions (LAPOP n.d.).

The recent wave of the Brazilian Electoral Study (Center of Studies and Public Opinion 2010), however, was designed to be representative at the regional level, and asked several questions about women's role in politics.[1]

---

[1] The "voter bias" indicator averages respondents' answers to the following three questions: "In general, men are more adequate for a political career than women," "In general, when

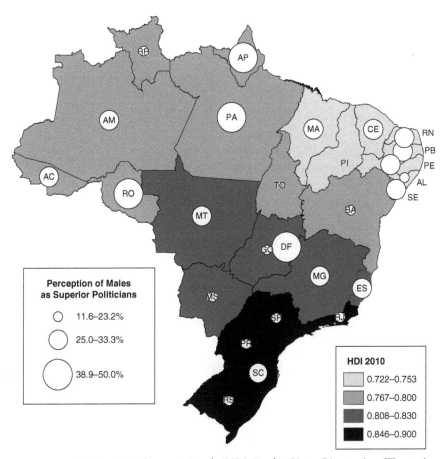

FIGURE 4.1 Do State Development Levels (HDI) Predict Voter Bias against Women?

As shown in Table 4.1, the data do not support the notion that the more developed southern and southeastern regions are more conducive to women's representation than the poorer regions. While respondents in southern states did express significantly lower levels of voter bias in 2010, that has not translated into more women politicians; the success of female candidates relative to male candidates (*Female–Male Success Rate Ratio*) is lowest in the South. Descriptive evidence thus suggests that machista voter attitudes may not predict women's electoral prospects in Brazil. Although residual voter bias against women does persist, several female candidates have nonetheless found a way to succeed electorally in inhospitable contexts, with some doing so even

elected, men govern better than women," and "Women still do not have sufficient political experience to govern well" (Center of Studies and Public Opinion 2010).

TABLE 4.1 *Women's Electoral Prospects (1994–2014) and Voter Bias (2010), by Region*

	Female Candidates	Female Deputies	Female Success Rate	Female–Male Success Rate Ratio	Voter Bias
North	557 (19.0%)	61 (15.6%)	11.0%	0.91	31.2%
Northeast	816 (14.3%)	44 (4.9%)	5.4%	0.42	23.4%
Center-West	372 (18.3%)	29 (11.8%)	7.8%	0.79	22.3%
Southeast	1998 (16.6%)	86 (8.0%)	4.3%	0.57	24.4%
South	549 (15.7%)	24 (5.2%)	4.4%	0.38	15.8%
BRAZIL	4292 (16.4%)	244 (7.9%)	5.7%	0.56	23.2%

Sources: Compiled by author with data from Center of Studies and Public Opinion (2010) and Tribunal Superior Eleitoral (1994–2016)

without the support of an institutionalized and women-inclusive party (illustrated in Chapter 6).

Interestingly, empirical work has actually revealed female candidates to be most successful in their bids for *local* elected office in Brazil's more traditional municipalities (Miguel and Queiroz 2006). Several of Brazil's most prominent female politicians do in fact come from the lesser developed northern and northeastern regions (e.g., Marina Silva of Acre, Heloísa Helena of Alagoas, Roseana Sarney of Maranhão), and those two regions have consistently had the greatest proportions of female mayors and municipal councilors (Miguel and Queiroz 2006; Tribunal Superior Eleitoral 1994–2016). Moreover, February 2009 and April 2013 public opinion polls suggest that the Northeast has the country's highest postulated support for women in politics, a hypothetical translated into action when northeastern electors voted in droves for Dilma Rousseff in the 2010 and 2014 presidential elections (Brazilian Institute of Public Opinion and Statistics 2009, 2013; Tribunal Superior Eleitoral 1994–2016). Together, those observations weaken the traction of the modernization hypothesis on the question of women's representation in Brazil.

Some analyses of aggregate level data, however, maintain that female candidates for national office should be most likely to thrive in the more developed regions of Brazil, with others finding no effect (Araújo and Eustáquio 2007). Table 4.2 depicts the variation in female candidacies and success rates across Brazil's five regions over the last six election cycles. While women have in fact struggled to gain national-level power in the impoverished Northeast, they also confront challenges in the more developed South. As shown in Table 4.2, women's political presence in the more developed southern and southeastern regions has actually rated lower—on several

TABLE 4.2 *Female Candidacies and Success Rates in the Chamber of Deputies, by Region*

	1994	1998	2002	2006	2010	2014
Women Candidates						
North	43 (11.6%)	49 (12.1%)	76 (13.8%)	84 (15.3%)	103 (23.0%)	202 (32.3%)
Northeast	30 (4.3%)	62 (9.2%)	99 (10.3%)	110 (10.2%)	151 (14.7%)	364 (28.5%)
Center-West	18 (7.4%)	38 (14.0%)	58 (15.1%)	57 (15.1%)	70 (20.5%)	131 (31.4%)
Southeast	71 (5.5%)	158 (10.4%)	199 (11.2%)	303 (13.3%)	455 (19.3%)	812 (28.6%)
South	23 (5.6%)	41 (8.3%)	48 (9.2%)	73 (10.9%)	150 (22.1%)	214 (29.9%)
Brazil	185 (6.2%)	348 (10.4%)	480 (11.4%)	627 (12.7%)	929 (19.1%)	1723 (29.4%)
Women Elected						
North	10 (15.4%)	5 (7.7%)	8 (12.3%)	13 (20.0%)	10 (15.4%)	15 (23.1%)
Northeast	3 (2.0%)	3 (2.0%)	8 (5.3%)	9 (6.0%)	11 (7.3%)	10 (6.6%)
Center-West	6 (14.6%)	7 (17.1%)	5 (12.2%)	3 (7.3%)	4 (9.8%)	4 (9.8%)
Southeast	11 (6.1%)	12 (6.7%)	15 (8.4%)	16 (8.9%)	15 (8.4%)	17 (9.5%)
South	2 (2.6%)	2 (2.6%)	6 (7.8%)	4 (5.2%)	5 (6.5%)	5 (6.5%)
Brazil	32 (6.2%)	29 (5.7%)	42 (8.2%)	45 (8.8%)	45 (8.8%)	51 (9.9%)
Female Candidate Success Rate						
North	23.3%	10.2%	10.5%	15.5%	9.7%	7.4%
Northeast	10.0%	4.8%	8.1%	8.2%	7.3%	2.7%
Center-West	33.3%	18.4%	8.6%	5.3%	5.7%	3.1%
Southeast	15.5%	7.6%	7.5%	5.3%	3.3%	2.1%

(continued)

TABLE 4.2 (*continued*)

	1994	1998	2002	2006	2010	2014
South	8.7%	4.9%	12.5%	5.5%	3.3%	2.3%
Brazil	17.3%	8.3%	8.8%	7.2%	4.8%	3.0%
Female–Male Success Rate Ratio						
North	1.39	0.61	0.87	1.38	0.61	0.61
Northeast	0.45	0.20	0.49	0.56	0.46	0.18
Center-West	2.14	1.27	0.78	0.44	0.42	0.24
Southeast	1.12	0.62	0.73	0.64	0.38	0.26
South	0.45	0.29	0.84	0.45	0.24	0.16
Brazil	1.02	0.52	0.69	0.66	0.41	0.27

Notes: Values in parentheses represent the percent of women among the region's total candidates and elected.
Source: Compiled by author with data from Tribunal Superior Eleitoral (1994–2016)

dimensions—than that of the lesser developed northern states of the Amazon region in all of the six recent elections under consideration.

Are there mass-level partisan patterns to voter bias against women politicians? If so, which parties' voters express the most support for assertions of male political superiority? Public opinion data permit some consideration of the question, although a-partisan tendencies of the electorate caution against over-interpreting the data. The 2010 Brazilian Electoral Study (Center of Studies and Public Opinion 2010) survey mentioned above asked 2,000 voters to identify which, if any, political party best represents their perspective. As demonstrated in prior studies and in line with other younger democracies (Samuels 2006), most Brazilians (57.9%) indicated that no party represented them. A subsequent question asking respondents to identify up to three parties they liked returned similar results; 51.7% of respondents said there is not a single party that they like.

Of the 39.2% of respondents who indicated a particular political party representing them, the majority (62.4%) listed the PT. Respondents listed 18 different parties, but just four parties had at least 50 respondents—the PT (489), PSDB (113), PV (74), and PMDB (54). Among those four parties, respondents' support for statements of male political superiority suggests that 36.7% of PSDB respondents, 30.8% of PMDB respondents, 19.6% of PT respondents, and 18.3% of PV respondents exhibit voter bias against women. Difference-in-proportions tests suggest that PSDB respondents tend to be significantly more skeptical (and PT respondents significantly less skeptical) of women's political capacity than the average respondent. Yet the small n for all parties other than the PT limits the representativeness of the finding.

Elite surveys preclude comparable analysis. A CFEMEA (2009) survey asked 321 elected deputies several questions related to proposed political reforms intended to increase women's representation. The raw data were unavailable so we cannot speak to partisan differences, but gender differences were stark. While 67% of female deputies supported (at least in part) the proposal for closed lists with zipper quotas, just 21% of male deputies supported the proposal. Requirements for the distribution of public resources (30% of party funds and HGPP time) yielded 89–93% support from female deputies and 61–63% support from male deputies. Exclusive public financing of campaigns returned a striking 93% full support from female deputies, and 73% support (including 71% full support) from male deputies.

Power and Zucco's Brazilian Legislative Survey (BLS) offers a proxy measure for elite support for women's rights with a question assessing parliamentarians' attitudes toward abortion rights ("Agree or disagree—Abortion should be banned in all circumstances"). Possible responses range from strongly disagree (1) to strongly agree (4). The average responses for congressional representatives from the four major parties in 2013 are as follows: PT (1.8), PSDB (2.6), PMDB (2.8), DEM (3.3), with an overall average of 2.8. As with the mass-level surveys discussed above, the gender ideology of *petistas* (members of the PT) tends to be more supportive of women's rights than that of *tucanos* (members of the PSDB) (Power and Zucco 2009, 2011). Such interparty variation lends additional support to this book's emphasis on party-level correlates of women's representation. The tentative evidence also reveals how the aggregate-level approach common to the literature (especially cross-national research, given data limitations) obscures important variation relevant for explaining women's political participation.

Given such mixed findings, this research seeks to clarify the relationship between state development level, public opinion, and women's representation by subjecting the hypothesis to empirical testing at the individual level. I first use public opinion data[2] from four nationally representative surveys conducted in 2001,[3] 2009,[4] 2010,[5] and 2014[6] to explore the covariates of voter hostility to women, and find that *machista bias* is more pronounced among respondents in lesser developed states. An even stronger predictor of that bias is the variable differentiating locales on the basis of size,[7] with male and female respondents in rural areas having a predicted probability of expressing *machista bias* of 0.53 and 0.36, compared to 0.39 and 0.24 in capital cities, even after controlling for respondent education, age, and income.

While the literature would therefore predict a positive influence of state development level upon the electoral performance of women (Inglehart and Norris 2003; Schmidt 2009; Thames and Williams 2010), with other studies restricting the relationship to women on the left (e.g., Avelar 2001), I expect that state *HDI* will nonetheless be an insignificant predictor of vote share for all candidates, including leftist women. As is discussed at length in Chapter 6, women have crafted means to thrive even in the context of machista electorates. Indeed, multivariate analyses (see Table 4.4) demonstrate that women in less developed districts nonetheless do not face an electoral disadvantage nor do women in more developed districts enjoy an advantage. As suggested by the negative main effect of the *HDI* (the effect of *HDI* for non-left men, when both *left* and *fem* [female] equal zero), for non-leftist men the effect of *HDI* is negative, with those candidates being worse off electorally in more developed states (even after controlling for district competitiveness). For leftist male

[2] I would like to thank Rachel Meneguello of UNICAMP's CESOP for making these data available.
[3] Survey, "The Brazilian Woman in the Public and Private Spheres," conducted by researchers from the PT's Fundação Perseu Abramo in October 2001 with 2,502 respondents in 187 municipalities throughout Brazil.
[4] Survey, "Women in Politics," conducted by the Brazilian Institute of Public Opinion and Statistics (Ibope) in February 2009 with 2,002 respondents in 142 municipalities throughout Brazil.
[5] Survey, "Brazilian Electoral Study," conducted by Vox Populi in November 2010 with 2,000 respondents in 149 municipalities throughout Brazil, and representative at the regional level.
[6] Survey, "The AmericasBarometer," conducted by the Latin American Public Opinion Project (LAPOP) in April 2014 with 1,500 respondents in 107 municipalities throughout Brazil (www.LapopSurveys.org).
[7] Ranging from 1 (capital/metropolitan area) to 5 (rural area).

TABLE 4.3 *Do More Female Contenders Translate into More Women Elected?*

Year	N Female Cands.	N Total Cands.	% Female Cands.	% Increase in % Fem Cands.	N Women Elected	% Women Elected
1994	185	3008	6.2	1%	32	6.2
1998	348	3357	10.4	69%	29	5.7
2002	480	4198	11.4	10%	42	8.2
2006	627	4946	12.7	11%	45	8.8
2010	929	4854	19.1	51%	45	8.8
2014	1723	5866	29.4	53%	51	9.9

Note: Cands. = Candidates. Source: Author calculation using data from Tribunal Superior Eleitoral (1994–2016)

candidates, the negative effect is reversed. But despite the literature's expectations to the contrary, the beneficial effect of district development for candidates in leftist parties does not appear to be gendered; interactions with *fem* are not significant, indicating that candidate sex does not moderate the effect of *HDI* on vote share. Nor does candidate sex mediate the negative effect of district development level on non-leftists' vote share. A breakdown of the marginal effects reveals that female and male candidates have the highest predicted vote share in states at the low level of development (1.01% and 0.94%, respectively), and the lowest predicted vote share in states near the mean level of development (0.66% and 0.75%, respectively).

The absence of a development-driven advantage for women is striking given the association of development level with machista bias and the survey data cited above about the persistence of machismo in Brazil (Fundação Perseu Abramo 2010). Why does such bias not appear to have depressed the vote share of female candidates? The fact that many of the women discounting machista voter attitudes in my interviews conformed to traditional gender roles and emerge from parties associated with more restrictive views on women's rights suggests that while voter bias did not prevent their election, it has certainly affected the dynamics of women's campaigns and political profiles (to be discussed in Chapter 6).

Deputy Rebecca Garcia of the conservative PP in the northern state of Amazonas thought being a woman actually helped her in the eyes of the elector, because she represented a fresh alternative to the corrupt, largely male status quo. Garcia also thought that given her pro-business stance, her gender enhanced her portrait of viability in the perspective of corporate funders, who were looking to back pro-business candidates but eager to endorse a novel candidate such as herself (young and female).[8] Deputy Iriny Lopes of the PT

[8] Interview, December 2008.

in Espírito Santo (Southeast) also said that she had never suffered gender discrimination from electors, but drew a sharp contrast to her experience with corporate donors, the media, and interactions in the legislature, where she reported being "a victim of prejudice."[9] Lopes' sentiment that the legislature was considerably more machista than the electorate was echoed in several interviews, and suggests a disconnect between the elected and the electors.

Others reported that they had confronted voter bias,[10] with even many women constituents being hesitant to vote for female candidates.[11] For Municipal Councilor Olívia Santana (PC do B-BA) and Deputy Benedita da Silva (PT-RJ)—Afro-descendant women from impoverished backgrounds—prejudice in the electorate was intensified by multiple and intersecting layers of marginality.[12] Santana felt that corporate donors were less receptive to her requests for funding due to her race and gender; she learned that the same donors who expressed reticence to finance her campaign gave generously to some of her white, male co-partisans also contesting the election. Santana's challenges acquiring corporate funding undermined her ultimately unsuccessful campaign by limiting her ability to reach her constituents across Bahia's more than 400 municipalities.[13] Another stereotype faced by female contenders, especially heightened for women candidates conforming to traditional ideas about beauty, is the challenge of being objectified and discredited (Murray 2010).[14]

In sum, the empirical evidence on voter bias is mixed. The interviews suggest that while many women have been affected in some way by voter bias, most white women do not think it has diminished their chances of election, a perception reinforced by the quantitative findings. In Chapter 6, I advance an explanation for the apparent inconsistency of machista attitudes in less developed states existing alongside the perceived and observed insignificance of development level for women's electoral prospects. By conforming to traditional gender norms, or campaigning collectively in a programmatic and supportive party, (some) women have managed to navigate the constraints of machismo.

ELECTORAL RULES: DISTRICT AND PARTY MAGNITUDE

An alternative explanation for women's representation focuses on the institutional rules of the game. The feature of electoral systems most commonly considered in cross-national analyses of women's representation

---

[9] Interview, December 2008.
[10] Interviews with Deputy Tonha Magalhães (PFL/PR-BA), November 2008; Deputy Ana Arraes (PSB-PE), March 2009; Deputy Fátima Bezerra (PT-RN), March 2009; Municipal Councilor Olívia Santana, April 2009.
[11] Interview with former Deputy Maninha (PT/PSOL-DF), April 2009.
[12] Interviews, April 2009; June 2009.
[13] Interview, April 2009.
[14] Interview with Deputy Rita Camata (PMDB/PSDB-ES), December 2008.

has been the allocation of seats per district (district magnitude).[15] As discussed in Chapter 2, a greater district magnitude is widely considered favorable for women's representation. When there are multiple vacancies on a party list, the resource of a candidacy is less scarce. Parties are therefore able to diversify their lists, including candidates from various societal sectors, constituencies, or groups.

Party magnitude brings the measure to the party level, accounting for the fragmentation of votes that results from the multiplicity of parties associated with high district magnitude elections (Duverger 1954). The predictive power of party magnitude for women's representation stems from the tendency of party leaders to place female candidates in unelectable positions at the bottom of their closed party lists (Matland 1998). As party magnitude increases, candidates in less desirable list positions enjoy a greater chance of election. That component of the explanation loses ground in OLPR elections, where voters rather than party leaders determine the rank order of candidates.

Indeed, Jones finds that party magnitude is an insignificant predictor of the proportion of women elected on party lists in recent OLPR elections in Latin America (2009). But party magnitude may retain relevance for strategic reasons. In a party that anticipates winning only one seat, the candidacies of women will in most instances be subordinated to candidacies of those with a proven track record of attaining votes and/or raising funds. In the Brazilian electoral system, prioritized candidates on the so-called "unofficial list" and particularly the *puxadores de voto*—candidates who enhance the electoral prospects of fellow partisans by virtue of their anticipated quantity of votes in excess of the electoral quotient—enjoy greater access to the state-funded electoral propaganda time (HGPE) allocated by the party, more support in producing their advertisements for HGPE and other campaign materials, and a greater chance of garnering organizational support and endorsement from their party's gubernatorial campaign (Matos 2008; Samuels 2003). A party that is fighting for a single seat will likely be hesitant to encourage and support additional candidacies, recruiting instead *candidatas laranjas* (sacrificial lambs and phantom candidates) intended solely to garner votes for the top (usually white male) candidate.

Conversely, a party that anticipates winning more seats in a state will be more willing to share party material resources such as campaign literature, time on and production assistance for HGPE, the highly-desired *dobradinha* in concurrent elections, and funds among its candidates. Such support generally parlays into a perception of viability in the media and electorate. Given those strategic considerations, I expect party magnitude—lagged to account for the anticipatory quality of the effect—to exert a positive influence on women's

[15] Given the widespread diffusion of quotas in the last two decades (Krook 2009), most cross-national analyses now also incorporate a measure of quota systems among their institutional variables.

electoral performance in Brazil. I expect that parties that anticipate winning less than two seats (based on prior performance in a district) will not support outsider candidacies and will therefore disadvantage most female contenders.

Of the 3,581 state parties that ran in six election cycles (1994–2014) across Brazil's 27 statewide multimember districts, with more than 20 parties in each election, 1,294 won at least one seat. Only 476 (36.8%) of those successful state parties elected any female deputies, with 818—more than 63%—electing exclusively male delegations.[16] A pairwise correlation demonstrates a slight positive relationship between a party's seat share and the number of women elected, and the parties with women in their congressional delegation tend to be those with a party magnitude of two or more (16.9% of the total) rather than one. Yet, the fact that some of the numerous all-male delegations hail from parties enjoying higher party magnitudes suggests that other factors, such as the biases confronted in the electorate (machista attitudes) and among party elites (the "good ole boys' club"), must also be considered.

I use the wide range in district and party magnitudes in Brazil's Chamber of Deputies (ranging from 8 to 70, and 0 to 20, respectively), to empirically test their effects on female candidates' electoral prospects. Although most prior studies of women's representation and district and party magnitude contend that both measures of magnitude are positively correlated to women's electoral success, I argue that it is a logical leap to expect that more female candidates presumed to result from greater district magnitude will automatically lead to the election of women.

On the contrary, as depicted in Table 4.3, the only two elections in contemporary Brazilian politics in which the percentage of women deputies decreased or stayed the same were 1998 and 2010, the two elections where the increase in female candidacies was the greatest (with the exception of 2014).[17] Increases in the number of female candidates have not automatically translated into more female deputies.

I therefore expect *district magnitude* to have a negative influence on candidate electoral performance, irrespective of sex, due to the greater number of candidates and thus more competitive electoral contexts in states with higher district magnitudes. I also include the effective number of candidates (*effective n cands*) *running* in each state (1 divided by the sum of

---

[16] When including those state parties that competed but won no seats, that number jumps to 2,954; in other words, 82.5% of all state parties contesting the 1994–2014 Chamber of Deputies elections did not elect a single woman.

[17] Each of the elections with marked increases in female candidacies took place in the wake of the gender quota implementation and subsequent reforms. In the 2014 elections, the first federal elections in which the quota mandate was widely enforced, the boost in female candidacies delivered only modest results. The apparent underperformance of women candidates is due largely to the widespread offering of female *candidatas laranjas* (sacrificial lambs and phantom candidacies) by parties resisting formal institutional change (Wylie 2011; Wylie, Marcelino, and dos Santos 2015).

TABLE 4.4 *Multivariate Analysis of Vote Share (1994–2010)*

Fixed Effects	Model 1—Rivals			Model 2—Controls			Model 3—Wylie		
	Coef.	SE	sig.	Coef.	SE	sig.	Coef.	SE	sig.
Level 2 District Variables									
For Intercept (β_{oj})									
Intercept (γ_{oo})	0.018	(0.001)	***	0.019	(0.002)	***	0.021	(0.002)	***
HDI (γ_{o1})	−0.001	(0.001)		−0.002	(0.001)	**	−0.002	(0.001)	**
District magnitude (γ_{o2})	−0.001	(0.000)	***	−0.001	(0.000)	***	−0.001	(0.000)	***
Effective n cands. (γ_{o3})				0.000	(0.000)		0.000	(0.000)	
Cross-Level Interactions									
For Female slope (β_{1j})									
Intercept (γ_{10})	−0.005	(0.001)	**	−0.004	(0.002)	*	−0.007	(0.003)	**
HDI (γ_{11})	0.000	(0.001)		0.000	(0.002)		0.000	(0.002)	
District magnitude (γ_{12})	0.000	(0.000)		0.000	(0.000)		0.000	(0.000)	
Effective n cands. (γ_{13})				0.000	(0.000)		0.000	(0.000)	
For Left slope (β_{2j})									
Intercept (γ_{20})	−0.005	(0.000)	***	−0.005	(0.001)	***	−0.006	(0.001)	***
HDI (γ_{21})	0.002	(0.000)	***	0.003	(0.000)	***	0.003	(0.000)	***
For Fem*Left slope (β_{3j})									
Intercept (γ_{30})	0.003	(0.001)	**	0.003	(0.001)	*	0.001	(0.002)	
HDI (γ_{31})	−0.001	(0.001)		−0.001	(0.001)		−0.001	(0.001)	
Level 1 Party Variables									
Party magnitude (β_{4j}, γ_{40})	0.001	(0.000)	***	0.001	(0.000)	***	0.001	(0.000)	***
Fem*P.mag$_{(t-1)}$ (β_{7j}, γ_{70})	0.000	(0.000)		0.000	(0.000)		0.000	(0.000)	

(continued)

TABLE 4.4 (continued)

Fixed Effects	Model 1—Rivals			Model 2—Controls			Model 3—Wylie		
	Coef.	SE	sig.	Coef.	SE	sig.	Coef.	SE	sig.
PII (β_{8j}, γ_{80})							−0.001	(0.000)	***
Fem*PII (β_{9j}, γ_{90})							0.001	(0.001)	
C.Mass (β_{10j}, γ_{100})							−0.002	(0.001)	*
Fem*C.Mass (β_{11j}, γ_{110})							−0.005	(0.003)	*
Fem*PII*C.Mass (β_{13j}, γ_{130})							0.002	(0.001)	*
Level 1 Candidate Controls									
Education level (β_{14j}, γ_{140})				0.001	(0.000)	***	0.001	(0.000)	***
Feeder occupation (β_{15j}, γ_{150})				0.000	(0.000)	±	0.001	(0.000)	±
Incumbent (β_{16j}, γ_{160})				0.012	(0.000)	***	0.012	(0.000)	***
Campaign finance (β_{17j}, γ_{170})				0.000	(0.000)	***	0.000	(0.000)	***
Random Effects	*Var.*	*SE*	*sig.*	*Var.*	*SE*	*sig.*	*Var.*	*SE*	*sig.*
Intercept (u_{0j})	0.000	(0.000)	***	0.000	(0.000)	***	0.000	(0.000)	***
Female slope (u_{1j})	0.000	(0.000)	***	0.000	(0.000)	***	0.000	(0.000)	***
Level-1 (r_{ij})	0.000	(0.000)	***	0.000	(0.000)	***	0.000	(0.000)	***
N	17355			11211			10855		
LL	49542			32295			31238		
AIC	−99047			−64542			−62411		
BIC	−98908			−64366			−62178		

***p<0.001 **p<.01 *p<0.05 ±p<0.10 (one-tailed tests)

Notes: Dependent variable is candidate's proportion of valid votes; cands. = candidates.

the squared vote share of all candidates running per state), which accounts for the fragmentation of the vote resulting from the mass of candidates in Chamber of Deputies elections (Moser and Scheiner 2004; Taagepera and Shugart 1989). Multivariate analyses (see Table 4.4) lend support to my expectation, with *district magnitude* exercising a negative and statistically significant effect on vote share that is not differentiated by candidate sex. *Effective n cands*, which is highly correlated with *district magnitude*, is not statistically significant.

I hypothesize that once district competitiveness and seat availability are taken into account through *effective n cands* and *district magnitude*, we will see a positive relationship for *party magnitude*, with candidates emerging from parties with greater seat shares enjoying superior electoral performance. I estimate multivariate models with party magnitude from both the current and prior election (as a lag, or $p.mag_{t-1}$).[18] Again, given the open lists, I expect party magnitude to exercise an effect that is anticipatory in quality; parties that do not expect to win many seats (based on their district performance in past elections) will therefore have a scarcity of resources and be less likely to support outsider candidacies. I expect the effect of lagged party magnitude to be positive for all candidates, but especially salient—and thus elevated—for female candidates because they are less likely than are male candidates to run as the consummate insider of the "unofficial list," and therefore stand to gain more from the potential of shared party resources. Although this expectation runs contrary to Jones's (2009) finding that party magnitude does not predict a coalition's proportion of women elected in OLPR elections, I contend that we must subject those hypotheses to testing at the individual level in order to elucidate the conditions under which individual women can thrive.[19]

Yet multivariate results (see Table 4.4) indicate that neither party magnitude nor its lag exercise a gendered effect on candidate vote share. While the main effect (*party magnitude*) is positive, with a smaller and negative coefficient for the lag ($p.mag_{t-1}$) suggesting a slighter diminished positive effect for party magnitude at the last election, their interactions with *fem* were not statistically significant. An analysis of the marginal effects disaggregated by party magnitude and candidate sex demonstrates that the latter does not mediate the effect of the former, with the vote share of men and women increasing with party magnitude (with considerable variation among women at the upper bounds of party magnitude). While the findings run contrary to the literature's expectations, they do offer suggestive evidence that a party having

---

[18] Because I am using the lag of party magnitude, the 1994 elections are excluded from the multivariate analyses due to limited data availability from 1990 elections.

[19] While Jones's party/coalition list-level analysis represents a significant and commendable advance from the bulk of studies that aggregate at the country level, it cannot tell us how those factors affect individual women. Moreover, it is unclear how he codes "left" for Brazil's rarely ideologically coherent coalitions (2009).

the capacity to support female candidacies is not sufficient to bring about women's effective participation; it must also have the will. That corresponds to interview findings; although I explicitly asked candidates and party officials about electoral rules, few respondents actively engaged the question. Two exceptions were to contrast the Chamber of Deputies rules with those for majoritarian/plurality elections (the subject of Chapter 5) and in discussion of political reforms under debate (discussed further in Chapters 7 and 8).

To recap, neither state development level nor district or party magnitude has exercised a statistically distinct effect on the vote share of male and female candidates, with all of their interactions with *fem* being insignificant. Moreover, two of those overall effects operate in the opposite direction expected by the cross-national literature on women's representation. Candidate vote share—female and male—declines as the development (for non-leftists) and electoral size of one's district increases. Vote share does increase with the electoral fortunes of a candidate's party (captured in party magnitude), but that effect is not significantly amplified for female contenders. Therefore, two conventional explanations for women's overall representation—district development and district/party magnitude—appear not to be mediated by gender at the candidate level. Female candidates fare no better electorally in more developed and larger districts than in districts with lower development levels and magnitudes. Next, I discuss party characteristics that do operate in gendered ways to predict female candidates' electoral prospects.

THE GOOD OLE BOYS' CLUB: PARTY INSTITUTIONALIZATION AND LEADERSHIP

The literature on Brazilian electoral politics emphasizes the weakness of most Brazilian parties and thus tends to discount their role in explaining electoral outcomes (e.g., Ames 2001; Mainwaring 1995, 1999; Samuels 2003, 2008). Yet most comparative studies of women's representation point to political parties as the key gatekeepers (Caul 1999, 2001; Childs and Murray 2014; Kittilson 2006, 2013; Lovenduski and Norris 1993; Wiliarty 2010; Wolbrecht 2000). Parties' (albeit varied) roles in candidate recruitment, capacity-building, and resource allocation are understood as critical to the development of viable female candidacies in both party- and candidate-centered contexts (Burrell 2006; Crowder-Meyer 2013; Lawless and Fox 2005; Sanbonmatsu 2006).

I bridge those seemingly disparate literatures to explain precisely how the abovementioned weakness of many Brazilian parties has undermined their capacity to recruit, develop, and support viable female candidacies. I use interparty variation to explain which of Brazil's parties have proven most conducive to women's electoral prospects, finding that rather than ideology per se, party institutionalization and inclusion or exclusion of women into the "good ole boys' club" (party leadership) best predict the electoral performance of female candidates.

Ideology

Ideology's role as a conventional predictor of women's electoral fortunes derives from the left's historical emphasis on social equality and a platform of active policies intended to realize equality (e.g., Duverger 1955). Due in part to the professed ideological commitment to equality by parties on the left, non-leftist parties are presumed more likely than leftist parties to be dominated by men. Those (male) leaders will fight to maintain their status and therefore tend to be unsupportive of female candidacies (Duverger 1955).

The causal process through which leftist ideology should exercise a positive effect on the electoral prospects of women candidates is not entirely clear in extant work. Most explanations point to the left's historical emphasis on egalitarianism, but discussion of the precise mechanisms substantiating the relationship at the individual level is elusive. Kenworthy and Malami argue that the strength of leftist parties can predict overall women's representation because leftist parties' ideological commitment to reducing inequality should lead them to nominate more women candidates, with the assumption being that more female candidates will translate into more women elected (1999, 238).[20] Have Brazil's leftist parties run and elected more female candidates?

In the 1994–2014 elections, 17.2% of leftist candidates were female, compared to 15.9% percent for non-leftist parties. When looking at only elected deputies, we see that 11.4% of deputies elected by leftist parties are female, compared to only 6.3% for non-leftist parties. Those observed differences between left and non-leftist parties' advancement and election of female candidates are statistically significant (at the $p<0.01$ and $p<0.001$ levels). But the question remains—what is it about running with a leftist party that seems to benefit female contenders? Is the apparent electoral advantage in fact a product of the left's egalitarian ideology, and therefore universal to leftist parties?

The potential for a "contagion from the left" effect, whereby the initial promotion of female candidates by leftist parties drives other competitive parties to do the same, gives us reason to expect ideology will lose predictive power over time (Matland and Studlar 1996). Given the gender quota, especially in the wake of reforms that enable its enforcement, as well as great diversity among women and an electorate that is right-of-center, I do not expect the circumstance of running with a leftist party per se (after controlling for other

[20] As noted above and depicted in Table 4.3, that assumption has not held in Brazilian elections (1994–2010), with the only two elections suffering decline or stagnation in the proportion of women elected to the Chamber of Deputies coming in precisely those years where the increase in the share of female candidates was greatest (1998 and 2010).

key party characteristics) to advantage female candidates. I contend that it is the institutionalized structure and incorporation of women in leadership that is common—but not universal—to leftist parties that enables and motivates their effective promotion of women's participation.

Among the 2,180 state parties that competed in the 1998–2010 elections, *left* is indeed positively correlated (at the *p*<0.001 level) with my index[21] of party institutionalization (*PII*) (ρ=0.15), as well as *proportion of women leaders* (ρ=0.21) and *c.mass* (ρ=0.26). A logistic model of critical mass—measured here as whether a state party has at least 25% women in its leadership—demonstrates that leftist parties are much more likely than non-leftist parties to have a critical mass of women leaders, with an odds ratio of 3 to 1 (see Appendix 4.3).

Given those observations, and the theoretical expectations outlined in Chapter 2, I argue that while the mass and participatory character and ideological commitment to equality of most leftist parties have given them a head start on effectively promoting women's participation, leftist ideology *per se* is neither a necessary nor sufficient condition for women's electoral success. I find that party institutionalization and the incorporation of women in party leadership yield superior analytical leverage for explaining variation in women's electoral prospects. The effect on female candidates of leftist ideology is *indirect*, with parties with a mass and participatory orientation more conducive to institutionalization, and those supporting egalitarianism more likely to incorporate women in top decision-making structures.

Multivariate analyses (see Table 4.4) demonstrate that in Brazil's right-of-center electorate, *left* exercises a negative effect on candidate vote share. For women, that negative effect is mitigated. Disaggregating the marginal effects reveals that for non-leftist candidates, men have a higher predicted vote share; but among leftist candidates, this is reversed, with women enjoying the greater predicted vote share.[22] Yet as expected, that positive interaction of *fem**left dissipates with the introduction of *PII* and *c.mass* (whether measured continuously or dichotomously); the main effect of *left* remains negative, but its interaction with *fem* loses significance. Leftist ideology *per se* has not yielded superior electoral gains among Brazil's female candidates. Instead, it is the combination of a structure favorable to outsiders and the presence of actors willing to mobilize resources on their behalf. Moreover, multivariate analyses demonstrate that neither party capacity (*PII*) nor will (*c.mass*) are sufficient on their own; rather, their positive effects on women's vote share are contingent

---

[21] The party institutionalization index (PII) is an original measure capturing electoral stability, societal roots, and party organization at the state party level with an additive index that combines information on electoral volatility, party membership, party age, party finances, party municipal presence, and alternation in party leadership. For more information, see Appendices 4.1–4.2.

[22] The predicted vote share for female and male non-leftists is 0.83 and 0.88%; for female and male leftists, it is 0.75 and 0.68%.

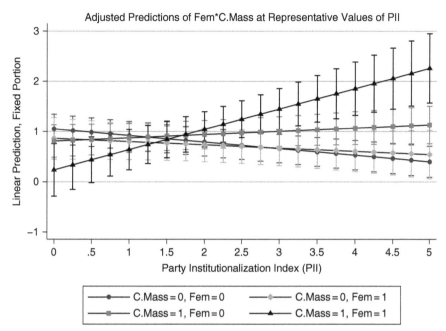

FIGURE 4.2 The Interactive Effect of Party Capacity and Will on Female Vote Share (1994–2010)

upon their joint occurrence.[23] Figure 4.2 plots the three-way interaction effect of *fem * PII * c.mass*, and illustrates how the advantage conferred to women by *PII* is conditioned by *c.mass*; without women leaders to mobilize resources on behalf of female candidates, the benefits of party capacity do not accrue to women. Next, I recall the discussion from Chapter 2 outlining my argument why well-institutionalized parties with women leaders improve the electoral prospects of female contenders, and offer descriptive and qualitative evidence to further substantiate the claims.

Transparency and the Norm of Compliance

Formal institutional change is often insufficient to induce meaningful change, especially when those reforms challenge the status quo (Mackay 2014; Mackay et al. 2010; Mackay and Waylen 2014). Rather than a wholesale shift in the rules of the game, such formal change often maintains intact "tenacious"

---

[23] Two-way interactions between *female* and each of the constitutive terms (*PII* and *critical mass*) either lose significance or become negative upon introducing the three-way interaction (*female*PII*critical mass*), which consistently returns a positive and significant effect on vote share. See Table 4.4 for model results.

informal norms (North 1990), and can occur in a gradual process that allows actors to nominally accommodate demands for change while maintaining their power (Thelen 1999). Moreover, as a burgeoning literature on feminist institutionalism compellingly demonstrates, processes of institutional change (particularly in the case of gender reforms) are inherently gendered (Kenny 2013; Krook and Mackay 2011; Mackay et al. 2010). Mackay explains how gender reforms are especially "vulnerable to regress," with gendered implications of the "nested newness" inherent to institutional change, which infuse the process of institutional layering with gender relations and norms that serve to hinder (or facilitate) genuine change (2014). Studies by Bjarnegård (2013), Franceschet (2010), Kenny (2013), Lovenduski (1998, 2005), Mackay (2014), Waylen (2017), and others speak to the gendered interplay between formal and informal institutions, "highlight(ing) the operation of informal mechanisms that shape institutional processes, developments and outcomes" (Mackay et al. 2010, 581).

It follows that formal institutional change cannot be understood in a vacuum, and in the case of status-quo changing gender reforms, it will often face resistance and backlash (Krook 2015a). Such limitations are especially heightened in an inchoate context where formal laws are regularly flouted and informal norms carry the day. Institutionalized parties are more likely to cultivate an environment in which the rules of the game are transparent, and where there is a reasonable expectation that such rules will be respected by all. The implications for women's electoral prospects are many, with two being particularly salient. First, institutionalized parties will be more likely to abide by a norm of compliance with internal and external formal rules, and thus more compelled to comply with the gender quota than will parties in which formal rules are regularly flouted.[24] When decisions are made within an exclusive realm of state party elites rather than according to clearly defined rules of the game, transparency and accountability suffer. The propensity of party leaders in inchoate parties to dominate internal decision-making and act with total impunity spills over into the realm of external rules. This is particularly true in the case of the Brazilian quota, which until the 2009 mini-reform provided ample loopholes for circumventing the law (Wylie and dos Santos 2016).

Indeed, domineering white, male leaders of Brazil's inchoate parties have acted with impunity in their resistance to the legislated gender quota. Even in the wake of the 2009 electoral reform strengthening the measure, only a quarter of state parties met the 30% target for female candidates in the 2010 elections. A striking 268 of the 607 (44%) state parties running did not advance a single female candidate. From 1998–2014, the party with the second worst record of

---

[24] As discussed in Chapter 2, this logic derives from findings in the international organizations literature that constitutional constraints on states instill a norm of compliance that carries over to the international realm, inducing compliance with rarely enforced international laws (Dixon 1993; Simmons 1998).

quota compliance and the lowest average in the proportion of women contenders is the PP, a notoriously inchoate party with domineering male leadership. The PP has the second lowest mean on the party institutionalization index (1.38), a critical mass of women leaders in less than one-fifth of its state organizations (as of 2010) and a NEC with only 8.3% women (2014), and only complied with the quota on 20 of its 135 state party lists (1998–2014).[25] The majority of the PP's state party lists have been exclusively male, with an average share of female candidates of just 12.2%.[26] A clear portrait of the PP's disregard for formal laws is its maintenance of provisional commissions in an average of 70.7% of the municipalities across its state organizations despite having the second greatest average share of affiliated voters.[27] As of 2010, leadership had remained monopolized by one or two individuals over at least two election cycles in 21 of its 27 state party organizations.

In contrast, when parties have a propensity to abide by their own transparent internal rules, the norm of compliance extends to external rules. As a result, institutionalized parties are more likely than are inchoate parties to make a good-faith effort to comply with the gender quota. As mentioned in Chapter 2, the odds that an institutionalized party (party institutionalization=3) will comply with the quota, relative to a weakly institutionalized party (party institutionalization=1), are approximately 2 to 1.25, with a one-unit increase in party institutionalization yielding a 25% increase in the odds that a party will meet the quota target (see Appendix 4.3). To illustrate, the more institutionalized PC do B (2.07), with a critical mass of women leaders in three-quarters of its state organizations in 2010, complied with the quota in 44% of the elections it contested and ran an average of 29.2% female candidates (1998–2014).

The evidence offered above suggests that the likelihood of compliance with the quota varies predictably across Brazilian parties. Logistic regression analysis of state party quota compliance (clustered by state party) provides additional support; the state parties most likely to meet the quota target are those that are institutionalized, and those with a critical mass of women in party leadership (measured continuously or dichotomously).[28] Regina Perondi, Vice-President

---

[25] Notably, 13 of those 20 compliant lists were in 2014; this means that from 1998–2010, the PP met the quota target on just 6.5% of its state party lists.

[26] This is the third lowest proportion of female candidates among 37 parties (1998–2014). Again, pre-2014 numbers were significantly lower, with the PP state party organizations running on average 7% women from 1998–2010, the second lowest overall.

[27] The legitimate use of the provisional commissions clause is for parties in the process of building their membership, with a certain number of affiliated voters required before a municipal directorate can be established (Guarnieri 2011).

[28] Notably, the effect of *left* on quota compliance is not robust (its significance is contingent upon the measure of women's leadership and the inclusion of year dummies), and *party magnitude* exercises a negative effect (see Appendix 4.3).

of the women's organ of the strongly-institutionalized PMDB,[29] confirmed the importance of women in party leadership for meeting the quota. Under her leadership, PMDB Women set out to meet the quota target by the 2012 elections through "occupying spaces throughout the party," pushing for an internal quota, and establishing a national PMDB female working group (Interview, July 2009). Perondi traveled throughout the country seeking to embolden state-level PMDB female working groups, with an eye on consolidating the national PMDB female working group to enhance their bargaining power in top party decision-making circles (Interview, July 2009). Her efforts were ultimately successful, with the national working group since being reinforced and advancing a national strategic plan for furthering women's participation that includes capacity-building courses designed to incentivize female candidacies. In June 2012, PMDB Women compelled a guarantee from the national executive commission that it would comply with the mini-reform's requirements to devote HGPP time and publicly-provided party funds to advancing women's participation (PMDB Mulher 2012).

Although the PMDB has long counted on active women's sectors (Perondi 2007), women have been underrepresented in the upper echelons of the party's leadership,[30] and the promotion of women's political participation had therefore not been prioritized. As Perondi stated, "the biggest obstacle is precisely the men in the party, they don't want to listen to us. They think that we want to take control of the party, they don't perceive it as a way to democratize the party" (Interview, July 2009). As a result of the failure to incorporate women in top party leadership and thus absence of an effective commitment to furthering women's candidacies, less than 14 percent of state parties complied with the quota in the 1998–2010 elections to the Chamber of Deputies. In our 2008 interview, Deputy Rita Camata expressed frustration with what she perceived as disregard for the quota among PMDB leadership; the men "não vão abrir a mão,"[31] or will not give up their power and privileges, and, she continued, do not seek out female candidates until the last hour in a meaningless gesture toward the quota with no intent of supporting their candidacies (Interview, December 2008).

In 2010, the PMDB's rate of quota compliance doubled to 25.9 percent, but much work remains. To be developed in Chapter 5, from 1994–2010, the PMDB did not elect a single female senator despite winning nearly a quarter of the senate seats, and elected only 36 women deputies of a total 433 (8%). My analysis suggests that the limited presence of women in party leadership is responsible for their poor record electing women. Although the PMDB is

---

[29] The overall mean party institutionalization index score for the PMDB across the states (1998–2010) is 2.29, with 63.9% of state parties scoring at least two. For party and state averages, see Appendix 4.2.

[30] As of 2010, the median proportion of women in PMDB state party leadership was only 12.5%, with an average of 8.8% and less than 8% of its state parties incorporating a critical mass of women leaders.

[31] Literally, "will not open (or extend) their hand," a Brazilian expression that illustrates stinginess.

sufficiently institutionalized in most states, with the largest share of affiliated voters of any party, and active party directorates in most municipalities in 19 of 27 states (average 61.1%) with very few provisional commissions, and is thus both rule-bound and capable of fulfilling the quota, it has simply not been a priority for male leaders who refuse to "abrir a mão" to women. However, the bold initiatives recently introduced by Regina Perondi, former President of PMDB Women and Deputy Maria Elvira, and Deputies Fátima Pelaes, Rose de Freitas (now Senator), and Marinha Raupp to hold the party publicly accountable to the women-friendly provisions of the 2009 mini-reform helped to change that pattern (PMDB Mulher 2012). Among the 608 variations on the PMDB's multiparty coalitions for October 2012 elections to municipal councils across Brazil, the average proportion of female candidates is 31.3%, a striking 44% increase from 21.7% women among their 2008 municipal councilor candidates (Tribunal Superior Eleitoral 1994–2016). In 2014, the PMDB ran 97 female candidates (29.7%) for federal deputy (seven won election), with 13 of its 27 state party organizations complying with the quota, and the party also elected its first two female senators since redemocratization.

Women party leaders can pressure leadership to recruit and support female candidacies. As stated by Deputy Luiza Erundina, many parties have not complied with the quota due to a "lack of commitment to questions of gender" (Questionnaire, April 2009). Responding to a question about the quota law, Deputy Roberto Santos (PSDB-BA) of the Special Commission of Electoral and Party Legislation stated, "It is only the leaderships in favor of women that end up (improving the political process for women)" (quoted in Araújo 1999, 125). Once women leaders reach a critical mass, they are able to explicitly incorporate gender into party decision-making, and hold the party accountable to the pro-women provisions of the electoral law. If the party then has sufficient resources to recruit and develop women's candidacies, genuine quota compliance is within reach.

The frequent malleability of formal laws among Brazil's weakly institutionalized parties poses a second hurdle for women; absent a universally understood set of rules and a norm of compliance, those new to or low in the party ranks cannot anticipate the path of ascension within the party. This means that women and other outsiders will have a difficult time attaining intermediary leadership positions as well as candidacy.

If top party leaders regularly circumvent elected delegations and conventions for the purpose of candidate nomination, political aspirants must cozy up to those party leaders to attain the nomination and subsequent campaign support, rather than cultivate a broad base of support within the party (Braga 2008; Guarnieri 2011). As stated by Mainwaring, party conventions are often "a formality behind which the 'real' mechanism of candidate selection is controlled by a small group of party leaders" (1999, 253). The fact that the upper echelons of party decision-making in most parties remain largely white and male means that most women—especially women of color—are insufficiently connected to such "good ole boy" networks, and therefore less likely to have success ascending the ranks of inchoate parties. On the contrary, where parties make a concerted effort to comply with the quota and exhibit clear processes for ascending to candidacy, women are able to work their way up through the party, with party leaders seeking to meet the quota target eager to capitalize on their potential.

The story of Deputy Jô Moraes of the PC do B in Minas Gerais illustrates how universal criteria for party ascension can illuminate the path to power for outsiders. Moraes climbed her way up the PC do B ranks by "working through party structures," regularly attending meetings and mobilizational events, and participating in leadership roles in panels whenever possible (Interview, March 2009). A member of the then underground PC do B since 1972, Moraes served as a staff member for party members in municipal government, and was eventually elected Municipal Councilor in 1996 and 2000, State Deputy in 2002, and Federal Deputy in 2006 and 2010. She is state president of the PC do B for Minas Gerais, a member of the National Directorate, and has served as Vice-Leader of the governing coalition and Leader of the PC do B in the Chamber of Deputies (Chamber of Deputies 2015).

Moraes knew that her party militancy and demonstrated base in the community would garner party support, and in 2006, she earned the privilege of being the party's priority candidate. Priority status secured human and material resources for the campaign, including the coveted "6565" campaign number (Interview, March 2009). The party chose Moraes to run for mayor of the capital city, Belo Horizonte, in 2008, although the campaign ultimately proved unsuccessful. In 2010, 45.4% of her rather sizeable campaign budget (R$861,148, more than twice the state mean) came from the party. Moraes stated that the strong party militancy and deliberate treatment of gender in the PC do B—which she argued had created "a virtuous cycle" furthering women's empowerment—were critical for her electoral successes (Interview, March 2009). She has demonstrated her militancy and electoral viability at each level, inching her way to the top and developing a solid base.

Such an orderly progression through the party ranks is unlikely in inchoate parties, where candidacies are not cultivated according to clear guidelines. The candidacy of Deputy Rebecca Garcia of the PP, for example, emerged in 2006 when her father decided not to run for reelection[32] to the Chamber of Deputies and suggested she leave her position in the family-owned media outlet to contest the election (Interview, December 2008). That is hardly a replicable path for the vast majority of party newcomers, and can prove daunting for actual outsiders who lack the economic and/or familial capital to convert into political capital.

---

[32] Francisco Garcia ran instead as 1st Substitute on the unsuccessful reelection campaign of Senator Gilberto Mestrinho. In his 2010 campaign, again as the 1st Substitute, that time on a successful senate ticket, his declared assets exceeded $12 million (Tribunal Superior Eleitoral 1994–2016).

The Psychology of Self- vs. External Nomination

In Brazil's entrepreneurial electoral context, where party organizations are often a "few-man-show" rather than a collective and well-structured organization, self- rather than external nomination is the norm (Samuels 2008). It is up to candidates to get themselves on the party list, which will most often simply be presented—as is—at a ceremonial convention (Braga 2008; Mainwaring 1999). That is problematic for women's representation in part because of the constructed gender gap in political ambition, with women socialized to perceive their appropriate societal role as in the home. Despite the fact that women are transcending such constructed barriers, are the head of household in 37.3% of Brazilian homes (Portal Brasil 2015)—often times the manager of family funds (with 94% of the Bolsa Família transfers benefitting millions of Brazilian families going to women (Leonardi 2011)), and comprise the majority contingency of many if not most social movements, many women maintain a distance from formal politics.

This is a result of a complex and gendered interconnected web of factors, including traditional gender socialization, disillusionment with pervasive political corruption, and the inherent risks of the campaign. As illustrated in Chapter 2, traditional gender socialization has left women largely responsible for domestic duties, with the vast majority of women who work outside the home having to take on a "triple shift" in order to be active in party life. That has a fundamental influence on the kind of women seeking and winning election. Women deputies are far less likely than their male counterparts to be married (CFEMEA 2009; Tribunal Superior Eleitoral 1994–2016) and have young children while serving (CFEMEA 2009), and if they do have a family at home, they must have the conditions to contract household help in their stead. With societal gender norms still privileging women as mothers, a family supportive of female political ambition—which if successful, will result in her spending a sizeable portion of her time away from home—is not a given.

Several women I interviewed spoke of the difficulties in reconciling family life and a political career, and the double/triple shift it entailed (e.g., Interviews with Emília Fernandes, April 2009; Jô Moraes, March 2009; Maninha, April 2009; Raquel Teixeira, April 2009; Rita Camata, December 2008; Serys Slhessarenko, December 2008). Tonha Magalhães (PFL/PR-BA), who is from a modest background and acquired her political capital heading up a neighborhood association and then in municipal politics, lamented that her children were practically raised by a maid (Interview, November 2008).[33] District Deputy Eliana Pedrosa (PFL-DF) actually lost her marriage over the time and energy she committed to politics rather than spending time at home; only two years into her mandate, her husband (also in

---

[33] Magalhães has no relation to Bahia's longtime dominant Magalhães family. She has belonged to a number of parties, moving from the PMDB→PMB→PFL→PDT→PP→PFL→PR.

politics) delivered an ultimatum—either politics or their marriage. She chose politics (Interview, July 2009). Deputy Iriny Lopes (PT-ES) confirmed the importance of a supportive network for her electoral successes, with fellow party militants even helping to care for her children when necessary. Lopes stated, "The militancy and level of solidarity in the PT has no substitute" (Interview, December 2008).

Moreover, women are often reluctant to make such a sacrifice to enter an arena they perceive as corrupt and ineffective. Earlier waves of public opinion data demonstrate statistically significant gender gaps in trust in and satisfaction with the country's political institutions. In 2008, more than a third of female respondents indicated that they had absolutely no trust in parties, 20.6% reported no trust whatsoever in elections, and 41.2% said they were unsatisfied with the functioning of Brazilian democracy (LAPOP n.d.). Interestingly, by 2014, the gender gaps appeared to have dissipated; nevertheless, dissatisfaction was even higher, with 45.8% and 31.7% of women reporting absolutely no trust in parties and elections, respectively, and 59.8% saying they were unsatisfied with the functioning of Brazilian democracy (LAPOP n.d.). An oft-repeated expression characterizes politics as dirty and a man's world, a bastion of corruption and masculinity that women are frequently reluctant to confront. Add to those already powerful deterrents the expense and combative character of campaigns alongside gendered and racialized wage inequities, and the disincentives for women to self-nominate are evident. Without the strong encouragement and assurance of support from her party, most women will be hesitant to embark on such an endeavor that is fraught with abundant risk and questionable rewards.

Women in general also have a greater affinity for parties that recruit *loyalists* rather than *entrepreneurs*, with women being "more likely to try to obtain their party's nomination when a *loyalist* is the type of deputy the party commonly wants" (Escobar-Lemmon and Taylor-Robinson 2008, 347). The probability of combative intraparty competition tends to deter women, with experimental evidence suggesting that women typically prefer being a part of collective team-based strategies "rather than intraparty competition that directly pits co-partisans against each other" (Ellis 2002; Escobar-Lemmon and Taylor-Robinson 2008, 350).

Affirming the weight of such constraints, the vast majority of the women I interviewed said they never intended to get involved in politics. All but two (Judge Denise Frossard[34] and Emília Fernandes[35]) said that the decision to be

---

[34] Judge Denise Frossard is an exceptionally ambitious individual. Her experience in the magistrate —which she contended was significantly more egalitarian than electoral politics, and national fame after her involvement (and death threats thereafter) in bringing down 14 figures in organized crime—augmented her self-confidence and self-perception of viability. She ran for governor in 2006, but lost in the second round.

[35] Emília Fernandes said the firing of her colleagues (fellow teachers) after their participation in a strike provoked her and led to her first candidacy for city councilor in 1982 with the PTB (she is now with the PT).

a candidate was not "their decision," but was externally made, providing strong support for the importance of external rather than self-nomination. Women in institutionalized parties most often said it was their party that pushed them to candidacy, with those running in weaker parties saying it was their group (association/movement) and one telling me "o povo" (the people) that decided she should be a candidate. Deputy Emília Fernandes (PT-RS) corroborated the importance of external nomination for women, saying that female candidacies "have to be stimulated" by parties, who play a fundamental role in building the self-esteem and audacity of potential female aspirants (Interview, June 2009). In contrast, a young male deputy and son of the longtime president of the PMDB in Rio de Janeiro highlighted the typical male experience when he proclaimed cavalierly that he had always liked politics and wanted to be a politician, so decided to run for office (Interview, December 2008).

Although party support for the decision to run is critical, parties "do not offer conditions for women to be candidates ... many times ... lacking a structure that facilitates their participation." Even with the quotas, the majority of parties "do not seek to incentivize enhanced participation by women" (Governor Ana Júlia Carepa, PT-PA, quoted in Paiva 2008, 34–35). Senator Patrícia Saboya Gomes (PDT-CE) explained, "among the principal (obstacles) is the lack of party investment in women ... It is fundamental to stimulate the entrance of women ... which necessitates a greater party investment in women's sectors and a change in the mentality regarding the importance of women's participation" (Questionnaire, April 2009). Deputy Thelma Oliveira echoed that sentiment, placing the onus directly on party structures, "You do not have this reasonable number of women launching their campaigns because of the lack of party support ... the party has to first make their presence possible ... the party has to invest in women" (Interview, December 2008).

Without influential women in the party pressuring leadership to make that investment and develop and recruit female candidates, those (men) in power will seek to maintain the status quo. "The parties need to perceive that it is time to invest in women" (Peron 2012, paraphrasing José Eustáquio Alves). Armed with favorable public opinion data, a (recently) enforced quota law, and the impressive electoral showing of women throughout the country at various levels (six were the top vote earners in their state in 2014 Chamber elections), women in party decision-making structures can convince male leaders of the electoral utility of cultivating viable female candidacies. The female leaders of PMDB Women are perhaps the foremost example of the importance of such pressure. Fighting to change the status quo of male dominance in their party by infiltrating party leadership and recruiting and training more women members, their goal of genuine quota compliance is within reach (Interview with Regina Perondi, July 2009).

Women running in weakly institutionalized parties are likely to be those that either possess family or converted political capital independent of their party (to be discussed in Chapter 6), or those that have been tapped at the last moment as *candidatas laranjas* (sacrificial lambs and phantom candidates) intended to garner votes for the priority (usually male) candidate(s) while allowing the party to feign an attempt at compliance with the gender quota. The latter candidate will be poorly equipped for the campaign and have no party support, with any success achieved by the former candidate done so in spite of her party.

In institutionalized parties, on the other hand, municipal party organizations collect suggestions for candidates, with leaders from the women's and organizational sectors often approaching women leaders in the community about considering a run well in advance of the election (rather than at the last minute solely to gesture at the gender quota). Nominations are evaluated by municipal and state party leadership, and then a unified party ticket is presented at an inclusive state party convention, where popularly elected delegates are allowed to propose and debate changes to the party slate, after which the final candidate list is voted upon (Braga 2008). Those conditions are propitious for women because they externalize the decision to run—with being selected itself serving to boost women's self-confidence and thus viability. Greater vetting by an active party organization is also likely to result in a more qualified candidate pool, leading to greater prospects of electoral success among women candidates from such parties.

The PC do B is exemplary of the ability of female leaders in institutionalized parties to further the electoral prospects of women through active recruitment. It is well-institutionalized and as of 2010 had 25.9% women in its NEC, an average of 27.1% women in state party leadership, and five state committees presided by women.[36] Accordingly, it has run an average of 29.2% female candidates in the 1998–2014 Chamber of Deputies elections (67% higher than the national mean of 17.5%), complied with the quota in 44% of those elections, and enjoys an impressive success rate of 22.3% among its female candidates (the national success rate for female candidates is just 5.2%).

As discussed above, the PC do B operates a thorough recruitment and training process for candidates. Female leaders such as Nereide Saviani, Director of the PC do B's National Training School (ENF), have mobilized that infrastructure with a particular emphasis on women, offering courses that prioritize women's participation, gender equality issues, and even provide day care for children during the course, alleviating in each instance prominent impediments to women's participation analyzed here (PC do B 2009a; PC do B 2011). Such efforts are at the heart of the PC do B's success promoting women, and should continue to bear fruit through future elections. After the PC do B's Second National Conference on the

---

[36] São Paulo, Minas Gerais, Rio de Janeiro, Santa Catarina and Sergipe.

Emancipation of Women, Liège Rocha, the party's National Secretary of Women commented, "I think that women and the Party itself are more alert for this necessity of the promotion of women and the guarantee of female candidates for the Party" (PC do B 2012).

Without active measures to recruit and promote female candidacies, the socialized gender gap in political ambition is likely to remain intact and women's disproportionately limited participation in formal politics will persist. Well-institutionalized parties have proven more conducive to women's political participation because their recruitment process externalizes the decision to seek office and mitigates the constructed gender gap in political ambition. When female leaders mobilize supportive party networks to recruit, train, and campaign for women, they provide significant psychological incentives for women's participation. Parties lacking such resources favor entrepreneurial candidates who must fend for themselves in the absence of any real party recruitment effort or organization in general. The result is an individualistic campaigning effort that tends to deter most female aspirants (Escobar-Lemmon and Taylor-Robinson 2008).

Organizational Support

Institutionalized parties also provide opportunities for newcomers to cut their political teeth. Whereas inchoate parties often have only a couple of offices that remain in the hands of a few leaders, more institutionalized parties have various sectors that are represented by internally elected leaders, with regular alternation. The range of electable internal party positions affords aspirants a lower risk opportunity to gauge their support within the party and explore their broader electability, with those elected having the chance to learn the ropes and eventually demonstrate their political prowess to co-partisans. Frequent meetings and mobilizational events are other means through which active party organizations facilitate the acquisition of political skillsets by their members.

As illustrated in the discussion of the PC do B above, institutionalized parties also often offer courses designed with candidate capacity-building in mind. For example, some parties offer "political capacitation" courses early in the year of elections. They explain what is in the purview of each office, what to expect in the campaign, give lessons in rhetoric, and review key party policy positions (if applicable). Since the 2009 mini-reform, which in part requires parties to spend 5% of their publicly-provided funds on promoting women's participation, several parties have adopted such courses and incorporated gender into the program. In the PC do B's courses at the ENF, participants are required to read over 100 pages of Marx and Engels as well as the resolutions of recent party congresses and excerpts from assessments of socialism and capitalism in the 21st century, with units on philosophy, class, political economy, socialism, gender, and race and ethnicity (PC do B 2009b). Such opportunities demonstrate both the *how* and *what* of politics.

As discussed above, women are in general predisposed to collective strategies based on constructive ideas rather than combative and individualistic campaigns (Escobar-Lemmon and Taylor-Robinson 2008). Particularly given the intraparty competition prevalent in Chamber of Deputies elections, the ability to campaign on party (or faction) ideals and proposals, rather than clientelistic strategies that favor incumbents, is advantageous for female contenders. An institutionalized party has clearly identifiable policy positions, with participation in party events providing on-the-ground training allowing women to adopt and articulate those positions. Political training and capacity-building courses such as those discussed above educate women on their collective party platform.

By offering candidates the chance to develop political wherewithal, institutionalized parties enhance their candidates' electoral viability. In contrast, a weakly institutionalized party is problematic for women because it lacks coherent platforms, and offers little or no opportunities for outsiders to acquire the necessary skillset. With a party organization that is fleeting at best, candidates are left to fend for themselves. One result of that extremely entrepreneurial setting is that many of the few successful female candidates have developed their political capital in alternate spheres rather than coming up through the party ranks (see Chapter 6).

Organizational support from one's party can also have a psychological effect, with women unlikely to contest an election for which they feel unqualified. Fox and Lawless's surveys of men and women from the "candidate eligibility pool" in the US (law, business, education, political activism) reveal that women are significantly more likely than men to doubt their qualifications and capacity for both electoral politics and the campaign itself (Fox and Lawless 2004, 2011; Lawless and Fox 2005, 2010). I expect the same dynamic of "gendered evaluative standards" to hold in Brazil, where socialized gender norms are equally (if not more) resilient despite recent progress.

The acquisition of knowledge and sense of community prepares female political aspirants both organizationally and psychologically, instilling self-confidence and a potentially powerful boost to their political ambition. Sílvia Rita Souza, a veteran congressional staffer and former Executive Secretary of PSDB Women, emphasized the importance of familiarity with the "how and what" of party politics for success, and the power of such knowledge to enhance women's self-confidence and electoral viability (Interview, December 2008). Souza conveyed the difficulties women often confront, and the importance of party support for overcoming them, "The parties in general have not invested in building the capacity of female candidates. After having the courage to run, women often become lost with the instruments of the campaign, principally the media" (Quoted in *Jornal Cidade* 2008). Responding to the limited accessibility of such information, Souza self-financed the publication of a brief and easy-to-understand non-partisan book on the process titled, *The Woman Candidate: A Guide to Dispute Elections* (2008), and has served as a consultant in capacity-building courses for women.

In sum, the solid party organizations of well-institutionalized parties are conducive to the participation and electoral success of outsiders because they provide lower stakes opportunities for newcomers to acquire the political skillset, and can offer capacity-building courses that further awareness of party platforms and aspirants' sense of preparedness. But as I discuss next, the prospect for learning party platforms depends, of course, on their presence. If a party exists as a mere electoral vehicle and lacks coherent, shared positions, there is little for women (or any candidate) to latch onto (Interview with Deputy Rita Camata, PMDB-ES, December 2008). Thus inchoate parties are detrimental to any candidate unable to marshal a suite of individual or familial resources.

Personalist vs. Programmatic Politics and Material Support

The prospect of programmatic campaigns rather than personalist politics is far greater in institutionalized parties than in inchoate parties (Ames 2001; Guadagnini 1993). Programmatic politics facilitate collective, ideas-based strategies, with candidates running in such parties able to emphasize party policy positions rather than their own personal appeal. That may in turn lead the elector to evaluate a candidate on the basis of her articulated policy positions rather than personal traits such as gender (Valdini 2013a). An ideas-based evaluation can mitigate the potential for voter bias against women, which is elevated in electoral systems such as Brazil's (Valdini 2013a), where open-list electoral rules and large district magnitude foment intraparty competition (Shugart, Valdini, and Suominen 2005).

In contexts where party platforms remain elusive, a candidate's campaign will be based more on accumulated personal political capital than collective party ideas. In contrast, candidates running with more institutionalized parties are able to count on a loyal base engaged with the party platform. Senator Fátima Cleide (PT-RO) stated, "I know no name in the PT that you could point to as elected by his or her own force and individual expression with no help from the party."[37] Candidates' campaigns in the PT and other institutionalized parties are more collectively-run endeavors, with the party often establishing a common platform to which it holds its candidates accountable, and providing campaign materials and assistance with the production of candidates' segments on the HGPE (publicly-funded electoral propaganda hour) that reiterate the collective campaign message. Former Deputy Maninha reported that PT financing of electoral flyers and

---

[37] Questionnaire, May 2009.

her HGPE spot[38] was fundamental for her 2002 victory. She contrasted that campaign to her under-funded and unsuccessful 2006 campaign with the then nascent PSOL, which still lacked the infrastructure to support her candidacy.

In the face of intraparty competition, weakly institutionalized parties only exacerbate the potential for personalist politics, favoring those with accumulated personal political capital—which as a result of constructed gender roles and racial hierarchies, are primarily white men (or women relatives of white male politicians). While candidates in weakly institutionalized parties will have to themselves hire most of their campaign staff and thus independently garner extensive campaign funding, institutionalized parties with strong party organizations can provide female candidates with funding and militant (wo)man power to overcome their probable finance deficit. Indeed, among the candidacies studied here, as party institutionalization increases, the proportion of campaign contributions financed by one's party grows. But as party institutionalization decreases, the proportion of campaign funds coming from the candidate herself and from corporations increases. Absent the support of an institutionalized party, candidates must fend for themselves.

In spite of women's substantial advances in education and workforce participation, they continue to receive less remuneration for equal work—with wage discrepancies that are amplified for women of color—and perform the vast majority of unpaid labor in the home (Institute for Applied Economic Research 2012).[39] That means that most women will simply not possess the material capital to bank a campaign, and thus be dependent upon the availability of party or external (corporate, individual) funding. A well-institutionalized party will have both party funds and militants at its disposal, which can provide women with much needed material support for the campaign.

A materially well-off campaign (whether through money or [wo]manpower) is essential due to the vast numbers of candidacies and often extensive territory within a district. Parties can assist with the acquisition of necessary resources

---

[38] Maninha said the PT spent R$700,000 producing the HGPE spot (it was unclear whether this was just her ad, or for all 10 candidates in the district). Because this expenditure is indirect (by the party, not the candidate) it does not appear in reported campaign contributions. This is one reason, along with *caixa dois*—under the table campaign finance—why the quantification of party funding is challenging (Interview, April 2009).

[39] In 2009, the average reported weekly hours on domestic duties for women aged 16 and older was 26.6 hours, compared to only 10.5 weekly hours for men aged 16 and older. Only 49.9% of men (compared to 89.9% of women) affirmed that they took care of any household labor (Institute for Applied Economic Research 2012). Among those aged 10 and older, the average weekly hours was 20.6 for white and Asian-descendant women, 22.5 for Afro-descendant women, 9.2 for white and Asian-descendant men, and 9.8 for Afro-descendant men (Departamento Intersindical de Estatística e Estudos Socioeconômicos 2011).

and otherwise help to orient newcomers to the nuances of a daunting electoral arena that privileges incumbents (Araújo and Alves 2007) and others possessing political and/or economic capital (Avelar 2001; Pinheiro 2007). Party (and external) funds help to produce electoral propaganda and stage and attend political rallies, parades, and other events over the course of the campaign. Candidates without such campaign materials and/or events will be lost in a sea of competitors and thus have little to no chance of election. While there are several deputies who have won election with limited funds, campaign finance remains one of the strongest predictors of an individual candidate's chance of success (Samuels 2001a, 2001b; author calculations).

Nearly all of the women I interviewed spoke of the difficulty posed by campaign finance. Deputy Luiza Erundina, the women's caucus's most vocal and informed advocate within Congress for political reforms to enhance representativeness, emphasized "Without a doubt the financing of campaigns is the most difficult problem," with the related lack of party support being the second most pressing challenge (Questionnaire, April 2009). In weakly institutionalized parties, the problem is compounding—the campaigns are often more expensive as candidates spend to distinguish themselves as individuals rather than as part of a collective campaign, and inchoate party organizations often suffer from a resource disadvantage and therefore cannot fund their candidates' campaigns. Pairwise correlations lend support to that argument, with party institutionalization being positively correlated to the proportion of campaign contributions from parties, and negatively correlated to the proportion financed by corporations or the candidate herself. The magnitude of those correlations grows when looking at female candidates only. With a gendered discrepancy both in professional wages at large and in candidates' proportion of campaign contributions from corporate donors, the need to depend on self and corporate financing in inchoate parties bodes poorly for women.

Former Deputy Rita Camata also considered campaign resources one of the most significant obstacles to women's representation, saying women "do not have the culture of power," with men having an easier time asking for money (Interview, December 2008). Municipal Councilor Olívia Santana (PC do B) reported difficulties in raising money for her campaign for federal deputy, saying businessmen preferred to fund male candidacies (Interview, April 2009). According to Deputy Iriny Lopes, businesses commonly discriminate in their donations, giving male candidates much higher contributions than they do female candidates (Interview, December 2008). Parties with limited funds cannot compensate, and even where party resources are available, those without women-friendly leadership may not avail the resources for women.

While the relationship between women party leaders and financing for female candidates' campaigns is not determinative, with all rational leaders hesitant to divest resources from their own or close allies' campaigns on behalf of untested newcomers, the overall pattern suggests that the presence of a critical mass of women in leadership does increase the likelihood that female candidacies will receive funding. In 2010, the average share of state funding among female candidates in well-institutionalized parties was significantly greater among parties with a critical mass of women leaders than those without. If women have an effective voice in party leadership, they can pressure party leaders to distribute funds more equitably. The PSDB's National President Sérgio Guerra recently echoed that sentiment when responding to the publicized finding that the PSDB ran 20.4% women candidates in 2010, but dedicated only 1.7% of their dispersed funds to these women—"This pattern will only change with more mobilization and pressure by women" (Quoted in Mendonça and Navarro 2012). Notably, the women-inclusive PC do B actually gave proportionately more money to the campaigns of female candidates than to men (Mendonça and Navarro 2012).

As the ultimate "fortress of machismo" (phrase stated in several interviews), even many institutionalized parties have remained closed to women, with the vast majority of state parties still led by men. As of 2010, the average percentage of women in state party leadership was 17.33, with four of the five major parties falling well below this (PFL: 10.6%; PMDB: 8.8%; PSDB: 11.6%; PP: 10.7%). The fact that the leading PSDB had only one state party leadership with a critical mass of women (Roraima) is appalling. Several of the parties that have incorporated women into their leadership such as the PRB and the PRTB have yet to institutionalize adequately and are thus unable to provide the conditions ripe for women to thrive in Brazil's candidate-centered electoral system.

The lack of party support diminishes women's viability while also discouraging female aspirants from waging future campaigns (Special Secretariat for Policies for Women 2014). As CFEMEA stated, "The electoral campaigns of women tend to receive less support and sustenance from parties and to have less visibility than the campaigns of men, and consequently, to receive less support and votes from electors" (Fêmea 2006, 11). Often, parties will recruit female candidates as *laranjas* (sacrificial lambs and phantom candidates), only to satisfy the quota requirements for their party. Many ambitious and respected female party activists I interviewed indicated their own reluctance to run, knowing well from their front-row seat to the paucity of party support that their party's initial encouragement would ring empty during the campaign and in the end, they would confront an uphill battle on their own, committing their personal time and money for an endeavor fraught with risks. For a campaign to be viable, a candidate needs material and human resources that endure.

In sum, "women need to have concrete investment from the parties" (Laisy Moriére, National Secretary of Women of the Workers' Party, quoted in Paraguassu 2008, 31). CFEMEA summarizes the conundrum,

The parties have not undertaken the challenge to stimulate and contribute substantively to the increased political participation of women. In this sense, very few have adopted gender quotas for the composition of party leadership and, in general, they [parties] do not have policies to devote resources and media time to the promotion of women's political participation. They are masculine institutions whose functioning and structure make female participation difficult. It is necessary to democratize the party life and structures. (Fêmea 2004, 5)

Women in Party Leadership

The *capacity* to recruit and promote female candidacies, however, is only effectuated with the endorsement and active support of party leadership. When women attain a "critical mass" among party leadership, they are able to lobby for the active promotion of women's participation (Agência Patrícia Galvão 2011; Kittilson 2006).[40] Once reaching a critical mass, and therefore less hindered by the constraints of token minority status and thus better situated to amplify each other's voices, women in party leadership can use their awareness of the barriers confronted by female contenders to introduce a gendered frame of reference and carry out a number of "critical acts" (Dahlerup 1988). As illustrated in Figure 2.2, women leaders can pressure parties to adopt women-friendly policies, hold parties accountable to the quota, serve as mentors for women aspiring to ascend within the party, recruit and recommend women for inclusion on candidate lists, lobby for and host capacity-building events, and mobilize party resources to support female candidacies. Such critical acts, which help women overcome an array of obstacles, are less likely to be promoted by male party leaders, who are often incognizant of the significance of such acts for women and/or unwilling to support efforts that may ultimately dilute their own influence.

Former Deputy, Mayor, Senator, and Governor Mário Covas' (PMDB/PSDB-SP) characterization of the PMDB is typical, "Women have political space in the party. But for me, a woman is a politician not a woman politician, it is not a question of being a woman or not ... Politics is all equal and the space is open to anyone. It would be highly improbable that the PMDB, in any way, made the (political) life of women difficult" (Quoted in PMDB 1986, 234). Contrary to Covas' statement—the sentiment of which was echoed in my interviews with male party leaders across the ideological spectrum, male and female contenders do not compete on a level playing field. The interrelated implications of traditional gender socialization—the wage gap, women's disproportionate burden of domestic responsibilities, aversion to risk, and

---

[40] In an event history analysis of the adoption of candidate gender quotas in sixty parties in ten Western European democracies, Kittilson found that even after controlling for several party and electoral system variables, "for each percentage point gain in the proportion of women among the party's leadership, or national executive committee, the likelihood that the party will adopt quotas increases by almost 8% in the first model (1975–1995) and by 13% in the second model (1985–1995)" (2006, 60).

distaste for the corrupt formal political sphere—as well as the combative electoral climate of Chamber of Deputies elections create powerful disincentives for women to participate. Yet, Covas' statement is indicative of the failure of many male leaders to comprehend the necessity for parties to actively intervene on behalf of women; "parties have to make [women's] presence possible" (Interview with Deputy Thelma Oliveira, December 2008). Women in party leadership can introduce a gendered frame of reference that conveys to male leaders the obstacles confronted by women and the means for overcoming them.

While female presence in party leadership can be a potent mechanism for enhancing women's legislative representation, acquiring power within those largely male decision-making circles is difficult (Htun 2005). According to Kittilson's study of several Western European parties, the parties most likely to have women in their high-level party leadership structures are those that have internal party quotas, are centralized, have New Left values, and are fractionalized with strong external ties (2006).[41] As discussed in Chapter 1, women's presence on the national executive committees (NECs) of most Brazilian parties remains minimal, with women at least approximating 25% in only eight parties (left: PT, PC do B, PPS, PSOL, PV; non-left: PMN, PRTB, PTB). While there are several outliers at the national and state levels, with even those eight parties having some state organizations with few women and other leftist parties having only minimal representation of women in their national and state leadership, it is noteworthy that leftist parties are three times more likely to have a critical mass of women leaders in state leadership than non-leftist parties (1998–2010). Another telling indicator is that among the major non-left parties (PFL, PMDB, PP, PSDB), which together have 35% of the current seats in the Chamber of Deputies, the average proportion of women on their NEC is a paltry 9.8 percent (2014).

Ideology thus retains an indirect influence, with leftist parties being more likely to provide the initial conditions propitious for women. Under historical conditions of inclusion, women in leftist parties are more likely to have developed critical organizing experience allowing them to ascend the party ranks, as the case of Jô Moraes illustrates above. In short, there is a certain degree of path dependence, with leftist parties traditionally more conducive to women's participation than non-leftist parties. Yet while that in part illuminates why leftist parties have been overall more likely than non-leftist parties to incorporate women in their leadership structures, it is less convincing for explanations of women's electoral prospects. I maintain that the fact of not being leftist does not itself lead a party to defy the quota law while diminishing its own electoral conquests by squandering candidate slots. Rather, domineering male party leaders evade efforts they perceive will dilute their

---

[41] O'Brien (2015) finds that women's access to top party leadership positions is inversely related to parties' electoral fortunes.

influence and/or lack awareness of how they can effectively recruit and develop viable female candidacies.

A critical mass of women in state party leadership facilitates a greater commitment of resources toward women. For instance, two critical acts that women in party leadership can perform are to hold party leaders accountable to the quota and recruit female candidates. A logistic model of a state party's odds of complying with the gender quota (1998–2010) demonstrates that state parties with a critical mass of women are 75 percent more likely to comply with the gender quota than are parties lacking a critical mass of women in their leadership.[42] As mentioned above, a one-unit increase in *PII* is associated with a 25 percent increase in the odds that a party will comply with the quota. Notably, upon the introduction of *c.mass*, the effect of *left* loses statistical significance. That offers additional evidence that it is the inclusion of women in party leadership rather than leftist ideology per se that is more important for quota compliance.

So while leftist parties are in general considered to be more women-friendly, with parties being constrained in their ability to respond to new demands by their historical ideological orientation (Kitschelt 1994), leftist ideology is an insufficient condition for a party to be deemed open to women. Leftist ideology per se does not have a monopoly on enabling female political aspirants; the party institutionalization and incorporation of women in party leadership more common to parties on the left, however, have proven women-friendly in recent elections. As chronicled throughout this book, those two distinct mechanisms— a party's capacity to provide conditions propitious to women, and their will to mobilize that capacity on behalf of women—enable the electoral success of female political aspirants in Brazil. The following discussion of the Workers' Party, which underwent two distinct episodes of leadership diversification, allows me to trace the process unfolding over time and thus address concerns about the potentially tautological relationship between female party leaders and women's electoral prospects.

A Glimpse at the Workers' Party through the Lens of Women

Brazil's largest leftist party has since its founding reached out to women (Macaulay 2003).[43] Leading *petistas* such as Bete Mendes and Benedita da Silva have figured prominently in the party, establishing the importance of women's participation for the PT since its founding while also serving as role models for aspiring female politicians. Coordination between female leaders and women's sectors has enabled effective pressure on party leadership to create women-friendly policies such as the leadership quota, and to host capacity-

---

[42] See Appendix 4.3 for model results. The robust standard errors adjust for clustering among a state party over time.

[43] Interview with Senator Marta Suplicy, May 2015.

building opportunities and otherwise empower female candidacies.[44] The PT's embrace of women stands in sharp contrast to the right-wing Democratas party (PFL), where women have had a minimal role since its inception (which has its roots in the military regime) with very few female politicians who are not the wife or daughter of a prominent male politician.

In spite of the historical involvement of women in the PT—sustained in part by the party's affinity with social movements, where women's participation is far less constrained (Alvarez 1990)—and their strength among the party rank and file, in 1990, women comprised less than 10% of party leadership compared to around 40% of total party affiliates. In response to that disparity, the proposal of a quota for party leadership was introduced at the PT's Second National Women's Congress in 1988, and debated and finally approved at the party's Third National Women's Congress in 1991 (Godinho 1996, 1998). Feminist party activists waged a rigorous fight for a voice in the party's top decision-making circles, strategically targeting all major PT factions and using the slogan "sex inequality does not rhyme with democracy" to frame the campaign, and won approval for the pioneering 30% gender quota for all instances of party leadership at the National Party Congress later that year (1991) (Santos 2009; Godinho 1996). Female presence in the PT's national directorate catapulted from 6.1% in 1990 to 29.8% in 1993 (Godinho 1996; Macaulay 2003, 7).

According to Tatau Godinho, then Secretary of Organization of the PT's National Executive Committee, the results were profound. Women *petistas* exercised their strengthened collective voice and the demand for more women in elected office "became more frequent" and gained traction and visibility, persuading both the men in leadership and female political aspirants themselves of the importance and viability of women as political subjects in general and candidates in particular (Godinho 1996, 153; 1998, 29). In the 1994 elections, the proportion of women in the PT's congressional delegation doubled, up from 8.3% in the 1990 to 16.7% Tribunal Superior Eleitoral 1994–2016). Again citing Godinho, of all the mechanisms considered for enhancing women's participation, "none have altered the access and role of women in the party as significantly" as the PT's quota for leadership positions (1996, 156; 1998, 31). According to Deputy Benedita da Silva, "We, PT women, engaged in this debate about the question of gender in whatever space we were in, whether in the community, church, or samba schools" (PT 2017a). The summary produced of the 3rd National Meeting of PT Women explained, "The organization of women within the party was important for the advance of discussions about gender. ... They contributed to allow other women to have contact with feminism. ... It was important for the elaboration of public policy related to women. [It contributed to the] elaboration of electoral platforms for municipal and state governments and for the presidency" (cited in dos Santos 2009, 73).

---

[44] Interviews with Laisy Moriére, May 2015, and Tatau Godinho, August 2014.

By 2011, with nearly two decades of a critical mass of women throughout PT party directories (if not executive commissions) under their belt, and the party's 2010 election of the country's first female president, female leadership was becoming normalized in the PT. Female *petista* leaders coordinated with the party's women's sectors to pressure party leadership to create and support women-friendly initiatives such as capacity-building workshops and recruit and support viable female candidacies. But barriers remained. Observing the limitations of the party's 1991 gender quota for leadership and the national candidate quota, female party leaders and women's sectors mobilized for gender parity in leadership (Interviews with Laisy Moriére, May 2015, and Tatau Godinho, August 2014). At the PT's 4th National Congress in 2011, the party's pioneering parity statute for all instances of party leadership was approved, to be implemented in the 2013 internal party elections (Agência Patrícia Galvão 2011).

Women *petistas* played a key role in winning approval of the parity quota, with a coordinated campaign of female *petista* leaders and women's sectors working together to strategically target individual *puxadores de legenda* (vote champions) for the party in advance of the National Congress and secure their support (Aggege 2011; Interview with Laisy Moriére, May 2015). According to the PT's National Women's Secretary Laisy Moriére, a group of around 50 women *petistas* physically delivered their parity proposal to key party leaders targeting all major factions and were a force to be reckoned with. She speculated that some of the leaders surely wanted to reject the proposal but "did not have the courage" to speak against their intrepid group (Moriére 2017, speaking at the May 2017 Seminar "Women and Participation in Politics: Challenges and Perspectives).

The parity proponents confronted an opportunity structure that was favorable for party change related to gender equality. Brazil had just elected its first female president, Dilma Rousseff, who viewed gender equality as a key component of her mandate (Jalalzai and dos Santos 2015). And when paired with traditional gender norms rooted in *marianismo*, which expect women to be moral and trustworthy motherly figures, the societal weariness with long-tolerated political corruption offered a context ripe for marketing women's political involvement. By incorporating women in their leadership, parties could present a novel face representing an alternative to corrupt politics as usual (Barnes and Beaulieu 2014; Goetz 2007; Valdini 2013b). As discussed above, opinion polls increasingly demonstrated a public eager for women to play a greater role in politics (Brazilian Institute of Public Opinion and Statistics 2009).

Legally, the 2009 mini-reform imposed changes to the gender quota law for legislative candidates that required parties to actually meet the quota target, which had been "a law on paper only" since its 1995 approval (Wylie and dos Santos 2016). The mini-reform also required parties to devote 10% of their publicly provided off-election year propaganda time and 5% of their publicly provided party funds to promoting women's representation (Wylie and dos Santos 2016). With those changes to the electoral law alongside increasingly gender egalitarian societal preferences, the writing was on the wall—parties would have to become more women-friendly.

The literature on party organizational change (e.g., Amaral 2013; Gauja 2017; Harmel 2002; Harmel and Janda 1994, Katz and Mair 1994; Kittilson 2006) suggests that the PT, as a centralized, factionalized, and institutionalized leftist party, with a history favorable to gender quotas, offers an internal party structure and ideology conducive to the change proposed by the gender parity rule. The 1991 quota, notwithstanding its limitations, put a critical mass of women in a position to pressure for changes. Female *petista* leaders were able to leverage that party context and general evolving societal and legal scenario described above to work collectively to convince the party leadership to support the parity proposal. The PT's 4th National Congress also saw the approval of quotas for age and race (Abreu 2011).[45] The statute changes promised a major shakeup in the PT's leadership composition, yielding expectations of further change.

The proponents of the parity provision had hopes that the introduction of new blood throughout PT leadership would be a catalyst for transformational change. Moriére anticipated a "radical transformation" as a result of the parity measure, facilitating "a new party vision" in which "parity is possible and is something that we can attain" (PT 2012b). Deputy and former Minister of Human Rights Maria do Rosário was similarly enthusiastic, saying "parity in the PT will have a great influence in the parliament" (PT 2011). Reflecting upon the parity principle, former Deputy and Minister of the Special Secretariat for Policies for Women Iriny Lopes stated "in our comprehension, parity is an instrument to transform the Workers' Party into a feminist party" (Lopes, May 2017 Seminar).

The PT's 2013 internal elections saw nine women elected with a specific office to the National Executive Commission (NEC)—39.1% of 23 members with an office, more than twice the national average across all parties with congressional presence (17.6%). It was a significant boost from 2010, when just two of the PT's 13 NEC titled (with a specific office) members were women (15.4%). The failure to meet the 50% target is reflective of the implementation of the PT's internal quota, which came to be considered satisfied with posts that do not actually have a specific office on the executive commission (in the role of *vogal*).[46] As findings from Verge and Claveria (2016) would predict, even some

---

[45] At least 20% of party leaders should be less than 30 years old, and at least 20% should be "in compliance with ethno-racial criteria to be defined by the National Directorate," based proportionally on the ethno-racial demographics of its membership (www.pt.org.br/estrutura-partidaria/).

[46] The 84-member National Directorate, which is elected by the full membership, and elects the National Executive Commission, does have 39 women (46.4%). When I refer to "leaders," I mean members of the executive commissions with a specific office.

women with titled posts would find their secretariat woefully under-resourced in comparison to the offices held by their male colleagues (PT Secretaria de Formação—Minas Gerais, May 2017 Seminar). Such subversion of the parity provision represents "informal and masculinist party practices" that illustrate the "'stickiness' of informal institutions, drawing attention to how 'old' ways of doing things have been reinvented and redeployed" (Bjarnegård and Kenny 2016, 17–18).

The numeric results of the parity clause nonetheless represent a significant advance; at the time of the 2010 elections, just over half of the PT state executive commissions had a critical mass of women leaders (at least 25%), ranging from 0 to 53.8%, with an average of 24.0%. In 2014, the average percentage of titled women on state level executive commissions was 40.0%, ranging from 20.0% to 63.6%. Perhaps more importantly, by 2014, 19/27 PT state party organizations were led by a female secretary general, president, or vice president.

Four years later, *petista* feminists credit the parity rule with changing the political culture of the party (PT 2017b, 2017c). "Now, we women have a greater protagonism, more respect, *we are more heard*, we have a more equal relationship" (Maristella Matos, PT's Secretaria Nacional de Mobilização, quoted in PT 2017b, emphasis mine). "Although it is not in the statute of the PT, today most panels are comprised with parity. There was a change in the greetings,[47] in the narrative of the party. *Women empowered themselves* and succeeded in politically capturing parity for a change in the political culture and everyday practices of the PT" (Vivian Farias, PT's Secretaria Nacional de Coordenação Regional, quoted in PT 2017c, emphasis mine). Such changes are indebted to the visible mobilization of women; as articulated by NEC member Anne Karolyne in her reflections on the PT's 6th National Congress, "It is the collective organization of women that allows us to give support so we advance in the occupation of spaces of power, which was on display at the Congress" (Karolyne 2017).

The expectation is that the equal presence of women will also facilitate a more equitable distribution of party funds to female candidacies (this has yet to materialize), and will embolden efforts to hold the party accountable to its rhetoric of women's empowerment. One example of those efforts is the PT's thorough audit of the legislated 5 percent of publicly provided party funds that must be devoted to promoting women's participation, per the 2009 mini-reform (PT 2012a). While many parties have neglected that requirement, choosing instead to incur a fine (deduction in publicly provided party funds in the next allocation), with other parties using the funds for dubious

---

[47] In greetings, *petistas* now tend to explicitly reference men and women, i.e., *companheiros e companheiras*, rather than the conventional use of the male form as universal. An English language parallel is the use of "you guys" to implicitly refer to women as well as men, which is a subtle linguistic form of rendering women invisible.

purposes, women PT leaders have demanded accountability in the spending of those funds.

May 31, 2017, the day before the PT's 6th National Congress was to begin, Moriére held the seminar, "Women and Participation in Politics: Challenges and Perspectives," with a goal to prepare women delegates to the 6th National Congress and discuss what has worked and not worked with regard to the gender parity rule. The seminar included women representing each of the major factions of the party (PT 2017e). Female *petistas* discussed the need to stand firm collectively to protect the parity rule, and push for its application to actual offices (rather than the disempowered *vogal* role). A central objective of the meeting was to discuss how to pressure the party to reconceptualize parity as a concept, rather than a number. Moriére lamented, "Parity cannot be just a number" (Moriére, May 2017 Seminar); "the number is not sufficient to give women the decision-making power and protagonism that they should have" (Moriére, quoted in Mazotte 2016). Moriére implored women *petistas* to "fight every hour, every moment for parity to stop being a number and become an everyday form or manner of militancy in the PT" (Moriére, May 2017 Seminar). Just days later, the PT elected its first woman national president, Senator and former Chief of Staff for President Rousseff, Gleisi Hoffmann (PT 2017f).

While there remains extensive work ahead for the PT to achieve parity in all instances of power in the party and in government, the parity rule has worked to disrupt masculinist party networks. All but one of the PT's 27 state executive commissions include at least 25% women (up from just 15/27 in 2010). After the 2014 Chamber of Deputies elections, for which most of its party tickets approximated the 30% quota, the PT had the largest share among elected female federal legislators; nine of the 51 women elected deputy were *petistas*.[48] Nevertheless, only 13.2% of its elected deputies were women. Moreover, an estimated 28.4% of the PT's female candidates in the 2014 Chamber of Deputies elections were *laranjas* (sacrificial lambs or phantom candidates) with no party support and no chance of election (Wylie, Marcelino, and dos Santos 2015). So although the PT has made significant advances in mitigating the structural disparities confronted by women, inequities remain. Moriére points to the persistent weight of traditional gender roles, which result in party politics being a *triple shift* for women (alongside formal employment and unpaid household labor); when party meetings run late or kids get sick, it is the women who leave the meeting. And when women do actively contribute to meetings, they are sometimes

---

[48] One of those nine women switched parties (to the PC do B) and two renounced their position to serve in subnational government, one as state Secretary of Education, and another as mayor. Of the 45 women to ever serve in the Senate, 13 were elected (counting two *suplentes* or substitutes) as *petistas* (28.9%). Not counting Marta Suplicy, who left the PT (for the PMDB) after her election, 3 of the 13 female senators in the 55th Congress are from the PT (23.1%).

disrespected by male colleagues. This all serves to disincentivize women's participation in party politics (PT 2017d).

Women's hard-fought gains in PT leadership have offered them a space to visibly contend for a "party without machismo" and work collectively to "create a feminist political culture inside and outside the PT" (Karolyne 2017; Moriére 2015). Yet organizational inertia and masculinist informal party practices hinder party organizational and cultural change (Wylie 2017). Moreover, the incentives toward intraparty competition in the Chamber of Deputies loom large for all parties, including the parties heretofore most successful in recruiting and electing women, the PT and PC do B. To further the analysis, in the following chapter, I contrast the experiences of the PT and other major parties across the Chamber of Deputies and Senate, bringing into focus how electoral rules incentivizing either intraparty competition or party support affect parties, and in turn, the electoral prospects of women.

CONCLUSIONS

While parties that have historically incorporated women such as the PT and the PC do B enjoy a head start in women's participation, the findings presented here suggest that parties without such women-friendly legacies can overcome their historical deficits in women's presence. By developing a clear and universal set of rules for party ascension (including candidate selection) that furthers a norm of compliance, a recruitment network, and training and capacity-building programs, while also cultivating a programmatic party platform, parties can provide women with critical psychological, organizational, and material support that will facilitate their successful participation. Those tools for enhancing women's empowerment are not monopolized by leftist parties in general, or the PC do B and PT in particular, but are available to any party seeking to at once comply with the electoral law while enhancing its electoral fortunes, representativeness, and accountability to the electorate. Parties that are well-institutionalized and incorporate a critical mass of women in their decision-making structures provide the conditions most propitious for the mobilization of such resources on behalf of women.

Although the obstacles to women's representation are formidable, parties can empower women to overcome them. In spite of the incentives for intraparty competition induced by the open-list electoral system and related weakness of the gender quota law discussed in Chapter 3, when parties are well-institutionalized and have a critical mass of women in their leadership, they can level the playing field for female contenders. Psychological, organizational, and material support mitigates the constructed gender gap in political ambition, enabling women to acquire the necessary political skillset and participate in a collective, ideas-based campaign.

Voter bias does persist, especially in Brazil's less developed and rural areas, but this has not precluded women's electoral success. As I demonstrate in

Chapter 6, that is because women have crafted profiles enabling them to thrive in spite of such bias, either by working through parties to convert their own experiences in informal politics into political capital driven by programmatic linkages, or in the absence of party support, by conforming to the traditional gender norms. The conventional explanations for women's representation centered on electoral rules such as district and party magnitude do not consistently hold for women. That is because many of Brazil's most electorally successful parties (e.g., PSDB) remain dominated by men at the upper echelons of party decision-making and are thus difficult for women to infiltrate.

Leftist parties have certainly reached out to women more than non-leftist parties, ultimately, but running as a leftist woman in Brazil—where the median voter is right-of-center and traditional gender norms persist—is hardly a generalizable winning strategy. More generally, the literature and evidence presented here suggests that in the current era of increasing awareness of gender inequality and a growing commitment to mitigate inequities through state policies such as gender quotas, the explanatory power of party ideology may be waning. Leftist parties in Brazil and elsewhere have historically been more institutionalized with internal ranks more open to women than non-leftist parties. Part of that reality stems from the distinct gendered networks tapped by leftist and non-leftist parties; the affinities between leftist parties and social movements, and between non-leftist parties and business elites fuels a gendered path dependence that has resulted in more opportunities for women and other outsiders on the left. But leftist ideology is neither a necessary nor sufficient condition for inclusion. What facilitates women's participation is not ideology per se but rather the mobilization of party resources to recruit them and support their candidacies. That support is more likely (but not guaranteed) to be availed by parties with female leaders. In the case of Brazil's Chamber of Deputies and other contexts with intraparty competition, well-institutionalized parties with programmatic platforms tend to have the resources capable of mitigating the gendered constraints of a combative electoral climate.

As I illustrate further in Chapter 5, rather than negating the role of parties, the intraparty competition incentivized by the Chamber of Deputies' open-list electoral rules introduces great variation in women's electoral prospects across parties, with the few well-institutionalized parties with women in leadership being willing and able to work toward closing the gender gaps in formal political ambition and legislative presence. I contrast women's electoral performance in the Senate and Chamber of Deputies to reveal how the presence or paucity of party support can modify the effect of candidate sex on electoral outcome, with the Senate's ostensibly greater electoral hurdle overcome by party support. The result is that women senatorial candidates have enjoyed greater success than women seeking a seat in the Chamber of Deputies, where a combative climate of intraparty competition undermines women and other outsiders by intensifying personalist politics, with inchoate and male-led parties being ill-equipped and/or unwilling to recruit and support female contenders in their efforts to confront such an entrepreneurial system.

That party does matter in the Brazilian context is the key contribution of this chapter. Bridging the Brazilianist literature—which downplays or even negates the gatekeeping role of parties—with the women's representation literature's emphasis on parties as the key gatekeeper, I have demonstrated that Brazil's extreme underrepresentation of women can be explained by the prevalence of weak parties and disproportionately male party leadership. But the overall pattern obscures variation in those party characteristics, which when uncovered, helps to explain how Brazil's few female politicians have managed to defy the odds and attain office.

I thus recast the assumption that Brazil's often amorphous parties exert little or no explanatory capacity in its candidate-centered electoral context, a finding which was generated from disproportionately male samples unrepresentative of the experiences of women. Honing the analysis to the candidate (rather than legislator, party, or aggregate) level and explicitly incorporating women demonstrates how parties do, in fact, have an essential gatekeeping role to play in Brazilian electoral politics. That finding has fundamental implications for reform efforts in Brazil and beyond, which must target political parties rather than just electoral rules, if they are to enhance the representativeness and accountability of democracy.

5

Electoral Rules, Party Support, and Women's Unexpected Successes in Elections to the Brazilian Senate

> Electoral institutions should be seen as part of a self-reinforcing equilibrium that also includes voters and party organizations. Although they are widely treated as key explanatory variables, electoral institutions are probably the weakest and least important of these three.
>
> (Desposato 2006, 1028)

In all six election cycles since 1994, a greater proportion of women have attained seats in Brazil's more powerful and prestigious legislative chamber—the *Senado Federal*—than in the Chamber of Deputies. Although senatorial candidates confront an evidently greater electoral hurdle than do candidates to the Chamber of Deputies, the Senate's low district magnitude plurality elections generate incentives for unified party support for candidates. Senate seats are valuable partisan assets, and parties are normally generous in their investments of time and money. From the moment of nomination through election day, party elites, organizations, and activists rally behind their candidate(s), mobilizing substantial unified party support to further their campaign. The Senate's electoral context stands in contrast to the high-district magnitude OLPR elections to the Chamber of Deputies, which motivate substantial intraparty competition (Ames 2001; Carey and Shugart 1995; Desposato 2006; Nicolau 2006). This chapter uses the variation in electoral rules as a natural laboratory to explore their direct effects on women's representation, the (dis)incentives that those varying rules yield for party support, and the implications thereof for women's electoral prospects, holding constant an array of potentially confounding factors. I find that the varying incentives for party support explain women's unexpected relative successes in the Senate, where women candidates confront a more level playing field than their counterparts in the Chamber of Deputies.

After discussing the contributions and limitations of the extant literature on electoral institutions and women's representation, I elucidate why the Brazilian

Congress offers a particularly compelling environment for testing how rules and parties interact to affect women's representation. Next, I discuss the electoral rules in Senate elections, differentiating them from those of the Chamber of Deputies described in Chapter 3, and compare the incentives for party support generated by each. I then conduct multivariate analyses of candidate electoral performance in four concurrent elections to the Chamber of Deputies and Senate (1998–2010).

The cross-chamber comparison in turn assesses the explanatory capacity of conventional wisdom and my central argument—that psychological, organizational, and material support mobilized by women leaders of institutionalized parties enables female candidates to overcome the barriers posed by the entrepreneurial electoral context of the Chamber of Deputies. If the standard explanations of women's underrepresentation regarding voter bias, party ideology, and electoral institutions rang true in Brazil, women's electoral prospects in the Chamber of Deputies should exceed those in the Senate, given the latter's greater prestige and the higher electoral hurdle of its low magnitude plurality elections. But contrary to conventional wisdom, there is a record of consistently greater proportions of women elected to the Brazilian Senate than to the Chamber of Deputies. Moreover, while candidate sex exercises a negative and statistically significant effect on women's electoral prospects in the Chamber, it loses its predictive power for candidacies in Senate elections. I attribute women's greater levels of electoral successes in Brazil's upper rather than lower house to the more forthcoming unified party support typically enjoyed by candidates to the Brazilian Senate.

My multilevel analysis reveals two key elements: the Senate's favorable electoral structure, and its amplification of the positive effects of women-friendly party leadership, which together enhance women's electoral prospects. The presence of a critical mass of female leaders affords women a say in candidate selection and the distribution of party resources, enabling them to mobilize unified party support on behalf of other women. But when parties lack a viable female presence in party decision-making circles, I expect they will be less likely to develop, advance, and support women candidates in the lower magnitude Senate elections, where candidacy itself is a scarce and prized resource.

In sum, electoral rules and parties interact to generate varying incentives for party support and thus, women's electoral success. Whereas tendencies toward intraparty competition in the Chamber of Deputies OLPR elections substantially undermine women's electoral prospects in all but the most institutionalized and women-friendly parties, the concentration of party support in Senate elections provides a more propitious context for female contenders. Parties with women in party leadership are well-positioned to capitalize on the favorable electoral environment with viable female candidacies.

UNDERSTANDING THE EFFECTS OF ELECTORAL RULES

As stated in Chapter 3, the literature on women's representation is no exception to the general primacy of electoral institutions for explaining political outcomes in contemporary political science. Electoral rules figure prominently in explanations of women's (under)representation, with the implication being that the rules of the game can be modified to augment the political participation of women and other marginalized groups (Larserud and Taphorn 2007; Matland 2005). Amassing considerable evidence, several cross-national studies have affirmed that countries with closed-list proportional representation and gender quotas with placement mandates tend to elect more women (Htun and Jones 2002; Krook 2009; Moser 2001a; Schwindt-Bayer 2010; Tremblay 2008; Tripp and Kang 2008). Accordingly, international organizations and NGOs seeking to advance female political participation advocate for the adoption of such measures, with a growing number of countries following suit (Dahlerup 2006b; Krook 2009; Schwindt-Bayer 2010; Tripp and Kang 2008).

Yet, results of such efforts to fast-track women's representation have been neither uniformly positive nor as "fast" as anticipated (Htun and Jones 2002; Franceschet, Krook, and Piscopo 2012; Schwindt-Bayer 2010). Such mixed evidence on the effectiveness of quotas stems from wide variation in quota design and implementation as well as the compatibility of quotas with particular electoral and party systems. Indeed, the case of Brazil's *Lei Eleitoral de Cotas* discussed in Chapter 3 demonstrates how negotiated compromises, OLPR electoral rules, and intransigent party elites conspired to reduce the Brazilian quota to a mere symbolic measure. It is critical, therefore, that analyses of electoral rules account for the specifics of the party system in which they operate.

Studies of the institutional factors underpinning women's (under) representation tend to face two key limitations: (1) they analyze electoral rules in a vacuum, with at best tenuous controls for the sociocultural and historical contexts in which such rules are embedded, and (2) they infer the effects of electoral rules on individual women's electoral prospects from aggregate level analyses of women's representation in legislatures; i.e., they commit an ecological fallacy.

Following Moser and Scheiner (2012), the current chapter avoids those two shortcomings with an individual-level, controlled comparison analysis of women's electoral prospects in the Brazilian Chamber of Deputies and Senate. Similar to analyses of the effects of electoral rules in mixed electoral systems, the comparison of Brazil's two legislative chambers allows me to hold constant innumerous site-specific (and often unquantifiable) confounding explanations while providing rich variation on the traditional institutional predictors of women's representation—ballot structure, district magnitude, and quotas—and the incentives those electoral rules generate for parties. The intranational, bicameral analysis thereby affords great variation across both parties and electoral rules, focusing on their interaction. Comparing the effects of electoral rules on legislative party cohesion and discipline in the Brazilian Chamber of Deputies and Senate, Desposato demonstrated how such a setting yields "a powerful opportunity for testing and inference" (2006, 1018).

Moreover, this analysis of women's electoral prospects in the Brazilian Chamber of Deputies and Senate advances an interesting puzzle. The electoral rules for ascension to the Senate—i.e., plurality elections with a low district magnitude and no gender quota—are widely considered disadvantageous for women's representation (Duverger 1955; Kittilson 2006; Rule and Zimmerman 1994; Schwindt-Bayer 2010). Further, upper chambers in the Americas are the more prestigious legislative arena (Desposato 2006; Lemos 2008; Money and Tsebelis 1992), with an issue domain traditionally gendered masculine (Kahn 1996). Indeed in most bicameral legislatures, women's presence is greater in the lower house than in the upper house (Inter-Parliamentary Union 2017). Yet in the 2014 congressional elections, 18.5% of those elected senator and just 9.9% of those elected federal deputy were women. As shown in Table 1.4, the proportion of women elected to Brazil's Senate has over the last six elections consistently exceeded the proportion elected to its Chamber of Deputies.

I explain the apparent puzzle by honing the analysis to the candidate level, and thus leveraging interparty variation in women's electoral performance across Brazil's bicameral legislature. This approach illuminates how parties mediate the effects of electoral institutions, in particular, how the differing electoral rules in the Senate and Chamber generate distinct incentives for party support, and the implications thereof for women's chances of election. I thus respond to several recent studies on electoral systems and women's representation that call for consideration of not only electoral rules per se but also the party system in which they are embedded (Jones 2009; Krook 2009; Krook and Zetterberg 2014; Moser 2001a; Moser 2003; Moser and Scheiner 2004, 2012).

With few exceptions,[1] most quantitative studies of the effects of electoral systems on women's representation are conducted at the aggregate level, employing the percentage of women in the legislature as the dependent variable to be explained. In response, Schwindt-Bayer, Malecki, and Crisp recently asserted that the dominance of the aggregate-level approach explaining women's overall descriptive representation "has nearly precluded research on other equally essential and related questions" (2010, 693).

How do electoral systems and other hypothesized obstacles to women's overall representation affect the electoral prospects of female candidates? To infer such effects on women's electoral performance from aggregate country-

---

[1] Moser and Scheiner (2012) conduct a legislator-level study, analyzing the chance that a given legislator is female, and Jones (2009) conducts an analysis of the percent of women elected on a party/coalition-list.

level analyses is to commit an ecological fallacy (King, Keohane, and Verba 1994; Robinson 1990). Recall (from the discussion in Chapters 2 and 4) the mechanisms linking voter bias and ideology, for example, to the proportion of women in the legislature are distinct from those substantiating the effects of these barriers on individual women's electoral success.[2] Only with a candidate-level analysis can we elucidate their actual effects on the electoral performance of female contenders. Lost within aggregates are the individuals that run for, and sometimes win elected office, as is any variation across parties.

Moreover, most of the cross-national studies on women's representation analyze the data as static rather than longitudinal—adjusting for temporal effects rather than modeling them—and thus cannot illuminate change over time (see Hughes and Paxton 2008; Kittilson 2006; McConnaughy 2007).[3] The introduction of gender quotas in many countries will—once sufficient time has passed to allow several pre- and post-treatment observations—provide a sort of natural experiment, where researchers can isolate the actual effects of changes in electoral systems on women's representation. In the meantime, scholars of mixed electoral systems have conducted innovative analyses that exploit the laboratory-like setting, contrasting women's representation in distinct tiers within countries to infer their effects (Fortin and Eder 2011; Moser 2001a; Moser 2003; Moser and Scheiner 2004, 2012).

CONTROLLED COMPARISON ANALYSIS

The within-country, controlled comparison approach allows for variation across electoral rules while holding constant a range of potentially confounding explanations such as political culture and historical background, many of which are simply unquantifiable. Several scholars have employed the natural experiment-like approach to enrich our understanding of electoral rules and their implications for legislative party discipline and cohesion (Desposato 2006; Ferrara 2004; Haspel, Remington, and Smith 1998), for representation in the context of inchoate parties (Moser 2001b), and how the mixed electoral system can, under the condition of a weakly institutionalized party system, create a mandate divide (Thames 2005). This chapter extends that line of research by analyzing the electoral performance of female candidates to each

---

[2] For instance, the strength of leftist parties in parliament is a common predictor variable in studies of the overall proportion of women legislators. The mechanisms linking a country's affinity for leftist parties to women's representation are their support for welfare state policies, which can incorporate women in the paid workforce and in turn change their interests and induce an ideological gender gap, leading parties to compete for women's votes by advancing more female candidates (Rosenbluth, Salmond, and Thies 2006). That logic does not readily extend to explaining individual women's electoral prospects, but must be re-theorized to apply to candidates, and then tested at the appropriate level.

[3] Paxton, Hughes, and Painter's (2011) latent growth curve model of changes in women's representation over time represents an important advance on this front.

house of the bicameral Brazilian Congress, attentive to the distinctions in electoral rules. I investigate why women have enjoyed relatively more electoral success in the Senate than in the Chamber, first revealing observed differences across candidacies to the two chambers, and then discussing the effects of differences in candidate qualities, ideology, electoral rules, and party support on the electoral prospects of women.

LESSONS FROM THE BRAZILIAN LEGISLATURE

Female candidates to both houses of the Brazilian Congress confront a preferential electoral system that, in contrast to closed-list PR elections, is candidate- rather than party-centered. Such candidate-centered campaigns tend to undermine women, who—studies show—are generally predisposed to collective, rather than individualistic, endeavors (Escobar-Lemmon and Taylor-Robinson 2008), and because voters in such elections typically rely on heuristics such as gender and thus potentially negative stereotypes in choosing candidates (Shugart, Valdini, and Suominen 2005; Valdini 2013a).[4] Therefore, neither the Senate nor the Chamber of Deputies provides an ideal environment for women contenders. Yet, I marshal evidence to argue that willing parties can go a considerable way toward overcoming those obstacles. Compared with the lower house, the potential positive effect of party support for women is heightened in the Senate's low magnitude plurality elections, where all parties play a greater and more unified role in the electoral process. In what follows, I compare the electoral rules of the Senate and Chamber, their varying incentives for party support, and their anticipated effects on women's electoral prospects.

By most considerations, gaining election to the Senate should be more difficult—especially for women—than acquiring a seat in the Chamber of Deputies. Enjoying exclusive jurisdiction over impeachment, international financing, and setting debt limits for federal, state, and municipal spending, as well as eight-year mandates, Brazil's upper house is the country's more prestigious legislative chamber (Desposato 2006; Lemos 2008). Comparisons of the recent legislative agenda in the Chamber of Deputies and the Senate (when not in joint session) suggest more appointments and treatment of fiscal and trade policy in the Senate. Such issues are traditionally gendered masculine (Kahn 1996), which along with the greater prestige of the office, poses a disadvantage to female candidates (Bohn 2007). Indeed, only 45 women have ever served in the Senate.[5] With most of the politicians occupying Senate seats

---

[4] Recall from preceding chapters, OLPR rules also undermine the gender quota.
[5] This count excludes the first female senator to serve, the Imperial Princess Isabel from the late nineteenth century. With a long era of exclusively male senators during the Old Republic, the Vargas Era, the Second Republic, and the military regime (one woman, Eunice Michiles, was elected as a substitute for the ARENA, and served from 1979–1987), women's participation in the

being "veterans," both in terms of their record of elective or executive office and their age[6] (Lemos and Rainicheksi 2008, 100), such a cycle of exclusion is difficult to break.

The Senate's Heightened Electoral Threshold

Given the discussions of electoral systems in prior chapters, the electoral rules of the Senate should also disadvantage women contenders. Whereas multiple available seats and vote pooling across parties/coalitions mean that candidates often win a seat to the Chamber of Deputies with less than 1% of the statewide vote, Senate candidates must themselves win a plurality of votes, with no vote pooling. In 2014, the average winning vote share of Chamber of Deputies candidates was 3.3%, compared to 51.9% in the Senate elections.[7] The higher candidate vote threshold and expense that requirement entails (Lemos 2008) will surely prove prohibitive for most outsiders.

While both chambers have statewide districts, candidates to the Chamber of Deputies can win a seat with votes in only a few municipalities. Senate candidates, on the other hand, undertake the prohibitive expense of having to garner votes throughout the state. Given the often extensive geographies and precarious highway infrastructure, statewide campaigns are costly. Moreover, candidates to the Senate must seek to represent a diversity of constituents rather than electoral niches, as is common in the Chamber of Deputies. Figure 5.1 maps a characteristic municipality-breakdown of winning candidates' electoral performance in the Chamber of Deputies (Alice Portugal) and Senate (Lídice da Mata) in the northeastern state of Bahia, demonstrating the necessarily broader appeal of Senate candidates.

Varying Incentives for Party Support

These characteristics of the Senate create an environment disadvantageous to women and other outsiders. Yet, the low magnitude plurality rules generate greater incentives for party support than do the Chamber of Deputies' high magnitude OLPR elections. With the forthcoming analysis, I argue that this more salient and unified role of parties in Senate elections provides a context more propitious for female candidates, allowing women in party leadership to capitalize on their potential. In contrast, the combative climate of intraparty competition in the Chamber of Deputies means that only well-institutionalized

---

Senate has grown significantly in the New Republic (1985–present), with the first two women (Júnia Marise and Marluce Pinto) elected in 1990 (Senado Federal 2004).

[6] While the electoral law requires Chamber of Deputies candidates to be 21 years of age, Senate candidates must be at least 35 (Lemos and Rainicheksi 2008, 101).

[7] In the 2010 elections, when two Senate seats were up for grabs in each district, the average winning vote share was 31.9% (compared to 3.4% for elected deputies).

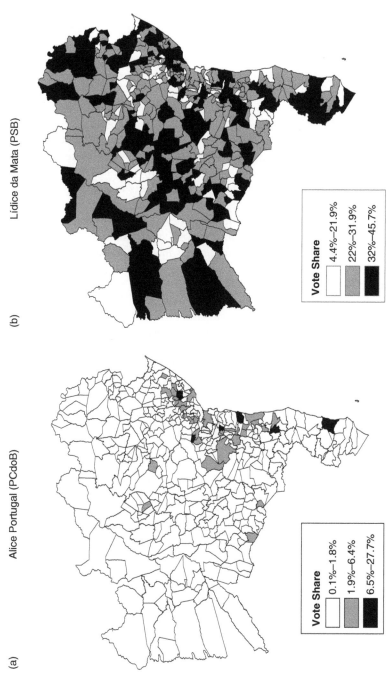

FIGURE 5.1 Statewide Constituencies in the Brazilian Congress for (a) the Chamber of Deputies (Alice Portugal) and (b) Senate (Lídice da Mata)

and women-friendly parties will have the capacity and/or will to mobilize resources to recruit women candidates and provide them with the psychological, organizational, and material party support necessary to thrive in the entrepreneurial electoral context. Next, I compare the electoral rules of the two houses—focusing on district magnitude, ballot access, and votes—and the incentives they generate either for party support or intraparty competition (Carey and Shugart 1995).

The Senate has significantly lower district and party magnitudes than the Chamber of Deputies. As discussed in Chapter 3, district and party magnitude in the Chamber of Deputies varies from 8 to 70, and 0 to 20 (in 1994–2014 elections), respectively. Each district elects three senators, who serve staggered eight-year terms. Every four years (concurrent with elections for president, governor, federal and state deputy), each district elects one or two senators. Elections in 1994, 2002, and 2010, sat two-thirds (54) of the Senate; elections in 1998, 2006, and 2014 selected one-third (27). In other words, district magnitude in the Senate varies from one to two. Looking back on the literature discussed in Chapter 2, that lower magnitude—especially in the elections with a district magnitude of one—should diminish women's representation because it makes candidacy itself a scarce resource.

Conversely, higher district magnitudes entail a dizzying number of candidates. This is especially true in elections to the Chamber of Deputies, where parties are permitted to run 16 candidates in the smallest districts (8*2) and 105 candidates in the largest district (70*1.5).[8] Under the condition of intraparty competition (i.e., OLPR), the vast quantity of candidacies in high district magnitude elections intensifies the incentive to cultivate a "personal vote" as candidates work to differentiate themselves from the masses of candidates on their list and others (Carey and Shugart 1995; Shugart et al. 2005).[9] Such tendencies dilute party support across candidacies, with most parties strategically devoting disproportionate party resources to the favored *puxadoras de votos* or vote champions, who, by virtue of their votes in excess of the electoral quotient, can elect other candidates on the party list.

In elections to the Senate, however, parties tend to concentrate their efforts on a single seat. That means that the party elite, organization, and militants campaign collectively for their candidate, and that a spot on the party's gubernatorial ticket presented at rallies and on campaign materials is assured (recall the *dobradinha*). In those elections with a district magnitude of two, voters have two votes (which they cannot give to the same candidate), so even if parties do advance two candidates in such elections, there remain substantially

---

[8] As discussed further in Chapter 3, until the 2015 mini-reform, coalitions were permitted 24 candidates in the smallest districts (8*3), and 140 candidates in the largest district (70*2).

[9] This contrasts with closed-list PR, where higher district magnitudes decrease the incentives to cultivate a personal vote (Carey and Shugart 1995; Shugart, Validini, and Suominen 2005).

fewer incentives for intraparty competition in Senate elections (Desposato 2006).

Ballot access for Senate elections is controlled by the state party leaders. A few parties are considering the introduction of primaries to extend the selectorate (Fonseca 2012), but the majority of candidate selections for plurality/majoritarian elections have heretofore been conducted in the proverbial smoke-filled rooms (Braga 2008).[10] While I dispute the portrayal of Chamber of Deputies elections as "open for easy ascent" (Schedler 1995, 18; Samuels 2008) and maintain that parties do exercise a gatekeeping role, party leaders certainly exercise less formal control over access to Chamber candidacies, with 1–2 Senate candidacies being far more scarce and contested. Parties do not present a fixed ballot in elections to either legislative chamber, with the rules allowing voters to "disturb" the party list. In the Chamber's OLPR elections, that means that in contrast to closed-list PR elections, the end ranking of candidates on the party list is determined by voters. For the Senate, it means that when two-thirds of the seats are up for grabs, voters can divide their two votes among parties.

Because voters can "disturb" the party list for both houses, personalist politics and thus intraparty competition is implied in each system. Yet for the Senate, that only applies in the elections for two-thirds of the seats, where parties can advance two candidates. And again, even in the elections allowing more than one candidate per party, there are no real incentives for intraparty competition because voters command two votes that cannot be cast for the same candidate. In elections to the Chamber, however, voters cast a single ballot, and each party's numerous candidates seek to differentiate themselves from and outperform their co-partisans. This breeds an every-man-for-himself mentality and diminishes party support for all but the most favored candidacies. Interviews and analyses of campaign finance suggest that many candidates to the Chamber receive absolutely nothing from the party organization beyond the party label itself.

The lesser scarcity and control of ballot access in the Chamber elections also raises the premium on personal reputation relative to party reputation, leading once more to intraparty competition. With so many candidate slots available, there are often candidacies advanced that the party organization has absolutely no intention of supporting. In contrast, in the Senate, party support is always unified behind their 1–2 candidates with any intraparty competition having been hashed out prior to nomination.

In sum, the lower district magnitude, fewer candidacies, multiple votes, and restricted ballot access in elections to the Senate generate considerably more

---

[10] While the Workers' Party (PT) has formal guidelines requiring a broader approval and are thus more inclusive than most parties, state PT leaders retain considerable influence (Álvares 2004; Braga 2008). Of the major parties, the conservative PFL/Democratas and Progressive Party (PP) have the most exclusive candidate selection procedures (Braga 2008).

TABLE 5.1 *Varying Incentives for Party Support in Elections to the Brazilian Congress*

	Senate: Unified Party Support	Chamber of Deputies: Intraparty Competition
Women Inclusive Party Leadership	#1 Most women-friendly: Women leaders mobilize forthcoming party support and level the playing field	#2 Intraparty competition difficult, but women leading institutionalized parties mobilize party support and help to overcome
Male Dominated Party Leadership	#4 Least women-friendly: Scarce resource unlikely to be mobilized for women	#3 Parties unwilling (and often ill-equipped) to mitigate intraparty competition

incentives for unified party support than elections to the Chamber of Deputies, where the rules tend toward intraparty competition. If women can acquire access to the restricted and scarce resource of candidacy in the Senate, they stand to benefit from forthcoming party support. I expect that their likelihood to do so is significantly greater among parties with a critical mass of women in their leadership. Conversely, the greater scarcity of candidacies and more restrictive ballot access for the Senate will, I expect, disadvantage female political aspirants if women lack a voice among party leadership.

Given the heightened incentives for intraparty competition in the Chamber relative to the Senate, I anticipate that female candidates bulwarked by a party organization with a critical mass of women leaders will enjoy the most success in elections to the Senate. In parties where women lack a voice in decision-making, however, successful female Senate candidacies are unlikely. And as demonstrated in Chapter 4, female candidates to the Chamber enjoy the most success when running in parties that have women in party leadership, and are sufficiently institutionalized to overcome the vast incentives toward intraparty competition that deter most female political aspirants. In elections to the Brazilian Congress, women's electoral prospects are shaped by the interaction of incentives for party support or intraparty competition and the will of party leadership to mobilize that party support on behalf of women, which in the Chamber, mitigates the difficulties of intraparty competition. Table 5.1 outlines these expectations.

So although the Senate is more prestigious than the Chamber of Deputies, candidacy is a scarcer resource, the electoral threshold is higher, campaigns are more expensive, and ballot access is tightly regulated, with no gender quota,[11] I argue that unified party support mobilized by women in party leadership helps

---

[11] As elaborated in preceding chapters, the quota law for proportional elections remains a *lei que não pega*—merely nominal, and flouted by the vast majority of political parties. Therefore, the

TABLE 5.2 *Women's Success Rates in the Brazilian Congress (1994–2014)*

	Senator				Federal Deputy			
Election Year	Fem Cands	Fem Elected	Fem S Rate	FMSR Ratio	Fem Cands	Fem Elected	Fem S Rate	FMSR Ratio
1994	7.3%	7.4%	23.5%	1.01	6.2%	6.2%	17.3%	1.02
1998	14.0%	7.4%	8.7%	0.49	10.4%	5.7%	8.3%	0.52
2002	12.4%	14.8%	21.1%	1.23	11.4%	8.2%	8.8%	0.69
2006	16.8%	14.8%	12.5%	0.92	12.7%	8.8%	7.2%	0.66
2010	12.7%	14.8%	29.6%	1.20	19.1%	8.8%	4.8%	0.41
2014	20.4%	18.5%	14.7%	0.89	29.4%	9.9%	3.0%	0.27
1994–2014	13.3%	12.9%	18.1%	0.96	16.3%	7.9%	5.7%	0.44

Notes: Success rate ("S Rate") = number of (women) elected / number of (women) candidates. A Female–Male Success Rate Ratio ("FMSR Ratio") greater than 1 indicates that women candidates have a higher success rate than male candidates. In 1994, 2002, and 2010, each state elected two senators.

Sources: Tribunal Superior Eleitoral (2015); CFEMEA. Calculations by author.

female aspirants overcome all of those obstacles. Because intraparty competition disincentivizes party support for most individual candidates in the Chamber, women running in all but the most institutionalized and women-friendly parties essentially undertake the campaign alone. The Senate, however, poses a different incentive structure whereby party support is more forthcoming. It is the distinction in party support that explains women's unexpected electoral successes in Brazil's upper chamber. Next, I discuss the observed differences across chambers in the success rates of female candidates.

Women's Success Rates in the Brazilian Congress

Looking at women's success rates across the two chambers, we see that female candidates to the Senate have enjoyed more electoral success than have women running for the Chamber of Deputies (Table 5.2). Even when taking into consideration women's relative competitiveness through the Female–Male Success Rate Ratio, the Senate has proven more conducive to women's success than has the Chamber in recent elections. That discrepancy remains despite the Chamber's gender quota. That women candidates perform their best in the legislative chamber lacking a quota suggests that the quota's effects have been neither forthcoming nor direct.

Overall, women's impressive success rates in Senate elections (18.1%) refute the enduring argument that the electorate is reluctant to elect women

absence of a gender quota in Senate elections has not posed a stark disadvantage for female candidates.

politicians. In the multivariate analyses that follow, I control for observed differences in candidate quality and explore the effect of candidate sex on electoral outcomes in the Brazilian Congress. Drawing on the statistical findings and interviews with female candidates to both chambers, I explain how, even in Brazil's candidate-centered electoral context, party support makes the difference for women contesting electoral office. Yet as displayed in Table 5.3, there remains substantial interparty (and regional) variation within and across chambers.

EXPLAINING WOMEN'S UNEXPECTED SUCCESSES IN THE SENATE

Analyzing both chambers simultaneously, I employ institutional variation that reveals how distinct electoral rules affect women's electoral prospects in Brazil while controlling for a barrage of potentially confounding variables. I assess variation within and across chambers, using hierarchical modeling to explore how gender (or more precisely, sex) interacts with electoral rules and particular individual-, party-, and district-level factors to predict candidate electoral success. Given the sizeable discrepancy in the electoral threshold across the Senate and Chamber, which renders incomparable the traditional vote share variable, I code electoral outcome dichotomously, with those elected coded "one," and all others coded "zero." For details on the hierarchical logit model specification, see Appendix 5.1. Table 5.4 displays the results.

As argued above, because the extensive intraparty competition incentivized by the electoral rules in the Chamber of Deputies concocts a disadvantageous environment for women and other outsiders, *fem* exercises a negative effect on the electoral prospects of candidates in the Chamber of Deputies. Yet because party support is more forthcoming in elections to the Senate, with competition fiercer between parties rather than within, *fem* has an insignificant effect on candidate electoral outcomes in the Senate. A disaggregation of the marginal effects of an underspecified bivariate analysis reveals that the difference in predicted probabilities of male and female candidates gaining election is statistically significant in the Chamber, but approximates zero in the Senate. Male and female candidates to the Senate, respectively, are 1.43 and 1.79 times more likely to win election than male candidates to the Chamber, who in turn are almost twice as likely to get elected than female candidates to the Chamber. Public discontent with the corruption scandals of recent years and societal perceptions of women as novel candidates who are more honest and less corrupt (however essentialist) contribute to making women competitive contenders for the Senate, particularly under the condition of party support, which helps to project an image of viability.

It is suggestive that the inclusion of controls for electoral rules—district magnitude group (*dmag group*), *effective n cands*, and *quotas*, and district development (*HDI*) hardly improved the model fit to the data (although it did reduce the district-level error term). Moreover, Wald tests of the joint

TABLE 5.3   *Women in the Senate and Chamber of Deputies, by Party, Ideology, and Region (1994–2010)*

PARTY / REGION	WOMEN SENATORS		WOMEN DEPUTIES	
	Candidates	Elected	Candidates	Elected
LEFT	87 (16.9%)	15 (25.4%)	1053 (14.3%)	86 (11.1%)
PT	23 (22.3%)	11 (36.7%)	249 (13.8%)	41 (11.1%)
PC do B	7 (25.0%)	1 (50.0%)	75 (23.3%)	19 (33.3%)
PDT	6 (9.2%)	0 (0.0%)	155 (10.2%)	7 (5.3%)
PPS	5 (12.2%)	1 (25.0%)	101 (12.3%)	2 (3.7%)
PSB	7 (14.3%)	1 (11.1%)	151 (12.6%)	15 (12.8%)
PSOL	12 (27.3%)	1 (50.0%)	82 (18.3%)	1 (16.7%)
PV	2 (5.3%)	0 (—)	181 (17.4%)	1 (2.9%)
NON-LEFT	50 (8.3%)	11 (7.1%)	372 (11.5%)	106 (5.9%)
PFL/DEM	5 (6.0%)	5 (13.2%)	97 (8.4%)	20 (5.2%)
PMDB	3 (2.7%)	0 (0.0%)	195 (11.3%)	36 (8.3%)
PMN	0 (0.0%)	0 (—)	94 (15.8%)	1 (7.1%)
PPR/PPB/PP	4 (8.3%)	1 (11.1%)	95 (8.6%)	11 (4.6%)
PP (1994)	1 (11.1%)	0 (0.0%)	7 (4.2%)	1 (2.9%)
PSDB	7 (9.1%)	3 (9.7%)	177 (12.6%)	24 (6.8%)
PL/PR	2 (7.7%)	0 (0.0%)	96 (10.9%)	3 (2.6%)
PRB	1 (50.0%)	0 (0.0%)	29 (19.0%)	0 (0.0%)
PSC	4 (21.1%)	0 (0.0%)	101 (13.1%)	3 (9.4%)
PTB	4 (12.1%)	2 (22.2%)	133 (12.0%)	3 (2.3%)
PTC	2 (25.0%)	0 (—)	68 (17.9%)	1 (25.0%)
PT do B	1 (9.1%)	0 (—)	48 (11.8%)	1 (25.0%)
NORTH	33 (14.3%)	9 (16.4%)	355 (15.3%)	46 (14.2%)
NORTHEAST	37 (10.4%)	7 (9.9%)	452 (10.2%)	34 (4.5%)
CENTER-WEST	14 (9.5%)	4 (12.5%)	241 (14.9%)	25 (12.2%)
SOUTHEAST	29 (12.5%)	2 (6.3%)	1186 (12.9%)	69 (7.7%)
SOUTH	24 (16.0%)	4 (16.7%)	335 (12.1%)	19 (4.9%)
TOTAL	137 (12.3%)	26 (12.0%)	2569 (12.6%)	193 (7.5%)

Note: Values in parentheses represent the proportion of the party/region's candidates and elected that are women

TABLE 5.4 *Multilevel Analyses of the Chance of Election of Congressional Candidates (1998–2010)*

Fixed Effects	Model 1 Coef.	SE	sig	Model 2 Coef.	SE	sig	Model 3 Coef.	SE	sig	Model 4 Coef.	SE	sig
Level 2 District Variables												
For Intercept (β_{oj})												
HDI (γ_{01})	0.539	(0.073)	***				0.763	(0.043)	***	0.630	(0.052)	***
District magnitude (γ_{02})							1.159	(0.079)	*	0.760	(0.082)	**
Effective n cands (γ_{03})							0.998	(0.002)		1.008	(0.003)	**
Cross-Level Interactions												
For Female slope (β_{1j})												
Intercept (γ_{10})				0.453	(0.069)	***	1.510	(0.793)		0.510	(0.337)	
HDI (γ_{11})							0.911	(0.164)		1.111	(0.226)	
District magnitude (γ_{12})							0.928	(0.202)		1.048	(0.282)	
Effective n cands (γ_{13})							0.994	(0.006)		0.996	(0.008)	
For Left slope (β_{2j})												
Intercept (γ_{20})				0.609	(0.029)	***	0.479	(0.036)	***	0.642	(0.082)	***
HDI (γ_{21})							1.279	(0.069)	***	1.243	(0.099)	**
For Fem*Left slope (β_{3j})												
Intercept (γ_{30})				1.644	(0.264)	***	1.179	(0.304)		0.672	(0.285)	
HDI (γ_{31})							1.368	(0.251)	*	1.301	(0.334)	
Level 1 Variables												
Quotas2 (β_{4j}, γ_{40})	1.433	(0.122)	***	1.819	(0.186)	***	0.736	(0.044)	***	0.940	(0.054)	
Fem*Quotas2 (β_{5j}, γ_{50})							0.560	(0.130)	**	0.775	(0.149)	
Senate (β_{6j}, γ_{60})	1.788	(0.450)	*	1.753	(0.665)	±	1.700	(0.273)	***	1.625	(0.327)	*
Fem*Senate (β_{7j}, γ_{70})							0.642	(0.364)		0.107	(0.246)	
Left*Senate (β_{8j}, γ_{80})				0.515	(0.100)	***	0.546	(0.106)	**	2.646	(1.516)	*

(continued)

	Var	SE	sig	Var	SE	sig	Var	SE	sig	Var	SE	sig
Fem*Left*Senate ($\beta 9j$, $\gamma 90$)				1.362	(0.706)		1.398	(0.724)		13.348	(21.628)	±
C.Mass ($\beta 10j$, $\gamma 100$)										0.649	(0.152)	*
Fem*C.Mass ($\beta 11j$, $\gamma 110$)										1.419	(1.002)	
Fem*C.Mass*Senate ($\beta 13j$, $\gamma 130$)										152.4	(500.4)	
PII ($\beta 14j$, $\gamma 140$)							1.159	(0.079)	*	0.954	(0.047)	
Fem*PII ($\beta 15j$, $\gamma 150$)										1.133	(0.186)	
Level 1 Candidate Controls												
Education level ($\beta 16j$, $\gamma 160$)										1.362	(0.086)	***
Feeder occupation ($\beta 17j$, $\gamma 170$)										1.352	(0.111)	***
Incumbent ($\beta 18j$, $\gamma 180$)										8.265	(0.612)	***
Campaign finance ($\beta 19j$, $\gamma 190$)										1.000	(0.000)	***
Random Effects	Var	SE	sig	Var	SE	sig	Var	SE	sig	Var	SE	sig
Intercept (u_{0j})	0.058	(0.019)	***	0.061	(0.020)	***	0.029	(0.012)	***	0.047	(0.024)	***
Female slope (u_{1j})	0.273	(0.131)	***	0.279	(0.133)	***	0.201	(0.118)	***	0.004	(0.016)	***
N	21478			21478			21478			11174		
LL	−8130			−8053			−8000			−3511		
AIC	16274			16128			16047			7100		
BIC	16329			16216			16047			7386		

Notes: ***$p<0.001$, **$p<0.01$, *$p<0.05$, ±$p<0.10$ (one-tailed tests). Cands = Candidates.

significance of the interaction of *fem* with *dmag group* and *effective n cands* after all three full models suggests that together, those predictors do not gain much traction in explaining the variation in electoral outcome. Yet, once I introduce the party characteristics of *c.mass* and *PII*, the model fit improves by one-third. That suggests that for women's electoral prospects, those factors operate most significantly through their effects on political parties. In turn, party characteristics such as institutionalization and women in leadership positions have mediated their response to the incentives generated by electoral rules. Put simply, I find that supportive parties are pivotal to women's electoral success (see Table 5.4).

These findings demonstrate how party characteristics mediate institutional variables to influence women's electoral prospects and therefore suggest that the generic application of quotas in high district magnitude PR elections is insufficient to enhance women's electoral prospects. By holding constant the context in which those electoral rules operate, their assumed universal effects dissolved. My findings then deviate from those first generated from samples in Western Europe and later confirmed through aggregate level cross-national analyses. Rather, this analysis demonstrates that the effects of electoral rules on women's electoral prospects in Brazil are mediated by party characteristics, with important variation across political parties. It is critical then to consider interactions between those rules and the political and historical contexts in which they operate, with variation across parties, states, and women themselves explaining those disparities in findings. Indeed, as demonstrated with statistical analysis and corroborated in interviews, electoral rules exercise their effects on women's representation in Brazil indirectly, through the incentives they generate for intraparty support or competition, and are mediated by party characteristics such as party institutionalization and the incorporation of women in party leadership.

Even after controlling for the differences in electoral rules between the chambers (*dmag group, effective n cands, quota, senate*), as well as the effects of ideology (with more leftist women in the Senate) and the superior candidate quality of Senate candidates (*education level, feeder occupation, incumbent, campaign finance*), findings demonstrate that women in the Chamber face a gendered disadvantage not shared by their female colleagues seeking a seat in the Senate. Once we take party characteristics into consideration, the implications of the two chambers' varying incentives for party support come into focus. Because the electoral rules in the Chamber incentivize intraparty competition, the effect of *fem*PII*c.mass* is heightened in the Chamber, with institutionalized parties able to mitigate the tendencies toward combative, personalist politics and women mobilizing this capacity on behalf of female candidates. As discussed in Chapter 4, the positive effects for female candidates of women in party leadership are contingent upon *PII*, with institutionalized parties able to facilitate the provision of psychological, organizational, and material support critical for women to thrive in the entrepreneurial context.

In the Senate, *PII* loses salience, since the electoral rules generate broad incentives for unified party support of candidates across parties. Findings support the argument advanced above—that such party support is especially likely to be galvanized in the name of recruiting, developing, and supporting female candidacies when women have a voice in party leadership; when bulwarked by a women-friendly party, female candidates thrive in the context of unified party support.[12] The principal finding that emerges is that, although the electoral rules of both chambers are less than ideal for women, female candidates to the more prestigious Senate actually face a more viable campaign than do female candidates to the Chamber. Even after controlling for differences in candidate quality and a range of other factors, the negative effect of being a woman that we see in Chamber of Deputies elections is rendered null for Senate candidates.

My interviews with party officials and candidates throughout Brazil affirmed that candidates in majoritarian/plurality elections can count on significantly more party support than candidates in proportional elections. Former Senator, Governor, Minster, and current Deputy Benedita da Silva (PT-Rio de Janeiro) stated, "the party has to invest in majoritarian campaigns, but in the proportional (campaigns) it does not pass (along) resources, it is your campaign."[13] Emília Fernandes (PT-Rio Grande do Sul) emphasized the issue of factional support in the PT, which is divided into "tendencies" or factions. "In majoritarian elections, it's more about the party, but in proportional elections, only your party faction supports you," with municipalities governed by a mayor of a faction other than your own being considered off-limits.[14] In 2002, then State Deputy Serys Slhessarenko (PT-Mato Grosso) wanted to run for reelection, but "the party said Senate or nothing."[15]

Parties acting strategically generally prevent their candidates from the same municipality and/or base from contesting the same proportional election (which would lead them to split the vote). The candidacies given the go-ahead are most often male, at times regardless of seniority. According to a PT state party official in São Paulo, this was the cause for former three-term city councilor and then two-term Deputy Iara Bernardi's defeat in her reelection campaign in 2006—the party launched another candidate (from a different faction) in Sorocaba, her municipality.[16] Former Governor Wilma de Faria (PSB—Rio Grande do Norte) echoed this sentiment—in 1986, she proposed to run for State Deputy, but her

---

[12] An analysis of the marginal effects of *fem*c.mass*senate* demonstrates the magnitude of the positive effect of critical mass in the Senate—women's predicted probability of election in parties without a critical mass (0.17) is half that of female candidates running in parties with a critical mass of women leaders (0.35).

[13] Interview with Deputy Benedita da Silva (PT-RJ), June 2009.

[14] Interview with Deputy Emília Fernandes (PT-RS), April 2009.

[15] Interview with Senator Serys Slhessarenko (PT-MT), December 2008.

[16] Interview with party staffer (PT-SP), June 2009.

party denied her request, in an effort to consolidate votes for her (male) partisans. Presuming she had no chance, they allowed her an open spot on the party's candidate list for federal deputy in the Constitutional Assembly; in the end, she was the most voted in her party.[17]

Former Senator Fátima Cleide (PT-Rondônia) indicated that in her two races for the Senate and one for governor, party support—including that of various party factions—was "importantíssimo."[18] All but one of the 14 female candidates to both the Senate and Chamber included in my sample affirmed that the party played a fundamental role in their candidacy, with the majority pointing to a lack of party support as the most important barrier facing women in Brazilian politics. With difficulties obtaining financial resources as the second most frequently stated obstacle, and party support retaining at minimum an indirect role in the acquisition of resources, parties hold the key to enhancing women's representation.

Yet as many women attested, most of Brazil's political parties remain machista. Several interviewees said they confronted far more gender bias in their parties and the Congress than in the electorate. When women acquire a space in party decision-making the overwhelming male dominance in leadership is mitigated, and they are able to "let the ladder down" to female political aspirants. Indeed, as verified above, female candidates are significantly more likely to win election when running with parties that have a critical mass of women in their leadership. The data also demonstrate that such women-friendly parties are more likely to comply with the quota in the Chamber elections and have higher female candidate success rates and more favorable success rate ratios than do parties lacking women leaders. In sum, parties that afford women a real voice in decision-making more effectively promote female political participation, and when the electoral rules incentivize party support, that potential is optimized.

CONCLUSIONS

This chapter used the variation in electoral rules across Brazil's legislative chambers as a natural laboratory to examine the interacting effects of electoral institutions and party support/competition on women's electoral prospects. I found that the explanatory power of those electoral rules for the electoral successes and failures of female candidates is mediated by party characteristics. In spite of the Senate's greater prestige and higher electoral threshold relative to the Chamber of Deputies, female candidates to the Senate have had higher probabilities of electoral success, even after controlling for a range of potentially confounding factors. The Senate's low magnitude plurality elections with more restricted ballot access and multiple

---

[17] Interview with Governor Wilma de Faria (PSB-RN), July 2009.

[18] Questionnaire with Senator Fátima Cleide (PT-RO), May 2009 (answered before her failed reelection campaign in 2010).

votes incentivize unified party support, while the Chamber of Deputies' high magnitude OLPR elections yield intraparty competition.

In both chambers, the presence of a critical mass of women in party leadership induces the will to support female candidates, but in the Chamber, that effect is contingent upon party institutionalization, which affords parties the capacity to overcome the implications of intraparty competition. In contrast, the forthcoming party support in the Senate has a powerful effect on female candidates when women have a voice in party decision-making, regardless of party institutionalization. In the end, the effect of being a woman on one's chance of election is negative for the Chamber and insignificant in the Senate. While the salience of party institutionalization for women's electoral prospects does then hinge on the electoral system's incentives for intraparty support or competition, the role of female party leaders is robust. Across electoral contexts, the presence of a critical mass of women leaders in party decision-making structures tends to improve the electoral prospects of women.

In conjunction with the hierarchical logit analyses, interviews with women politicians who have run for both offices corroborate my findings. Based on that evidence, I contend that the greater successes of women in Senate elections despite an ostensibly difficult electoral context is attributable to the greater incentives for party support for Senate candidates, which motivates parties to rally behind their candidate(s). That stands in stark contrast to the Chamber, where intraparty competition results in an internal struggle for organizational and material resources. As demonstrated in Chapter 4, women can still succeed in the context of intraparty competition, albeit at lower ratios of success, but require an institutionalized party—which enjoys the means to recruit and support candidates and to execute programmatic campaigns—and women in party leadership willing and able to extend resources to female contenders. In Chapter 6, I advance this argument with case studies of women who have worked with or around their parties to navigate the constraints of intraparty competition in the face of bias in the electorate and/or among party elites.

The findings produced here have implications for proponents of an institutional design approach to resolving gender inequities. Countries do not adopt electoral institutions tabula rasa, but rather layer them upon layers of existing formal and informal institutions in a graduated process of change (Thelen 1999; Waylen 2017). Ample consideration of the sociocultural, historical, and political contexts in which electoral rules are/will be embedded is imperative before invoking generic recipes for success. After all, those electoral rules are endogenous to social and historical legacies (Desposato 2006).

This is not to say, however, that electoral rules do not matter, but rather, that they do not act in a vacuum. The same formal institutions may function differently in distinct contexts. Desposato drives home the point by contrasting the functioning of OLPR in Finland and Brazil, with the former having an institutionalized party system "while Brazil has been labeled the 'anti-party system'" (2006, 1019). The factors thought to enhance women's overall representation have not played out for female candidates in Brazil because of the particularities of the parties and party system to which those rules are endogenous.

As other controlled comparison analyses of electoral rules in recently (re) democratized nations have shown (e.g., Moser 2001b), the institutionalization of parties and the party system can have drastic effects on the operation and implications of electoral rules. While the inchoate character of most Brazilian parties has led many Brazilianists to discount the role of parties in elections, we must not simply footnote the exceptionally strong parties, but instead seek to explain variation among parties and the implications for political recruitment and representation.

6

Supermadres, Lutadoras, and Technocrats: The Bounded Profiles of Brazil's Female Politicians

Society is evolving, but the political structure still isn't.
(Deputy Manuela d'Ávila, 2010)

The findings of preceding chapters on the only recently emboldened gender quota, incentives for intraparty competition in the Chamber, importance of party support, preponderance of inchoate and male-led parties, and residual machista bias in Brazil beg the question of how women have attained even the measly 10.8 percent of the seats in Congress. In the current chapter, I explain how the relatively few women who have acquired elected office in Brazil have done so largely by following one of three pathways to power. The *supermadre, lutadora,* and technocrat profiles have enabled women to overcome women-adverse districts and/or parties and afforded female candidates improbable electoral success. Yet the bounding of potential profiles viable for Brazilian women limits their possibilities, constricting and conditioning their political aspirations and trajectories. This chapter explores those profiles, asking whether the country's female politicians have progressed beyond simple extensions of traditional domestic roles (Chaney 1979).

I find that women seeking electoral success in inhospitable district and party contexts often do remain squarely in the mold of the *supermadre* (literally, "super mother"), substantiating their political presence with feminine, maternal perspectives. But when bulwarked by a supportive party, *lutadoras* (female fighters) have deviated from traditional gender norms still prevalent, particularly in lesser developed states. Working with their party to transform experiences in informal politics into the requisite political skillset while confronting voter bias, such women are enjoying electoral success while expanding the political possibilities for women. Another novel pathway to power is that of the technocrat, prominent in more women-friendly districts absent the party support generally extended to the *lutadora*. Technocrats demonstrate professional competence, and thrive by converting area-specific expertise from the professional world into political capital. That helps technocrats to convince male party elites of their relevant skills and electability, overcoming the challenges of an unsupportive or deficient party organization. When women run in both parties and districts that are open to women, however, the bounding of profiles ceases and they are free to pursue any path to power.

I draw on expectations from the literature on women's representation discussed in Chapter 2, as well as aggregate cross-national data and descriptive evidence to advance a typology of the "women-friendliness" of statewide electoral districts and parties, thus exploiting the interstate and interparty variation discussed throughout the book. I then deploy my typology to explain how intersecting anti-women biases among voters and party elites have constricted the profiles viable for female contenders. I apply the findings of the multilevel analyses from Chapters 4 and 5 and interviews with candidates and party elites to delineate three electorally viable ideal types of profiles for women under the constraints of Brazilian politics—the *supermadre*, the *lutadora*, and the technocrat. Finally, I illustrate each profile with case studies of female political aspirants in Brazil. In illuminating the circumscribed paths to power, this chapter provides further evidence that parties are the gatekeepers that can mitigate Brazil's persistent gender gap in formal political power by expanding the opportunities available for women. More generally, the chapter reveals how women can thrive even in contexts the literature considers disadvantageous.

OBSTACLES TO WOMEN'S EMPOWERMENT

The explanations for women's underrepresentation highlighted in the literature have long emphasized voter hostility, electoral institutions, and the "male conspiracy" (i.e., political parties dominated by male elites who act to maintain their own power) (Duverger 1955). Yet as discussed in the preceding chapters, while numerous cross-national studies have analyzed the relative weight of such cultural, structural, and political factors in explaining women's underrepresentation, findings on their predictive powers remain mixed (Kenworthy and Malami 1999; Matland 1998; Salmond 2006; Schmidt 2009; Tripp and Kang 2008). The analysis in Chapter 4 and description of women's profiles below explain the disparity in results by moving beyond the common assumption of a homogenous electoral experience for women and revealing the causal heterogeneity at work. I show how different profiles have enabled women to thrive not only in contexts the extant literature predicts to be women-friendly, but also in those that it has deemed disadvantageous for women (or "women-adverse").

Although multivariate analyses discussed in the preceding chapters demonstrate the insignificance of district development levels and associated machista voter bias for female candidates' electoral prospects in

Brazil,[1] I contend that this does not mean those attitudes do not persist in Brazil, but rather that (some) women have found a way around them. Next, I use Brazil's extensive variation in levels of state development, state party institutionalization, and proportion of women in state party leadership to identify the intersecting constraints confronted by female contenders. I advance a typology of women-friendly and women-adverse contexts, and then detail how women have crafted viable political profiles allowing them to thrive even in inhospitable conditions, before illustrating their experiences with case studies of *supermadres, lutadoras*, and technocrats.

Machista Voter Attitudes and State Development

In line with the modernization hypothesis and the analysis of the covariates of machista voter bias in Chapter 4, I expect that Brazil's less developed states will be ostensibly less women-friendly than the more developed states. While machista voter bias has not predicted female candidates' electoral prospects, the fact that less developed states rank the highest in perceived male political superiority (LAPOP n.d.; Center of Studies and Public Opinion 2010) suggests that women in such districts are somehow circumnavigating machista voter bias. Of the 27 statewide districts, 14 fall below the national average in HDI in at least one of the five election years under consideration, and are thus coded as less developed. As displayed in Figure 4.1, the correlation with development and region is perfect, with the less developed states found exclusively in the north and northeastern regions—where clientelistic politics have historically dominated in a predatory cycle of local political bosses (*coronéis*) enriching themselves at the expense of the impoverished masses (Hagopian 1996; Montero 2010). Women may then be doubly disadvantaged in such contexts, with an electorate harboring traditional ideas about gender norms and a largely male political and economic elite maintaining power among themselves.

Party Elites and the "Good Ole Boys' Club"

As declared by Duverger decades ago, the "male conspiracy" poses an important obstacle to women seeking to enter politics (1955). In spite of the provocative term, Duverger's argument is more rationalist than conspiratorial, contending that predominantly male party elites are hesitant to share their power and therefore resist newcomers who may dilute their influence.

---

[1] Recall, 23.2% of respondents agreed or strongly agreed with the statement of male political superiority in 2010 (down from 33.5% in 2008), an average proportion that obscures great variation—while only 6.7% of respondents in Mato Grosso agreed with the statement, 55% of those in Sergipe did (Center of Studies and Public Opinion 2010; LAPOP n.d.). So while machista voter bias has not predicted female candidates' electoral prospects, it remains present. The current chapter explains this apparent anomaly.

Although many de-emphasize the power of most parties by contending that "the candidate nomination process is wide open and that candidates self-select" in Brazil's candidate-centered legislative elections (Samuels 2008, 84), I have demonstrated throughout this book that the "entrepreneurial" system and gendered structural disadvantages together render the support of an institutionalized party critical for women.

To connect parties with profiles, it is necessary first to summarize the relevance of institutionalization. To recall, previous research from the United States has shown that a party's promotion of female political participation is essential in overcoming a constructed gender gap in political ambition (e.g., Lawless and Fox 2005). By providing opportunities for political training and offering party funds and campaign materials, parties can stimulate female candidacies. Further, whereas inchoate parties are prone to personalist campaigns, well-institutionalized parties typically provide a coherent ideological platform, allowing women to deflect personal characteristics such as gender and focus the campaign instead on concrete policy proposals (Valdini 2013a). Such a collectivist endeavor is in general more palatable for women than the individualistic campaigns common to weaker parties (Escobar-Lemmon and Taylor-Robinson 2008).

Regardless of a party's capacity to promote women, however, without an earnest commitment, the women-adverse exclusionary incentives discussed above prevail and women's participation remains marginal. Based on arguments outlined in the preceding chapters, I contend that the parties least susceptible to exclusionary tendencies are those that have a critical mass of women in party leadership bodies (Duverger 1955; Kittilson 2006). When women have a real voice in party leadership they are able to perform critical acts, lobbying for the promotion of women-friendly policies and providing the necessary opportunities to minimize a socialized gender gap in political ambition (Kittilson 2006). While the relationship is not determinative, women leaders are more likely than male leaders to possess the know-how and the will to cultivate viable female candidates, particularly once they supersede token status.

In determining which of Brazil's many parties can be considered women-friendly or adverse, I employ as the key predictors whether a party is (1) well-institutionalized[2] and (2) the proportion of women in its leadership is greater than or equal to 25 percent. Because congressional campaigns in Brazil are state-centered rather than national affairs, I incorporate original state-level measures of party institutionalization and women in party

---

[2] As discussed in Appendix 4.1, I consider a state party to be "well-institutionalized" if it exceeds the mean (mean=1.9) level of state party institutionalization in Brazil. To recall, my 5-point index of party institutionalization (PII) incorporates each state party's relative measures on electoral volatility, age, membership, funds, active municipal organizations, and propensity of leadership to alternate.

leadership.[3] According to those criteria (state party institutionalization and leadership composition), of the 607 state parties that advanced female candidates in the 2010 elections, only 105—17.3%—can be considered women-friendly. Across the 1998–2010 elections, the numbers fall, with 331 of the 2,383 (13.9%) state parties participating in election rating as women-friendly. The state parties most often enjoying a level of institutionalization and women in leadership that qualify them as women-friendly are the PC do B, the PMN, and the PT. Notably, less than 5% of the elections contested by four of the major five parties—PFL, PMDB, PP, and PSDB—were done so under conditions propitious for female contenders. That is suggestive of the difficult battle confronted by female political aspirants and illustrates why women remain so underrepresented in the formal political sphere. The puzzle of this chapter thus becomes not why there is such extreme underrepresentation of women in Brazilian politics, but rather, how the few successful female politicians have defied the odds and acquired office.

I incorporate the expectations from the gender and politics literature regarding the obstacles to female political aspirants and the findings of preceding chapters to surmise that Brazil's most "women-friendly" states will be those with a development level above the national average (where machista voter attitudes are hypothesized to be less prevalent), while the most women-friendly parties will be those that are well institutionalized, and that have a critical mass of women in their leadership (whether through a quota or organically). After identifying the intersecting constraints confronted by women, I delineate particular profiles that have enabled (some) female candidates to overcome those obstacles.

The map (Figure 6.1) below applies the typology of women-friendliness to the Brazilian case. The bolded line divides the northern and northeastern states (which have below-average HDI levels and are thus coded as "women-adverse") from the remaining "women-friendly" states (with above-average HDI levels). The map uses shading to depict the proportion of each state's participating parties that, by virtue of their institutionalization level and inclusion of at least 25 percent women in state-level party executive commissions, qualify as "women-friendly" parties.

As Figure 6.1 depicts, women by and large confront rather hostile contexts in their bids for political power. From 1998–2010, the percentage of parties running in Chamber of Deputies elections and qualifying as "women-friendly" across all the states averaged only 11.7%, ranging from 1.3% in Alagoas to 24.4% in Piauí. That means that the vast majority of parties contesting the Chamber of Deputies

---

[3] That being said, state-level information on party leadership structures is often exceedingly difficult to attain. Future applications of the typology may therefore choose to apply the proportion of women on parties' national executive committees (NECs). That strategy is most appropriate in more centralized party systems.

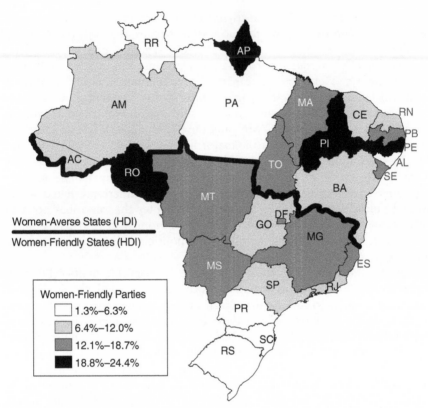

FIGURE 6.1 Percent of Women-Friendly Parties Contesting Chamber of Deputies Elections, by State (1998–2010)

elections are inchoate and/or top heavy with men. Figure 6.1 also displays the interesting interstate variation, with several less developed states actually enjoying higher proportions of women-friendly parties (darkest shading) than the more developed states. Such variation is reflective of the limitations of a singular emphasis (i.e., on development) or excessive aggregation when explaining women's political prospects. As I explain in the following section, some women have managed to overcome seemingly formidable obstacles, gaining office not only in the rare contexts that the literature expects to be women-friendly, but also in Brazil's most conservative states and inchoate and male-led parties.

CIRCUMVENTING THE OBSTACLES IN BRAZIL

In spite of the plethora of women-adverse contexts confronted by female political aspirants, several pioneers have blazed trails into the still male dominant arena of Brazilian politics. Of the 161 instances (2,052 possible) women were elected to the Brazilian Chamber of Deputies during the 1998–2010 period (104 women, with several gaining reelection), an astonishing 93.8% came from districts and/or parties predicted to be women-adverse. Slightly less than one-fifth of the successful candidacies emerged from the ideal condition of a women-friendly party. This means that most of Brazil's few female politicians have boldly confronted extremely difficult conditions, in turn illuminating the understandable reluctance of many would-be candidates to throw their hat in the ring.

The constraints confronting female candidates to the Chamber of Deputies are profound, with electoral rules that promote combative intraparty competition and expensive campaigns, weak parties lacking strong organizations and programmatic platforms (and thus susceptible to personalist politics), male-dominant party leadership structures, and non-negligible levels of voter skepticism regarding women's political role, fabricating a formidable electoral climate. The puzzle then shifts from why there is such an extreme underrepresentation of women in Brazil to how the few female politicians have been able to overcome electoral and party structures seemingly rigged against them. As I show, women have forged novel paths to power to achieve improbable electoral successes in Brazil. By crafting certain profiles, those pioneers have expanded the realm of possibilities for female political action by mitigating the impediments posed by biases and institutional arrangements.

While the profiles are neither necessarily mutually exclusive nor consistently adopted by the women in each context, I delineate three ideal types (see Table 6.1) that are most likely to afford women electoral success in the face of these obstacles: (1) the *supermadre* profile affords women electoral success in women-adverse parties and districts, (2) the *lutadora* profile is viable for women running with the support of a women-friendly party but in women-adverse districts, and (3) the technocrat profile enables women who are lacking party support to win in women-friendly districts. The "open" designation for women in women-friendly districts and parties means women in these contexts are open to pursue any (mix of) profiles.

The fact that the vast majority of Brazil's numerous parties remain weakly institutionalized with few women leaders means that most female candidates

TABLE 6.1 *Ideal Types of Viable Profiles in Women-Adverse and Women-Friendly Contexts*

	Women-Adverse Districts	Women-Friendly Districts
Women-Adverse Parties	SUPERMADRES	TECHNOCRATS
Women-Friendly Parties	LUTADORAS	OPEN

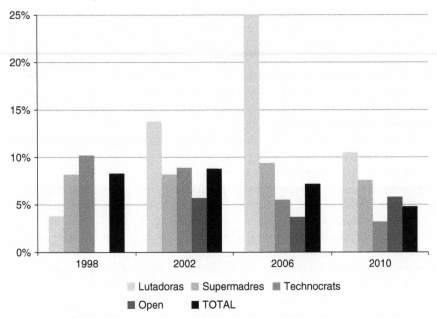

FIGURE 6.2 Profile Ideal Types by Success Rate (Percent Elected), 1998–2010

have run without the support of a women-friendly party.[4] Of the 2,384 women seeking election to the Chamber of Deputies (1998–2010), 84.9% did so in inchoate and/or male-run parties. Interestingly, 17 of the 136 women running in a women-adverse district but friendly party were elected for a success rate (n female elected / n female candidates) of 12.5 %, which is 67% higher than the women's overall success rate (See Figure 6.2).[5] As I discuss below, those women likely achieved such success as *lutadoras*, defying traditional gender norms and running collective, ideas-based campaigns. But the *lutadora* path is contingent on party support, so in order for the profile to prove viable for more contenders across Brazil, reforms must emphasize institutionalizing parties and incentivizing their inclusion of female leaders and active promotion of and support for female candidacies. The success of *lutadoras* provides yet another piece of evidence suggesting

---

[4] Officials and politicians from several parties revealed the disconcertingly common practice of parties including women on their candidate lists in a post-hoc manner to simply pay lip service to the gender quota, only recognizing the void at the final hour (when lists are due to the electoral court) with little or no effort to actively recruit and support female candidacies.

[5] The drop in success rates in 2010—when credible threats of enforcement of the gender quota strengthened in the 2009 mini-reform to Brazil's electoral code prompted a widespread offering of *candidatas laranjas* (sacrificial lambs and phantom candidates) by many parties (Wylie 2011; Wylie, Marcelino, and dos Santos 2015)—reveals the futility of mere symbolic gestures and the imperative of sincere party involvement on behalf of women.

that the problem of women's underrepresentation in Brazil is fundamentally political rather than societal.

Below, I discuss how the three profiles have afforded women political space in such inhospitable contexts. I draw upon my original database of several individual-, party-, and district-level characteristics of the 20,363 candidates to the Chamber of Deputies (1994–2010) and over 100 interviews with both failed and elected women candidates as well as party staff and activists conducted in 11 states across Brazil. I selected interview participants to ensure representation from each of the country's five regions and seven major parties (PFL/DEM, PC do B, PMDB, PP, PSB, PSDB, PT), and variation on the women-friendliness of districts and parties. In the discussion below, I will refer to Table 6.2—which includes the averages for several characteristics of women candidates and elected deputies across the women-friendly and women-adverse contexts.

First, to establish a baseline for comparison, I discuss the political trajectory of Judge Denise Frossard, an ambitious woman exemplary of the kind of self-promoting individual capable of thriving independently in Brazil's entrepreneurial electoral system. Judge Frossard gained her entrée into electoral politics five years after convicting 14 members of an organized crime ring involved in the *Jogo do Bicho*, a lottery of sorts that infamously launders money and has been implicated in a number of corruption scandals. Undeterred by death threats and determined to fight against corruption, Judge Frossard decided to join the Socialist People's Party (PPS—a leftist but anti-PT party) and run for the Senate in 1998, obtaining fourth place with 635,415 votes.

Judge Frossard was one of only two women I interviewed who said the decision to run for office was hers alone, with no party role. She ran again in 2002, that time with the PSDB, and earned the highest vote share of all 560 candidates in Rio de Janeiro, winning an impressive 5.21% of the valid vote (the average vote share was 0.18%). As Judge Frossard herself said, she was larger than either of her two parties, and did not need them to advance or sustain her candidacy.[6] Indeed, she received no campaign funds from the party for her Chamber candidacy. In 2006, Judge Frossard ran a competitive campaign for governor, but was ultimately defeated by Sérgio Cabral in the second round of elections.

Judge Frossard entered party politics with vast self-confidence, political interest and knowledge, and name recognition already under her belt. With fifteen years of experience in the state government magistrate, which Judge Frossard accredited as significantly more equitable than the machista parties and parliament, she was able to thrive in the absence of any party support mobilized on her behalf.[7] Judge Frossard launched her own candidacy,

[6] Interview with former Deputy Judge Denise Frossard (PPS-RJ), June 2009.
[7] Interview with former Deputy Judge Denise Frossard (PPS-RJ), June 2009.

TABLE 6.2 *Individual Characteristics of Women Running in Women-Adverse and Women-Friendly Contexts (1998–2010)*

	Wmn-Adverse District		Wmn-Friendly District	
	WF Party	WA Party	WA Party	WF Party
CANDIDATES				
Electoral Perf.	0.14	0.08	0.06	0.05
Pct Vote Share	1.53%	0.81%	0.26%	0.35%
Pct Elected	12.50%	8.36%	5.89%	4.46%
Education	3.64	3.55	3.56	3.65
Pct Feeder Occup.	64.62%	58.61%	54.54%	54.02%
Pct Incumbent	8.09%	6.35%	5.19%	2.68%
Pct Married	40.00%	46.57%	45.23%	34.91%
CF	R$ 97,843	R$ 86,668	R$ 78,667	R$ 87,502
Pct CF from Corps	12.17%	14.32%	14.21%	11.52%
Pct CF from Ind	35.75%	36.39%	31.22%	36.64%
Pct CF from Party	32.41%	30.16%	39.51%	31.81%
Pct Left	69.12%	33.11%	34.78%	85.27%
Ideology	2.98	4.26	4.14	2.86
Pct Wmn Leaders	33.80%	15.59%	12.98%	31.65%
ELECTED				
Electoral Perf.	0.84	0.58	0.59	0.81
Pct Vote Share	9.54%	5.62%	2.67%	5.50%
Education	3.94	3.82	3.79	3.60
Pct Feeder Occup.	94.12%	87.76%	83.13%	80.00%
Pct Incumbent	52.94%	46.00%	46.43%	40.00%
Pct Married	52.94%	62.00%	52.56%	30.00%
CF	R$ 336,542	R$ 381,939	R$ 458,206	R$ 906,416
Pct CF from Corps	29.37%	32.55%	43.89%	40.96%
Pct CF from Ind	24.83%	35.19%	34.04%	33.14%
Pct CF from Party	32.65%	17.87%	11.52%	19.42%
Pct Left	82.35%	26.00%	45.24%	90.00%
Ideology	2.93	4.47	3.90	2.18
Pct Wmn Leaders	34.04%	15.28%	11.66%	33.88%

advanced her own already well-developed anti-corruption platform, raised her own funds, and depended upon her own cultivated base. This is indicative of the path to power pursued by entrepreneurial candidates with independent converted capital, and is unlikely for women who lack the intense ambition, independent fame, connections, and resources of Judge Frossard. Next, I discuss the profiles more commonly pursued by female contenders, and how they have navigated the constraints of women-adverse contexts.

Supermadres

Historically, women have typically lacked the consummate insider status discussed above, and with female political aspirants often confronting both districts and parties adverse to women. Yet, women facing those constraints can and have for generations in countries around the world managed to chip away at the monolith of male political dominance. As elaborated in the fundamental text on women politicians in Latin America, the profile most likely to succeed in such a situation has been that of the *supermadre*, whereby women politicians extend their role in the private sphere to the public sphere (Chaney 1979; Franceschet 2005).[8] Given that the inegalitarian attitudes and resultant *machista* biases persistent in less developed areas are generally associated with traditional beliefs regarding the societal roles of women (Inglehart and Norris 2003), *supermadres* can strategically leverage the maternalist frame to mitigate the effects of such biases by conforming to traditional gender norms (Franceschet, Piscopo, and Thomas 2015).

The primary emphasis on the role of familial connections in the extant literature on women politicians in Brazil (e.g., Araújo 2001a, 2001b; Avelar 2001; Haas 2001) is reflective of the capacity of such connections to minimize the threat to traditional gender norms posed by female political aspirants. By running as the wife or daughter of a male politician, those privileged female candidates corroborate the patriarchal order found in women-adverse contexts. Furthermore, the wives and daughters of male politicians can employ their family name and experience in politics to assuage the fears of biased voters and elites about the political ineptitude of women. Because they have already experienced a life of politics, male politicians' wives and daughters may also be deemed more "fit" for politics than the average woman. If so, women candidates with familial connections may be relatively exempt from the persistent biases in women-adverse districts and parties, therefore hastening their electoral success in such contexts. And even in the context of such biases, access to familial capital can catapult women to

---

[8] Although the term denotes a maternal association, *supermadre* was initially coined to suggest that women remained confined to an extension of their role in the home, not necessarily—but usually—as mother. In my reading of Chaney (1979), women are conceptualized as *supermadres* regardless of their actual maternal status but rather as their exemplification of the traditional feminine (which due to traditional gender roles, is associated with motherhood). In this sense, a more appropriate label would perhaps be "superfeminine," but I stick to the term *supermadre* here to maintain consistency with Chaney's concept.

insider status through political endorsements, financial backing, and the family name (Hinojosa 2012).

Of the 598 female Chamber of Deputies candidates (1994–2010) in women-adverse states and parties, 50 women were (re)elected, with 29 being the wives or daughters of a male politician. The concentration of wives and daughters winning amidst those constraints has remained constant over time, at 56–58% of the women elected in women-adverse districts and parties, which exceeds the proportions found in other contexts. Two interrelated factors explaining this pattern are the ability of familial capital to assuage and/or overcome voter bias against women, and the persistence of oligarchic clientelist politics dominated by a handful of political families in the less developed states, particularly the northeast (Congresso em Foco 2011; Costa and Cornwall 2014).

This is not to say that the fit between familial ties and the *supermadre* profile is perfect, as many women with connected family members develop their own political capital rather than simply inheriting it from their father or husband. For example, two influential female senators are the (ex-)wife of prominent male politicians, but those women (Marta Suplicy and Gleisi Hoffmann) cut their political teeth outright as activists in the student movement and eventually in party politics. While Suplicy's fame as a televised sexologist propelled her directly to the Chamber of Deputies in 1994, Hoffmann worked her way up through the party ranks, serving as advisor in several administrative and campaign roles, and as the state party president before entering electoral politics as a mayoral candidate in 2008. In 2017, Hoffmann was elected National President of the PT (PT 2017f). Whether their independent capital-building efforts will be supported is a product of their party and district constraints, with such independence perceived as a threat in inegalitarian contexts. Notably, Suplicy and Hoffman both come from more developed states (São Paulo and Santa Catarina) and at least a nationally supportive party (PT).[9]

But women lacking familial ties can withstand gender inegalitarian electorates and elites by conforming to traditional gender norms through other means. Because traditional gender norms confine the areas of expertise of women to issues such as education, health care, and non-feminist women and children's rights,[10] voter and elite biases in women-adverse states and parties may be attenuated for women with traditionalist prior careers in education, health, and social work. Of the 2,569 female candidacies from 1994–2010, at least 28.5% emerged from those professions.[11] Another viable means of

---

[9] Suplicy was a longtime *petista* and switched to the PMDB in 2015 shortly before announcing her candidacy for mayor of São Paulo.

[10] For analyses on how gender norms have influenced committee and ministerial assignments, see Escobar-Lemmon and Taylor-Robinson (2005).

[11] The total of female candidates excludes candidates that did not report their occupation. Also included in this calculation are other occupations conforming to traditional gender roles, such as model, nun, housewife, and receptionist.

conforming to traditional gender norms is for women candidates to employ their church connections (i.e., with the *bancada evangélica* or *comunidades eclesiais de base*). Indeed, among the 50 women elected (and reelected) in women-adverse states and parties from 1998–2010, all but seven report such *supermadre* backgrounds.

In interviews I conducted with women conforming to the *supermadre* trajectory, they consistently justified their political presence through the maternal, more humane perspective they felt they, as women, could bring to politics. The goal repeatedly expressed was *cuidar* (to care) for their constituents. Jusmari Oliveira, former deputy for the conservative PFL and mayor of a town in the interior of Bahia, believed that women politicians should emphasize social issues, arguing "God gave us greater sensitivity, an understanding of the suffering of humanity." Accordingly, Oliveira prioritized social issues while in the Chamber of Deputies and deemed her mayoral administration the "Governo Cidade Mãe" (Government Mother City).[12] Next, I demonstrate how one deputy has had mixed results complying with traditional gender norms in her women-adverse state and party.

BEL MESQUITA: A PROUD SUPERMADRE

Building on the political capital of her ex-husband as well as her own political capital developed while serving as municipal president of the Foundation of Social and Cultural Action[13] under his administration, Bel Mesquita followed her husband's mayoral mandates with two of her own and subsequently served as federal deputy for the centrist PMDB in the northern state of Pará. She firmly believed in her responsibility to *cuidar* for her district and to "humanize" politics, enthusiastically affirming her role as the supermadre of her constituents.[14] Mesquita's sentiment was echoed in an interview—when the reporter asked about the appointment of ten women (including Mesquita) to President Dilma Rousseff's cabinet, Mesquita declared, "I have conviction that women were born with the gift of management, organization, and administration. She takes care of the kids, [and] is able to provide for her family with what little resources she can have ... she knows what to do" (Diário do Turismo 2011). As a *supermadre*, Mesquita draws a direct parallel between overseeing a home and overseeing a federal government.

In contrast to the movement and party-based path to power of the *lutadora* discussed below, Mesquita—a psychologist by training—inherited her capital from her husband, further cultivating it while serving in his

---

[12] Interview with Deputy Jusmari Oliveira (PFL/PR-BA), November 2008.
[13] Such posts are extremely common for first ladies; in interviews, many former first ladies stated that their role in the positions served as a catalyst for the development of their own political aspirations.
[14] Interview with Deputy Bel Mesquita (PMDB-PA), December 2008.

Foundation of Social and Cultural Action (1989–1992) and as the Municipal Secretary of Health (1992) under his administration. Initially a member of the PSDB from 1995–1999, Mesquita soon joined the PTB, under which she served as municipal party president from 1999–2004. She was first elected mayor with the PSDB in 1996—in a municipality that she and her husband helped to create—and then gained reelection under the PTB. While the party tends to be central to the success of *lutadoras*, as discussed below, Mesquita succeeded in spite of only fleeting party ties.

After completing her second mayoral mandate, Mesquita joined the PMDB. Soon thereafter, she ran an ultimately successful campaign for federal deputy, earning over 44,000 votes, the 21st in her state (of 137 candidates) and 5th (of 12) in her party, which ran without a coalition. Mesquita ran under the number 1501, and won a majority of the vote in her small town, Parauapebas, and more than 10% of the statewide vote in five nearby municipalities. With nearly 70% of her campaign contributions originating from individuals, and only 12% from the party, Mesquita went it alone in the campaign. As shown in Table 6.2, women who have succeeded under the constraints of a women-adverse district and party on average draw greater share of funds from individuals than do women in the other contexts.

It must be noted, however, that Mesquita did benefit from running in the PMDB in Pará, which has long been dominated by the Barbalho family. Jader Barbalho alone won 1.7 times the electoral quotient (183,438), with his wife Elcione[15] also winning election with over 114,000 votes of her own. As such, women who anticipate no party support are wise to run on party lists headed by such *puxadoras de voto*, and thus squeeze some benefit yet from the unsupportive party.

As Deputy, Mesquita served in the Commissions on Education and Culture, and Social Security and Family, as the president of a congressional inquiry on missing children, and as the *Procuradora-Adjunta Especial da Mulher* (Assistant Special Solicitor General of Women). She remained pinned to issues conforming to the traditional feminine, with the vast majority of her 132 proposed pieces of legislation concerning missing and exploited children (Chamber of Deputies 2012). Although Mesquita herself embraced the *supermadre* role, it has not parlayed into more recent electoral success. While representing the interests of children is generally uncontroversial, it has left neither electors nor corporate backers with much (pork) to rally behind. With minimal support from the PMDB, Mesquita subsequently lost three sequential bids for mayor, state deputy, and vice-mayor (Rodrigues 2012).

In sum, Mesquita's political ascendance appears to have been restricted. So while the *supermadre* path has increased access to a political arena long-dominated by men, it remains restricted and maintains a "commitment to the eternal feminine" (Bourque and Grossholtz 1998, 25), with motherhood rather

---

[15] Elcione Barbalho ran under the highly sought "1515" number.

than citizenship providing "the principal mobilizational referent for women's participation" (Alvarez 1990, 50). The issues and political arenas perceived societally to be "appropriate" for women to engage are thus tied inextricably to motherhood, effectively preventing women's unfettered participation in the formal sphere.[16] Women are, however, no longer confined to the *supermadre* mold and have instead transcended the private–public dichotomy by concerning themselves with a diversity of issues, including the economy, foreign policy, and national and public security in addition to health care, education, and women's and children's rights (Schwindt-Bayer 2006).[17] Building on that finding, I contend that the *supermadre* pathway is but one of the available avenues of political ascension for women in Brazil—neither women nor the obstacles they confront is monolithic. Next, I discuss how women have worked with supportive parties to parlay their party/movement activism into political capital.

Lutadoras

Female candidates in less developed states often conform to traditional gender norms in their campaigns, as elaborated in the discussion of the *supermadre* profile above. But when bolstered by a supportive party, women contenders can deviate from the traditional notion of femininity embodied by the *supermadre* and still thrive in women-adverse districts. To overcome (rather than conform to) the gender biases persistent in such states, women must be resilient and battle-proven, thus the designation *lutadora*—or female fighter. *Lutadoras* typically earn their stripes and demonstrate their political prowess through party militancy and activism in labor unions or popular social movements. By actively participating in such arenas, *lutadoras* gain political and social capital and signal their viability to party leaders open to recruiting female candidates for office. A women-friendly party—well institutionalized and with women in party leadership—is most likely to (at least attempt to) comply with the gender quota and has clear processes for the party to recruit and select its candidates. *Lutadoras* are thus well positioned for advancement, having proven their commitment to the party and broader social causes while demonstrating their base of support in the community.

A deep connection to the community helps stimulate political ambition and often leads parties to recruit women for candidacy, but the ultimate decision to run is always personal and fraught with economic risk. Many of the women

---

[16] For a discussion of the resilience of traditional gender norms rooted in motherhood in Brazil, see Pinheiro (2007).

[17] While Schwindt-Bayer finds reported attitudes/preferences among male and female legislators to be similar, thus her conclusion that women are not "still supermadres" in Latin America, she also finds gendered patterns of bill initiation that she attributes to the marginalization of women by male legislators who perceive their powers to be threatened by the increasing presence of women (2006).

interviewed across seven states qualifying as women-adverse expressed their unwillingness to run a campaign in such a context if the party had no intention of supporting her, with one woman declaring she would not "take bread off the family table" to serve as a *candidata laranja* (sacrificial lamb or phantom candidate).

When parties have the resources to allocate and the will to do so, however, *lutadoras* are well-prepared for the challenge. Institutionalized parties with a critical mass of women in their leadership prove helpful for female candidates seeking to solidify their platform because these parties are more likely to advance capacity-building programs that cultivate women's political ambition by enhancing their sense of preparedness. They teach female aspirants the scope of the office at stake as well as party positions on key issues, thus enabling them to run knowledgeable and ideologically grounded campaigns. In weakly institutionalized parties, ideological roots are elusive, leaving women contenders with nothing collective to latch onto.

A firmly rooted ideological platform that she can present to voters skeptical of her political aptitude is a critical component of the *lutadora*'s toolkit. Where intense voter bias against women exists, women's representation will be lower in electoral systems that incentivize the personal vote (Valdini 2013a). The emphasis on policy positions rather than personal traits such as gender allows the *lutadora* to recast the campaign around policy debates rather than personal characteristics, in turn diminishing the elector's prospect of employing negative gender stereotypes. When prompted in interviews for advice for less electorally fortunate women, successful female politicians often highlighted the importance of defining one's *bandeiras* (central campaign themes) and related community activism.[18]

For Municipal Councilor Olívia Santana (PC do B-Salvador) and Deputy Benedita da Silva (PT-RJ), both of whom are Afro-descendant women from impoverished backgrounds, party support formed a psychological and organizational bulwark against prejudice—among both the electorate and corporate donors—rooted in intersecting layers of oppression.[19] *Lutadoras* have at their disposal extensive mobilizational resources such as footwork by party and movement militants that can help to overcome gendered and racialized deficits in financial resources, a prominent obstacle impeding most female political aspirants. Campaign finance is particularly important given the growing expense of elections in Brazil; in 2010, the average in campaign contributions for winning candidates to the Chamber of Deputies was more than R$1.1 million,[20] with the overall average

---

[18] Interviews with Deputy Ana Arraes (PSB-PE), March 2009, Deputy Fátima Bezerra (PT-RN), March 2009, Deputy Alice Portugal (PCdoB-BA), December 2008.

[19] Interviews with Deputy Benedita da Silva (PT-RJ), June 2009, and Municipal Councilor Olívia Santana (PC do B-Salvador, BA), April 2009.

[20] The average campaign contributions for winning candidates jumped to R$1.43 million in 2014 (Tribunal Superior Eleitoral 1994–2016).

jumping 106% from the 2006 average.[21] When party militants are encouraged and willing to mobilize on behalf of women and help to wage labor-intensive *corpo a corpo* (person to person) campaigns, the effects of campaign finance discrepancies between men and women and leftists and non-leftists can be mitigated, enabling female candidates to thrive even in women-adverse states.[22]

Candidates are increasingly relying on party funding for their campaigns, with an average of 43.5% of candidates' contributions coming from party organizations in the 2010 Chamber of Deputies elections. Women consistently draw even more of their funding from party organizations— 57.3% on average in 2010—reflecting gendered wage discrepancies in the workforce and the difficulty many women have in attaining funds from large donors. For women winning in women-adverse districts but women-friendly parties in the 2010 Chamber of Deputies elections, the mean proportion of campaign funds from their party was 27%, significantly higher than the overall proportion for successful women candidates (16.2%). Whether in the currency of foot soldiers or finance, party support helps to level the playing field for any female candidate.

Although this path is still significantly less pursued than that of the *supermadre*, many of Brazil's most prominent female politicians—including Marina Silva and Heloísa Helena—are *lutadoras*. Those pioneers from Brazil's north (Acre) and northeastern (Alagoas) regions have represented their historically women-adverse states as social movement and PT militants,[23] municipal councilwomen, state deputies, senators, minister (Silva), and presidential candidates, serving as role models for *lutadoras* to come. Moreover, the *lutadoras* exemplify a female insurgency in the male-dominant system; as suggested by Table 6.2, women running with women-friendly parties in women-adverse districts have consistently enjoyed the highest overall success rates, vote shares, and incumbency rates.

---

[21] Those figures become even more striking when one considers the state-funded air time and compulsory voting law (Tribunal Superior Eleitoral 1994–2016).

[22] In 2010, the averages in campaign contributions were R$273,595 for male candidates, R$126,323 for female candidates, R$264,950 for non-leftists, and R$227,089 for leftists. In 2014, those averages were R$308,868 for male candidates, R$87,711 for female candidates (reflecting the widespread offering of *candidatas laranjas*), R$265,830 for non-leftists, and R$213,208 for leftists. Difference in means tests show the gendered differences were statistically significant at the $p<0.001$ level, and the ideological differences significant at the $p<0.05$ and $p<0.01$ levels, respectively.

[23] Both Helena and Silva were early members of the PT, but have since joined other parties (PSOL and the Green Party). Helena was expelled from the party in 2003 for voting against more than a dozen measures backed by the Lula administration, in particular the pension privatization. Silva left the party in 2009, disillusioned by the inadequate attention given by the Lula administration to issues of sustainable development. In October 2015, Silva's Sustainability Network gained formal approval from the TSE; she has been in the process of founding the party for the past two years. Helena announced that she will leave PSOL to join Silva's Sustainability Network (Novaes 2015).

Most of the 17 successful female candidacies in women-adverse districts but women-friendly parties epitomize the *lutadora* profile. One woman has drawn heavily on familial political capital,[24] and two women qualify as technocratic types, new to party life and effectively leveraging their professional experiences, but the others are long-time party militants with active union and popular movement backgrounds. The late Francisca Trindade joined the PT at an early age, serving as two-term municipal councilor of the capital city of her northeastern state of Piauí, state deputy, and candidate for vice-mayor before winning a seat to the Chamber of Deputies. Perpetua Almeida and Vanessa Grazziotin have been members of the Communist Party of Brazil (PC do B) since the 1980s, both serving as municipal councilors before becoming federal deputies of their northern states in the Amazon region. Grazziotin was elected to the Senate in 2010 (the PC do B's first-ever senator). Almeida ran a competitive election for the Senate in 2014 but ultimately lost. In the case study that follows, I show how party support helped one *lutadora* to overcome bias in the electorate and climb her way to the Chamber of Deputies, twice winning the highest vote total for federal deputy in her state, and recently gaining election as Senator.

DEPUTY FÁTIMA BEZERRA: THE ESSENCE OF A LUTADORA

A woman of humble origins in northeastern Brazil (Rio Grande do Norte), Deputy Fátima Bezerra confirmed the critical role of her background in social movements and support from movement and party militants in helping her to confront and transcend class and gender discrimination, pointing to movement and party militants as "shapers of opinion." In contrast, local political elites had at first only impeded Bezerra's political ambition, maintaining that the role of deputy was "predestined for the sons (and daughters) of traditional families." Yet, a lifetime of precarious living conditions in the rural northeast coupled with her experiences fighting injustices at the helm of several social movements emboldened Bezerra to pursue and eventually, with the encouragement of her party, fulfill her political ambitions.[25]

Like so many other (often leftist) female politicians, Bezerra cultivated her political aptitudes during the student movement of the 1970s. She participated in the National Student Union's (UNE) formative 1979 Congress in Salvador, where UNE was restructured in the wake of its weakened status during the military regime. Later drawing on her experience in the student movement and as a public school teacher, Bezerra founded and presided over a prominent teacher's union, served as the secretary general of another, and was a two-term president of the influential Union of Education Workers.[26]

---

[24] Interview with Deputy Ana Arraes (PSB-PE), March 2009.
[25] Interview with Deputy Fátima Bezerra, March 2009.
[26] http://portal.fatimabezerra.com.br/p/perfil

During that time Bezerra joined the then nascent PT, which was closely aligned with union activity on behalf of education. When asked whether she got involved in party life in 1981 with an idea of being an elected official, she responded "I confess to you, this never even crossed my mind" (TV Seridó 2009). But seeking to make headways in state and local politics, the PT tapped Bezerra's considerable clout in the education community and encouraged her to run for the state assembly. Bezerra recalled that her candidacy for state deputy in 1994 "was a fruit of my involvement in the social movements and at the same time, a necessity of my party (PT) to advance candidacies in the state legislatures."[27] She recognized the fundamental role of the party in recruiting her into party politics and enabling her success, "The PT was certainly the most responsible for me having entered in party politics and also for me having arrived to this stage" (TV Seridó 2009).

Bezerra served two terms as state deputy and leader of her state party delegation, in her first term winning awards for the Deputy of the Year in 1996 and Best Deputy of the Legislature (1995–1998). She gained ideological coherence, demonstrated her political skills, and shored up the good will of her fellow members, forming a support base that would enable her to thrive even in her less developed district.[28] In 2002, the PT advanced Bezerra's name for the Chamber of Deputies, and she won the most votes of all of the 74 candidates in her state, 12.3% of the statewide vote. Bezerra won the honor again in 2010, when she competed against 59 other candidates and captured an impressive 14.6% of the statewide vote, winning more than 15% in nearly one-fifth of her state's 167 municipalities and over 23% of the vote in the capital city (Tribunal Superior Eleitoral 1994–2016). She just missed the second round of mayoral elections in 2008, winning 36.8% of the vote and losing to Green Party candidate Micarla de Sousa, who allied with several right-wing parties (DEM, PP, PR, PTB) to win a narrow majority of votes in the first round.

Bezerra's roots in the social movements are enduring and have informed her legislative efforts. She has remained involved with the education unions, was elected president of the Chamber's Commission on Education and Culture, and is an active proponent of education issues such as establishing a minimum wage for public school teachers, protecting the right to strike, and improving access to quality education. Most of her more than 400 legislative proposals in the Chamber of Deputies relate to education, the rights of marginalized populations (primarily LGBT, women, indigenous, domestic workers, Afro-Brazilians, and the impoverished), and regional development (Chamber of Deputies 2015). She was a delegate to the pivotal Beijing Conference in 1995 and to the first and second iterations of the World Social Forum in 2001 and

---

[27] Interview with Deputy Fátima Bezerra, March 2009.
[28] As stated by President Lula at a 2008 rally for Bezerra's mayoral bid, you need "character of force (to govern), and this lady here has that in excess" (Ribeiro 2008).

2002.[29] Bezerra has also served in the state and national leadership of the PT, remains active in the mayoral campaigns of her co-partisans throughout Rio Grande do Norte, and was Vice-Leader of the PT's Chamber caucus. She was elected to the Senate in 2014 with 54.8% of the valid vote, is the Vice-President of the Senate's Commission of Education, Culture, and Sports, and was nominated Vice-Leader of the PT's Senate caucus.[30]

The ability of Bezerra to thrive in Rio Grande do Norte, where 33.3% of survey respondents agreed or strongly agreed with the statement that men make better politicians than do women (LAPOP n.d.), is quite remarkable given her deviation from the elite and traditional feminine. As a never-married 60-year old woman who promotes the civil rights of marginalized populations and a far-reaching education agenda, Bezerra bucks the traditional perception of femininity in the less developed northeast. She has been a "victim of hateful prejudice" (President Lula, quoted at a rally for Bezerra's ultimately unsuccessful 2008 mayoral bid), with an alarming rejection rate of 23% in the run-up to the 2008 mayoral elections (Macedo 2008). But campaigning on the issues for which she had earned great credibility, and relying on a strong party organization, Bezerra has overcome such bias, twice the most voted deputy in her state and most recently elected Senator. Running under the coveted "1313" campaign number, and receiving R$235,000 from the party organization (42.4% of the overall contributions from her extremely successful 2002 and 2010 campaigns), Bezerra benefited extensively from PT support.[31] Alternately, as we see next, to achieve election without the support of a strong party, women have used their expertise in the professional world to convince women-adverse party elites of their political potential.

Technocrats

Among all female candidates, the most common predicament in which women candidates find themselves is that of a women-friendly district and a women-adverse party (59.8% from 1998–2010). As stated by Manuela d'Ávila, popular federal deputy, former city councilwoman, and mayoral candidate for the PC do B in the developed southern region (Rio Grande do Sul), "society is evolving but the political structure still is not," with the PC do B being one of the few parties in which traditional outsiders have a shot.[32] In order to thrive in this context, where hostilities from party elite have persisted in spite of an evolution in gender norms and women's progress in society at large, women must convert their

[29] http://portal.fatimabezerra.com.br/p/perfil
[30] http://portal.fatimabezerra.com.br/p/perfil
[31] It is telling that in the 2006 elections, when the party played a lesser role in Bezerra's campaign—donating zero funds—she fell to 6th place in the state (4th in her coalition). This is in spite of raising overall nearly three times more funds than she raised in 2002, and only 36% less funds than she did in 2010.
[32] Interview on blog *Eleições* (2010): *Ascensão da Mulher na Política* (2010).

intellectual and experiential capital into political capital. By employing the knowledge and skills they are increasingly acquiring in the workplace, women technocrats demonstrate their area-specific expertise and can convince stubborn party elites of their capacity for politics.

Technocrats may also enjoy a fundraising advantage. Candidates with higher than average educational attainment (i.e., those with university education) are in general more adept at forging connections with the predominantly male political and economic elite, and thereby more likely to be successful in attaining campaign contributions (Avelar 2001, 155). Indeed, as shown in Table 6.2, women succeeding under the constraints of a women-adverse party in a women-friendly state received, on average, a significantly greater proportion of their campaign contributions from corporate donors (43.9%) than did women in the other contexts. An exceptional educational and vocational background is particularly helpful for female candidates that lack familial or party ties, with their knowledge and skills compensating for their politically unconnected status. Although they will likely lack leadership experience in their male-dominant parties or may not be partisans at all, female political aspirants in women-friendly states can use skills acquired in the professional world to demonstrate competence and viability.

While not all women running in women-friendly districts and women-adverse parties do so as technocrats, and a few technocrats have found success in women-adverse districts, the profile is more common in the context of developed states and inchoate and/or male-led parties. This is because women in such states are more likely to have developed professional skills, with a greater insertion into the paid workforce than women in less developed states. Moreover, women running in weak, male-dominant parties will have been unable to work their way up through the party ranks and thus have to convert their political capital from the professional arena. Alternatively, female candidates amidst such constraints will draw on familial political capital, which is more prevalent in but certainly not exclusive to the less developed northeast. Of the 84 women elected in women-friendly districts despite their women-adverse parties, 31 (36.9%) are the wife or daughter of a male politician. This extent of women winning with family connections is less than the concentration found among women elected in women-adverse parties and districts, but significantly higher than what we see for deputies from women-friendly parties.

The overall success rate of women running in more developed states but inchoate and/or male-led parties is only 5.9 percent, which is significantly poorer than the success rate for female candidates in women-adverse districts. Several factors help to explain that weak performance, including the overall competitiveness of many of the women-friendly districts, the fact that women's insertion into the paid workforce and general societal progress is a relatively recent phenomenon, and most importantly, the absence of party support. Even though female candidates in more developed states enjoy an ostensibly less machista electorate, absent party support, they may be either unable or unwilling to navigate the contours of such a competitive electorate climate, particularly if they have better opportunities in the private sector or bureaucracy. Once again, we see that the problem of women's representation in Brazil appears to be political rather than societal. Next, I discuss two female technocrats who have managed to convert their successes in the professional world into political capital.

TUCANA (PSDB) TECHNOCRATS YEDA CRUSIUS AND RAQUEL TEIXEIRA

The technocrat profile is particularly amenable to the centrist PSDB, with its rhetorical emphasis on "good governance" and policymaking priorities such as administrative decentralization, economic growth, and the stemming of corruption. Although the party leadership at all levels remains dominated by men, with only a single state-level PSDB organization meeting the minimalist critical mass benchmark of 25 percent women among their leadership as of 2010, women have nonetheless begun to make inroads into the party by demonstrating technical prowess. Technocrat Yeda Crusius, former PSDB federal deputy and governor of Rio Grande do Sul, exemplifies the profile. A Vanderbilt-trained economist and professor of economics, Crusius converted capital acquired in her roles as an academic and then federal Minister of Planning, Budget, and Management. She then successfully parlayed her experience in the federal government into electoral mandates as federal deputy and governor.

Professor Raquel Teixeira, also of the PSDB, similarly gained entry into the political sphere through her area of expertise (education) and educational background. Teixeira earned her Ph.D. in linguistics from Berkeley in 1986, followed by a postdoctoral stint in Paris at the prestigious École des Hautes Études en Sciences Sociales in 1988. She was the Vice-President and President of the Instituto de Ciências Humanas e Letras at the Federal University of Goiás (UFG) (1989–94), and in 1997 contested the position of Dean of the university (UFG), an elected post which had been almost exclusively occupied by men. She served in the leadership of several state and national education organizations, including CNPq (National Council for Scientific and Technological Development) and Capes (Brazilian Federal Agency for Support and Evaluation of Graduate Education). Her extensive experience eventually landed her an appointment as the Secretary of Education of Goiás under PSDB Governor Marconi Perillo.

Typical of the technocrat experience, Teixeira was not a partisan, considering her work in the state bureaucracy to be *superpartidária* (above party lines), but was soon recruited by the governor to join the PSDB and run for office. While the invitation was perhaps intended solely to help the party image and make a feeble attempt at quota compliance while gathering a few votes for the five male politicians running in her coalition list,[33] Teixeira used her expertise to gain votes and in 2002 earned the third highest vote total in her state. She was reelected in 2006, falling to 12th place after being unjustly embroiled in a corruption scandal and essentially sacrificed by co-partisans.[34] Although Teixeira did win reelection, the betrayal left a bitter taste in her mouth, leading her to lament, "my party is very machista" and "party solidarity does not exist" (in the PSDB).[35]

When prompted for advice to female aspirants lacking family connections and party support, she said you can thrive "if you can construct your own path, but you have to work harder." Although she did not have the family connections of most other women politicians in her party, she did have her academic title, which she believes afforded her respect. By demonstrating her technical capacities and authority on her area expertise in academia and the state bureaucracy, Teixeira overcame party skepticism of her electoral viability. The small push from the gubernatorial candidate was all she needed to throw her hat in the ring. Teixeira received 31% of her 2002 campaign budget from the party, and ran a *corpo-a-corpo* (person-to-person) campaign in neighborhood meetings and the homes of friends, using fundraisers and donations from individuals to finance most of her extremely successful 2002 campaign.[36] In 2006, Teixeira received less than 13% of her budget from the PSDB, drawing instead on corporate donors.

Teixeira's slogan, *Uma vida pela educação* (A life for education), reflects the centrality of her area expertise for her mandate. The tendency to be confined to a single issue domain is a potential drawback of pursing a profile emphasizing one's area expertise—Teixeira entered on a platform of education, and remained largely focused on this issue. Importantly, however, she was not limited to manifestations of the traditional feminine, with Teixeira serving not only in the Commissions on Education and Culture, but also Science and Technology and Tourism and Sports, and in the Council of Advanced Studies.

---

[33] One such man proclaimed, "How great, you'll help the *legenda* (coalition list)!" In the end, Teixeira won more votes than the male candidate making this comment (Interview with Deputy Professor Raquel Teixeira, April 2009).

[34] Teixeira was approached as part of the *mensalão* scandal, in which allies of the Lula Administration bribed individual members of Congress in exchange for their support on the legislative floor. She was offered a monthly payment of R$50,000 and lump sum of R$1 million to switch to the PL, one of the parties in the government alliance. She immediately brought the information to Perillo, who instead of thanking Teixeira for her stand against corruption—a tenet of the PSDB—acted to make himself look good (now seemingly lost as his alleged connections to Carlos Cachoeira, a racketeer recently under trial, are exposed) and left Teixeira appearing guilty of non-disclosure. In the commission that voted on whether to expel Teixeira, two co-partisans actually voted against her, in an apparent pact to save Aécio Neves, the governor of Minas Gerais, to whom Perillo was somehow indebted (Interview with Deputy Professor Raquel Teixeira, April 2009).

[35] Interview with Deputy Professor Raquel Teixeira, April 2009.

[36] Interview with Deputy Professor Raquel Teixeira, April 2009.

Of the 272 pieces of legislation Texeira proposed, she considers those with the greatest potential to affect change to be her approved bill requiring children from age 6 to 9 enroll in school, and her proposed Law of Educational Responsibility (modeled after the Law of Fiscal Responsibility) (Chamber of Deputies 2015). Teixeira withdrew from the PSDB in June 2011 to assume the position of Executive Director of the Jaime Câmara Foundation, where she worked through local initiatives to improve primary education in Brazil (Almeida 2011). She was later reappointed to Secretary of Education, Culture, and Sports of Goiás under reelected PSDB Governor Marconi Perillo (Marcelo 2014).

STILL SUPERMADRES?

For District Deputy Eliana Pedrosa in the highly-developed Federal District, family ties initiated her political involvement. While at the helm of the small conservative Liberal Party (PL), Pedrosa's brother suggested she help the party fill the 30 percent candidate quota, expecting her to garner 800 votes or so. Building on the name of her brother and husband at the time, Pedrosa won more than 11,000 votes in 2002; she exercised leadership within the district assembly and was reelected in 2006 with the PFL, subsequently served in the Federal District bureaucracy as Secretary of Social Development and Cash Transfers, and returned to the district assembly in 2010, winning more votes than any woman in the history of that institution's elections.[37] What helped her confront the "largest fortress of machismo" found in party politics, which she called a *clube de bolinha* (essentially, good ole' boys' club), was at least initially her family name.[38] Indeed as mentioned above, family connections remain a viable means for thriving in the absence of party support even in a more developed state, with 31 of the 84 women elected (and reelected) in women-friendly districts but women-adverse parties being wives or daughters of a male politician.

Not all women in a context ripe for converting professional skills into political capital have pursued the technocratic path. Some women in women-adverse parties, such as Deputy Lauriete (PSC) of the southeastern state of Espírito Santo, remain in the *supermadre* mold despite having independent capital and hailing from a women-friendly district. Lauriete is the wife of a male politician but is also a famous evangelical gospel singer with significant convertible capital of her own, yet she campaigned in a way very consistent with the *supermadre* profile outlined above, using her 25 seconds of HGPE to stand alongside her husband while emphasizing "defense of life, family values, women, children, and adolescents."

---

[37] http://www.elianapedrosa.com.br/main/conheca-a-deputada/
[38] Interview with District Deputy Eliana Pedrosa (PFL-DF).

Although women such as Crusius and Teixeira have forged a new pathway for female aspirants lacking party support, demonstrating that women can nonetheless convert their professional experiences into political capital, the *supermadre* profile persists for women in both women-adverse and -friendly states. As the feminist movement marches on and the electorate's perceptions of female politicians continue to improve, women will be more equipped to translate their professional gains into political presence. Parties that seek to capitalize on those changes (and follow the electoral law) would be wise to invest in developing viable female candidacies and expanding the paths to power available to women.

The ideal context, after all, is one in which a woman contender can campaign without the threat of bias from either the electorate or party leadership. Under those conditions, women recognize and seize opportunities from within parties and society at large to develop their political capacities. The path to power pursued by Deputy Manuela d'Ávila represents the fruition of such forthcoming support.

Free to Succeed: Manuela d'Ávila

D'Ávila is a journalist by training, who, like many of the women politicians who preceded her, cut her political teeth in the student movement. Yet d'Ávila matured politically in a Brazil very different from that lived by women like Fátima Bezerra, Gleisi Hoffmann, and President Dilma Rousseff herself, who risked imprisonment, torture, and exile in their struggles against the military dictatorship of the 1970s. Coming of age in democratized and developed Rio Grande do Sul in the 1990s, d'Ávila was able to confront the remaining injustices. The PC do B and the developed state of Rio Grande do Sul had both long been open to the idea of women in politics, and without having to convince party leaders or her constituents of a woman's capacity for politics, d'Ávila quickly signaled her strength.

At 18 years of age, d'Ávila joined the Union of Socialist Youth (UJS), one of the nation's more influential student unions, and an affiliate of the PC do B. She officially became a member of the PC do B two years later, and soon acquired the requisite skillset of a political leader, immersing herself in politics. D'Ávila learned how to win elections, serving as a Councilor to the Federal University of Rio Grande do Sul, National Director and later State President of the UJS, and Vice-President of the National Union of Students (UNE). In 2004, at age 23, she was elected to the municipal council of Porto Alegre, winning the 8th most votes in the (capital) municipal—in a contest of 439 candidates for 36 seats—and becoming its youngest city councilor to date.

When asked of her decision to run, d'Ávila said, "It was not my candidacy, I did not want to be a candidate—it was the party that selected me." D'Ávila reported that it was "the type of party" that the PC do B is which enabled her to thrive. Its history of strong women's involvement nationally and in her state rendered tangible the possibility of women in power. According to d'Ávila, with greater internal democracy and a more just distribution of party resources, the PC do B enabled rather than impeded her political aspirations. Accordingly, her advice to unsuccessful female candidates was to commit to democratizing their party internally, which she considered the "decisive" factor in women's underrepresentation.[39]

In 2006, she ran a successful campaign for Federal Deputy. As the "priority candidate" of the PC do B, she had the full backing of the party, including ample time on the HGPE, assistance waging a free but intense internet campaign, and funding, with 43% of her campaign contributions coming from the party. Spending R$1.32 per vote won (more efficient than 66% of the candidates), d'Ávila and the PC do B ran an ideas-based, militant-driven campaign. Her tenure as Municipal Councilor and National Director of UNE gave her a strong base, and party support sustained the campaign logistics.[40] D'Ávila was the most voted of all 279 candidates in her statewide district, at 271,939 votes (almost 5% of candidate votes) (Tribunal Superior Eleitoral 1994–2016).

In an unsuccessful campaign for mayor of her state's capital and its most populous city, Porto Alegre, in 2008, d'Ávila competed against two other leftist women, Maria do Rosario (PT) and Luciana Genro (PSOL, former *petista*), ultimately knocking each other out of the race and enabling the reelection of the PMDB incumbent, José Fogaça. Undeterred, d'Ávila gained reelection with ease in 2010. She was once again the state's most voted, as well as the most voted female deputy in Brazil, doubling her prior vote total and breaking state records for a total of 482,590 votes (8.5% of candidate votes among 270 candidates). D'Ávila again ran for mayor in 2012 and although she commanded the lead in polls leading up to election, she ultimately lost to the incumbent mayor.[41] In 2014, d'Ávila decided to contest elections to the state assembly so she could be closer to home. She won a striking 4% of the valid vote in a contest with 670 candidates, earning more than twice the number of votes of her nearest competitor (Tribunal Superior EleitoralTSE 1994–2016).

Emerging from partisan and electoral contexts that cultivated, rather than debilitated, her political acumen, d'Ávila was never confined to a single or secondary issue and has thrived in a range of prestigious posts. She served as the President of the Commission of Human Rights, the Vice-President of the Commission on Labor, Administration, and Public Service, and as Vice-President of the Commission on Foreign Relations and National Defense. Less

---

[39] Interview with Deputy Manuela d'Ávila, March 2009.
[40] Interview with Deputy Manuela d'Ávila, March 2009.
[41] Fogaça renounced his post to run for governor, a race he lost. His vice-mayor José Fortunati (PDT) assumed the mayoral post in 2010, and defeated d'Ávila in the first round of the 2012 mayoral elections.

constrained by politicized gender roles, d'Ávila has also ascended among her peers, serving as Vice-Leader for the governing coalition in Congress. She has been active on the freedom of information campaign, and rights for youth, the LGBTQ population, and other minorities. D'Ávila was honored with Congresso em Foco awards in 2009 and 2011, indicated as one of the 100 most influential members of Congress by DIAP (100 Cabeças do Congresso), and named by *The Independent* as one of the principal future world leaders. In sum, d'Ávila and the PC do B represent the great possibilities of the combination of encouraged political ambition, party support, and a receptive electorate.

CONCLUSIONS

The recent wave of successful female presidential candidates throughout Latin America suggests that machista skepticism of female political leaders is diminishing. Argentina, Chile, Costa Rica, and Brazil have all elected women presidents in recent years. In Brazil, survey data suggest the electorate to be extremely receptive to women in politics, with three-quarters agreeing that true democracy only exists with the presence of more women in politics and other decision-making spheres (Brazilian Institute of Public Opinion and Statistics 2013). Yet despite such societal progress, hostilities among party elite persist. According to a report by the Feminist Center for Studies and Advisory Services (CFEMEA), Brazilian parliamentarians "seem disposed to perpetuate women's parliamentary underrepresentation," with the majority of deputies and senators surveyed disagreeing with various proposals designed to enhance women's legislative presence (2009, 39).

In sharp contrast, 8 out of 10 Brazilians surveyed in a nationally representative poll agreed that laws should change to guarantee gender *parity* in legislatures (Brazilian Institute of Public Opinion and Statistics 2013). Notably, respondents in the northeast in that survey reported the highest levels of support for the legal initiatives proposed to mandate parity, which calls into question any presumptions by party elite that voters throughout Brazil's lesser developed areas remain unwilling to support female politicians. When bulwarked by party support, women have achieved their greatest success rates in Brazil's less developed states. Parties wishing to capitalize on women's potential and conform to the electoral law must actively work to reconcile the yawning gap between societal preferences for more women in politics and the woefully scarce proportion of women among candidates and elected leaders.

Historically, to develop training opportunities for female political aspirants within parties, women have had to first acquire space in party decision-making organs. Yet by mandating that parties devote funds to the promotion of women's participation, the 2009 mini-reform has now incentivized all parties to implement such programs. Given that elite culture and party organizations are particularly resistant to change, with women-adverse parties thus unlikely to open up without some kind of exogenous stimulus, the mini-reform represents a promising step toward the meaningful inclusion of women in Brazilian politics. Only by incentivizing parties to cultivate and support the political ambitions of women can future reforms reconcile the discrepancies between elector and elected in their support of women in politics, and thereby engender a truly representative democracy. In the interim, female political aspirants in Brazil and elsewhere—even in contexts ostensibly adverse to women—should be emboldened by the trailblazing efforts of Brazil's *lutadoras* and technocrats.

7

Intersections between Race and Gender in Brazil's 2014 Chamber of Deputies Elections

> Sexism and racism are foundational ideologies of violence and are present in the daily lives of all Brazilians: in family, professional, and academic relationships and institutions; they produce and maintain perverse structural inequalities, whether symbolic or explicit, within Brazilian society.
>
> (Eleonora Menicucci, quoted in Marcondes et al. 2013, 9)

For the first time in the history of Brazilian elections, the 2014 electoral returns included candidates' self-declared racial identity. The data afford an empirical glimpse into the numerous ways in which power is raced and gendered in Brazilian politics. The disaggregation of candidacies by race thus allows me to address a major blind spot in the study thus far; as Beckwith and others have compellingly demonstrated, "the research on gendered political structures primarily concerns women in the aggregate and hence may underestimate or seriously misrepresent structural impacts on ethnic and/or racial minority women" (Beckwith 2015, 445; Bejarano 2013; Smooth 2006). Intersectional theorists have chronicled how race intersects with gender (and other dimensions of identity) to shape the differential experiences of oppression and privilege of white and nonwhite women (Collins 2000; Crenshaw 1995). Critically, the intersectional lens also enhances our understanding of the ways in which systems of power are mutually reinforcing, with an aim toward realizing social justice through broad coalition across difference (Cole 2008, 2015).

This chapter examines the construction of race in Brazil, finding persistent racial discrepancies in access to opportunity and power. After discussing the struggle to attain racially disaggregated data that would make such inequities visible, I present an array of indicators illustrating the heightened obstacles faced by Afro-Brazilian female political aspirants. The chapter concludes with an analysis of the role of race and gender in the 2014 legislative elections and a discussion of the implications of gendered institutions for Afro-Brazilian women.

THE CONSTRUCTION OF RACE IN BRAZIL

As in other nations, the social construct of race was created and imbued with privilege and oppression to sustain a white racial hierarchy in Brazil (Marx 1998). Yet with its history of miscegenation and consequent racial diversity that appeared to defy the binary reified in places like the United States and South Africa, a myth of racial democracy emerged (da Costa 2014; Marx 1998). Proponents of the understanding of Brazil as a racial democracy sought to differentiate the situation from more stark racial orders of institutionalized racism in the United States. Undeterred by the reality of more than five million enslaved Africans being trafficked to Brazil, the racial democracy myth perpetuated the claim that the Brazilian variant of slavery was less brutal and afforded its captives more agency relative to the reality of other colonial regimes (Eltis and Richardson 2010; Freyre 1933; Hébrard 2013).

To this day, the legacies of miscegenation and the myth of racial democracy pervade domestic and international perceptions of Brazil, challenging a cohesive Black identity and undermining collective action and state efforts to level the playing field. As explained by Sueli Carneiro, "Despite all the black movement's attempts to break the conspiracy of silence surrounding racism and racial discrimination, race persists as one of Brazil's greatest taboos" (1999, 221). Alexandre da Costa characterizes "racial democracy and mixture as enduring post-racial ideologies that continue to thwart anti-racist efforts and socio-economic transformation for Afro-descendants despite the increasing legitimacy of multicultural discourses and ethno-racial policies" (2014, 2). This is in spite of the fact that by any available measure of socioeconomic opportunities and outcomes, Brazilians of African descent fare markedly worse than their white counterparts (Alves 2014; da Costa 2014; Minority Rights 2015; Paixão et al. 2010; Silva and Goes 2013; see Table 7.1 below).

Such post-racial ideologies have also undermined empirical documentation and academic exploration of racial inequities. "The myth of 'racial democracy,' which reigned at least until the mid-1970s, permeated the social sciences, and only recently has racial discrimination been acknowledged and debated (Hasenbalg 1990)" (Goldani 1999, 180). Although the myth, emboldened by Gilberto Freyre's work and entrenched in the Vargas era nationalism, was increasingly contested by a growing body of scholars, "any attempt to continue researching Brazilian race relations came to an abrupt end" when the military overthrew Brazil's democratic regime in 1964 (Reiter and Mitchell 2010, 2). Therefore the oppression and disadvantage confronted by Brazil's Afro-descendant population has not always been visible in the official record, with historical resistance to the differentiation of socioeconomic indicators by race (Caldwell 2007; Carneiro 1999; Reiter and Mitchell 2010; Telles 2014). The release of data disaggregated by both race and sex has proven even more elusive, with the experiences of Afro-descendant women rendered "profoundly invisible and neglected, whether by public policy, academic work, or research institutions, which generally are not accustomed to evaluating the phenomenon of race/color and gender, but instead just one of those characteristics—to be Afro-descendant or to be a woman" (Romio 2013, 155).

While data on racial socioeconomic stratification have not been widely available until relatively recently, the Brazilian census has asked questions about respondents' "color" since its first iteration in 1872. From 1900–1930 and again in 1970, racial data (or census data all together in 1910 and 1930) were not collected. Since 1991 (with the collapse of the military regime in 1985), the census has asked respondents to indicate their "color or race" from five options: white, brown, black, yellow (people of Asian descent), or indigenous (Bailey and Telles n.d.; Brazilian Institute of Geography and Statistics 2008).[1] Classification based on color and race varies dramatically, however, with 190 different terms offered in response to an open-ended question on the National Household Survey (PNAD) in 1976, including such categories as coffee with milk and toasted (Hordge-Freeman 2015; Piza and Rosemberg 1999).

Distinguishing color—which tends to connote phenotype (physical appearance)—from race, the activists and researchers often collapse categories of *preto* (black) and *pardo* (brown) into a single racial identity referred to as *negro*, Afro-descendant, or Afro-Brazilian (Black Women of Brazil 2013; da Costa 2014; Hordge-Freeman 2015; Minority Rights 2015; Telles 2004, 2014, n.d.). In 2010, for the first time since the Brazilian census began (1872), the Afro-descendant population reached a majority (50.7%), outnumbering the white population (Black Women of Brazil 2013; Brazilian Institute of Geography and Statistics 2015; Phillips 2011). That majority has increased, with 2014 PNAD data indicating that 53.6% of the population is Afro-Brazilian (Brazilian Institute of Geography and Statistics 2015). Up from 44.7% in 2000, many credit the increase as "due mostly to the increased reclaiming of a black or brown racial identity long avoided by many Brazilians" (da Costa 2014, 3; Phillips 2011).

In the political realm, assessments of racial diversity (or the lack thereof) have focused on subsamples of elected officials or states and/or depended upon external or "hetero-classification" (Bueno and Dunning 2013; Johnson 1998, 2006, 2015; Mitchell 2009, 2010; Santos 2010; SEPPIR 2010). That approach was necessitated by the lack of candidate-level data on candidates' self-declared racial identity. Yet with the approval of TSE Resolution 23.405 in 2014, Luiza Bairros, former minister of the Special Office for the Promotion of Racial Equality (SEPPIR), won a long battle to have electoral candidates report their racial identity in candidate registries with electoral officials (Portal Brasil 2014). Edson Cardoso of SEPPIR explained, "with the inclusion of the item color/race

---

[1] Further, there exists inconsistency between respondents' and interviewers' racial classification, with interviewers at times reportedly imposing respondents' classification rather than allowing for self-classification, and a single family member sometimes providing data on behalf of the entire family (Telles n.d.).

in the personal data of candidates, essential for democracy and overcoming racial inequalities, the construction of a database becomes possible, which offers a dimension of not only elected candidates, but of all of those involved in the electoral dispute" (quoted in Portal Brasil 2014, 1). In the wake of Resolution 23.405/2014, candidate-level analyses have begun to emerge (Institute of Socioeconomic Studies 2014); the foregoing analysis is only possible by virtue of the empirical glimpse into the effect of candidates' racial identity on their electoral prospects afforded by these candidate-level data on color/race.

Such increasing data availability has at once enhanced our understanding of racially stratified opportunities and outcomes while invigorating mobilization efforts by Black power movements for the development of race-based affirmative action measures in Brazil (Reiter and Mitchell 2010). Comparatively, Brazil thus stands out among Latin American countries, where race-based initiatives have largely operated through (typically underfunded) government agencies rather than affirmative action policies (Hernández 2013).[2] With an explicit commitment to affirmative action measures in the International Convention on the Elimination of All Forms of Racial Discrimination, to which Brazil is a state party, alongside substantial mobilization by Afro-Brazilian social movements in the 2001 United Nations World Conference against Racism in Durban, Brazil implemented its first affirmative action policies in 2001 (Hernández 2013; Johnson and Heringer 2015; Paschel 2016). Controversy continues over affirmative action programs for university admission, with legal challenges and public resistance fueled by the enduring myth of racial democracy (Hernández 2013; Htun 2004, 2015; Roza 2009). In spite of persistent challenges to affirmative action, public opinion data suggest that most Brazilians acknowledge that racism remains a problem in Brazil (while simultaneously denying their own racist attitudes), with 66.2% of respondents in the 2010 AmericasBarometer poll agreeing (including 45.0% who strongly agree) that it is fair for universities to reserve seats for Afro-descendants (Hernández 2013; LAPOP n.d.; Smith 2010).

RACIAL INEQUITIES IN BRAZIL

Yet despite such government initiatives, the lived realities of Afro-Brazilians remain disproportionately oppressive. As displayed in Table 7.1, race and poverty are tightly correlated in Brazil. Afro-Brazilians are substantially more likely than whites to be poor, illiterate, lacking a college education, and employed in the informal economy (Brazilian Institute of Geography and Statistics 2013, 2015; Institute for Applied Economic Research 2014). Such inequities in opportunities and outcomes are exacerbated for Afro-Brazilian

---

[2] Colombia is an exception, with quota provisions for Afro-Colombians in several universities as well as the federal legislature (Hernández 2013, 148–149).

TABLE 7.1 *Racialized Opportunities in Brazil (2013–2014)*

	White	Afro-Brazilian
Income		
% in top 10%	16.0	4.9
% in bottom 10%	5.5	13.7
% <= min wage	18.6	37.3
Median monthly income (Reais)	R$ 1,517.70	R$ 876.40
Education		
% illiterate	5.2	11.5
Median years of study	8.8	7.2
% 18–24 with (some) college education	23.4	10.7
Employment		
% 16+ in informal economy	35.3	48.4

Sources: Brazilian Institute of Geography and Statistics (2013, 2014), Institute for Applied Economic Research (2013)

women, whose median monthly income is just 39.5% of that of white men (and 68.8% of that of Afro-Brazilian men) (Institute for Applied Economic Research 2014). Education has not closed that gap; college-educated Afro-Brazilian women earn just 40.6% of what college-educated white men make (Institute for Applied Economic Research 2014). Even Afro-Brazilian women working in public administration face a raced-gender wage gap; white men in public administration have a median monthly income (R$ 3,773) that is nearly double that of Afro-descendant women in the field (R$ 2,048) (Institute for Applied Economic Research 2014).

Public opinion data from the 2012 AmericasBarometer suggest that the majority of Brazilians acknowledge the structural causes of such persistent poverty, with 72.1% responding that the cause of Afro-descendants' impoverishment is the unjust way they are treated (LAPOP n.d.). Yet in spite of the incontrovertible racial stratification of opportunities and outcomes in Brazil, "antiblack racism and white supremacy remain so embedded in the social fiber of the region through stereotypes, language, violence, and a disregard for the centrality of race to black socioeconomic marginalization that the subordinated status of Afro-descendants is still viewed as logical and neutral" (da Costa 2014, 1).

The naturalized subordination of Afro-Brazilians manifests in pervasive everyday violence. In his article on racial terror by police-linked death squads in São Paulo, "Neither Humans nor Rights: Some Notes on the Double

Negation of Black Life in Brazil," Alves explains how "the lack of access to health care, mass incarceration, residential segregation, and police killings [constitute] ... some of the mundane practices that render Black life 'unlivable life' (Butler 2006)" (Alves 2014, 12). With a staggering 53,646 homicides in 2013, someone was killed every ten minutes; 68% of the victims were Afro-descendant and the majority were youth. Those figures amount to two young Afro-Brazilians being killed every hour (or two airplanes full of young adults every single week) (Borges 2015). The risk of death for Afro-descendant youth is substantially greater than the risk for white youth in all but Paraná, ranging from 1.4 times higher (Santa Catarina) to a startling 11.6–13.4 higher in two northeastern states, Pernambuco and Paraíba (*Índice de Vulnerabilidade Juvenil Violência e Desigualdade Racial* 2015).

Romio's descriptive analyses of 2009 PNAD data reveal that gender, race, and class clearly intersect to affect patterns of violence. Afro-descendant women report levels of perceived security lower than levels for Afro-descendant men or white women, higher levels of being the victim of physical aggression than white women at all income groups except the very highest (five times the minimum wage), higher rates of victimization by someone they knew (whereas white women were more likely than Afro-descendant women to be attacked by someone they did not know), and were less likely than white women to report the attack to the police (2013). Moreover, a report released in 2015 demonstrates that murder rates of Afro-Brazilian women rose 54.2% from 2003–2013 while rates for white women fell by 9.8% (Tavener 2015; Waiselfisz 2015). Bulwarked by such data, Romio issued a call for more disaggregated data to permit longitudinal analyses, and making the data accessible to civil society to facilitate inclusive approaches to developing public policies to address the raced-gendered injustices faced by Afro-descendant women (2013).

RACED-GENDERED POWER IN INFORMAL AND FORMAL POLITICS

In the face of such raced-gendered inequities, Afro-Brazilian women have mobilized within and beyond the predominantly white, male sphere of electoral politics. Women have long been considered leaders in the Black community, exercising leadership roles within Brazil's maroon communities and their descendants and in the Candomblé faith (Capone 2010; Goes 2015; Landes 1947; Minority Rights 2015; Parés 2013; Pinho 2010). In 1930, the *Frente Negra Brasileira*, or Black Brazilian Front, was founded with an explicit emphasis on intersections between racial and gender equality (but was banned in 1936 under Vargas' authoritarian *Estado Novo* regime), and in 1950, the *I Conselho Nacional da Mulher Negra*, or first National Council for Black Women, was established to advocate on behalf of Afro-descendant women (Minority Rights 2015; Reiter and Mitchell 2010).

As discussed below, Afro-descendant women were critical contributors in campaigns for both racial and gender justice. Yet in spite of their double militancy in the black movement and the women's movement, "their concerns about race largely went unheeded by the feminist movement, (and) their concerns about gender were often marginalized by the black movement" (Caldwell 2007, 155). Illustrating the insights elaborated by intersectional theorists such as Patricia Hill Collins (2000) and Kimberlé Crenshaw (1995), Sueli Carneiro, one of Brazil's leading critical race scholars and intersectional feminist voices, explains:

The classical feminist discourse on women's oppression fails to account for the qualitative differences in oppression suffered by black women, and the effects those multiple oppressions had and still have on black women's identity. Because the women's movement has failed to comprehend this, its victories tend to benefit white women. In a similar way, the minor gains made by Brazil's black movement have primarily benefited black men, who are still barely conscious of sexual discrimination (Carneiro 1999, 218).

Women activists played a pivotal role in the *Movimento Negro Unificado* (Unified Black Movement), the "most important contemporary national black movement in Brazil" (Paschel 2011, 34). Founded in 1978, the MNU aimed to consolidate black movement organizations throughout the country, which had operated underground during the dictatorship and/or recently (re)emerged with the gradual political *abertura* (opening, or political liberalization) (Covin 2006; Paschel 2011, 2016). The MNU functioned through "community nuclei created throughout popular neighborhoods," representing "the most serious effort to mobilize the masses of black Brazilians, many of whom did not identify with racialized struggle" (Paschel 2011, 35). Their consciousness-raising efforts were emboldened by emerging data that offered a counternarrative or "counterideology" of social exclusion to the dominant discourse of miscegenation that had long romanticized Brazilian race relations (Reiter and Mitchell 2010; Telles 2004, 2014, n.d.).

As in the US civil rights movement and many 'old left' political organizations (Barnett 1993; Crawford, Rouse, and Woods 1993; Kittilson 2006), women's broad participation in the rank-and-file of MNU stood in contrast to the organizational ranks, where patriarchal societal norms were replicated (Caldwell 2007; Carneiro 1999). Caldwell (2007) speaks to the male-dominant leadership structures of the MNU and other organizations of the black movement, and cites several interviews with women MNU activists relating experiences of machismo and sexism within the black movement.[3] She further examines gendered differences in responses to the forced

---

[3] Also corroborated in my interview with an advisor of the Women's Secretariat in the Chamber of Deputies and militant of the black movement, May 2015.

sterilization of Afro-Brazilian women as an illustration of the challenges Black women encountered in the movement (Caldwell 2007).

Similarly, while Afro-Brazilian women have long been active in the women's movement, racial injustices were often neglected or even tolerated by white feminists. Caldwell recalls insights from Black feminist Lélia Gonzalez who "lamented white feminists' failure to address the racism found in the women's movement" and denial of "the salience of race and its impact in black women's lives" (Caldwell 2007, 152). In 1975, the *Manifesto das Mulheres Negras* (Manifesto of Black Women) issued during the *Congresso das Mulheres Brasileiras* (Congress of Brazilian Women) formally brought racial inequities to the attention of the women's movement. "By calling attention to the specificities of black women's life experiences, representations and social identities, the manifesto underscored how practices of racial domination have shaped gender relations in Brazil" (Caldwell 2007, 151–152).

Racial divisions in the women's movement have proven difficult to uproot, however, with "markedly different social experiences and social locations" in post-abolition Brazil yielding racially disparate experiences of privileges and oppression and at times conflicting policy goals (Caldwell 2007, 153). In general, the demands of the women's movement, comprised in large part by middle- and upper-class women, were perceived as more palatable to mainstream society than the goals of the black movement, which sought more transformational change (Carneiro 1999). As "an advocate for a black population still imprisoned by the myth of racial democracy and the ideology of whitening," the black movement has been thwarted by "the taboo of race," with entrenched resistance to addressing racial injustices even in ostensibly progressive spaces such as the women's movement (Carneiro 1999, 221). Moreover, recent progress made on the front of gender equality has in many ways been limited to white women and contingent upon "the continued socioeconomic subordination of black women" whose cheap domestic service has enabled white women to enter the formal workforce (Caldwell 2007, 153; Gonzalez 1982).[4]

Given those limitations, Afro-Brazilian women cultivated autonomous movements of Black women in the early to mid-1980s, with the First National Meeting/Encounter of Black Women held in 1988 (Caldwell 2007; Carneiro 1999, 224). Several autonomous Black women's organizations were launched throughout the 1980s and 1990s, and continue to work to highlight the differential impact of issues including reproductive and sexual health, racial justice, and violence on Afro-Brazilian women (Caldwell 2007). Participants in the 1997 National Meeting of Black Women voted against centralizing the

---

[4] In 2001, 23.4% of formally employed Afro-descendant women (and 14.0% of white women) worked in domestic labor. As of 2014, more than 1 in 6 (17.7%) Afro-descendant women in the formal workforce remained employed in domestic labor, compared to 1 in 10 (10.1%) white women (Institute for Applied Economic Research 2014).

black women's movement, which has at once avoided bureaucratization while challenging national coordination and policymaking influence (Caldwell 2007). As is true with other social movements, Brazil's black women's movement has confronted internal divisions driven by socioeconomic, political, religious, and regional differences, among others. Yet while Black women are not homogeneous, the social construction of their identity has served as an impetus for group consciousness and collective organizing; "Similarities in black women's social identities and life experiences across classes and regions further underscore the existence of *mulheres negras* as a social group in Brazil" (Caldwell 2007, 174).

Such collectivity was apparent in the recent November 2015 March of Black Women, which was planned in three-year-long participatory processes by local groups around the country and culminated in a march on the capital of several thousand (estimates range from 4,000 to 30,000) Afro-Brazilian women and allies (Agência PT 2015; Geledés 2015b; Gonçalves 2015). As stated by activist Juliana Gonçalves,

We are youths, *quilombolas*,[5] students given access to the public university system by quotas, feminists, Christians, lesbians, party militants, trans women, anarchists, bisexuals, elderly women, representatives of traditional people of African origin, domestic workers, landless, favela residents, immigrants and refugees, rural inhabitants, mothers, autonomous ... Through its mobilization the march created opportunity for real dialogue among black women, with the mutual strengthening of our goals. That is, it permits a construction from what unites us rather than what separates us. (Gonçalves 2015, 1)

The *Carta das Mulheres Negras 2015* (Letter of Black Women 2015) demands "the end of the racism and violence that manifests in the genocide of black youth," calling for "the right to life, the right to humanity, the right to have rights, ... for justice, equity, solidarity, and well-being" (Geledés 2015a). The *Carta* spoke to the critical role of Black women's political participation in mitigating raced-gendered inequities, with March coordinator Clátia Regina Vieira affirming, "We will not change the lives of black women, the lives of black people, if we do not occupy seats in the legislature" (Geledés 2015b).

While most studies of Brazil's political and electoral institutions either do not engage or explicitly diminish the role of race in Brazilian politics, formal political power remains fundamentally racialized (Johnson 1998, 2006; Johnson and Heringer 2015; Mitchell 2009, 2010; Paixão and Carvano 2008; Reiter and Mitchell 2010). Ollie Johnson opens his 1998 article on Afro-Brazilian representation in the National Congress with an illustrative epigraph from then Senator Benedita da Silva, "There is a stereotype of who can be intelligent and competent, who can have power. In Brazil it is rich, white

---

[5] "*Quilombolas* are descendants of enslaved Africans that maintain cultural, subsistence, and religious traditions throughout the centuries," residents of *quilombos* or (former) maroon communities, many of which are recognized by federal and state governments (Fundação Cultural Palmares 2016).

men who represent the face of power" (Quoted in Johnson 1998, 97). Indeed, although white men are less than a quarter of Brazil's general population, they won 71.7% of the 540 congressional seats up for grabs in the 2014 elections (Brazilian Institute of Geography and Statistics 2015; Tribunal Superior Eleitoral 1994–2016).

The mobilization by black movements (including autonomous Afro-Brazilian women's movements) described above "contributed directly to the rise of the current group of black politicians" (Johnson 1998, 102). From 1987–1999, Johnson estimates that Black members held just 2.7% of seats in the Chamber of Deputies.[6] In spite of their numerically limited presence, Brazil's few Black parliamentarians left a mark, putting issues of racism and racial inequality on the congressional agenda (Johnson 1998). Johnson draws on his years of research on racial representation in the National Congress (using largely hetero-classification) and the newly available data on candidates' self-declared racial identity in the 2014 elections to examine trends over time, finding that while the percentage of Afro-Brazilian federal deputies has increased from 8% in 1998 to 20% in 2014, the underrepresentation of Afro-Brazilians persists. And as demonstrated in Table 7.2, the progress in Black representation in the Chamber of Deputies has been largely male; from 1998–2014, just 11.7% of Afro-Brazilian federal deputies were women, thus corroborating the general pattern of gendered representation that exists independent of race.[7] Interestingly, however, the 2002–2010 period saw a greater share of Afro-descendants among female deputies (24%) than among deputies overall (15%). Yet such numbers fall far short of the demographic reality in Brazil's Afro-descendant majority population and female majority electorate.

Such disproportionate whiteness of Brazil's formal power structures persists alongside public opinion data suggesting that Brazilians are not opposed to the hypothetical of Afro-descendants in power. In the 2012 AmericasBarometer survey, 93.0% of respondents disagreed (including 52.2% who strongly disagreed) with the statement that "people with dark skin are not good political leaders." Interestingly, a similar statement about women evoked significantly less opposition, with 83.4% disagreeing (including 36.6% who strongly disagreed) (LAPOP n.d.).[8] Experimental studies have also found "no discernible effects of candidate race on evaluations of candidates" (Dunning

---

[6] Interestingly, as is the case for women (see Chapter 5), during that time period, the percentage of Black senators was proportionately higher than the percentage of Black deputies (Johnson 1998).

[7] That figure is actually better than overall numbers; from 1998–2014, just 8.3% of elected deputies were women.

[8] There is also likely a social desirability bias at play in such surveys, with respondents hesitant to report answers that would be considered racist. Their greater likelihood of agreeing with such statements against women leaders is suggestive of a norm against explicitly hostile racism (that exists alongside pervasive implicit and "cordial racism") that is relatively stronger than norms against explicit sexism. Yet in spite of such norms, as this chapter makes clear and as most

TABLE 7.2 *Racial Representation in the Chamber of Deputies (1998–2014)*

	1998	2002	2006	2010	2014
Afro-descendant deputies (N total)	41	53	70	108	103
% Afro-descendant among deputies	8.0%	10.3%	13.6%	21.1%	20.1%
Afro-descendant deputies (N female)	2	7	10	15	10
% women among Afro-descendant deputies	4.9%	13.2%	14.3%	13.9%	9.7%
Female deputies (N total)	29	42	45	45	51
% Afro-descendant among female deputies	6.9%	16.7%	22.2%	33.3%	19.6%

Sources: Johnson (2015); Tribunal Superior Eleitoral (1994–2016)
Note: Count of Afro-descendant deputies 1998–2010 includes substitutes (Johnson 2015)

2010, 2), with resource disparities carrying more explanatory weight (Bueno and Dunning 2013).

Next, I deploy the 2014 data to describe and explain the influence of race and gender on the electoral prospects of Afro-Brazilian women. Table 7.3 depicts the results of three series of difference in means tests; the second column includes asterisks reporting the significance of differences between white women and Afro-descendant women, the third column compares Afro-descendant women to Afro-descendant men, and the final column compares Afro-descendant men to white men. I tested those differences among all candidates, and elected deputies only. Nearly all of the raced-gendered differences among candidates overall—which have heretofore been obscured by the lack of candidate-level data on race—are statistically significant, with Afro-descendant women faring worse off electorally on every dimension. The average vote share for white women (0.34%), Afro-descendant men (0.52%), and white men (0.75%), respectively, was 62, 148, and 257 percent greater than that of Afro-descendant female candidates (0.21%). One of the more pronounced differences revealed in Table 7.3 is that of campaign finance; Afro-descendant women candidates raised on average less than 10% of what white male candidates raised (and one-third of what white women raised and one-quarter of what Afro-descendant men raised). That finding lends support to Bueno and Dunning's (2013) emphasis on resource disparities in explaining Brazil's racial representational gap.

Nearly all of the raced-gendered disparities depicted in Table 7.3 lose statistical significance when looking just at elected deputies, with the notable exception of ideology. Significantly more Afro-descendant women deputies

Brazilians acknowledge, Afro-descendants experience rampant discrimination and everyday racism.

TABLE 7.3 *The Role of Race and Gender in Contesting and Winning Federal Deputy Elections, Difference in Means Tests (2014)*

	Women		Men	
	White	Afro-descendant	Afro-descendant	White
ALL CANDIDATES				
Vote Share (%)	0.34%	0.21% *	0.52% *	0.75% *
Elected (%)	4.17%	1.35% *	5.86% *	14.44%
College (%)	60.96%	51.08% *	53.84%	71.10% *
Feeder Occupation (%)	46.95%	41.64% *	54.85% *	64.87% *
Incumbent (%)	2.44%	1.22% *	5.19% *	10.95% *
Married (%)	41.69%	35.44% *	60.83% *	64.89% *
Campaign Funds	R$ 122,737	R$ 37,836 *	R$ 152,741 *	R$ 396,177 *
Left (%)	31.60%	37.87% *	32.75% *	32.68%
Ideology	0.181	−0.160 *	−0.121	0.174 *
N	981	742	1588	2555
ELECTED				
Vote Share (%)	3.63%	2.69%	3.34%	2.91%
College (%)	90.24%	90.00%	81.72%	88.35% *
Feeder Occupation (%)	85.00%	80.00%	83.13%	84.55%
Incumbent (%)	36.59%	60.00%	56.99%	55.28%
Married (%)	53.66%	50.00%	77.42% *	74.25%
Campaign Funds	R$ 1,431,538	R$ 717,717	R$ 1,035,953	R$ 1,554,921 *
Left (%)	34.15%	80.00% *	40.86% *	25.75% *
Ideology	0.348	−0.867 *	0.173*	0.542 *
N	41	10	93	369

Source: Author elaboration with Tribunal Superior Eleitoral (1994–2016) data
Note: Asterisk indicates one-tailed difference in means tests (between white and Afro-descendant women, Afro-descendant women and men, and Afro-descendant and white men) are statistically significant at the $p<0.05$ level.

(80%) hail from a leftist party than do white women (34%), Afro-descendant male (41%), or white male deputies (26%). That bivariate finding offers suggestive evidence that some of the party-level characteristics driving the gendered electoral inequities discussed throughout this book may also bear explanatory weight for understanding the electoral prospects of Afro-descendant women. Following the approach charted in prior chapters, I estimate a hierarchical linear model to evaluate the effect of candidate sex—

now interacted with a dichotomous measure of race—on vote share while controlling for traditional indicators of candidate quality[9] and the gendered hypothesized covariates of electoral success discussed in prior chapters.[10] I interact the race–sex interaction term with several party-level characteristics[11] to assess whether those variables exercise distinct effects on the vote share of Afro-descendant women.

Multivariate analyses of the 2014 elections indicate that Afro-descendant candidates—especially women—faced electoral disadvantages beyond the stark racial disparities in campaign finance displayed in Table 7.3. Even after controlling for traditional indicators of candidate quality (*education level, feeder occupation, incumbent, campaign finance*), and *party magnitude* and *p.mag$_{t-1}$*, and for the gendered effects of district competitiveness (*effective n cands*) and development level (*HDI*), and ideology (*left*), *Afro-descendant* and its interaction with *fem* both exercised statistically significant negative effects on candidate vote share (see Table 7.4). A breakdown of the marginal effects for that model demonstrates that holding all else constant, the predicted vote share of Afro-descendant female and male candidates, respectively, was 0.375% and 0.472%, compared to 0.583% and 0.629% for white female and male candidates.

Statistical power limitations[12] caution against overinterpreting the multivariate findings, but alongside the bivariate tests and qualitative evidence, they offer suggestive evidence that this book's argument about the importance of party capacity (party institutionalization) and will (women in party leadership) for the electoral prospects of female political aspirants may only partially apply to Afro-descendant women. Difference in proportions tests indicate that Afro-descendant candidates overall and among female candidates only are significantly more likely than white candidates to run and win in state parties that have had a critical mass of women leaders. While one in five white women elected in 2014 and 35% of Afro-descendant male deputies won election with a state party with a recent history of having a critical mass of women leaders, a striking 70% of Afro-descendant women deputies did so. Interestingly, mean party institutionalization scores are actually significantly

[9] *Education level* (alternatively estimated with a dichotomous variable *college*, coded 1 if the candidate has attended college, 0 otherwise) *feeder occupation, incumbent*, and *campaign finance* (and *campaign finance*^{2} to account for diminishing returns)

[10] District development (*HDI*) and competitiveness (*effective n cands*), and *party magnitude, p.mag$_{t-1}$*, and *left*.

[11] In addition to *party magnitude* and *ideology*, I include the 2010 state-level measures of *c.mass* and *PII* as proxies for women's leadership and party institutionalization in 2014.

[12] The new addition of racial data in 2014 means that any analysis of race necessarily includes returns from a single election. Evaluating those candidacies across 27 districts and at minimum 19 parameters with three-way cross-level interactions leads to statistical power limitations that pose a challenge to assessing the interaction of race and gender through multivariate analysis. Future analyses will have the benefit of additional data from forthcoming elections, and permit improved multivariate evaluation of intersecting inequities.

TABLE 7.4 *Accounting for Race and Gender in Multivariate Analyses of Vote Share in Chamber of Deputies Elections (2014)*

Fixed Effects	Model 1			Model 2		
	Coef.	SE	sig	Coef.	SE	sig
Level 2 District Variables						
For Intercept (β_{oj})						
Intercept $(\gamma 00)$	1.550	(0.128)	***	1.319	(0.145)	***
HDI $(\gamma 01)$ – Medium	−0.148	(0.151)		−0.129	(0.146)	
HDI $(\gamma 01)$ - High	−0.321	(0.164)	*	−0.303	(0.157)	*
Effective n cands $(\gamma 02)$	−0.019	(0.003)	***	−0.017	(0.003)	***
Cross-Level Interactions						
For Female slope (β_{1j})						
Intercept $(\gamma 10)$	−0.636	(0.108)	***	−0.551	(0.176)	***
Effective n cands $(\gamma 12)$	0.010	(0.001)	***	0.009	(0.001)	***
For Left slope (β_{2j})						
Intercept $(\gamma 20)$	0.022	(0.052)		−0.051	(0.054)	
Level 1 Party Variables						
Party magnitude $(\beta 4j, \gamma 40)$	0.045	(0.013)	***	0.079	(0.014)	***
P.mag$_{(t-1)}$ $(\beta 5j, \gamma 50)$	−0.053	(0.011)	***	−0.089	(0.012)	***
PII $(\beta 6j, \gamma 60)$				0.060	(0.035)	*
Fem*PII $(\beta 7j, \gamma 70)$				0.006	(0.064)	
C.Mass $(\beta 8j, \gamma 80)$				−0.314	(0.152)	*
Fem*C.Mass $(\beta 9j, \gamma 90)$				−0.259	(0.306)	
Fem*PII*C.Mass $(\beta 11j, \gamma 110)$				0.079	(0.145)	
Level 1 Race Variables						
Afrodesc $(\beta 12j, \gamma 120)$	−0.111	(0.056)	*	0.090	(0.134)	
Afrodesc*Fem $(\beta 13j, \gamma 130)$	−0.133	(0.104)	±	−0.159	(0.250)	
Afrodesc*Fem*Left $(\beta 15j, \gamma 150)$	0.212	(0.161)	±	0.158	(0.170)	
Afrodesc*Fem*PII $(\beta 17j, \gamma 170)$				−0.008	(0.111)	
Afrodesc*Fem*C. Mass $(\beta 19j, \gamma 190)$				0.059	(0.481)	
Afrodesc*Fem*PII*C. Mass $(\beta 21j, \gamma 210)$				0.053	(0.223)	

(*continued*)

TABLE 7.4 *(continued)*

Fixed Effects	Model 1			Model 2		
	Coef.	*SE*	*sig*	*Coef.*	*SE*	*sig*
Random Effects	*Var*	*SE*	*sig*	*Var*	*SE*	*sig*
Intercept (u_{oj})	0.079	(0.027)	***	0.072	(0.025)	***
Level-1 (r_{ij})	1.025	(0.024)	***	0.985	(0.024)	***
N	3636			3521		
LL	−5232			−4997		
AIC	10504			10058		
BIC	10628			10255		

***$p<.001$, **$p<.01$, *$p<.05$, ±$p<.10$ (one-tailed tests).
Notes: Dependent variable is candidate's percentage of valid votes. To preserve space, candidate controls for education (+), feeder occupation (n/s), incumbent (+), and campaign finance (+) and its square (−), and complete interactions are estimated but not displayed.

lower for Afro-descendant candidates (1.99) and deputies (2.11) than for white candidates (2.10) and deputies (2.33). Yet the average party institutionalization scores for Afro-descendant women candidates (2.05) and deputies (2.35) were not statistically different than scores for white women candidates (2.11) and deputies (2.24), and were higher than scores for male Afro-descendant candidates (1.97) and deputies (2.08, but not statistically significant given the limited N).

After introducing the proxies for women's presence in state party leadership and party institutionalization into the multivariate model (see Table 7.4 and Figure 7.1), an analysis of the marginal effects suggests that the positive effect of party institutionalization for women's predicted vote share is much greater for white women than Afro-descendant women. The predicted vote share of white and Afro-descendant women, respectively, increases from 0.413% and 0.381% at the lowest party institutionalization score to 0.828% and 0.468% at the highest party institutionalization score. By running with a state party with recent history of having a critical mass of women leaders, white and Afro-descendant women, respectively, increase their predicted vote share from 0.595% and 0.394% to 0.715% and 0.505%.

When we interact party will and party capacity, but do not disaggregate by racial identity, we find that women running in state party organizations that have been well-institutionalized with a critical mass of women leaders have a predicted vote share of 1.185%, compared to just 0.476% for women running in poorly institutionalized parties with less than 25% women leaders. Together, the bivariate and multivariate results suggest that Afro-descendant women stand to gain less from party institutionalization than do white women, with less clarity on the issue of women's leadership. The data suggest that women's

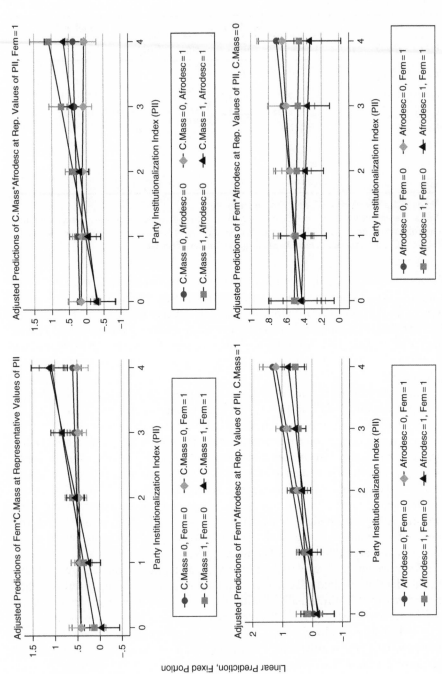

FIGURE 7.1 Intersectional Implications of Party Institutionalization and Leadership

leadership in state parties can level the playing field between male and female Afro-descendant candidates, but their predicted vote share (0.51% for men and women) nonetheless remains substantially lower than that of white candidates (0.84% for men, 0.72% for women). As further demonstrated in Figure 7.1, across those scenarios and particularly in parties without a critical mass of women leaders (bottom-right), the predicted vote share of Afro-descendant women candidates remains lower than that of white women. And while parties with inclusive leadership structures do seem to improve the electoral prospects of both white and Afro-descendant women at higher levels of party institutionalization, the steeper slope for white women suggests that the potential benefits of party capacity may be greater for white women (top-right).

The 2014 descriptive and multivariate statistics presented in this chapter thus corroborate what the few scholars studying racial representation in Brazil have long argued—access to political power is not equitable, with racial identity constituting a formidable barrier. In spite of apparently favorable public opinion data, Brazil's formal political power structures remain disproportionately white. Moreover, Afro-descendant women are doubly disadvantaged, faring worse electorally than Afro-descendant men, white women, and white men. While campaign finance disparities are one of the more egregious inequities in Brazilian electoral politics, the disadvantage confronted by marginalized groups—Afro-descendant men and women as well as white women—persists even once such disparities are controlled for in multivariate analyses. Yet the ability of institutionalized parties to mitigate such inequities by providing psychological, organizational, and mobilizational support to political aspirants does not appear to be a universal fix; while running with institutionalized state parties with women leaders increased the predicted vote share of women overall, the interaction loses statistical and substantive significance once measures of candidates' racial identity are introduced.

Several studies have shown that when policies designed to level the playing field for women do not expressly take into consideration the intersection of gender with other dimensions of identity such as race, benefits tend not to be uniformly distributed and often cluster to the dominant subgroup (Bird 2014; Holmsten, Moser, and Slosar 2010; Htun 2015; Hughes 2011; Krook and O'Brien 2010). Equity policies are not universal (Young 1989). Not surprisingly then, and as suggested by the array of empirical evidence on racial socioeconomic and political disparities discussed above, reforms that are to rectify the double disadvantage confronted by Afro-descendant women must be explicitly designed with that purpose in mind. Literature from the United States suggests that the gendered gap in formal political ambition may not apply to African American women (Moore 2005); in that scenario, an emphasis on financing the campaign may be more prescient than stimulating candidacy by externalizing the decision to run.

For PC do B (Salvador) Municipal Councilor and candidate for federal deputy Olívia Santana, "life itself" brought her into politics; as she developed consciousness about the problems confronted in her life, often connected by the recurring undercurrents of racism and sexism, she became convinced of the need to get involved politically to combat such inequities.[13] The daily injustices catalogued throughout this chapter often politicize the lived experiences of most women of color. Federal Deputy and former senator, governor, minister, and state secretary Benedita da Silva—whose grandparents were enslaved and at the time of our interview had only spent 10 of her 67 years not in a favela— reiterated Santana's statements about being politicized through her lived experiences and spoke of transforming the challenges of being a poor, Black women into her strong points. Yet as Benedita's own trajectory makes clear and as stated by Santana, the sheer difficulty of social ascension as a poor, Black woman is profoundly repressive.[14]

Against all odds, Santana entered the Federal University of Bahia (UFBa), passing the entrance exam without taking the expensive preparatory course students (especially those from public high schools) must typically invest in. At UFBa Santana assumed leadership roles in the student movement, black movement, and women's movement, and joined the PC do B. Although Santana's trajectory illustrates a growing political consciousness and ambition, it is important to again point out that formidable obstacles preclude such opportunities for most poor Afro-Brazilian women. And despite her clear ambition, the decision to run for office was ultimately not an individual choice. According to Santana, "it is the group that decides," with conviction from her party and the black movement that she had promise as a candidate propelling her candidacy.[15] For Benedita, her leadership in neighborhood associations and evangelical base communities and activism within the PT led fellow activists to recruit her to serve as a voice for popular movements within formal politics.[16] So while daily injustices and women's historical leadership roles within the Black community may help Afro-descendant women to counteract the socialization processes generally dissuading women from expressing political ambition, the path to power remains steep and uphill, and external support critical.[17]

Santana's social movement trajectory is common for women (and men) in the PC do B, but she drew an important distinction between her path to power and the party norm. While Santana's base came from popular movements—which tend to be the movements more open to marginalized groups—the better

[13] Interview with Municipal Councilor Olívia Santana, April 2009.
[14] Interviews with Secretaria Benedita da Silva, June 2009 and Municipal Councilor Olívia Santana, April 2009.
[15] Interview with Municipal Councilor Olívia Santana, April 2009.
[16] Interview with Secretaria Benedita da Silva, June 2009.
[17] Interview with advisor of the Women's Secretariat in the Chamber of Deputies and activist in the black movement, May 2015.

resourced (in human and financial resources) candidates drew on a syndical base instead. Candidates whose social movement trajectory is rooted in unions rather than popular movements enjoy (relatively) superior campaign structure and resources. Santana spoke several times about the financial precariousness of her campaigns, and the difficulties she faced in fund raising.[18] Benedita also pointed to the financial obstacles in running a campaign—especially for proportional races, where "it is your campaign" with party support less forthcoming (relative to majoritarian races). Such insights shared in interviews about the barrier posed by financial disparities are corroborated by the vast racial and gendered discrepancies in campaign finances demonstrated above in Table 7.3.

CONCLUSIONS

Together, the secondary sources, descriptive and multivariate analyses of the 2014 elections, and interviews examined in this chapter offer empirical evidence for the significance of race and gender in allocating formal political power in Brazil. Such racial disparities—which tend to fall doubly hard on women—have been neglected through the long-time invisibility of race in socioeconomic and political indicators, maintained by post-racial ideologies that undermine racial consciousness and perpetuate a delusion of racial democracy that stands in shocking contrast to the lived realities of Brazil's Afro-descendant majority.

Just as the black movement fought to disaggregate official socioeconomic indicators by race and thus permit the development of public policies oriented toward rectifying racial inequities, the new availability of self-reported data on candidates' racial identity yields a promising opportunity to offer concrete data on the extent, causes of, and solutions for racial underrepresentation. And as demonstrated above, the numbers are incontrovertible; formal political power is fundamentally raced and gendered in Brazil. The findings more generally remind us of the important role of the politics of knowledge, and the theoretical and practical salience of resisting hyper-aggregation and instead embracing complexity. As this study of the Brazilian case, echoing years of intersectional theory and praxis, makes clear, if reformers are to enhance inclusion, they must account for intersectional realities,

In future research, more emphasis should be given to the role of race and gender in candidate recruitment and selection processes; anecdotal evidence suggests that many parties may actually be receptive to the idea of Afro-descendant women candidates, who allow them to ticket balance on two fronts. Their will and capacity to actively recruit such candidates, however, remains questionable and far from universal. The internal climate of parties also merits further consideration. Several women I interviewed spoke of the explicit and implicit sexism, racism, homophobia, and classism they confronted within

---

[18] Interview with Municipal Councilor Olívia Santana, April 2009.

their party organization; as long as party leadership remains dominated by the (typically white, male) old guard, internal cultural changes are unlikely. But if parties can be compelled to adapt to societal demands for inclusion and changes in the electoral law mandating greater gender balance in their candidate slates, the chances for new, diverse voices in leadership—and in turn, a more representative and higher quality democracy—will be renewed.

8

Theoretical Implications and Comparative Perspectives

> What does a gendered lens teach us about party politics? A focus on gender highlights some important lessons: parties are still important to representation because they can and do change over time, and both formal and informal party institutions (the party opportunity structure) impact different sets of people in different ways.
>
> (Kittilson 2013, 547)

Beset by a crisis of representation, many third wave democracies remain undermined by weakly institutionalized political parties and the underrepresentation of marginalized groups. Citizen discontent with limitations to the quality of democracy is apparent, with a striking disconnect between their widespread protests and elite responses and maneuverings. While the extant literature tends to engage the dynamics of accountability and representativeness in isolation, this book uses extensive variation across Brazilian parties to explain how the two are related, employing mixed methods to analyze the relationship. Deviating from previous findings, this work demonstrates that party elites are the central gatekeepers of political power in Brazil, sending a clear message: reforms that strengthen parties and incentivize their promotion of women's participation in party leadership structures present a powerful remedy for the representative deficits in Brazilian democracy and beyond.

In exploring the connections between parties and representation in third wave democracies, the Brazilian case offers ample interparty variation as well as an interesting empirical puzzle, outside the conventional advanced-industrial context that tends to dominate extant studies. Despite substantial socioeconomic progress, effective and dynamic women's movements, an electorate increasingly receptive to female politicians, and a gender quota—factors that have furthered women's representation across Latin America—women remain scarcely represented in Brazilian electoral politics. This book marshals an extensive array of original qualitative and quantitative data to refute and recast the conventional explanations of women's (under) representation, concluding that the poor compatibility of quotas and open-list PR elections, voter bias, and district magnitude cannot fully explain the variation in electoral prospects of women across Brazil. These expectations of the literature emerge from aggregate-level findings that cannot be simply extended to the individual level. While such studies have contributed by exploring the conditions under which a country will elect more women, they have done little to theorize the conditions under which women will acquire election, which is a distinct question. Those extant findings also derive largely from Western Europe and the US, where parties tend to be far less inchoate and democracies more consolidated. My findings thus call into question the generalizability of such expectations for both the individual level and a recently (re)democratized and weakly institutionalized context.

Due to gendered social psychological processes and structural disadvantages, women tend not to possess the factors comprising the traditional recipe for success in entrepreneurial candidate-centered elections such as those to the Brazilian Chamber of Deputies: (1) a psychological affinity for self-promotion and thus aptitude to be an entrepreneurial candidate who self-nominates, (2) political interest and knowledge and the ability to use this to ascend within the party organization, or as is more often the case, to thrive independently in the absence of any real party organization, and (3) personal political (or otherwise converted) capital essential in personalist politics. Traditional gender socialization, the certain risk but uncertain reward of seeking election to an arena women perceive to be corrupt and ineffective, and increasing opportunities and responsibilities in the professional realm comprise part of an interconnected web of factors dissuading women from entering the formal political sphere. While Brazilianist studies of elections and representation have downplayed the importance of parties, I argue that political parties hold the key to enhancing the representation of traditionally marginalized groups such as women because they can mitigate the effects of these compounding factors of exclusion, providing outsiders with the psychological, organizational, and material support they need to thrive in Brazil's entrepreneurial system.

As documented in Chapter 2, orthodox explanations for understanding women's electoral prospects offer some contributions but face important limitations for the Brazilian case. While machista voter bias is a commonly employed explanation for the underrepresentation of women in Brazil's historically patriarchal cultural context, the contemporary electorate exhibits relatively moderate levels of gender stereotypes doubting women's capacity for the political realm. Moreover, many countries with more extensive gender bias have higher levels of women in politics, including others with preferential elections. Furthermore, Brazilian voters have expressed increasing levels of support for women in politics, suggesting that such gender bias is diminishing. Eighty-three percent of respondents in a 2009 nationally representative poll agreed that women's political presence improves the quality of politics, and three-quarters of respondents affirmed in 2009 and again in 2013 that true democracy exists only with the presence of women (Brazilian Institute of Public Opinion and Statistics 2009, 2013). Such postulated support for women in politics was corroborated in the 2010 and 2014 presidential elections, when 66.2% and 64.5% of voters, respectively, cast a vote for a woman, leading to the election and reelection of Dilma Rousseff, Brazil's first female president. Considering those recent developments, I surmise that Brazil's relatively moderate levels of machista voter bias cannot explain its drastic underrepresentation of women.

Electoral rules are another prominent explanation for women's representation, with most studies emphasizing distinctions between plurality and proportional representation rules, and in particular, the candidate- and party-centered elections they entail. Yet the implications of such expectations for female candidates in Brazil's Chamber of Deputies, which employs the open-list variant of PR elections, remain unclear. While increased numbers of candidacies and party seat share should make those resources less scarce and therefore more accessible for outsider contenders, they also tend to generate heightened incentives for intraparty competition, possibilities I explore in Chapters 4 and 5.

Party ideology and women in party leadership are the final two explanations I consider from the literature on women's representation. Again, Brazil's sizeable presence of leftist parties in government—the principal indicator for ideology's influence on women's overall representation—is not congruent with the paucity of women in Congress. There is, however, a close parallel between the low proportion of women in the national leadership structures of Brazilian parties—as of 2014, an average of 17.7% among the 28 parties with seats in the Chamber of Deputies—and in Congress (10%). A disaggregation of those numbers by parties reveals considerable interparty variation, which I describe, model, and explain in the analyses of Chapters 4, 5, and 6.

After discussing several other limitations of the extant literature and the contributions offered in my candidate-level analysis, I advance and substantiate an alternate explanation for Brazil's dearth of female politicians. I contend that it is the weak institutionalization and disproportionately male leadership of most Brazilian parties that has maintained women's political marginalization, and emphasize four mechanisms through which this relationship operates. First, inchoate parties suffer from a lack of transparency and accountability, with no clear guidelines for ascendance within the party and thus no norm of compliance with internal rules. Such parties, particularly those that are male dominant, are less likely to comply with the gender quota. Second, the reliance on candidate self-nomination in weakly institutionalized parties exacerbates a socialized gender gap in formal political ambition. External nomination through an active and women-inclusive recruitment network is more conducive to women's participation. Third, amorphous party organizations are ill-equipped to provide critical capacity-building opportunities for women. Finally, the rarity of programmatic appeals and dominance of personalist politics favor those with personal political and financial capital, which given wage discrepancies and the underrepresentation of women in appointed and elected posts, tends to be men.

The leadership of most Brazilian parties remains dominated by men, who even in well-institutionalized parties will be less likely than female party leaders to mobilize party support for women. Conversely, when women occupy a critical mass of leadership positions in institutionalized parties, they are afforded an effective voice in party decision-making, enabling them to amplify each other's voices and carry out a range of "critical acts." Although the relationship is not determinative, with women not necessarily acting for other women, female party leaders are more likely than male leaders to understand how to level the playing field for women contenders and to levy the party for resources for female aspirants.

As concluded in the development community and beyond, the effective mitigation of gender inequities necessitates an explicitly gendered frame of reference (Lovenduski 1998; Quinn 2009), whereby we consider the implications of and for gender in structures and processes. Female party leaders can introduce a gendered frame of reference in party decision-making, forcing leadership to stop functioning as an exclusively male domain and supporting each other, while raising awareness of gender inequities and means to resolve them. In particular, women in the leadership of institutionalized parties can hold parties accountable to the quota provisions, recruit and train female candidates, lobby for and host capacity-building opportunities for women, and mobilize party resources on behalf of female aspirants and their campaigns.

I thus integrate party institutionalization and the representation of women in party leadership and electoral politics to theorize that to effectively promote women's participation in a context of intraparty competition, parties must have both the capacity to recruit and provide female political aspirants with the psychological, organizational, and material support (forthcoming in appropriately institutionalized parties) essential for overcoming the combative entrepreneurial electoral climate, and the will to do so (heralded by women in party leadership).

I argue that it is capacity and will, rather than ideology per se, that substantiates leftist parties' apparent superiority in accommodating female candidates; with a mass and participatory character and historical emphasis on equality, leftist parties are more likely than non-leftist parties to be institutionalized and incorporate women in their leadership. Yet leftist ideology per se is neither necessary nor sufficient for women's electoral success. Parties must have both the structural conditions that provide the capacity to help women overcome the tendencies toward combative intraparty competition in the Chamber of Deputies, and the critical mass of women leaders likely to actualize this potential on behalf of female contenders through a series of critical acts; parties must be willing and able to promote women's participation. Thus women's representation is most effectively enhanced when a critical mass of women ascend to the leadership of an institutionalized party.

Those theoretical claims about capacity and will complicate the characterization by many observers that Brazil's extreme underrepresentation of women is easily dismissed by the poor fit of gender quotas for the open-list electoral context. While such a stance does offer merit, I elaborate in Chapter 3 that this is but one component of a more nuanced explanation. A singular focus on electoral rules holds limited weight for explaining the variation within Brazil. Brazil's open-list proportional representation (OLPR) electoral system does in fact dilute the potential of the gender quota to enhance women's representation, but Brazil actually ranks the worst among countries with candidate-based list elections, and the 6th lowest of the more than 60 countries with legislated gender quotas. Moreover, some Brazilian parties have had significantly greater success with quota compliance and the election of women than have others. Clearly then, there are other dynamics at play.

I establish for the reader a baseline understanding of legislative elections and parties in Brazil, and then explain why the OLPR system poses an obstacle to women's representation, focusing on the incentives it creates to cultivate a personal vote. I quickly review the historical role of women in Brazilian politics, the recent plateau in women's gradually progressing political presence, and the pervasiveness of male dominance in Brazilian politics. Next, I survey the global use of gender quotas to fast-track women's representation, and the process of quota implementation and reform in Brazil.

Following the arguments developed in Chapters 1 and 2, my analysis of the inadequacies of the Brazilian quota law bridges party institutionalization and the underrepresentation of women. It points to the preponderance of weakly institutionalized and male-led parties—which continue to resist complying with the quota law despite a recent reform expanding its reach—to explain the variation in quota compliance across parties and the failure (thus far) of quotas to empower women politically in Brazil. In the context of formally weak and robustly gendered institutions, formal institutional fixes are insufficient to induce real change and if the gender quota is to be effective, the *lei que não pega* (law on paper only) culture among party elites must be vanquished. This is best done by furthering party institutionalization and thus transparency, accountability, and a norm of compliance.

In Chapter 4, I subject the conventional explanations for the underrepresentation of women to empirical testing at the candidate level, in a context that is recently (re)democratized, has open-list elections, and a still inadequately institutionalized party system replete with inchoate parties. I integrate public opinion data with my multilevel database of candidacies to the Chamber of Deputies to assess the relative explanatory power of the rival explanations for women's underrepresentation—voter bias and development, electoral rules (district and party magnitude), and ideology—along with my argument that (a lack of) party institutionalization and women in party leadership are the key predictors of women's electoral prospects in Brazil.

I draw on interview findings, descriptive analyses of women's legislative presence and success rates throughout Brazil, public opinion data, multivariate analyses of candidate vote share, and documentary research to demonstrate that while residual machista voter bias does persist in less developed areas, it has not depressed women's electoral performance in the Chamber of Deputies. Rather, with the lone exception of male leftists, candidates actually have a higher predicted vote share in the less developed states than in the more developed states. I also find that the effects of district and party magnitude are not gendered, with the former exercising a negative effect and the latter a positive effect on candidate vote share overall but interactions with female consistently insignificant. So contrary to conventional wisdom, even when controlling for electoral competitiveness and a range of other factors, women (and men) running in more developed states with more seats up for grabs actually perform worse than those running in less developed and smaller states.

Employing descriptive analyses of party variation in quota compliance, female candidate success rates, and election of women, along with multivariate analyses of candidate vote share, interviews, and documentary research, I find strong support for my argument that women's electoral prospects are heightened in well-institutionalized parties with a critical mass of female leaders. It is not leftist ideology per se that improves the electoral prospects of women contenders, but rather the combination of a structure favorable to outsiders and the presence of actors willing to mobilize resources on their behalf. I use the experiences of two of Brazil's largest parties—the PMDB and PT—to illuminate the critical acts performed by women in party leadership. Women leaders are more likely to understand that it is insufficient to simply reserve candidate slots for women and allow them to go unfulfilled, and are more likely to then pressure other party leaders to provide conditions favorable to women's candidacies that will in turn facilitate compliance with the gender quota. By availing psychological, organizational, and material support to female political aspirants, women in the leadership of institutionalized parties can level the playing field for female contenders.

Chapter 5 uses variation in electoral rules across Brazil's bicameral legislature and the incentives for party support or intraparty competition that these differing rules generate to illuminate the interacting role of electoral rules and parties in explaining women's limited electoral presence in Brazil. The controlled comparison analysis provides a potent opportunity for testing the relative explanatory power of my central argument, as it allows me to control for a barrage of potentially confounding cultural and historical factors, while analyzing variation in electoral rules, incentives for party support or intraparty competition, and party characteristics. If party support is in fact critical for the development of viable female candidacies, the Senate's heightened incentives for such support should lead women congressional contenders to confront a more level playing field in the upper rather than lower house.

Indeed, in the last six elections, a consistently greater proportion of women have been elected to the more powerful and prestigious Senate than to the Chamber of Deputies. I advance background information on the varying electoral rules and incentives generated, descriptive analyses of interparty variation in the proportion of women they nominate and elect, cross-chamber multivariate analyses of candidates' chance of election, and interview data and documentary research to explain how the Senate's low magnitude, multi-vote plurality elections yield an electoral climate significantly more propitious to female contenders than do the Chamber of Deputies' high-magnitude OLPR elections. While the Senate rules generate incentives for unified party support, the electoral rules of the Chamber incentivize combative intraparty competition.

As demonstrated in Chapter 4, well-institutionalized parties are capable of overcoming those tendencies, but the potential is much more likely to be mobilized when a party has incorporated women in its decision-making structures. Party institutionalization is less important for women in the Senate due to the existing incentives for party support, but the scarcity of Senate candidacy and restrictive ballot access mean that those benefits of unified party support are unlikely to be mobilized on behalf of female contenders without women in party leadership. When women do have an effective voice in party decision-making structures, however, the Senate incentives for party support amplify the positive effects of critical acts performed by women leaders. So although the upper house is more prestigious and poses a higher electoral hurdle than does the lower house, incentives for unified party support in the Senate have been able—when mobilized by women in party leadership—to nullify the negative effect of gender on electoral outcome that persists in elections to the Chamber of Deputies. In sum, the conditions most favorable for the election of women are electoral rules that incentivize unified party support, and party leadership that carries out critical acts to cultivate viable female candidacies.

Given the importance of party support, incentives for intraparty competition in the Chamber, the preponderance of inchoate and male-led parties, and residual gender bias in Brazil, it is impressive that even the few female deputies were able to win election. In Chapter 6, I explain how, even under conditions of machista bias in the electorate and/or in party leadership, some women have cultivated particular profiles enabling them to overcome prejudices and attain office. By conforming to the traditional gender norms prevalent in some areas and therefore minimizing their perceived threat to the established order, or by working with supportive parties to transform their experiences in informal politics into the requisite political capital and run a collective ideas-based campaign, *supermadres* and *lutadoras* have managed to win election in less developed states, with *supermadres* doing so without the benefit of a supportive party.

As demonstrated in Chapter 4, women are not afforded any electoral advantage in developed districts. The scenario is particularly dire when such women run with parties that are, by virtue of their weak institutionalization and/or lack of female party leaders, women-adverse. Women running as technocrats have nonetheless succeeded under such constraints by converting their area-specific expertise acquired in the professional world into political capital and thus convincing reticent male party elites of their electoral viability. Chapter 6 tells the stories of women elected under those intersecting constraints, elucidating their paths to power and how they have managed to overcome the obstacles and gain election. These circumscribed profiles represent successful strategies in women's struggle to gain power in Brazil but come at the cost of constraining and conditioning their political participation, often reinforcing traditional gender roles.

Unfortunately, the inchoate character and/or male-dominant leadership of so many Brazilian parties means that the most women-friendly context of a supportive party and developed district persists as the least common among elected female deputies. That ideal of a women-friendly district and party simply remains a rarity in Brazilian elections, heretofore accessible to exceedingly few women. There is a degree of path dependence, with most of Brazil's few female politicians to date coming up either as *supermadres* or *lutadoras*. As demonstrated in Table 6.2, just 2.68% of female candidates running in a women-friendly district and party ran as incumbents, compared to 8.09% of women running with women-friendly parties in women-adverse districts. I predict that, as the "open" profile becomes more accessible through the strengthening of parties and incorporation of women in party decision-making, we will see more female candidates running and winning, which by de-normalizing the political exclusion of women, should contribute to the evolution of gender attitudes.

Bridging the women's representation literature that affirms the critical gatekeeping role of parties with the Brazilianist literature, which underestimates such a role due to the amorphous character of most Brazilian parties, I move parties to the center of the analysis and confirm that they are the key arbiters of women's political empowerment in Brazil. Indeed, in sharp contrast to the image of a minimal or non-existent gatekeeping role so often painted for Brazilian parties, every single female candidate I interviewed underscored the importance of party support. Within an entrepreneurial electoral context, weakly institutionalized and male-led parties exacerbate the socialized gender gap in formal political ambition and impede women's political prospects, while circumscribing their pathways to power. Well-institutionalized parties, however, provide a structure fit to overcome the tendencies toward intraparty competition, and women in party leadership are able to amplify each other's voices, incorporate gender considerations in party decision-making, and mobilize party resources on behalf of female political aspirants.

If development, electoral rules, and ideology were the most important factors for women's electoral prospects, we would need to accelerate economic growth in order to stimulate modernization, while also implementing a top-down quota or other requirement on non-left parties which are, the story goes, ideologically opposed to the incorporation of women. Indeed, this has been the approach of most advocates for enhancing women's representation in Brazil. The analyses advanced here suggest that such an approach is misguided. Rather, gender-friendly reformists must align their interests with those seeking to enrich the quality of Brazilian democracy in other ways. Foremost are reforms that strengthen and democratize political parties.

Even when faced with an unfavorable entrepreneurial electoral system, Brazil's few female politicians have proven themselves capable of electoral success. Women's shared history of structural disadvantages, the societal weight of traditional gender socialization, and an affinity for the collective often leave female contenders wary of self-promotion, "good ole' boy" networking, and personalist politics. Yet those traits describe precisely the political status quo maintained by Brazil's predominantly inchoate parties. When provided the opportunity to acquire political skillsets, bulwarked by a solid party organization, and able to run an ideas-based campaign, women's success in the political realm increases. In the absence of those conditions of party support, however, (some) women have enjoyed success by converting capital acquired elsewhere into sufficient political capital.

In sum, residual gender bias, a faulty electoral quota, and the plethora of non-left parties cannot fully explain Brazil's woefully scarce female political presence, nor can it explain variation among Brazilian parties in furthering women's participation. Rather, it is the rarity of institutionalized parties and prevalence of male dominance in party leadership that has sustained women's marginalization in the legislature. Therefore, only by strengthening parties and incentivizing their active promotion of women's participation within the party infrastructure and as priority candidates can Brazil (and other countries facing similar crises of representation) expect to level the biased playing field and enhance women's self-perceived and actual electoral prospects.

Building on the insights of intersectional theorists who point to the mutual constitution of salient identities like gender and race, Chapter 7 examines the construction of race in Brazil and advances an array of descriptive evidence on racial disparities to assess the intersection of race and gender in Brazilian society and politics. Applying newly available data on candidates' self-declared racial identity, I evaluate racial representation in the 2014 Chamber of Deputies elections, and present bivariate and multivariate analyses of the role of racial identity and its intersection with sex in predicting electoral prospects. The data are incontrovertible; power is fundamentally raced and gendered in Brazil. Even after taking into account vast racial discrepancies in campaign finance, Afro-descendant candidates face an electoral disadvantage, which is further heightened for Afro-descendant women.

Interestingly, as prior intersectional studies have demonstrated, the factors offering equalizing power to women's electoral prospects overall—institutionalized parties and women in party leadership—may not extend as readily to Afro-descendant women. The gains offered by party institutionalization were substantially greater for white women than Afro-descendant women. And although Afro-descendant women were disproportionately elected in state parties with a critical mass of women leaders, the small N and other data limitations prevent firm conclusions about how the gendered effects of such party characteristics may be mediated by racial identity. Future elections will only increase the number of cases and variation, and thus facilitate deeper exploration of the intersections of race and gender in electoral politics. In the interim, the evidence warrants two conclusions; first, Afro-Brazilian men and especially women face a series of societal and political obstacles that at once necessitate and impede their effective participation in formal politics, and second, reforms designed to mitigate gendered barriers must explicitly take into consideration the intersection of gender with race if they are to yield transformational change in the representativeness of Brazilian democracy.

THEORETICAL IMPLICATIONS

The approach and findings of this book speak to some of political science's most enduring questions. We remain engaged in debate on the form representation should take; for example, must representatives mirror their constituents (descriptive representation) to represent their interests adequately? The point of departure of this book is that democratic representation does indeed entail descriptive representation, which in turn engenders a powerful socializing effect through symbolic representation. Brazil's 2010 election and 2014 reelection of its first female president has ruptured any vision of political power as exclusively masculine, but the impeachment process against Dilma signaled the precariousness of those gains and the extent of good ole' boy networks dominating the formal political arena. Moreover, an electorate that is majority female and Afro-descendant is still "represented" by a Congress that remains 90 percent male and 80 percent white. This book helps to illuminate the conditions under which white, male dominance of political institutions can be assuaged.

A greater perception of representativeness may increase citizen satisfaction with democracy (Schwindt-Bayer 2010). If so, enhanced representativeness might increase the currently dire levels of trust and confidence in political parties and parliament in Brazil and beyond. Indeed, three-quarters of Brazilian respondents in a recent nationwide poll agreed that there is only true democracy with the presence of women in spaces of power and decision-making, with 80 percent agreeing that half of the candidates on party lists should be women (Brazilian Institute of Geography and Statistics 2013). While the Brazilian electorate has exhibited itself to be open to electing women, both in public opinion polls and in elections, political parties have resisted. How can political parties be held accountable to evolving societal preferences in a context where the party label is of dubious significance?

When parties are weakly institutionalized, accountability suffers. Limited party identifiability undermines voters' efforts to reward or punish politicians and their parties, and campaign rhetoric tends to focus on individuals rather than programmatic party platforms. What are the conditions under which parties might embrace changes evoked in response to societal preferences? Conventional wisdom on party change suggests a general aversion to change within party organizations (Harmel and Janda 1994; Panebianco 1988). Party change is facilitated by leadership change or a changing factional distribution of power within the party organization, and/or external stimuli (Harmel and Janda 1994; Svåsand 1994). For electorally competitive parties, external stimuli or environmental changes may result from updated electoral incentives driven by factors such as shifting economic conditions, a contagion effect, or constitutional reforms (Harmel and Janda 1994; Hunter 2010; Matland and Studlar 1996). In the Brazilian case, as this book has demonstrated, domineering (mostly white male) leaders of inchoate parties act unencumbered by electoral reforms and societal preferences for more representative candidate slates, while women leaders in more institutionalized parties have worked to recruit and support more diverse tickets. Below, I outline the case for inducing party change with incentives for more diverse internal leadership structures.

Another fundamental question engaged in this book is the power of institutions to induce change. The implementation and reform of Brazil's quota law was a clear instance of graduated change, where power holders sought to nominally accommodate societal demands for change while maintaining their power (Thelen 1999). Yet Brazil's gender quota represents just one layer of several layers of formal and informal institutions, and it has been unable to reach a new equilibrium amidst a plethora of inchoate and male-led political parties. In the more rule-bound context of Brazil's few well-institutionalized parties, however, the introduction of new actors—a critical mass of women leaders—has induced a genuine shift in party decision-making, which has in turn had important implications for women's electoral prospects. This case illustrates the difficulty of institutionally-driven change in the context of weak institutions, as well as the gendered character of institutional change. Gender-negligent accounts of institutional change will tend to overpredict the prospects for real change, with insufficient attention given to the gendered embodiment of political power in the formal and informal rules of the game and the actors who implement (and resist) them. Reformers must seek to trigger a new equilibrium by not only changing the formal institutions to incentivize stronger parties, but also introducing new actors capable of generating a sufficient shock to break from the multiple layers of informal institutions that continually reproduce the political arena as a white masculine domain.

Indeed, the crux of this book and so many other social science analyses is that structures and actors interact to produce outcomes, and that we are remiss to consider those fundamental pieces in isolation. I demonstrate that neither electoral rules nor party institutionalization have proven independently capable of empowering women, but rather must be mobilized by willing party leaders. More generally, electoral rules do not function in a vacuum, but are endogenous to and interact with the actors that created and sustain them. Future reform efforts in Brazil and beyond must therefore consider not only electoral rules but also the political parties that will mediate the effects of those rules.

REFORMS TO ENHANCE BRAZILIAN DEMOCRACY

This book bridges two critical challenges confronting many third wave democracies—the weak institutionalization of parties and party systems and the underrepresentation of marginalized groups—and demonstrates that reforms aimed at strengthening parties can go a long way toward resolving both manifestations of the crisis of representation. My analysis suggests that stronger parties would enhance both accountability and representativeness, two virtues of democratic governance historically considered to exist as tradeoffs.

But proposals for electoral and political reforms have been at the forefront of the legislative agenda—in rhetoric if not action—since the return to democracy in the 1980s. Indeed, David Fleischer has characterized the ongoing reform attempts as a "never-ending story" (2011, 2016). While the 1987–88 Constitutional Assembly achieved substantial gains (Fleischer 2011), as articulated by Power (2000), the outcome left standing three critical challenges for the Brazilian party system and resultant quality of democracy: party (in)fidelity, campaign finance, and the open-list format of proportional elections. Most of the rules governing those issues are resolved through the Electoral and Party Legislation, continually updated by the Congress (Power 2000). It is hardly surprising then that elected officials have not voted to change the laws under which they themselves were elected. Civil society groups have, however, mobilized under a "Platform for Reform to the Political System," gathering signatures and pressuring elected officials to undertake a series of reforms. A similar collaborative civil society effort, which drew on 1.3 million signatures and mass mobilization, resulted in the significant accomplishment of the approval in 2010 and judicial declaration of constitutionality in 2012 of Ficha Limpa, an anti-corruption law.[1] Such success suggests that reform is

---

[1] For more information, see the campaign's website, www.fichalimpa.org.br.

possible, but requires substantial collaboration among civil society and with the various branches of government.

As discussed by Power, the fact that party fidelity measures had been imposed by the authoritarian regime spelled their undoing—the Brazilian Congress swiftly abolished party fidelity statutes after the return to democracy in 1985 (Power 2000, 118). Some progress toward reform was subsequently made by the Cardoso administration, which attempted to re-engineer electoral institutions so as to strengthen parties, not only imposing stricter standards for party fidelity but also adopting a threshold for representation that works against fragmentation, barring coalitions in proportional elections, and advocating greater transparency in campaign contributions (Mulholland and Rennó 2008).[2] Most of those measures were rejected, however, and it was not until a series of judicial rulings in 2007 that enhanced standards for party fidelity enjoyed the force of law. The Supreme Electoral Court ruled in March 2007 that federal and state deputies and municipal councilors (later expanded to include those elected to majoritarian posts) switching parties after election would forgo their mandate. So-called "party migrations" decreased substantially in the wake of the court decisions—51 in 2007 and just 1 in 2008—and a few switchers unable to prove just cause[3] for jumping ship actually did lose their mandate (Cunow 2010).

With progress on party fidelity underway, much of the current reform effort is focused on instituting public financing of campaigns. As documented throughout this book, Brazilian electoral campaigns are expensive, draw on significant corporate funding, and serve to reproduce societal inequities resulting from raced-gendered disparities in wages and wealth. In sum, (most) non-white and/or female candidates do not confront a level playing field, a fact that deters many would-be political aspirants from throwing their hat in the ring. Such an imbalance, which confines allegedly representative spaces to the privileged few, could be rectified through the mechanism of exclusive public campaign financing. Although the use of public funds for campaigning would be a significant investment of state resources, in the words of one former deputy and mayor, who had recently changed her mind on the proposal, "the democratic process is the biggest public works project of all."[4]

While a great distrust of political parties has provoked skepticism in the electorate of the reform agenda, public financing enjoys greater support than does the proposal to shift to closed lists (discussed below). Of 1,073

---

[2] Two important and successful Cardoso-era reforms not discussed here are the reelection provision for executive posts and the Law of Fiscal Responsibility (Mulholland and Rennó 2008).

[3] If the politician can prove that the party with which (s)he won election substantially changed its platform or s(he) faced personal discrimination, switching can be deemed justifiable by the electoral court (Cunow 2010).

[4] Interview with former Deputy Jusmari Oliveira, November 2008.

callers to the Chamber of Deputies hotline,[5] 37% were in favor of and 57% opposed to public financing of campaigns (Agência Câmara de Notícias 2011b). Although Fleischer's prediction is that such a proposal would not be adopted (2011, 2016), it actually enjoys significant support within the Congress, with 58.7% of parliamentarians surveyed in a more representative sample in favor of exclusive public financing of campaigns and only 15.3% supporting the current system (Institute of Socioeconomic Studies 2009). The PT's Rapporteur on Political Reform, Deputy Henrique Fontana stated, "Exclusive public financing, through the reduction of the prices of campaigns, which each time are more expensive and unattainable for most of the population, is one of the measures with the greatest impact in fighting corruption, in addition to guaranteeing more autonomy for the governments" (Quoted in Agência Câmara de Notícias 2011b).

Despite such ostensible support for reforming the campaign finance system in Brazil, the former President of the Chamber of Deputies, Eduardo Cunha, rallied to retain corporate contributions to elections. Under Cunha's lead, the Chamber of Deputies passed Law 13.165/2015, which included a questionable fix to the ills of corporate financing by barring candidates but not parties from receiving corporate contributions. Cunha pushed through that legislation in an apparent attempt to entrench corporate financing in the law before a long-awaited decision by the Supreme Court on its constitutionality could be issued. But in rather quick succession (especially given the slow-moving saga of political reforms), the Chamber of Deputies passed Law 13.165/2015, the Supreme Court declared corporate financing of campaigns unconstitutional, and Rousseff vetoed the parts of the legislation speaking to campaign finance (Benites 2015; Congresso em Foco 2015). The October 2016 municipal elections were thus free of (legal) corporate financing, significantly reducing costs (Tribunal Regional Eleitoral de Alagoas 2017), but the playing field remains far from level; individual and self-financed donations are still allowed, which will continue to favor the more connected candidates with accumulated political and/or financial capital.

A current proposal from Vicente Cândido (PT-SP), head of the Special Commission of Political Reform in the Chamber of Deputies, seeks to create a public Special Fund for the Financing of Democracy (FFD) that would finance the 2018 elections. Cândido argues that "the cost of corruption is much larger than the R$ 3.5 billion of the national budget that will be destined for the fund" (quoted in Bezerra 2017). The proposal would also restrict self-

---

[5] "Disque-Câmara" is a service created in 2003 facilitating constituent communication with deputies. They receive hundreds of thousands of calls and emails each year with solicitations, complaints, denouncements, and compliments. The hotline is staffed Monday through Friday, 8am to 8pm (Agência Câmara de Notícias 2008).

financing and donations from individuals.[6] Controversially, the bulk (98%) of the FFD would be allocated to parties based on their congressional presence, and would afford party leaders discretion in the internal distribution of those funds. Concerns about the fiscal viability of combining exclusive public financing with the OLPR system also abound, and the approval of the former could motivate earnest consideration of the latter.

Yet as with the proposal for exclusive public financing, constituents' profound distrust for politicians and their parties has substantially undermined support for closing candidate lists and giving parties the ultimate say on the ordering of lists. Although closing the lists would strengthen parties and enable them to enforce the gender quota, many fear that in the interim, weak parties dominated by personalist leaders would simply elect their cronies, thus depriving the electorate of the ability to order the lists. Moreover, as discussed above, in the absence of placement mandates party leaders tend to cluster female candidates at the bottom of party lists. In sum, the closing of party lists, if accomplished, must be done so judiciously, requiring transparency in party selection of candidates and guidelines for establishing representative lists. In any case, there is scant support for such a proposal in the electorate and the Congress, and despite propositions from leaders of former and current iterations of the Special Commission of Political Reform in the Chamber of Deputies, we are unlikely to see such a wholesale shift in the electoral system any time soon. More plausible is the so-called *distritão*, which would maintain multimember districts but election would be determined by individual candidate votes with no pooling to the party/coalition list (an "every man for himself" model), or graduated adoption of a mixed electoral system, combining a tier of single member districts with a tier of seats allocated through proportional representation. Although Deputy Cândido's report recommended that the proportional tier be closed-list, with placement mandates requiring that every third candidate be a woman, it is also possible that the mixed system would be adopted while maintaining OLPR rules for the proportional tier or that the *distritão* would win approval, both of which would only exacerbate the ills of personalism that have undermined the accountability and representativeness of Brazilian democracy.

---

[6] The proposal would "maintain donations by individuals up to 10% of their declared income," or R$10,000, whichever is lesser, with a ceiling of R$10,000 per electoral contest. "Candidates for proportional positions (municipal councilor and deputies) in the 2018 elections could finance up to 5% of the campaign costs with their own money. But that would be forbidden for majoritarian posts (mayor, governor, president and senator)." Other reforms being seriously considered by the special commission are the gradual move to a mixed electoral system for currently proportional elections (municipal councilors and federal and state/district deputy), more stringent minimum thresholds for parties to access public resources (at least 2% [increased to 3% in 2020] of valid votes in 14/27 statewide districts), and an end to coalitions for proportional elections (Câmara Notícias 2017b).

The fact that any eventual shift to a closed-list or mixed system would entail a rather shaky transition if executed by weak parties, means that reform efforts should focus on other means to strengthen parties. The party fidelity measures discussed above represent a promising first step, but is at risk of reversal in the current political reform discussions. Party members and citizens in general must also demand accountability of party leaders. As Deputies Fontana and Cândido and countless others have argued, the public financing of campaigns is one such way to enhance accountability to constituents by removing the need for candidates to curry favor with corporations and wealthy individuals to run a viable campaign. Exclusive public financing of campaigns would also reign in ever-growing campaign budgets, thus counteracting another troubling side effect of open-list elections. Another option discussed below is increasing the "Party Fund," which directs state subsidies (with oversight) for party organizations, and would enable parties to develop more complex organizational structures capable of providing psychological, organizational, and material support to female political aspirants.

While the adoption of closed-list elections and allocation of more public funds to parties and campaigns remain a tough sell to the electorate, there already exists broad societal support for reforms requiring parties to strengthen the gender quota. According to a nationally representative survey in April 2013, eight out of ten Brazilians support the adoption of legislative measures to guarantee gender equity in elected office (Brazilian Institute of Public Opinion and Statistics 2013). An earlier survey in February 2009 found that 75% support the quota law, with a striking 86% indicating that parties that do not comply with quotas stipulated by the electoral law should be punished. Such support exists across Brazil's five regions, and is only slightly lower for male respondents (Brazilian Institute of Public Opinion and Statistics 2009, 2013). But when asking parliamentarians similar questions, support plummets (Center for Studies and Advisory Services 2009), yet another demonstration of the fact that the problem of women's extreme representation in Brazil is fundamentally political rather than societal.

The 2009 mini-reform and subsequent decisions by the electoral courts to enforce the quota provisions represent substantial progress in the battle for women's representation in Brazil. But as I have argued throughout this book, it is not enough to change the formal rules of the game; reformers must also target informal norms among party elites. Deputy Luiza Erundina's 2002 proposal (6216/2002) addresses precisely this concern by requiring parties to devote: (1) 30% of their federally-allocated funds for party organization to the promotion of women's participation and (2) 30% of their publicly-funded television and radio propaganda time to women (in both election and non-election years). The accomplishments of the 2009 mini-reform were more limited, however, devoting only 5% of party organization funds and 10% of propaganda time in non-election years to the promotion of women's participation, with only nominal oversight of the regulations. A largely overlooked component of

Deputy Cândido's final report to the Special Commission on Political Reform addresses women's participation, supporting Deputy Erundina's proposal that 30% of HGPE/HGPP be allocated to women, and also recommending that 5% of the Party Fund be destined for the individual campaigns of female candidates, and in Senate elections with two seats up for grabs, that each party/coalition list include a candidate from "each sex" (Câmara Notícias 2017a). The likelihood of approval of these essentially neglected elements of the proposal approximates zero.

Future reforms must achieve more—they must change the incentive structure adequately so as to make it irrational for parties to not invest in cultivating viable female candidacies, forcing their hands to promote women's political empowerment. The electorate appears poised to respond favorably to party advancement of quality female candidacies, but most party elites remain slow to adapt. The literature on party change and the evidence advanced here suggest that Brazil's male-dominant inchoate parties can be incentivized to change by reforms that introduce new diverse party leadership and increase public funds for parties and oversight of those funds. The new leadership will enable a break from organizational inertia and critically, incorporate more diverse voices in party decision-making. As this book has demonstrated, women leaders in Brazilian parties have often used their position of influence to "let the ladder down" to other female and Afro-descendant political aspirants.

We have also seen the general weakness of party organizations and the overwhelming raced-gendered discrepancies in campaign finance. Exclusive public financing of campaigns and increased state subsidies for party organizations can serve to level the playing field for candidates while also allowing parties to cultivate more complex organizations that offer training opportunities, a network for recruiting candidates, and an internal structure that provides political aspirants a chance to cut their political teeth, factors that can close the socialized gender gap in political ambition. But oversight of those funds is essential; explicit requirements for their allocation (as proposed by Deputy Luiza Erundina) would push parties to use campaign and additional party funds to enhance representativeness and organizational strength. In sum, reforms incentivizing diverse internal leadership structures and explicit provisions for resource allocation along the lines of Deputy Erundina's proposal would help to jumpstart party change, thus diminishing the yawning gap between electorate expectations and party elites, and improving the quality of Brazilian democracy.

COMPARATIVE PERSPECTIVES

The ability of institutionalized parties with women in party leadership to further women's empowerment even in Brazil's entrepreneurial OLPR elections is encouraging. But does this story of capacity and will have broader applicability? The preliminary findings presented in Chapter 7 call into question whether that combination of structure and agency is sufficient to also further the representation of other marginalized groups. Does it apply beyond Brazil? If so, institutionalized parties with women in party leadership should prove capable of and willing to facilitate women's political participation. In line with the argument of Chapter 5, where there are lesser incentives for intraparty competition, such as in the Brazilian Senate and even more so in closed-list PR elections, women in party leadership rather than party institutionalization should be most salient for predicting women's electoral prospects.

In Peru's open-list PR elections, women have enjoyed unanticipated successes, winning 29.2% of the congressional seats in the 2006 elections, placing the country among the top ten in the IPU rankings of women's parliamentary representation just fifty years after the country extended suffrage rights to women (Inter-Parliamentary Union 2017; Schmidt 2012). Although progress seems to have plateaued, with 27.7% women elected a decade later in the 2016 elections, Peru's share of female legislators has since 2000 consistently remained above the global average (Inter-Parliamentary Union 2017). In this mini-case study of Peru, I explore the role of voter bias, formal electoral institutions, and party-level characteristics in explaining the country's unexpectedly strong performance in women's representation, in turn assessing the generalizability of my argument about the role of party capacity and will in mitigating the constraints of OLPR elections.

A simple emphasis on national level of development would yield expectations of a less than favorable national gender ideology in Peru, where the 2015 HDI was 0.740, earning an 87th place ranking, just below Brazil's 79th place value of 0.754 (United Nations Human Development Report 2016). Yet as in Brazil, modernization-based arguments about the correlation between development, national gender ideology, and women's representation do not seem to hold in Peru, which is ranked 55th in women's parliamentary presence (Inter-Parliamentary Union 2017). Data from the World Values Survey depict a national gender ideology that while not egalitarian, has levels of disagreement with statements of male occupational, educational, and political superiority that exceed global averages (World Values Survey 1981–2014).[7]

LAPOP surveys suggest that the Peruvian electorate is actually quite supportive of female politicians; just 2.4% of respondents strongly agreed with the standard question asserting male political superiority, with 81.5% of respondents disagreeing (including 19.0% who strongly disagreed) (LAPOP

---

[7] Among Peruvian respondents, levels of agreement with several WVS questions constituting a restrictive national gender ideology were as follows: men should be prioritized when jobs are scarce (17.4%), women earning more than men is almost certain to cause problems (25.0%), a university education is more important for a boy than a girl (14.1%), men are better political leaders than women (18.7%). Per difference in means/proportions tests, those levels of agreement are significantly lower than averages for all other countries (World Values Survey 1981–2014).

n.d.).[8] Moreover, when asked about mandating reserved positions for women on electoral lists, Peruvians responded affirmatively, with 30.4% strongly agreeing (and an additional 43.3% agreeing in part) and just 2.9% strongly disagreeing with the idea of a quota (LAPOP n.d.). Differences in means tests suggest that minimal gender differences in those responses were statistically insignificant. Respondent level of education and demographic size of locale (but not income) was correlated with perception of women politicians, with higher levels of disagreement with male political superiority among the more educated respondents and those in large urban municipalities than the less educated respondents and those in rural municipalities. Even so, as Chapter 6 illustrates for the Brazilian case, some Peruvian women have made inroads in ostensibly hostile electoral contexts by conforming to traditional gender norms via the *supermadre* profile (Chaney 1979; Rousseau 2009).

The small but non-negligible levels of voter bias against women in Peru could nevertheless pose a challenge in its preferential elections, as discussed in Chapter 3 (Valdini 2013a). But as explained by Schmidt, the Peruvian version of preferential elections—the "double optional preferential vote" (DOPV) system—attenuates the expected disadvantages for women. First, the DOPV elections feature a party/ alliance vote accompanied by the often unexercised *option* to also cast up to two votes for specific candidates on that list (Schmidt 2012). Whereas in the Brazilian system, seats are allocated to parties/alliances based on pooled candidate votes (in addition to the rarely exercised party *legenda* votes), in Peru's DOPV elections, parties/alliances' seat allocation is directly determined by the electorate's party/ alliance votes. Yet in both systems, the preference votes determine which candidates win those seats. Nevertheless, Peruvian voters—especially poor voters—may neglect to cast their candidate votes. According to Schmidt (2012), the result is that Peru's legislators are by and large chosen by "a more affluent and better educated *subelectorate* ... (with) more progressive attitudes toward the political participation of women than the overall Peruvian electorate" (Schmidt 2012, 172; LAPOP n.d.).[9]

The DOPV system also constitutes an important check on intra-list competition. Schmidt (2012) explains how the presence of two votes makes the campaign less of a zero-sum endeavor despite the open-list electoral rules. Proponents of women's representation can emphasize equity rather than displacing men; feminist non-governmental organizations advocated, "Of your two preferential votes, cast one for a woman" (Schmidt 2012). As discussed in Chapter 5, the mitigation of incentives for intraparty

[8] As reported in Table 1.2, the WVS found levels of strong agreement with that statement that were slightly higher (4.1%), but still comparatively low (World Values Survey 1981–2014). A probable source of that slight discrepancy is the overwhelming gender imbalance of the 2014 LAPOP data; just 333 out of 1,451 Peruvian respondents identified as male (LAPOP n.d.).

[9] I thank Gregory Schmidt for clarification on the DOPV (G. Schmidt, personal communication, August 14, 2017).

competition can benefit women. Furthermore, the double vote option helps to assuage voter concern that a vote for a woman is a wasted or risky vote (Schmidt 2012). In elections to the Brazilian Senate, female candidates have been more successful in the two-seat elections (see Table 5.2); from 1994–2010, 24.4% of female candidates in two-seat Brazilian Senate elections won compared to just 10.9% of female candidates in the single-seat elections. Of the 31 successful female candidacies in the 1994–2014 Brazilian Senate elections, 20 (64.5%) were won in two-seat elections.

That distinction between single and double preferential vote elections is not the district magnitude, per se, but rather, the incentives it yields for parties and voters. Indeed, cross-national analysis and a subnational analysis of Peru both suggest that effective magnitude (in most cases equal to a country's average district magnitude) is not a significant predictor of women's parliamentary presence (Schmidt 2009; Schmidt and Saunders 2004), and the above analyses of candidate performance reveal that district magnitude does not predict women's vote share in Brazil. In Peru, district magnitude is 36 for Lima and Peruvians living abroad and the average across other districts is 3.8. While Peru's larger districts (Lima and Callao) had tended to elect more women than the other (typically rural) districts, Schmidt (2012) attributes that greater performance to cultural and structural (i.e., implications for traditional gender roles of occupational opportunities) rather than institutional factors. And in 2006, the gains in women's representation harkened from outside Lima-Callao (Schmidt 2012). Furthermore, Schmidt (2012) finds that bivariate correlations between women's legislative representation and district magnitude in four election cycles from 1985–2006 are statistically insignificant.

The duality feature of Peru's DOPV system somewhat tempers the tendencies of preferential elections toward personalism. While individual campaigns can and do distribute electoral propaganda, "the leaders of Peruvian parties have usually placed limits on individual campaigns," with a norm against individual television commercials, "which is the most effective way of reaching the electorate" (Schmidt 2012, 167). Such constraints on intra-list competition result in part from "the FREDEMO debacle" of 1990, where intralist competition among candidates from the four parties running on the ticket of presidential candidate and novelist Mario Vargas Llosa's Democratic Front (FREDEMO) took a particularly "tasteless" and ideologically incoherent turn and undermined the presidential candidate's electoral chances (Schmidt 2012).

In 1995, during the tenure of Peru's populist president Alberto Fujimori, the country approved a candidate gender quota for elections, with support from feminist organizations citing the forthcoming Beijing Platform, as well as many female legislators, the national Ombudsperson, and the president himself, whose backing was decisive (Blondet 2000; Flores 2004; Hurtado 2005). The quota was first applied to municipal council (closed-list PR) elections in 1998 and to national congressional elections in 2000 (Rousseau 2009; Schmidt 2017). As discussed in Chapter 3, the effectiveness of quotas in countries with preferential elections is limited by the role of candidate votes in ultimately determining which candidates win seats; parties can put forth 30 percent female candidates and still not elect a single woman. The Peruvian quota has, however, helped to stimulate female candidacies and normalize women in politics (Rousseau 2009). The first congressional elections (2000) after quota implementation yielded more than twice as many female candidates and doubled the proportion of women in the legislature (Flores 2004; Schmidt and Saunders 2004). The quota seemed to have the most pronounced direct effect in the closed-list municipal elections with smaller district magnitudes (in provincial councils and in district councils outside of Lima), where the 30 percent candidate quota becomes an "effective quota" of 40 percent in the standard 5-seat elections (2/5 candidates) (Schmidt 2003a, 2003b, 2012; Schmidt and Saunders 2004). Schmidt and Saunders (2004) attribute gains in Lima's larger district councils to mobilization by feminist activists with the NGO project, PROMUJER (Promotion of Women's Political Participation), who pressured party leaders to nominate women in excess of the quota target and place them in favorable list positions.[10] Moreover, Rousseau cites surveys from Calandria (2000) suggesting that the quota was associated with an "increase in the percentage of Peruvians supporting women's active role in politics" (Rousseau 2009, 133). Yet the country's numerous subnational executive posts, which are not subject to a quota, remain overwhelmingly male dominated; men won 94–97% of the subnational chief executive positions in the 2014 municipal elections (Schmidt 2017).

As with the Brazilian case, the most characteristic element of Peruvian political institutions stems from the party system. In the 1980s to 1990s, the Peruvian party system collapsed; the collective vote share of the country's leading four parties went from 97% in 1985 to only 6% in 1995 (Levitsky 2013). After a brief authoritarian turn under Fujimori, who was twice elected with a personalistic electoral vehicle rather than a party, various electoral reforms were implemented with an eye toward strengthening parties (Levitsky 2013). Yet the seeming "'rebirth' of established parties was illusory," and Peru has since existed as a "democracy without parties" (Levitsky 2013, 294). Even more so than in Brazil, elections in Peru are entrepreneurial endeavors, with individual candidates working with "political operators" and once elected, functioning as "free agents" who "strategically defect" or switch parties to maximize their electoral prospects (Levitsky 2013, 297; Muñoz 2013, 2014). Thus as explained above for Brazil's inchoate parties, political aspirants in Peru have no party organization to depend upon for psychological, organizational, and material support. "Politicians cannot rise up 'through the ranks,' from party activist to local and then national politician. With the partial exception of APRA, 'the ranks' simply do not exist" (Levitsky 2013, 300; Muñoz 2013).

[10] In the 2000 municipal elections, 59% of women candidates were placed by parties in the last half of their lists (Rousseau 2009).

Tellingly, the national parties' share of subnational executive offices has declined; since 2010, most elections for regional president and provincial and district mayor are won by "other political organizations" including regional movements, provincial organizations, and district organizations (Schmidt 2017). The victors of such a fragmented, entrepreneurial system tend to be those who possess independent capital; "they must make a name for themselves or accumulate resources *prior* to entering the political arena" (Levitsky 2013, 300).

That reality bodes poorly for women, who enjoy fewer opportunities to accumulate resources that could be converted into political capital. In Peru men on average earn 20 percent more than women for the same work, and a pervasive raced-gendered "inequality of opportunities" keeps the wage gap intact (Gestión 2014; Gonzalez 2015). Per the argument articulated in this book, this brief analysis of Peru suggests that the country's party organizations lack the capacity to recruit and support viable female candidacies. What then is the source of Peru's relatively strong record on women's representation (27.7%)?

While most "Peruvian parties are notoriously ad hoc and personalistic, they may nevertheless offer varying degrees of support to women running for office" (Schmidt and Saunders 2004, 717). What does party support look like in the Peruvian context, where parties lack organizations? Some examples of that support include help with the congressional campaign; although the bulk of propaganda materials are produced and distributed by candidate campaigns and financed by their personal funds, the party often handles painting walls and radio spots. And parties are responsible for the closed-list municipal council campaigns, in which women tend to perform best with national parties, with higher rates of candidacies and reelection relative to other political organizations (G. Schmidt, personal communication, August 14, 2017; Schmidt 2017).

The parties most likely to extend such resources to women are the national parties. The national parties retain relevance in Lima, where they won 93% of the district mayorships in 2014 (in contrast to just 29% of those posts outside of Lima) (G. Schmidt, personal communication; Schmidt 2017). As suggested by the Brazilian case, women's leadership in those less inchoate organizations may help to explain Peruvian women's unanticipated successes in descriptive representation. Historically, Peru's dominant parties (APRA and *Acción Popular*, AP) "never inserted women on equal terms into their rank and file," and resisted the 1994 proposal by a forum of feminist NGOs, *Foro-Mujer*, supported by an estimated 82.3% of Peruvians, to implement a quota for internal party elections (Rousseau 2009, 132, 143). The intraparty democracy initiative was finally approved in the 2003 provision of the Law of Political Parties, Article 26, which requires parties to include at least 30% women in elections for party leadership (as well as their candidate lists for legislative elections) (Apra 2012; Escobar 2004). Although parties vary in their commitment to those mandates (Manuela 2008), the inclusion of women in party leadership may have, at minimum, created a reservoir of female eligibles to serve as a candidate pool that could be tapped by political organizations seeking to comply with the gender quota.

A glimpse at data from the 2011 elections is suggestive. The participation of women in the executive commission, among candidacies, and elected deputies for the "major" national parties—*Fuerza 2011* (later renamed *Fuerza Popular*), *Perú Posible*, and the Nationalist Party[11]—were, respectively: 44.0/38.0/50.0 percent women in their national executive commissions, 40.7/38.6/40.0 percent women among their congressional candidates, and 24.3/9.5/16.7 percent women among their elected deputies (Inter-American Development Bank 2015). While all three parties met the leadership and candidate quotas, the end result (women elected) varied markedly, with the *Fuerza Popular*'s proportion of female deputies more than doubling the share among *Perú Posible*. The superior performance of the *Fuerza Popular*'s female candidates might be explained by support from party leader, Keiko Fujimori, the daughter of former president Alberto Fujimori, and two-time finalist for president in 2011 and 2016. *Fuerza Popular* doubled its delegation in the 2016 elections, winning a majority (73) of the country's 130 congressional seats and continuing to outperform other parties in terms of women elected. Of the 71 deputies currently serving, 24 (33.8%) are women, and those 24 women are two-thirds of the 36 women elected (*Perú—Congreso de la República, Congresistas* 2017).

By 2012, the average proportion of women in parties' national executive commissions was 40.6%, with a range from 35.7–50.0%, placing Peru at the top of regional assessments, second only to Costa Rica (Llanos and Roza 2015, 12). Yet country experts caution against overinterpreting formal indicators; the reality on the ground is that such party offices typically lack authority or may not even exist. Paula Muñoz characterized Peuvian parties as an "artifact" of the Law of Political Parties rather than genuine organizations (Levitsky 2013; P. Muñoz, personal communication, August 10, 2017).

Yet several women have exercised powerful roles in their parties / electoral vehicles. The 2016 presidential elections were contested by Keiko Fujimori (she also contested the 2011 presidential elections), president of *Fuerza Popular* and Verónika Mendoza, leader of *Frente Amplio*, an alliance of leftist parties (as well as the ultimately victorious male candidate, Pedro Pablo Kuczynski or PPK of *Peruanos Por el Kambio*, a new party with the same acronym). Women

---

[11] Peru has seen substantial volatility in party representation, with the Aprista party, which had been around since 1924, suffering serious setbacks in recent years, and *Cambio 90*, which was formed as an electoral vehicle for Alberto Fujimori in 1990, inconsistent. *Fuerza Popular* is a right-wing party affiliated with Keiko Fujimori. *Perú Posible* is centrist and affiliated with former president Alejandro Toledo. The Nationalist Party is leftist and the party of former president Ollanta Humala.

served as president of the legislature under much of Alberto Fujimori's presidency, and during one year of Ollanta Humala's presidency. PPK's cabinet comprises 31.5 percent women, all in stereotypically feminine posts (education, health, women, environment, justice and human rights, development and social inclusion) (Péres Llosa 2016; Post 2016).

This mini-case study of women's representation in Peru suggests that the country's surprising success is in part associated with the *will* of critical actors to promote women's political participation. In the Brazilian case, I explain how *will* is enabled by women's share of state party offices, with women party leaders well-positioned to perform critical acts advocating to recruit and support viable female candidates. The role of institutionalized parties in furnishing that support for women has proven especially important for mitigating the Brazilian Chamber of Deputies' electoral context ripe with combative intraparty competition. In Peru, as in the Brazilian Senate, constraints on intraparty competition have diminished the salience of party institutionalization for women's electoral prospects. But the willingness of critical actors to perform critical acts supporting women remains pivotal. In the Brazilian Senate, those critical actors tend to be women in party leadership structures. In Peru's "democracy without parties," the critical actors are prominent individuals and feminist NGOs; the presence of Peruvian parties' critical mass of women leaders is suggestive but their precise role in recruiting and supporting female candidates remains unclear.

Female-inclusive decision-making bodies are more likely than male-dominant ones to be knowledgeable of, advocates for, and receptive to measures to enhance women's political participation. Yet as articulated in prior chapters, the presence of female party leaders is not a sufficient condition for the execution of critical acts. Sometimes, as is the case for Peru's gender quota, men emerge as key protagonists in the struggle for women's participation, typically in response to a perceived electoral benefit to be gained from their inclusion. Alberto Fujimori's backing of Peru's gender quota law was essential to its approval, and his general support for women's leadership was conducive to the normalization of women's role in politics (Rousseau 2009).[12] In the post-Fujimori era of "democracy without parties," political elite again saw the electoral utility of including women, who offer political organizations a more novel and honest face to an electorate socialized in *marianismo* and disaffected with formal politics. And the leadership quota for internal party elections has created a pool of eligibles for parties / alliances to tap when creating their candidate lists. A frequent complaint of (predominantly male) party elite in Brazil is that they cannot find women interested in running.

---

[12] Critics counter that Fujimori's emphasis on women's issues served to coopt women voters and the women's movement while currying favor with international audiences, with the goal of expanding his base and legitimizing his increasingly authoritarian regime (Blondet 2000, 2004; Rousseau 2009).

As explained above, such searches are often unsuccessful in inchoate, male-dominant parties because they tend to happen at the final hour with no offer of party support for the candidacy. Peru's quota for internal party elections may appease such grievances by male party elite by offering a visible set of party women—low-hanging fruit even—for the least inclusive political organization.

The work of PROMUJER has also been pivotal in encouraging women to run, training viable female candidates, and helping them to negotiate favorable list positions (Schmidt 2003b; 2017). Although as argued throughout this book, strengthening parties would be a boon to women's participation (Schmidt n.d.), in the interim, the ability of feminist NGOs to fill the gap left by the absence of real party organizations in Peru offers cause for optimism. More generally, discontent with formal politics beckons enhanced participation from civil society. In the United States, feminist NGOs such as EMILY's List (Early Money Is Like Yeast) have played an important role in stimulating and supporting viable female candidacies. In the four months following the election of Donald Trump, EMILY's List was contacted by 10,000 female aspirants, ten times as many as the prior two years combined (Corasaniti 2017). Such increased interest in EMILY's List and similar NGOs is illustrative of how political organizations independent of (or lateral to) traditional political parties can perform critical acts that further inclusion, even in Peru's post-party reality.

While Peru has enjoyed surprising relative successes in women's representation, Panama, which also employs a variant of open-list PR elections for its multimember districts (in addition to a tier elected through single member districts), only recent outranked Brazil in women's parliamentary representation. The 2014 elections doubled Panama's proportion of women elected, rising from 8.5% to 18.3% (Inter-Parliamentary Union 2017). In the 2009 elections, the participation of women in the executive commission, among candidacies, and elected deputies for the top three parties (together winning 87% of the seats)—the *Partido Revolucionario Democrático, Partido Político Panameñista*, and *Cambio Democrático*—were, respectively: 11.1/ 6.7/20.0 percent women in their national executive commissions, 14.3/2.9/12.3 percent women among their congressional candidacies, and 7.7/0.0/16.7 percent women among their elected deputies (Género y Partidos Políticos en América Latina n.d.).

Two tentative patterns emerge from the above data points from Panama and Peru—first, there is substantial interparty variation within Panama, with the party with the highest proportion of women leaders (*Cambio Democrático*—a right-wing party) performing significantly better in terms of women's participation than its coalition partner, the *Partido Político Panameñista*, which had only minimal women in its leadership and an ultimately all-male congressional delegation. Second, the contrast with the Peruvian case is stark—Panama has significantly fewer women in party leadership and in Congress than does Peru despite sharing the open-list electoral context. A key distinction, brought into focus by contrasting among parties within Panama and overall with Peru, is the proportion of women in party leadership. Moreover, as discussed by Schmidt (2003a, 2012, 2017), the excesses of intraparty competition in the Peruvian system are mitigated by party leaders and the dual vote. Yet the party-level data available for the Panamanian case are from 2009 and merit reconsideration in the wake of its 2014 boost in women's legislative representation.

The above discussions of women's political presence in Peruvian and Panamanian parties lend tentative support to my finding that women in party leadership can overcome the problems posed by intraparty competition and improve the situation for female candidates. While we lack cross-national party-level data on party institutionalization, the Peruvian case speaks to the importance of party support even amidst a weakly institutionalized party system and thus echoes the findings of the cross-chamber comparison of women's performance in Chapter 5; the combination of women in party leadership and incentives for unified party support is conducive to the election of women. A quick glance at women's representation in Nicaragua's closed-list elections affirms the generalized relevance of women in party leadership, illustrating the broad scope conditions of that claim.

The Sandinista National Liberation Front (FSLN) adopted a parity statute in all instances of party leadership and candidacies in February 2011 (Radio Primerisima 2011). In November 2016, the FSLN elected a record 36 women deputies—58% of its 62-member delegation, catapulting Nicaragua to 45.7% women in the legislature (up from 21.6% in 2006), 5th in global rankings (Inter-Parliamentary Union 2017). For a point of comparison, in the 2006 elections, Nicaragua's Independent Liberal Party (an offshoot of the Constitutional Liberal Party, which suffered a dramatic defeat in the 2011 elections) had 14.3% women in its national executive committee and elected only 9.1% women of its 22-member delegation.

In sum, preliminary evidence from Latin America provides tentative support for the central findings of this book: (1) parties mediate the effects of electoral rules and are thus the key gatekeepers of political power in Brazil and beyond, and (2) reforms that strengthen parties and incentivize their active promotion of women's political participation within party leadership and as candidates offer the most effective tools for remedying the democratic deficits confronting many countries of the third wave. The comparison with Peru and data points from Panama and the FSLN, together with the Chamber–Senate comparison of Chapter 5 and the intersectional analysis from Chapter 7 yield broad support for the claim that women in party leadership can enhance descriptive representation in legislatures within a variety of electoral contexts. Absent party organizations, NGOs can fill the gap and help women to negotiate with their party/alliance. The scope conditions of the argument about party institutionalization, however, are more limited; strongly institutionalized parties improve the electoral prospects of white women in the context of intraparty competition. When incentives for intraparty competition are mitigated by electoral rules and/or party norms, as in the Brazilian Senate and Peru's DOPV legislative elections, the salience of party institutionalization dissipates.

FUTURE RESEARCH

In a 2008 report on political parties and gender equity, the Inter-American Development Bank (IDB) issued several recommendations of how parties can facilitate the participation of women, drawing on successful examples from throughout the hemisphere. These can be considered "critical acts" (Dahlerup 1988), most likely performed by women in party leadership, which help to introduce a gendered frame of reference to the party. In Costa Rica, the electoral court "established that parties should include in their statutes mechanisms that assure principles of gender equality and non-discrimination and also parity in all party structures (at all levels), and signaled that that it will not register or renew the registration of parties not in compliance with these principles" (Llanos and Sample 2008, 71). Note that gender parity in party leadership is a critical component of this apparent formula for success.

Most of the recommendations echo the findings of this book. Parties should (1) be aware of the electoral utility of reaching out to women, (2) bring women's voice to the decision-making table, (3) incorporate a gendered frame of reference in party statutes and programs of government and require party leadership to endorse those policies, (4) monitor the distribution of public resources such as electoral propaganda time and party funds, (5) devote a party organ to monitoring party compliance with an electoral quota if applicable, (6) mobilize resources for women's participation, (7) empower women's sections, (8) enhance contact with civil society, (9) publicize women's participation, and (10) recruit local leaders (Llanos and Sample 2008, 29). Those recommendations for Latin America and the Caribbean are precisely the kinds of critical acts I have outlined in the discussions above. Yet, many of those critical acts presume a viable party infrastructure, which is not addressed. Future research should embark on a collaborative effort among country experts throughout Latin America to investigate variations in party capacity for executing the critical acts advocated above, the role of party institutionalization in enhancing such capacity, and the implications thereof for the representation of women and minoritized groups.

Moreover, future studies must explicitly consider how political barriers impeding women affect other outsider groups, such as Brazil's marginalized Afro-descendant majority. While this book has illuminated the conditions under which women can(not) acquire political power in the context of candidate-centered elections, Chapter 7 demonstrated the particular barriers confronted by Afro-descendant women, which necessitate a differentiated approach to empowerment capable of mitigating centuries of specifically raced-gendered oppression. An extensive body of literature on intersectionality attests that gender and race cannot be understood independently, and the preliminary analyses offered in Chapter 7 suggest that while the potential gains of democratizing party leadership structures may be beneficial to Afro-descendant and white women, the improved electoral prospects yielded by strengthening parties appear to accrue primarily to white women. Moore's findings on race, gender, and political ambition in the US, where men and women of color were significantly more likely to report political ambition than white respondents (Moore 2005), are suggestive and raise questions about how the various factors constraining and cultivating women's political ambition discussed above might be racialized. Finally, Holmsten, Moser, and Slosar's analysis of ethnic parties' tendency to elect fewer women (2010), and Hughes's cross-national analysis of quotas and minority women's political representation remind us that parties and electoral institutions often affect majority women, minority women, and minority men differently (2011). Future studies should more explicitly examine how various dimensions of marginality intersect and the implications for representation.

Finally, at the root of the literature on women's representation lies a drive to enhance female empowerment. We strive to uncover the often subtle obstacles to women's political empowerment and the paths to surmounting those barriers so as to improve the lot of women, not just in formal politics, but in life. Yet our ability to further such bold objectives is seriously hampered by a sole emphasis on elite political institutions. We must investigate the conditions under which gender equity is broadly realized, integrating studies of formal and informal politics while forging hybrid institutional, agentic, structural, and cultural approaches. The feminist institutionalist (FI) project offers a promising theoretical foundation, and the latest generation of FI scholarship is working to broaden our understanding of political empowerment (Alexander et al. 2016, forthcoming; Majic 2013; Verge and de la Fuente 2014). As posed by Cecilia Blondet, "how do we bridge the chasm, common in our countries, between 'formal' democracy and real democracy, the one in which we live our daily lives, and not just during electoral periods or within the confines of Congress?" (2000, 6). Women's political empowerment cannot be realized until we illuminate, while centering intersectional realities, viable reciprocal mechanisms for connecting societal progress and political presence.

APPENDICES

APPENDIX 4.1

Operationalizing Party Institutionalization and Women in Party Leadership

I operationalize the concepts underlying the two key causal mechanisms examined in this book with original measures based on state parties' organizational reports to the Tribunal Superior Eleitoral (TSE), and assess their impact on women's electoral prospects. My party institutionalization index (PII) is motivated by the widely accepted measure of party system institutionalization advanced by Scott Mainwaring (1999), which helps to compare across countries' party systems rather than across parties within those systems. With 32 decentralized political parties, most of which have 27 distinct state party organizations, national measures of Brazilian parties and the system overall are inherently limited. The PII thus incorporates three of the central mechanisms constituting the concept—electoral stability, societal roots, and party organization (Mainwaring 1999)—into a state party-level measure, lending visibility to both inter- and intra-party variation. It represents a more comprehensive measure, moving beyond the common tendency to use electoral volatility, or the swing in the party vote and seat share from election to election (Pedersen 1979), as a proxy for party institutionalization (e.g., Booth and Robbins 2010; Braga 2010; Mainwaring and Zoco 2007; Tarouco 2010). While electoral volatility is certainly the most amenable to quick quantification, it fails to capture the totality of the concept; an exclusive "focus on volatility would therefore yield important blind spots" (Luna and Altman 2012, 22). By integrating party organizational characteristics into its operationalization, the PII reconstitutes the concept of party institutionalization, joining the growing body of work re-engaging party organization (Scarrow, Webb, and Poguntke 2017).

As discussed in Chapter 2, I conceptualize institutionalized parties as those with established value infusion (Huntington 1968; Janda 1980; Levitsky 1998) and internal "systemness" (Panebianco 1988; Randall and Svåsand 2002). Along with electoral volatility, I incorporate party membership and party age to get at the societal perception or "value infusion" of a party (Ferreira, Batista, and Stabile 2008). A party with no real platform or established significance in the public imagination will be unlikely to attract a consistently sizeable membership or vote/seat share over time, but rather be contingent upon a particular politician/state/time. It will then, as discussed above, be susceptible to personalist politics and less conducive to women's participation. Moreover, a party unable to predict its electoral fortunes across Brazil (due to volatility, newness,[1] and/or a lack of on-the-ground information from members) will be less able to recruit and support candidates.

I measure the internal systemness of each state party by the funds it has at its disposal (Braga and Bourdoukan 2009), its presence throughout the state, and an original measure of whether there exists an alternation in state party leadership. Parties with limited funds (measured relatively, as a state party's share of all party funds in the state) are poorly situated to recruit candidates or provide training opportunities and campaign assistance, and thus lack the capacity to promote women's participation. Candidates running in such parties will be dependent upon their own capital, which due to an un-level playing field is likely to disadvantage women contenders.

I expect that parties with a weak municipal presence—based on the proportion of municipalities in which a party has an active municipal party directorate (not provisional commission)—will be ill-equipped to actively recruit candidates, which will disadvantage women. Parties with a more extensive presence throughout the state will have more contact with municipal leaders and a better network for recruiting potential candidates. Because of the constructed gender gap in political ambition discussed above, parties with no statewide network—which will have to rely largely on self-nomination—are less favorable for women. Parties with a limited municipal presence will also be less able to support candidate campaign efforts, which will deter female contenders by undermining the prospect of a collective campaign.

For the PII's final indicator, I analyzed state party leadership rolls to determine whether there exists alternation in state party leadership. A party that remains dominated by the same president and/or secretary general and vice-president over time is likely to be subordinate to the leader(s), and unlikely to develop as an institution in its own right. Such weakly institutionalized parties will be more dependent upon their leader(s)' image and charisma than on programmatic policy positions and will be highly susceptible to personalist politics, which will disadvantage (most) women contenders. Moreover, because the electoral appeal of such a party is likely contingent upon the particular leader, it is not sustainable. Finally, the leader will fight to maintain his power rather than work to recruit and support independent female candidacies. As discussed further in Appendix 4.2, these six dimensions—volatility, membership, age, funds, municipal presence, and alternation in

---

[1] This raises the question of newness vs. institutionalization, which are distinct. Nevertheless, a truly new party (i.e., did not merely change its name) will likely pose similar barriers to outsider candidates, because they often lack a consolidated party organization to recruit and support candidacies. It is important to note, however, that new parties may very well have a programmatic platform and potentially inclusive structure.

leadership—are each transformed into a 0–1 scale and then summed up to constitute a cumulative index of party institutionalization (PII).

Data on women in party leadership come from the state party leadership rolls, which I use to manually code each individual's sex and the proportion of women. I work with both the proportion of women in state party leadership and a dichotomous coding based on the critical mass approach discussed in Chapter 2; state parties are coded 1 for *critical mass* if at least 25% of their leadership is female.[2]

As we can see from the tables in Appendix 4.2, there is extensive variation in these central variables of interest across Brazilian parties and states. Although the success rate of all female candidates to the Chamber of Deputies is 7.51%, that number conceals a low of 0% in various parties and a high for the PC do B, which has managed to elect more than a quarter of its female candidates. Also evident is that such electoral success is not simply a question of ideology, with more than 20% of the PFL/Democratas female candidates winning election. Yet the measure of candidate success rate by party also obscures relevant information; the parties with more female candidates running will inevitably have a higher denominator in the calculation of success rate, regardless of their actual electoral outcomes. That means that parties running fewer female candidates might enjoy higher success rates. For example, the PFL's 20% success rate belies the fact that a mere 8% of its 1,150 candidates to the Chamber were women, which pales in comparison to the PC do B, which advanced 23% women among its 322 candidates.

Variation across party averages on the PII demonstrates that it is not merely a question of electoral strength, with several small parties such as the PMN (Party of National Mobilization), PSC (Social Christian Party), and PTC (Christian Workers' Party) scoring relatively well. The PP (Progressive Party) and PR (Party of the Republic) are two parties that are fairly strong electorally, each with 8% of the seats in the 2011–15 Chamber of Deputies, but are extremely low on the party institutionalization index, hovering just above one (on a scale of six).

The tables below also show the proportion of parties' state executive commissions across Brazil with a critical mass of women leaders. At the time of the 2010 elections, just over half of the PT state party organizations had a critical mass of women leaders. This is reflective of both the nature of their internal quota, which can be satisfied with posts that do not actually have a voting position on the executive commission, and the relatively large size of their state party leaderships. The two parties that had the highest proportion of state organizations with a critical mass of women are leftist (PSTU and PC do

---

[2] I estimate all models with both the continuous and dichotomous rendering of women in party leadership. While I acknowledge concerns over what is a rather arbitrary cutoff point (25%), I found no statistically significant differences across the estimations, and so report using critical mass, which facilitates interpretation of three-way interactions.

B), but the non-leftist PRTB also performs quite well on this front, with 58% of its state party organizations having at least 25% women, an average proportion of 27%, and 10% comprised by a female majority.

The variation across states in the variables of interest is evident from the tables in Appendix 4.2. The northeast has both the fourth highest success rate—Rio Grande do Norte at 18.9%, and many of the lowest success rates, with only 3–5% of female candidates in three northeastern states winning election and not a single woman winning in Sergipe. The highs for female candidate success rate (Amapá) and average vote share (Acre) are both in the northern Amazonian region. The low average vote share for female candidates in São Paulo reflects the large number of candidates; in 2010, 1,017 candidates sought one of its 70 seats up for grabs.

Variation averaged across state parties on the PII is less informative, since the measure includes each state party's share of statewide affiliates and funds. But the tables in Appendix 4.2 do reveal significant variation in the presence of women in party leadership. The fact that women have struggled to gain election among the more developed southern states is less puzzling once we appreciate women's limited presence in its state party organizations—only 8–20% have a critical mass of women! In contrast, all but two of the eight states in which at least 40% of the party organizations include at least 25% women in their leadership are in the lesser developed northern and northeastern states.

In particular, the tables in Appendix 4.2 display what I argue throughout the book—that there exists significant variation across and within parties, thus rendering inadequate the traditional cross-national aggregate approach. Brazil with its numerous parties is simply not the US, UK, or Mexico. Rather, it implores a lower level analysis that uses the rich interparty variation to illuminate the relationship between parties, voters, and representation. Such variation renders Brazil an excellent selection for the analysis of individual women's representation. Next, I employ that variation to analyze how the central explanatory factors of the literature on women's representation interact to affect individual women's prospects outside the traditional developed and institutionalized contexts.

APPENDIX 4.2

Party Institutionalization Index, Women in Party Leadership, and the Success of Female Candidates to the Chamber of Deputies, by Party and by State (1998–2010)

TABLE A.4.2(a) *Party Institutionalization Index, Women in Party Leadership, and the Success of Female Candidates to the Chamber of Deputies, by Party (1998–2010)*

Party	Average Female Candidate Vote Share	Female Candidate Success Rate	Party Institutionalization Index	Proportion with Critical Mass of Women
PAN	0.02%	0.00%	—	—
PC do B	1.65%	25.33%	2.07	0.75
PCB	0.07%	0.00%	1.68	0.19
PCO	0.01%	0.00%	1.42	0.43
PDT	0.40%	4.52%	2.08	0.25
PFL	1.45%	20.62%	1.70	0.15
PGT	0.05%	0.00%	—	—
PHS/PSN	0.10%	0.00%	1.77	0.13
PMDB	1.43%	18.46%	2.29	0.07
PMN	0.15%	1.06%	2.07	0.64
PP (1994)	2.62%	14.29%	—	—
PP/PPB	0.74%	11.58%	1.38	0.19
PPS	0.25%	1.98%	1.74	0.19
PR/PL	0.23%	3.13%	1.44	0.19
PRB	0.03%	0.00%	1.36	0.48
PRN	0.02%	0.00%	—	—
PRONA	0.08%	1.82%	—	—
PRP	0.04%	0.00%	1.88	0.43
PRTB	0.07%	0.00%	1.68	0.58
PSB	0.62%	9.27%	1.81	0.38
PSC	0.17%	2.97%	2.09	0.09
PSD	0.36%	5.88%	—	—
PSDB	0.83%	13.56%	2.36	0.04
PSDC	0.04%	0.00%	1.60	0.47

(*continued*)

TABLE A.4.2(a) *(continued)*

Party	Average Female Candidate Vote Share	Female Candidate Success Rate	Party Institutionalizati-on Index	Proportion with Critical Mass of Women
PSL	0.11%	0.00%	1.62	0.32
PSOL	0.15%	1.22%	1.82	0.46
PST	0.78%	7.14%	—	—
PSTU	0.06%	0.00%	1.70	0.80
PT	0.86%	16.87%	3.17	0.56
PT do B	0.24%	2.08%	1.65	0.38
PTB	0.26%	2.26%	1.89	0.32
PTC	0.10%	1.47%	2.09	0.18
PTN	0.02%	0.00%	1.76	0.20
PV	0.07%	0.55%	1.81	0.47
Total	0.53%	7.51%	1.90	0.34

TABLE A.4.2(b) *Party Institutionalization Index, Women in Party Leadership, and the Success of Female Candidates to the Chamber of Deputies, by State (1998–2010)*

State	Average Female Candidate Vote Share	Female Candidate Success Rate	Party Institutionaliz-ation Index	Proportion with Critical Mass of Women
Acre — N	2.41%	17.95%	2.02	0.29
Alagoas — NE	1.07%	9.76%	1.69	0.28
Amazonas — N	1.73%	15.00%	2.01	0.33
Amapá — N	2.31%	22.45%	1.98	0.45
Bahia — NE	0.33%	12.70%	1.59	0.31
Ceará — NE	0.14%	3.08%	1.94	0.26
Distrito Federal — CO	0.79%	7.69%	1.98	0.41
Espírito Santo — SE	1.47%	21.05%	1.91	0.47
Goiás — CO	1.49%	20.75%	2.09	0.25
Maranhão — NE	0.66%	9.52%	1.85	0.41
Minas Gerais — SE	0.11%	4.83%	1.86	0.24
M.Grosso do Sul — CO	0.66%	4.48%	2.02	0.30

(continued)

TABLE A.4.2(b) *(continued)*

State	Average Female Candidate Vote Share	Female Candidate Success Rate	Party Institutionaliz-ation Index	Proportion with Critical Mass of Women
Mato Grosso — CO	1.19%	10.71%	2.03	0.23
Pará — N	0.81%	10.81%	1.81	0.33
Paraíba — NE	0.45%	6.06%	1.99	0.35
Pernambuco — NE	0.30%	4.29%	1.82	0.46
Piauí — NE	0.60%	4.26%	2.06	0.39
Paraná — S	0.14%	2.78%	1.77	0.08
Rio de Janeiro — SE	0.12%	5.81%	1.67	0.37
R.G. do Norte — NE	1.89%	18.92%	1.73	0.37
Rondônia — N	1.51%	9.43%	1.89	0.44
Roraima — N	1.18%	10.20%	1.56	0.55
Rio Grande do Sul — S	0.37%	8.33%	2.25	0.20
Santa Catarina — S	0.38%	4.82%	2.42	0.16
Sergipe — NE	0.30%	0.00%	2.02	0.48
São Paulo — SE	0.07%	4.47%	1.81	0.36
Tocantins — N	1.62%	7.84%	1.80	0.30
Total	0.53%	7.51%	1.90	0.34

APPENDIX 4.3

Which Parties Comply with the Gender Quota? (1998–2010)

A.4.3 *Which Parties Comply with the Gender Quota?*

	Model 1			Model 2		
	Odds Ratio	Robust SE		Odds Ratio	Robust SE	
Left	1.417	(0.185)	**	1.262	(0.164)	
Critical mass	—	—		1.750	(0.226)	***
Party institutionalization	1.252	(0.125)	*	1.254	(0.127)	*
N	2192	(691 clusters)		2180	(683 clusters)	
Pseudo R^2	0.008	—		0.019	—	

Note. ***$p<0.001$ **$p<0.01$ *$p<0.05$ (two-tailed tests)

APPENDIX 5.1

Modeling Cross-Chamber Comparison of Women's Electoral Success

The central dependent variable of interest is candidate electoral success. As shown in Figure 5.1, there is a sizeable discrepancy in the electoral threshold across the Senate and Chamber, rendering incomparable the traditional vote share variable. Instead, I code electoral outcome dichotomously, with those elected coded one, and all others coded zero. Given the binary outcome variable, I estimate the below hierarchical logit model, where π_{ij} denotes the probability of individual i in district j getting elected, and u_{ij} is assumed to be normally distributed $(0, \sigma^2)$:

$$log[\pi_{ij}/(1 - \pi_{ij})] =$$

Individual-level model: $\beta_{0\,j} + \beta_{1\,j}$ female$_{ij}$ + $\beta_{2\,j}$ left$_{ij}$ + $\beta_{3\,j}$ female*left$_{ij}$ + $\beta_{4\,j}$ quotas2$_{ij}$ +

$\beta_{5\,j}$female*quotas2$_{ij}$ + $\beta_{6\,j}$senate$_{ij}$ + $\beta_{7\,j}$female*senate$_{ij}$ +
$\beta_{8\,j}$left*senate$_{ij}$ + $\beta_{9\,j}$female*left*senate$_{ij}$ + $\beta_{10\,j}$ c.mass$_{ij}$ +
$\beta_{11\,j}$female*c.mass$_{ij}$ + $\beta_{12\,j}$ c.mass*senate$_{ij}$ +
$\beta_{13\,j}$female*c.mass*senate$_{ij}$ + $\beta_{14\,j}$PII$_{ij}$ + $\beta_{15\,j}$female*PII$_{ij}$ +
$\beta_{16\,j}$education level$_{ij}$ + $\beta_{17\,j}$feeder occupation$_{ij}$ + $\beta_{18\,j}$incumbent$_{ij}$ +
$\beta_{19\,j}$campaign finance$_{ij}$ + $\beta_{20\,j}$campaign finance$^2_{ij}$

District-level model:

$\beta_{0j} = \gamma_{00} + \gamma_{01}$HDI group$_j$ + γ_{02}dmag group$_j$ + γ_{03}eff n cands$_j$ + u_{0j}
$\beta_{1j} = \gamma_{10} + \gamma_{11}$HDI group$_j$ + γ_{12}dmag group$_j$ + γ_{13}eff n cands$_j$ + u_{1j}
$\beta_{2j} = \gamma_{20} + \gamma_{21}$HDI group$_j$
$\beta_{3j} = \gamma_{30} + \gamma_{31}$HDI group$_j$
$\beta_{4j} = \gamma_{40}$
$\beta_{5j} = \gamma_{50}$
$\beta_{6j} = \gamma_{60}$
$\beta_{7j} = \gamma_{70}$
$\beta_{8j} = \gamma_{80}$
$\beta_{9j} = \gamma_{90}$
$\beta_{10j} = \gamma_{100}$
$\beta_{11j} = \gamma_{110}$
$\beta_{12j} = \gamma_{120}$
$\beta_{13j} = \gamma_{130}$

$$\beta_{14j} = \gamma_{140}$$
$$\beta_{15j} = \gamma_{150}$$
$$\beta_{16j} = \gamma_{160}$$
$$\beta_{17j} = \gamma_{170}$$
$$\beta_{18j} = \gamma_{180}$$
$$\beta_{19j} = \gamma_{190}$$
$$\beta_{20j} = \gamma_{200}$$

List of Interviews

* Indicates that the Senator/Deputy responded to my interview questions via questionnaire.

Adami Santos, Regina Célia Santanna. Parliamentary Advisor for the Special Secretariat for Policies for Women. Brasília, Distrito Federal. August 2014; May 2015.

Aleluia, Caroline (PFL-BA). Pre-candidate for Federal Deputy, daughter of longtime politician José Carlos Aleluia. Salvador, Bahia. July 2010.

Almeida, Mônica, and Rose Barreviera (PSB). Parliamentary Assistants to Deputy Sandra Rosado, then President of the Women's Caucus. Brasília, Distrito Federal. December 2008; March 2009; July 2010; April 2012.

Álvares, Dr. Maria Lúcia. Scholar of women and politics. Belém, Pará. May 2009.

Araújo, Dr. Clara. Scholar of women and politics. Rio de Janeiro, Rio de Janeiro. June 2009.

Araújo, Cristina. Activist in the women's movement. Brasília, Distrito Federal. June 2015.

Arraes, Ana (PSB-PE). Federal Deputy. Brasília, Distrito Federal. March 2009.

Ávila, Betânia. Coordinator of SOS Corpo, activist in the women's movement. Recife, Pernambuco. May 2009.

Barbalho, Elcione (PMDB-GO). Brasília, Distrito Federal. August 2014.

Bernardi, Iara (PT-SP). Cabinet Staff. Brasília, Distrito Federal. August 2014.

Bezerra, Fátima (PT-RN). Federal Deputy. Brasília, Distrito Federal. March 2009.

Biancarelli, Aureliano, and Mariangela Ribeiro. Journalists at Instituto Patrícia Galvão. São Paulo, São Paulo. June 2009.

Born, Dr. Kátia (PMDB, PSB). Former two-term mayor, municipal councilwoman (president), unsuccessful candidate to the Chamber of Deputies, president of CUT/AL, State Secretary of Health; then State Secretary of Science, Technology, and Innovation. Maceió, Alagoas. May 2009.

Brietenbach, Zila (PSDB). Two-term State Deputy, PSDB State Secretary General. Porto Alegre, Rio Grande do Sul. June 2009.

Buarque, Cristina Maria. State Secretary of the Special Secretariat for Policies for Women, President of State Council of Women's Rights, scholar of women and politics, activist in the women's movement. Recife, Pernambuco. May 2009.

Callegaro, Vera Lúcia Maróstica (PSDB). President of PSDB Women. Porto Alegre, Rio Grande do Sul. June 2009.

Camata, Rita (PSDB, PMDB-ES). Federal Deputy. Brasília, Distrito Federal. December 2008.

Campos, Eugênia (PSDB). State President of Provisional Commission of PSDB Women. Salvador, Bahia. July 2010.

Campos, Dr. Gervasio (PSDB). Candidate for Federal Deputy. Salvador, Bahia. July 2010.

Cardoso, Ana Cristina Telles (PFL/DEM). State President of Women Democrats. Porto Alegre, Rio Grande do Sul. June 2009.

Carneiro, Professor Aroldo (PC do B). PC do B Secretary of Organization. Belém, Pará. May 2009.

*Cleide, Fátima (PT-RO). Federal Senator. Brasília, Distrito Federal. May 2009.

Cordero, Iara (PT-DF). Assistant to the Secretary of Women—Chamber of Deputies, party militant. Brasília, Distrito Federal. May 2015.

Corrêa, Rosemary (PSDB). President of the State Women's Council, former State Deputy, helped to open the first women's police stations. São Paulo, São Paulo. June 2009.

d'Ávila, Manuela (PC do B-RS). Federal Deputy. Brasília, Distrito Federal. March 2009.

da Costa, Dr. Ana Alice (PT). Scholar of women and politics, activist in the women's movement. Salvador, Bahia. November 2008; April 2009; July 2010.

da Mata, Lídice (PSB-BA). Federal Senator. Salvador, Bahia. April 2009.

da Silva, Benedita (PT). Former Senator, Federal Deputy, Governor, federal Minister, then State Secretary of Social Assistance and Human Rights. Rio de Janeiro, Rio de Janeiro. June 2009.

de Faria, Wilma (PSB). Governor, former Federal Deputy. Natal, Rio Grande do Norte. July 2009.

de Freitas, Rose (PMDB-ES). Federal Deputy, Senator. Brasília, Distrito Federal. December 2008; August 2014.

de Oliveira, Thelma (PSDB-MT). Federal Deputy. Brasília, Distrito Federal. December 2008.

de Souza, Micarla (PV). Former State Deputy, then Mayor. Natal, Rio Grande do Norte. July 2009.

de Souza, Sílvia Rita (PSDB). Assistant to Senator Marisa Serrano, former President of PSDB Women. Brasília, Distrito Federal. December 2008.

Diogo, Cida (PT-RJ). Federal Deputy. Brasília, Distrito Federal. March 2009.

do Amaral, Telma Lililan (PT). PT Secretary of Popular Social Movements. Rio de Janeiro, Rio de Janeiro. June 2009.

Dorigo, Cristina (PT). PT Women's Secretary. Rio de Janeiro, Rio de Janeiro. June 2009.

*Erundina, Luiza (PSB-SP). Federal Deputy. Brasília, Distrito Federal. April 2009.

Fernandes, Angélica (PT). PT State Secretary of Political Formation, member of National Collective of PT Women, party militant, activist in the women's movement. São Paulo, São Paulo. June 2009.

Fernandes, Emília (PTB, PT-RS). Federal Deputy. Brasília, Distrito Federal. April 2009.

Ferreira, Dr. Maria Mary. Scholar of women's participation, activist in the women's movement. São Luis, Maranhão. May 2009.

Freire, Amélia (PSB). State Coordinator of the Special Secretariat for Policies for Women, activist of the women's movement, President of Maria Maria Institute of Studies, Research, and Citizenship. Natal, Rio Grande do Norte. July 2009.

Frossard, Judge Denise (PPS, PSDB). Former Judge, Federal Deputy, candidate for Senate and governor. Rio de Janeiro, Rio de Janeiro. June 2009.

Galvão, Vânia (PT). Municipal councilwoman, PT1 Municipal President. Salvador, Bahia. Trailed campaign September–October 2008; Interviewed July 2009.

Garcia, Rebecca (PP-AM). Federal Deputy. Brasília, Distrito Federal. December 2008; August 2014.

Genro, Luciana (PT, PSOL-RS). Federal Deputy. Brasília, Distrito Federal. December 2008.

Godinho, Tatau (PT). Secretary of Policies for Work and Economic Autonomy for Women for the Special Secretariat for Policies for Women, party militant. Brasília, Distrito Federal. August 2014.

*Gomes, Patrícia Saboya (PDT-CE). Federal Senator. Brasília, Distrito Federal. April 2009.

Helena, Maria (PSDB). State Women's Coordinator. Porto Alegre, Rio Grande do Sul. June 2009.

Henriques, Lurdinha (PSDB-RJ). Party leader, various governmental posts. Rio de Janeiro, Rio de Janeiro. August 2014.

Hoffmann, Gleisi (PT-PR). Senator, party leader, former Chief of Staff for President Dilma Rousseff, candidate for governor. Brasília, Distrito Federal. June 2015.

Jorge, Márcia Andreia (PT). State Coordinator of the Promotion of Women's Rights. Belém, Pará. May 2009.

Jurema, Dr. Solange (PSDB). Former (first) president of the National Council of Women, then State Secretary of Social Assistance and Development. Maceió, Alagoas. May 2009.

Kokay, Erika (PT-DF). Federal Deputy. Brasília, Distrito Federal. August 2014.

Lima, Lenilda (PT). Former candidate for governor, party militant, leader of CUT/AL. Maceió, Alagoas. May 2009.

*Lobão, Nice (PFL-MA). Federal Deputy. Brasília, Distrito Federal. June 2009.

Lopes, Iriny (PT-ES). Federal Deputy. Brasília, Distrito Federal. December 2008.

Madeira, Augusto (PC do B). PC do B Chief of Staff in the Chamber of Deputies, Member of the PC do B Central Committee, party militant. Brasília, Distrito Federal. July 2009.

Magalhaes, Eliana. Political Assistant for the Institute for Socioeconomic Studies (Inesc). Brasília, Distrito Federal. December 2008.

Magalhaes, Tonha (PFL, PR-BA). Federal Deputy. Brasília, Distrito Federal. November 2008.

Maggessi, Marina (PPS-RJ). Federal Deputy. Brasília, Distrito Federal. November 2008.

Marcio (PSDB). PSDB Administrative Secretary, Secretary of Organization. São Luis, Maranhão. May 2009.

Marinho, Gesane (PDT, PMN, PSD). State Deputy (PDT). Natal, Rio Grande do Norte. May 2009.

Martins Caldas, Domingas de Paulo (PT). PT District President, State Women's Secretary, former Secretary of Organization. Belém, Pará. May 2009.

Menezes, Vanda (PDT). Activist in the women's and Black movement, party militant, and former President of the Municipal Council of the Female Condition, State

Secretary of the Special Secretariat for Policies for Women, candidate for vice-mayor. Maceió, Alagoas. May 2009.

Mesquita, Bel (PMDB-PA). Federal Deputy. Brasília, Distrito Federal. December 2008.

Moraes, Jô (PC do B-MG). Federal Deputy. Brasília, Distrito Federal. March 2009.

Morière, Laisy (PT). National PT Women's Secretary. Brasília, Distrito Federal. July 2009; May 2015.

Motta, Diana (PSDB). Omsbudwoman of the National Secretariat of PSDB Women, Director of Management of the Paulista Company Project of Metropolitan Planning and Development, Brasília, Distrito Federal. July 2010.

Nunes, Etelvinio de "Oliveira" (PC do B). PC do B Secretary of Organization, party militant. São Luis, Maranhão. May 2009.

Oliveira, Jusmari (PFL, PR-BA). Federal Deputy. Brasília, Distrito Federal. November 2008.

Paraguassu, Mara (PT). Assistant to former Senator Fátima Cleide and Deputy Padre Ton, scholar of women and politics, party militant. Brasília, Distrito Federal. April 2009; May 2012.

Pedrosa, Eliana (PFL-DF). District Deputy, District Secretary of Tourism. Brasília, Distrito Federal. July 2009.

Pereira, Dâmina (PMN/PMB/PSL-MG). Federal Deputy. Brasília, Distrito Federal. May 2015.

Perondi, Regina (PMDB). Vice-President of PMDB Women, National and State Party Leader. Brasília, Distrito Federal. July 2009.

Picciani, Leonardo (PMDB-RJ). Federal Deputy. Brasília, Distrito Federal. December 2008.

Pietá, Janete Rocha (PT-SP). Federal Deputy. Brasília, Distrito Federal. December 2008.

Pinheiro, Luana. Scholar of women and politics, official at the Federal Secretary of the Special Secretariat for Policies for Women and IPEA. March 2009.

Pinheiro, Telma (PSDB-MA). Former Federal Deputy, unsuccessful candidate for reelection. São Luis, Maranhão. May 2009.

Pinto, Laurinda (PC do B). PC do B State Women's Secretary, PC do B Municipal Secretary of Formation (Training), party militant. São Luis, Maranhão. May 2009.

Portugal, Alice (PC do B-BA). Federal Deputy. Brasília, Distrito Federal. December 2008; August 2014.

PT. Salvador, Bahia. Informal interviews with numerous leaders and members at 2008 municipal campaign events and 2010 state party convention. September–October 2008; July 2010.

Querino, Ana Carolina. Coordinator of Economic Rights Thematic Area for UN Women. April 2012.

Rangel, Patrícia. Researcher at the Feminist Center for Studies and Advisory Services (CFEMEA). September 2008; March 2009.

Rigo, Roseangela Maria. Director of the Subsecretary of Institutional Articulation and Thematic Actions. National Secretary of the Special Secretariat for Policies for Women. April 2012.

Rios, Ana (PMDB). State President of PMDB Women, Director of Loreta Valadares Center of Reference (for victims of domestic violence). July 2010.

Ruiz, Nilmar (PFL-TO). Federal Deputy. Brasília, Distrito Federal. November 2008.

Saiki, Madalena (PFL). President of Women Democrats. Brasília, Distrito Federal. June 2009.

Salazar, Sandro (PMDB). PMDB Coordinator of Working Groups for the National Directorate, party militant, active on women's issues. Brasília, Distrito Federal. July 2010; April 2012.

Santos, Ana Cristina (PC do B). Communications Assistant to Deputy Luciana Santos (PC do B-PE), party mlitant. Brasília, Distrito Federal. May 2012.

Santos, Joseanes (PT). Assistant to the Secretary of Women—Chamber of Deputies, party militant, activist in the women's movement, black movement, and autonomous black women's movement. Brasília, Distrito Federal. May 2015.

Santos, Luislinda Dias de Valois (PSDB-BA). Candidate for Federal Deputy, judge, Secretary for Racial Equality—Ministry of Justice and Citizenship. Salvador, Bahia. August 2015.

Santos, Soraya (PMDB-RJ). Federal Deputy. Brasília, Distrito Federal. May 2015.

Serrano, Marisa (PSDB-MS). Federal Senator. Brasília, Distrito Federal. April 2009.

Silva, Clovis (PC do B). PC do B State Secretary of Unions, party militant. Porto Alegre, Rio Grande do Sul. June 2009.

Slhessarenko, Serys (PT-MT). Federal Senator. Brasília, Distrito Federal. December 2008.

Soares, Cecilia Teixeira. State Superintendent of Women's Rights, President of State Council of Women's Rights. Rio de Janeiro, Rio de Janeiro. June 2009.

Sousa, Regina (PT-PI). Federal Senator, party leader. Brasília, Distrito Federal. May 2015.

Souto, Dona Isabel (PFL). Wife of longtime politician Paulo Souto. Salvador, Bahia. July 2010.

Starling, Sandra (PT). Former Federal and State Deputy, party founder and national and state leader, Municipal Secretary of Education. July 2009.

Suplicy, Marta (PT/PMDB-SP). Senator, former Minister of Culture, Minister of Tourism, Federal Deputy, and Mayor, party leader. Brasília, Distrito Federal. May 2015.

Tabak, Dr. Fanny. Scholar of women and politics, activist in the women's movement. Rio de Janeiro, Rio de Janeiro. June 2009.

Tavares, Dr. Rebecca Reichmann. Regional Director of UN Women. April 2012.

Teixeira, Professor Raquel (PSDB-GO). Federal Deputy. Brasília, Distrito Federal. April 2009.

Vebber, Celica (PT). PT Women's Secretary. Porto Alegre, Rio Grande do Sul. June 2009.

Viana, Raquel (PT). Municipal Special Coordinator of the Special Secretariat for Policies for Women. Fortaleza, Ceará. May 2009.

Viera, Patrícia (PC do B). PC do B State Secretary of Organization, State Coordinator of the Union of Brazilian Women. Salvador, Bahia. July 2009.

Bibliography

Abreu, Cida. 2011, October 5. "Cotas Étnico-Raciais, Por Quê?" *Teoria e Debate* 93. Retrieved from https://teoriaedebate.org.br/2011/10/05/cotas-etnico-raciais-por-que/ (Accessed September 6, 2017)

Acker, Joan. 1990. "Hierarchies, Jobs, Bodies: A Theory of Gendered Organizations." *Gender & Society* 4 (2): 139–158.

——— 1992. "From Sex Roles to Gendered Institutions." *Contemporary Sociology* 21 (5): 565–569.

Affonso, Julia. 2014, October 22. "Procuradoria Revela 31 Candidaturas Fictícias de Mulheres em Minas." *Estadão*. Retrieved from http://politica.estadao.com.br (Accessed August 14, 2015)

Agência Câmara de Notícias. 2008, January 22. "Cidadãos Também Pedem Soluções para Problemas Municipais." Retrieved from www2.camara.leg.br/agencia/ (Accessed March 8, 2018)

——— 2011a, June 16. "Deputada Defende Cotas para Mulheres na Reforma Política." Retrieved from www2.camara.leg.br/agencia/ (Accessed March 8, 2018)

——— 2011b, August 17. "Pesquisa com Disque-Câmara Revela Preferências sobre Reforma Política." Retrieved from www2.camara.leg.br/agencia/noticias.html (Accessed March 8, 2018)

Agência de Notícias da Justiça Eleitoral. 2010a, August 3. "TRE-SP Define Não Obrigatoriedade da Cota de 30% dos Registros de Candidatura para Mulheres." Retrieved from http://agencia.tse.gov.br (Accessed May 15, 2012)

——— 2010b, August 12. "TSE Determina que o PDT-PA Cumpra os Percentuais Mínimo e Máximo de Candidatos por Sexo." Retrieved from http://agencia.tse.gov.br (Accessed March 8, 2018)

Agência Patrícia Galvão. 2010. "Agora é para Valer: Cota de 30% de Mulheres será Exigida nas Eleições de 2010." Retrieved from https://agenciapatriciagalvao.org.br (Accessed March 8, 2018)

——— 2011, September 5. "Com Mais Mulheres na Direção dos Partidos, Haverá Mais Mulheres no Executivo e no Legislativo, Diz José Eustáquio Diniz Alves." Retrieved from http://agenciapatriciagalvao.org.br (Accessed March 8, 2018)

Agência PT. 2015, 18 November. "Em Ato Histórico, Marcha das Mulheres Negras Reúne mais de 4 Mil em Brasília." Retrieved from https://pt.org.br (Accessed May 3, 2016)

Aggege, Soraya. 2011, September 3. "No PT, Mulheres Tomam o Poder." *Carta Capital.* Retrieved from https://cartacapital.com.br (Accessed March 8, 2018)

Alexander, Amy, Catherine Bolzendahl, and Farida Jalalzai. 2016. "Defining Women's Global Political Empowerment: Theories and Evidence." *Sociology Compass* 10 (6/June): 432–441.

2018. *Measuring Women's Political Empowerment across the Globe: Strategies, Challenges and Future Research.* New York: Palgrave Macmillan.

Almeida, Cleomar. 2011, June 6. "Raquel Teixeira Troca Política pela Fundação Jaime Câmara." *Jornal Opção.* Retrieved from https://jornalopcao.com.br (Accessed March 8, 2018)

Álvares, Maria Luzia Miranda. 2004. "Mulheres na Competição Eleitoral: Seleção de Candidaturas e o Padrão de Carreira Política no Brasil." Ph.D. Dissertation, IUPERJ.

Alvarez, Sonia. 1990. *Engendering Democracy in Brazil: Women's Movements in Transition Politics.* Princeton, NJ: Princeton University Press.

Alves, Jaime Amparo. 2014. "Neither Humans nor Rights: Some Notes on the Double Negation of Black Life in Brazil." *Journal of Black Studies* 45 (2): 143–162.

Amaral, Oswaldo E. do. 2013. *As Transformações na Organização Interna do Partido Dos Trabalhadores entre 1995 e 2009.* São Paulo: Alameda/Fapesp.

Ames, Barry. 1995. "Electoral Strategy under Open-List Proportional Representation." *American Journal of Political Science* 39 (May): 406–433.

2001. *The Deadlock of Democracy in Brazil.* Ann Arbor, MI: University of Michigan Press.

Anzia, Sarah, and Christopher Berry. 2011. "The Jackie (and Jill) Robinson Effect: Why Do Congresswomen Outperform Congressmen?" *American Journal of Political Science* 55 (3): 478–493.

Apra. 2012. "En Pos de la Igualdad de Resultados." Retrieved from https://apra.org.pe/dest_p_equidad.asp (Accessed March 8, 2018)

Araújo, Clara. 1999. "Cidadania Incompleta: O Impacto da Lei de Cotas Sobre a Representação Política das Mulheres no Brasil." Ph.D. dissertation, Universidade Federal do Rio de Janeiro (UFRJ).

2001a. "Potencialidades e Limites da Política de Cotas no Brasil." *Revista Estudos Feministas* 9 (1): 231–252.

2001b. "As Cotas por Sexo para a Competição Legislativa: O Caso Brasileiro em Comparação com Experiências Internacionais." *Dados* 44 (1). Retrieved from http://ref.scielo.org/jdqtz6 (Accessed July 15, 2015)

2005. "Partidos Políticos e Gênero: Medições nas Rotas de Ingresso das Mulheres na Representação Política." *Revista de Sociologia e Política* 24 (June): 193–215.

2017. "Electoral Quotas at the National Level in Brazil: An Arduous Road to Nowhere?" In Adriana Piatti-Crocker, Gregory D. Schmidt, and Clara Araújo *Gender Quotas in South America's Big Three: National and Subnational Impacts.* Lanham, MD: Lexington Books, 77–96.

Araújo, Clara, and Jose Eustáquio Diniz Alves. 2007. "Impactos de Indicadores Sociais e do Sistema Eleitoral sobre as Chances das Mulheres nas Eleições e suas Interações com as Cotas." *DADOS – Revista de Ciências Sociais* 50 (3): 535–577.

Araújo, Clara, and Ana Isabel Garcia. 2006. "Latin America: The Experience and the Impact of Quotas in Latin America." In Drude Dalhrup (ed.) *Women, Quotas, and Politics.* New York: Routledge, 83–111.

Avelar, Lúcia. 2001. *Mulheres na Elite Política Brasileira* (2nd edn). São Paulo, Brazil: Fundação Konrad Adenauer.

Avon Institute / Ipsos. 2011. "Pesquisa Percepções sobre a Violência Doméstica contra a Mulher no Brasil." Survey, conducted January 31–February 10. Retrieved from http://compromissoeatitude.org.br/wp-content/uploads/2012/08/Avon-Ipsos-pesquisa -violencia-2011.pdf (Accessed March 8, 2018)

Bailey, Stanley R., and Edward E. Telles. n.d. "From Ambiguity to Affirmation: Challenging Census Race Categories in Brazil." Retrieved from https://sscnet.ucla .edu/soc/faculty/telles/Paper_AffirmationandAmbiguity.pdf (Accessed December 10, 2015)

Baldez, Lisa. 2004. "Elected Bodies: The Gender Quota Law for Legislative Candidates in Mexico." *Legislative Studies Quarterly* 29 (2): 231–258.

Ballington, Julie, and Azza Karam (eds.). 2005. *Women in Parliament: Beyond Numbers* (2nd edn). Stockholm: International Institute for Democracy and Electoral Assistance.

Barnes, Tiffany, and Emily Beaulieu. 2014. "Gender Stereotypes and Corruption: How Candidates Affect Perceptions of Election Fraud." *Politics & Gender* 10 (3): 365–391.

Banco Central. 2009. "Evolução do IDH das Grandes Regiões e Unidades da Federação." Boletim Regional do Banco Central do Brasil. Retrieved from www .bcb.gov.br (Accessed March 8, 2018)

Barba, Mariana Della. 2014, December 18. "Lei Abre Brecha para Desrespeito à Cota de Candidatas Mulheres." BBC Brasil. Retrieved from https://bbc.com (Accessed August 14, 2015)

Barnes, Tiffany D., and Emily Beaulieu. 2014. "Gender Stereotypes and Corruption: How Candidates Affect Perceptions of Election Fraud." *Politics & Gender* 10 (3): 365–391.

Barnett, Bernice McNair. 1993. "Invisible Southern Black Women Leaders in the Civil Rights Movement: The Triple Constraints of Gender, Race, and Class." *Gender & Society* 7 (2): 162–182.

Beckwith, Karen. 2005. "A Common Language of Gender?" *Politics & Gender* 1 (1): 128–137.

2007. "Numbers and Newness: The Descriptive and Substantive Representation of Women." *Canadian Journal of Political Science* 40 (1): 27–49.

2015. "State, Academy, Discipline: Regendering Political Science." *PS: Political Science & Politics* 48 (July): 445–449.

Beckwith, Karen, and Melody Cowell-Meyers. 2007. "Sheer Numbers: Critical Representation Thresholds and Women's Political Representation." *Perspectives on Politics* 5 (3): 553–565.

Bejarano, Christina E. 2013. *The Latina Advantage: Gender, Race, and Political Success*. Austin: University of Texas Press.

Benites, Afonso. 2015, September 17. "STF Decreta o Fim das Doações de Empresas para Campanhas Eleitorais." El País. http://brasil.elpais.com (Accessed September 2, 2016)

Bethell, Leslie, and José Murilo de Carvalho. 1985. "Brazil from Independence to the Middle of the Nineteenth Century." In Leslie Bethell (ed.) *The Cambridge History of Latin America, Vol. III: From Independence to c.1870*. Cambridge, UK: Cambridge University Press, 679–746.

Bezerra, Mirthyani. 2017. "Políticos Querem Fundo de R$ 3,5 Bi para Baratear Eleição de 2018. De Onde Vai Sair?" *UOL Notícias Política*. Retrieved from https://noticias .uol.com.br/politica/ultimas-noticias/2017/07/26/de-onde-os-politicos-querem-tirar-r-35-bi-para-financiar-a-campanha-de-2018.htm (Accessed September 30, 2017)

Bird, Karen. 2014. "Ethnic Quotas and Ethnic Representation Worldwide." *International Political Science Review* 35 (1): 12–26.

Bjarnegård, Elin. 2013. *Gender, Informal Institutions and Political Recruitment: Explaining Male Dominance in Parliamentary Representation*. New York, NY: Palgrave Macmillan.

Bjarnegård, Elin, and Meryl Kenny. 2016. "Comparing Candidate Selection: A Feminist Institutionalist Approach." *Government and Opposition* 51 (3): 370–392.

Black Women of Brazil. 2013, September 2. "According to Data, Brazil's Black Population has Surpassed 100 Million; As a Whole Brazil has Passed the 200 Million Mark." http://blackwomenofbrazil.co (Accessed November 19, 2015)

Blondet, Cecilia. 2000. "Lessons from the Participation of Women in Politics." In *Politics Matter: A Dialogue of Women Political Leaders*. Washington, DC: Inter-American Dialogue.

———. 2004. *Lecciones de la Participación Política de las Mujeres*. Geneva, Switzerland: Instituto de Investigación de las Naciones Unidas para el Desarrollo Social (UNRISD).

Bohn, Simone. 2007. "Women and Candidate Quality in the Elections for the Senate; Brazil and the United States in Comparative Perspective." *Brazilian Political Science Review* 1 (2): 74–107.

Booth, Eric, and Joseph Robbins. 2010. "Assessing the Impact of Campaign Finance on Party System Institutionalization." *Party Politics* 16 (September): 629–650.

Borges, Larissa Amorim. 2015. "Ações e Reflexões Sobre o Enfrentamento a Violência Contra a Juventude Negra." Presentation on behalf of the Special Secretariat for Policies Geared towards the Promotion of Racial Equality and the Secretariat of Affirmative Action Policies.

Bourdieu, Pierre. 1986. "The Forms of Capital." In J. Richardson (ed.) *Handbook of Theory and Research for the Sociology of Education*. New York, NY: Greenwood, 241–258.

Bourque, Susan, and Jean Grossholtz. 1998. "Politics an Unnatural Practice: Political Science Looks at Female Participation." In Anne Phillips (ed.) *Feminism & Politics*. New York, NY: Oxford University Press, 23–43.

Braga, Maria do Socorro Sousa. 2008. "Organizações Partidárias e Seleção de Candidatos no Estado de São Paulo." *Opinião Pública* 14 (2): 454–485.

———. 2010. "Eleições e Democracia no Brasil: A Caminho de Partidos e Sistema Partidário Inistitucionalizados." *Revista Brasileira de Ciência Política* 4: 43–73.

Braga, Maria do Socorro Sousa, and Adla Bourdoukan. 2009. "Partidos Políticos no Brasil: Organização Partidária, Competitição Eleitoral e Financiamento Público." *Perspectivas* 35: 117–148.

Brazilian Institute of Geography and Statistics (IBGE). 2008. "Histórico da Investigação sobre Cor ou Raça nas Pesquisas Domiciliares do IBGE." https://ibge.gov.br (Accessed December 10, 2015)

———. 2009. "Pesquisa Nacional por Amostra de Domicílios." Survey. Retrieved from www .ibge.gov.br (Accessed March 8, 2018)

2010. "Pesquisa Mensal de Emprego – Mulher no Mercado de Trabalho: Perguntas e Respostas." Survey. Retrieved from https://ibge.gov.br (Accessed March 8, 2018)

2013. "Pesquisa Nacional por Amostra de Domicílios (PNAD)." Survey. Retrieved from https://ibge.gov.br (Accessed March 8, 2018)

2015. *Síntese de Indicadores Sociais: Uma Análise das Condições de Vida da População Brasileira.* http://biblioteca.ibge.gov.br/visualizacao/livros/liv95011.pdf (Accessed December 10, 2015)

Brazilian Institute of Public Opinion and Statistics (IBOPE). 2009, February. *Mulheres na Política.* Retrieved from https://agenciapatriciagalvao.org.br (Accessed March 25, 2009)

2013. *Mais Mulheres na Política.* http://agenciapatriciagalvao.org.br/wp-content/uploads/2013/07/mais_mulheres_politica.pdf (Accessed December 10, 2015)

Brown, Nadia E. 2014. "Political Participation of Women of Color: An Intersectional Analysis." *Journal of Women, Politics & Policy* 35 (4): 315–348.

Bueno, Natália S., and Thad Dunning. 2013. "Race, Resources, and Representation: Evidence from Brazilian Politicians." Presented at the Universidade de São Paulo and the Annual Meeting of the Midwest Political Science Association, Chicago.

Burrell, Barbara. 2006. "Political Parties, Women's Organizations and Efforts to Recruit Women Candidates." In Susan J. Carroll and Richard L. Fox (eds.) *Gender and Elections: Change and Continuity.* New York, NY: Cambridge University Press, 184–202.

Cain, Bruce, John Ferejohn, and Morris Fiorina. 1987. *The Personal Vote: Constituency Service and Electoral Independence.* Cambridge, MA: Harvard University Press.

Caldwell, Kia Lilly. 2007. *Negras in Brazil: Re-envisioning Black Women, Citizenship, and the Politics of Identity.* New Brunswick, NJ: Rutgers University Press.

Câmara Notícias. 2017a, July 13. "Relator Apresenta Novo Texto da Reforma Política Que Prevê R$ 3,5 Bi para Financiar Eleições de 2018." *Câmara Notícias.* Retrieved from www2.camara.leg.br (Accessed September 30, 2017)

Câmara Notícias. 2017b, July 25. "Congresso Enfrenta Reforma Política Após o Recesso Parlamentar." *Câmara Notícias.* Retrieved from www2.camara.leg.br (Accessed September 30, 2017)

Campell, Rosie, and Sarah Childs (eds.). 2014. *Deeds and Words: Gendering Politics after Joni Lovenduski.* Colchester, UK: ECPR Press.

Capone, Stefania. 2010. *Searching for Africa in Brazil: Power and Tradition in Candomblé.* Durham, NC: Duke University Press.

Carey, John, and Simon Hix. 2011. "The Electoral Sweet Spot: Low Magnitude Proportional Electoral Systems." *American Journal of Political Science* 55 (2): 383–397.

Carey, John, and Matthew Soberg Shugart. 1995. "Incentives to Cultivate a Personal Vote: A Rank Ordering of Electoral Formulas." *Electoral Studies* 14 (4): 417–439.

Carneiro, Sueli. 1999. "Black Women's Identity in Brazil." In Rebecca Reichmann (ed.) *Race in Contemporary Brazil: From Indifference to Inequality.* University Park, PA: Penn State Press, 217–228.

Carroll, Susan, and Kira Sanbonmatsu. 2013. *More Women Can Run: Gender and Paths to State Legislatures.* New York, NY: Oxford University Press.

Carta Capital. 2015, July 15. "Temer Diz que PMDB Quer Ter Candidato Próprio à Presidência em 2018." Retrieved from https://cartacapital.com.br (Accessed July 16, 2015)

Carvalho, Eder Aparecido de. 2006. "O Sistema Eleitoral Brasileiro: Uma Análise sobre a Questão da Desproporcionalidade." Master's Thesis. Universidade Federal de São Carlos.

Caul, Miki. 1999. "Women's Representation in Parliament: The Role of Political Parties." *Party Politics* 5 (1): 79–98.

2001. "Political Parties and the Adoption of Candidate Gender Quotas: A Cross-National Analysis." *Journal of Politics* 63 (4): 1214–1229.

Celis, Karen, Silvia Erzeel, Liza Mügge, and Alyt Damstra. 2014. "Quotas and Intersectionality: Ethnicity and Gender in Candidate Selection." *International Political Science Review*, 35 (1): 41–54.

Celis, Karen, Johanna Kantola, Georgina Waylen, and S. Laurel Weldon. 2013. "Gender and Politics: A Gendered World, A Gendered Discipline." In Georgina Waylen, Karen Celis, Johanna Kantola, and Laurel Weldon (eds.) *The Oxford Handbook of Gender and Politics*. Oxford, UK: Oxford University Press, 1–26.

Center for Studies and Advisory Services (CFEMEA). 2009. *Como Parlamentares Pensam os Direitos das Mulheres?* Retrieved from https://observatoriodegenero.gov.br/menu/noticias/arquivos/pesquisa-cfemea-parlamentares (Accessed March 8, 2018)

Center of Studies and Public Opinion (CESOP), 2010. *Brazilian Electoral Study* (ESEB). Universidade Estadual de Campinas: São Paulo, Brazil.

Chamber of Deputies. 2012. Author Analysis of Legislative Proposals. Retrieved from https://camara.gov.br/sileg/default.asp (Accessed September 17, 2012)

2015. Author Analysis of Deputy Biographies. Retrieved from www2.camara.gov.br/deputados/pesquisa (Accessed March 22, 2016)

Chaney, Elsa. 1979. *Supermadre: Women in Politics in Latin America*. Austin, TX: University of Texas Press.

Childs, Sarah, 2013. "Intra-Party Democracy: A Gendered Critique and a Feminist Agenda." In William P. Cross and Richard S. Katz (eds.) *The Challenges of Intra-Party Democracy*. Oxford, UK: Oxford University Press, 81–99.

Childs, Sarah, and Mona Lena Krook. 2006. "Gender and Politics: The State of the Art." *Gender & Politics* 26 (1): 18–28.

2008. "Critical Mass Theory and Women's Representation." *Political Studies* 56: 725–736.

2009. "Analysing Women's Substantive Representation: From Critical Mass to Critical Actors." *Government and Opposition* 44 (2): 125–145.

Childs, Sarah, and Joni Lovenduski. 2013. "Political Representation." In Georgina Waylen, Karen Celis, Johanna Kantola, and Laurel Weldon (eds.) *The Oxford Handbook of Gender and Politics*. Oxford, UK: Oxford University Press, 489–513.

Childs, Sarah, and Rainbow Murray. 2014. "Feminising Political Parties." In Rosie Campbell and Sarah Childs (eds.) *Deeds and Words: Gendering Politics after Joni Lovenduski*. London: European Consortium for Political Research Press, 73–90.

Clayton, Amanda. 2014. "Beyond Presence: Gender Quotas, Female Leadership, and Symbolic Representation." Ph.D. Dissertation. University of Washington. https://digital.lib.washington.edu/researchworks/handle/1773/26160 (Accessed March 8, 2018)

Coelho, Mário, and Sylvio Costa. 2010, August 14. "TSE Exigirá Cumprimento de Cotas para Mulheres." Retrieved from http://congressoemfoco.uol.com.br (Accessed March 8, 2018)

Cole, Elizabeth R. 2008. "Coalitions as a Model for Intersectionality: From Practice to Theory." *Sex Roles* 59 (5): 443–453.

———. 2015, November 6. "Building 'Brave Spaces': Coalition across Difference in Social Justice Work." Keynote Address at Diversity Teach-In: Intersectionality In Action, James Madison University.

Collins, Patricia H. 2000. *Black Feminist Thought: Knowledge, Consciousness and the Politics of Empowerment*. London: Harper Collins.

Congresso em Foco. 2011, April 7. "Os Senadores e Seus Parentes na Política." Retrieved from http://congressoemfoco.uol.com.br (Accessed March 8, 2018)

———. 2012, June 4. "Quase 20% dos Congressistas Disputarão Prefeituras." Retrieved from http://congressoemfoco.uol.com.br (Accessed March 8, 2018)

———. 2014, December. *O Brasil que Esconde a sua Cor*. Retrieved from http://revista.congressoemfoco.uol.com.br/2014/12/revista-congresso-em-foco-no14/ (Accessed April 6, 2017)

———. 2015, September 29. "Dilma Sanciona, com Vetos, Projeto de 'Minirreforma Eleitoral.'" http://congressoemfoco.uol.com.br (Accessed September 2, 2016)

Corasaniti, Nick. 2017, March 22. "Roused by Trump, First-Time Female Candidates Eye Local Seats." *The New York Times*. https://nytimes.com/2017/03/22/nyregion/women-state-local-government.html (Accessed August 15, 2017)

Correll, Shelley, Sarah Thébaud, and Stephen Benard. 2007. "An Introduction to the Social Psychology of Gender." In Shelly Correll (ed.) *Social Psychology of Gender (Advances in Group Processes Volume 24)*. New York, NY: Elsevier, 1–18.

Costa, Ana Alice Alcântara. 2008. "Women and Politics: The Brazil Paradox." *Open Democracy*. Retrieved from https://opendemocracy.net (Accessed March 8, 2018)

Costa, Ana Alice, and Andrea Cornwall. 2014. "Conservative Modernization in Brazil: Blocking Local Women's Political Pathways to Power." *Revista Feminismos* 2 (2): 83–94.

Costa Benavides, Jimena. 2003. "Women's Political Participation in Bolivia: Progress and Obstacles." Presented at the International Institute of Democracy and Electoral Assistance Workshop, The Implementation of Quotas: Latin American Experiences, Lima, Peru.

Covin, David. 2006. *The Unified Black Movement in Brazil, 1978–2002*. Jefferson, NC: McFarland & Company.

Cox, Gary. 1997. *Making Votes Count: Strategic Coordination in the World's Electoral Systems*. Cambridge, UK: Cambridge University Press.

Crawford, Vicki L., Jacqueline Anne Rouse, and Barbara Woods (eds.). 1993. *Women in the Civil Rights Movement: Trailblazers and Torchbearers, 1941–1965*. Bloomington: Indiana University Press.

Crenshaw, Kimberlé W. 1989. "Demarginalizing the Intersection of Race and Sex: A Black Feminist Critique of Antidiscrimination Doctrine, Feminist Theory and Antiracist Politics." *University of Chicago Legal Forum* 139: 139–167.

———. 1995. "Mapping the Margins: Intersectionality, Identity Politics, and Violence against Women of Color." In Kimberlé Crenshaw (ed.) *Critical Race Theory: The Key Writings that Formed the Movement*. New York, NY: The New Press, 357–383.

Crowder-Meyer, Melody. 2013. "Gendered Recruitment without Trying: How Local Party Recruiters Affect Women's Representation." *Politics & Gender* 9 (4): 390–413.

Crowder-Meyer, Melody, Shana Kushner Gadarian, and Jessica Trounstine. 2015. "Electoral Institutions, Gender Stereotypes, and Women's Local Representation." *Politics, Groups, and Identities* 3 (2): 318–334.

Cunow, Saul. 2010. "Party Switching and Legislative Behavior: Evidence from Brazil's National and Subnational Legislatures of the Impact of Party Switching on Legislative Behavior." Presented at the Annual Meeting of the Midwest Political Science Association, Chicago, IL.

Czudnowski, Moshe M. 1975. "Political Recruitment." In Fred I. Greenstein and Nelson W. Polsby (eds.) *Handbook of Political Science*, Vol. 2. Reading, MA: Addison-Wesley.

Da Costa, Alexandre Emboaba. 2014. *Reimagining Black Difference and Politics in Brazil: From Racial Democracy to Multiculturalism*. New York, NY: Palgrave Macmillan.

Dahlerup, Drude. 1988. "From a Small to a Large Minority: Women in Scandinavian Politics." *Scandinavian Political Studies* 11 (4): 275–297.

2006a. "The Story of the Theory of Critical Mass." *Politics & Gender* 2 (4/ December): 511–522.

2006b. *Women, Quotas, and Politics*. New York, NY: Routledge.

Dalton, Russell, and Christopher Anderson. 2011. *Citizens, Context, and Choice: How Context Shapes Citizens' Electoral Choices*. New York, NY: Oxford University Press.

Darcy, Robert, Susan Welch, and Janet Clark. 1994. *Women, Elections, and Representation*. New York, NY: Longman.

Davidson-Schmich, Louise K. 2010. "Gender Quota Compliance and Contagion in the 2009 Bundestag Election." *German Politics & Society* 28 (3): 133–155.

Departamento Intersindical de Assessoria Parlamentar (DIAP). 2016, August 16. "83 Parlamentares são Candidatos às Eleições de 2016." Retrieved from https://diap.org .br (Accessed March 8, 2018)

Departamento Intersindical de Estatística e Estudos Socioeconômicos (DIEESE). 2011. *Anuário das Mulheres Brasileiras*. São Paulo: DIEESE.

Desidério, Mariana. 2011, August 9. "28% das Mulheres Assassinadas no País Morrem em Casa." *Folha de São Paulo*. Retrieved from https://folha.uol.com.br/ (Accessed March 8, 2018)

Desposato, Scott. 2006. "The Impact of Electoral Rules on Legislative Parties: Lessons from the Brazilian Senate and Chamber of Deputies." *Journal of Politics* 68 (4): 1018–1030.

Diário do Grande ABC. 2010, November 7. "Efeito Dilma Não Chega ao Congresso." Retrieved from https://dgabc.com.br (Accessed May 15, 2012)

Diário do Turismo. 2011, June 22. "Três Perguntas a Bel Mesquita, Secretária de Políticas de Turismo." Retrieved from https://diariodoturismo.com.br (Accessed May 15, 2012)

Dix, Robert. 1992. "Democratization and the Institutionalization of Latin American Political Parties." *Comparative Political Studies* 24 (4): 488–511.

Dixon, William. 1993. "Democracy and the Management of International Conflict." *The Journal of Conflict Resolution* 37 (1): 42–68.

Downie, Andrew, and Sara Miller Llana. 2009, October 13. "Latin America's Worst Wage Gap for Women and Minorities? Powerhouse Brazil." *Christian Science Monitor*. Retrieved from https://csmonitor.com (Accessed March 8, 2018)

Duerst-Lahti, Georgia, and Rita Mae Kelly. 1995.*Gender, Power, Leadership, and Governance*. Ann Arbor: The University of Michigan Press.

Dunning, Thad. 2010. "Race, Class, and Voter Preferences in Brazil." Presented at the Annual Meeting of the Latin American Studies Association, Toronto, Canada.

Duverger, Maurice. 1954. *Political Parties: Their Organization and Activity in the Modern State*. New York, NY: John Wiley and Sons.

1955. *The Political Role of Women*. New York, NY: Wiley and Sons.

Eckel, Catherine, and Philip Grossman. 2008. "Differences in the Economic Decisions of Men and Women: Experimental Evidence." In Charles Plott and Vernon Smith (eds.) *Handbook of Experimental Economics Results, Volume I*. North Holland: Linacre House, 509–519.

Eilperin, Juliet. 2016, September 13. "White House Women Want to Be in the Room Where It Happens." *The Washington Post*. Retrieved from https://www .washingtonpost.com (Accessed September 30, 2017)

Eleições 2010: Ascensão da Mulher na Política. 2010. Interview with Deputy Manuela d'Ávila. Retrieved from http://eleicoes2010mulhernopoder.blogspot.com (Accessed March 8, 2018)

Ellis, Melody. 2002. "Gender Disparity in Representation: The Effect of Preference Voting in Italy and Japan." Presented at the Annual Meeting of the American Political Science Association, Boston.

Eltis, David, and David Richardson. 2010. *Atlas of the Transatlantic Slave Trade*. New Haven, CT: Yale University Press.

Escobar, Guillermo. 2004. *II Informe FIO sobre Derechos Humanos: Derechos de la Mujer*. Madrid: Federación Iberoamericana de Ombudsman (FIO).

Escobar-Lemmon, Maria, and Michelle Taylor-Robinson. 2005. "Women Ministers in Latin American Government: When, Where, and Why?" *American Journal of Political Science* 49 (4): 822–844.

2008. "How Do Candidate Recruitment and Selection Processes Affect Representation of Women?" In Scott Morgenstern and Peter Siavelis (eds.) *Pathways to Power: Political Recruitment and Candidate Selection in Latin America*. University Park, PA: Penn State University, 345–370.

Farris, Emily M., and Mirya R. Holman. 2014. "Social Capital and Solving the Puzzle of Black Women's Political Participation." *Politics, Groups, and Identities* 2 (3): 331–349.

Federal Senate. 2015. Author Analysis of Senator Biographies. Retrieved from https:// www25.senado.leg.br/web/senadores (Accessed September 6, 2017)

Fêmea. 2004, July. Brasília: Center for Studies and Advisory Services (CFEMEA). Retrieved from https://cfemea.org.br/images/stories/colecaofemea/jornalfemea135 .pdf (Accessed March 8, 2018)

2006a, April–July. Brasília: Center for Studies and Advisory Services (CFEMEA). Retrieved from https://cfemea.org.br/images/stories/colecaofemea/jornalfemea150 .pdf (Accessed March 8, 2018)

2006b, August–December. Brasília: Center for Studies and Advisory Services (CFEMEA). Retrieved from https://cfemea.org.br/images/stories/colecaofemea/ jornalfemea151.pdf (Accessed March 8, 2018)

Ferrara, Federico. 2004. "Frogs, Mice and Mixed Electoral Institutions: Party Discipline in Italy's XIV Chamber of Deputies." *The Journal of Legislative Studies* 10 (4): 10–31.

Ferreira, Denise Paiva, Carlos Marcos Batista, and Max Stabile. 2008. "A Evolução do Sistema Partidário Brasileiro: Número de Partidos e Votação no Plano Subnacional 1982–2006." *Opinião Pública* 14 (2): 432–453.

Ficha Limpa. 2012. Retrieved from http://fichalimpa.org.br (Accessed September 22, 2012)

Figueiredo, Argelina Cheibub, and Fernando Limongi. 1999. *Executivo e Legislativo na Nova Ordem Constitucional*. Rio de Janeiro, Brazil: FAPESP/Editora Fundação Getúlio Vargas.

2000. "Presidential Power, Legislative Organization, and Party Behavior in Brazil." *Comparative Politics* 32 (2): 151–170.

Finamore, Claudia Maria, and João Eduardo Coin de Carvalho. 2006. "Mulheres Candidatas: Relações entre Gênero, Mídia e Discurso." *Estudos Femininstas* 14 (2): 347–362.

Fleischer, David. 2011. "Political Reform: A Never-Ending Story (1995–2009)." In Maurício Font and Laura Randall (eds.) *The Brazilian State: Debate and Agenda*. Lanham, MD: Lexington Books.

2016. "Attempts at Political Reform: (1985–2015): Still a 'Never Ending Story.'" Presented at the International Congress of the Brazilian Studies Association, Providence.

Flores, Rocío Villanueva. 2004. "Balance de la Aplicación de las Cuotas Electorales en el Perú." In Mónica Moreno Seco and Clarisa Ramos Feijóo (eds.) *Mujer e Participación Política*, Special issue of *Feminismo/s* June (3): 49–74.

Fonseca, Marcelo da. 2012, January 16. "PT e PSDB Devem Realizar Primárias para Escolha de Candidto a Prefeito só em Três Capitais." *Estado de Minas*. Retrieved from https://em.com.br (Accessed March 18, 2012)

Fortin, Jessica, and Christina Eder. 2011. "Mapping the Interactive Effects of Electoral Rules on Gender Representation in Mixed Member Proportional (MMP) Systems." Presented at the Annual Conference of the American Political Science Association, Seattle, WA.

Fox, Richard, and Jennifer Lawless. 2004. "Entering the Arena? Gender and the Decision to Run for Office." *American Journal of Political Science* 48 (2): 264–280.

2011. "Gendered Perceptions and Political Candidacies: A Central Barrier to Women's Equality in Electoral Politics." *American Journal of Political Science* 55 (1): 59–73.

Franceschet, Susan. 2005. *Women and Politics in Chile*. Boulder, CO: Lynne Rienner.

2010. "The Gendered Dimension of Rituals, Rules, and Norms in the Chilean Congress." *Journal of Legislative Studies* 16 (3): 396–406.

Franceschet, Susan, Mona Lena Krook, and Jennifer M. Piscopo. 2012. *The Impact of Gender Quotas*. New York, NY: Oxford University Press.

Franceschet, Susan, and Jennifer M. Piscopo. 2008. "Gender Quotas and Women's Substantive Representation: Lessons from Argentina." *Politics & Gender* 4 (3): 393–425.

Franceschet, Susan, Jennifer M. Piscopo, and Gwynn Thomas. 2015. "Supermadres, Maternal Legacies and Women's Political Participation in Contemporary Latin America." *Journal of Latin American Studies* 48 (1): 1–32.

Freedom House. 2016. *Freedom in the World 2016: Anxious Dictators, Wavering Democracies: Global Freedom under Pressure*. Washington, DC: Freedom House.

Retrieved from https://freedomhouse.org/sites/default/files/FH_FITW_Report_ 2016.pdf (Accessed March 8, 2018)

Freyre, Gilberto. 1933. *Casa Grande e Senzala*. Rio de Janeiro, Maia e Schmidt Ltda.

Fundação Cultural Palmares. 2016. Retrieved from https://palmares.gov.br (Accessed May 3, 2016)

Fundação Perseu Abramo. 2010. "A Pesquisa Mulheres Brasileiras nos Espaços Público e Privado." Survey.

Furlan, Juliana de Almeida. 2014. "Inclusão da Mulher na Política: Panorama Atual e Perspectivas." *Estudos Eleitorais* 9 (3): 62–90.

Gallagher, Michael, 2015. Election Indices Dataset. Retrieved from https://tcd.ie/ Political_Science/staff/michael_gallagher/ElSystems/index.php (Accessed August 14, 2015)

Garcia, Gustavo. 2017, September 28. "Senado Decide Colocar em Votação Ordem do STF para Afastar Aécio." *O Globo*. Retrieved from https://g1.globo.com (Accessed September 30, 2017)

Gatto, Malu. 2016. "Endogenous Institutionalism and the Puzzle of Gender Quotas: Insights from Latin America." PhD Thesis, University of Oxford, UK.

Gauja, Anika. 2017. *Party Reform: The Causes, Challenges, and Consequences of Organizational Change*. Oxford, UK: Oxford University Press.

Geledés. 2015a, November 18. "Carta das Mulheres Negras 2015." Retrieved from https://geledés.org.br (Accessed November 20, 2015)

2015b, November 20. "Mulheres Negras Querem Mais Espaço na Política." www .geledés.org.br (Accessed November 20, 2015)

Género y Partidos Políticos en América Latina (GEPPAL). n.d. Inter-American Development Bank and International Institute for Democracy and Electoral Assistance. Retrieved from https://iadb.org/es/investigacion-y-datos/geppal/inicio %2C18161.html (Accessed March 8, 2018)

Gestión. 2014, 25 April. "Brecha Salarial entre Mujeres y Hombres es de 20% en Perú." http://gestion.pe/empleo-management/brecha-salarial-entre-mujeres-y-hombres-20-peru-2095545 (Accessed August 7, 2017)

Godinho, Tatau. 1996. "Ação Afirmativa no Partido dos Trabalhadores." *Revista Estudos Feministas* 4 (1): 148–157.

Godinho, Tatau (ed.) 1998. *Mulher e Política: Gênero e Feminismo no Partido dos Trabalhadores*. São Paulo, Brazil: Editora Fundação Perseu Abramo.

Goes, Emmanuelle. 2015, November 26. "Mulheres Negras em Marcha, Esses Passos Vêm de Longe." Retrieved from https://geledes.org.br (Accessed April 3, 2016)

Goetz, Anne Marie. 2007. "Political Cleaners: Women as the New Anti-Corruption Force?" *Development and Change* 38 (1): 87–105.

Goldani, Ana Maria. 1999. "Racial Inequality in the Lives of Brazilian Women." In Rebecca Reichmann (ed.) *Race in Contemporary Brazil: From Indifference to Inequality*. University Park, PA: Penn State Press, 179–194.

Gonçalves, Juliana. 2015, November 16. "Marcha das Mulheres Negras, A Marcha que Faz Sentido." *Carta Capital*. Retrieved from https://cartacapital.com.br (Accessed April 3, 2016)

Gonzalez, Elizabeth. 2015. "Latin America's Wage Gap Greater among Top-Earning Women." *Americas Society Council of the Americas*. Retrieved from https://as-coa .org/blogs/latin-americas-wage-gap-greater-among-top-earning-women (Accessed August 7, 2017)

Grayley, Mônica Villela. 2012, July 12. "Ministra Diz que Partidos Não Facilitam Candidaturas de Mulheres no Brasil." *UN Radio News and Media*. Retrieved from https://unmultimedia.org (Accessed March 8, 2018)

Guadagnini, Marila. 1993. "A 'Partitocrazia' without Women: The Case of the Italian Party System." In Joni Lovenduski and Pippa Norris (eds.) *Gender and Party Politics*. London: Sage, 168–204.

Guarnieri, Fernando. 2011. "A Força dos Partidos 'Fracos'." *DADOS – Revista de Ciências Sociais* 54 (1): 235–258.

Haas, Liesl. 2001. "Changing the System from Within? Feminist Participation in the Brazilian Workers' Party." In Victoria González and Karen Kampwirth (eds.) *Radical Women in Latin America: Left and Right*. University Park, PA: The Pennsylvania State University Press, 249–271.

Hagopian, Fran. 1996. *Traditional Politics and Regime Change in Brazil*. Cambridge, UK: Cambridge University Press.

Harmel, Robert. 2002. "Party Organizational Change: Competing Explanations." In Kurt Richard Luther and Ferdinand Müller-Rommel (eds.) *Political Parties in the New Europe: Political and Analytical Challenges*. Oxford, UK: Oxford University Press, 119–142.

Harmel, Robert, and Kenneth Janda. 1994. "An Integrated Theory of Party Goals and Party Change." *Journal of Theoretical Politics* 6 (3): 259–287.

Haspel, Moshe, Thomas Remington, and Steven Smith. 1998. "Electoral Institutions and Party Cohesion in the Russian Duma." *The Journal of Politics* 60 (2): 417–439.

Hasenbalg, Carlos. 1990. "Notas sobre a Pesquisa das Desigualdades Raciais e Bibliografia Selecionada." Presented at the Seminário Interacional sobre Desigualdade Racial no Brasil Contemporâneo, Belo Horizonte.

Hawkesworth, Mary. 2003. "Congressional Enactments of Race-Gender: Toward a Theory of Raced-Gendered Institutions." *American Political Science Review* 97 (4): 529–550.

Hazan, Reuven Y., and Gideon Rahat. 2006. "Candidate Selection: Methods and Consequences." In Richard S. Katz and William J. Crotty (eds.) *Handbook of Party Politics*, Thousand Oaks, CA: SAGE, 109–121.

Hébrard, Jean M. 2013. "Slavery in Brazil: Brazilian Scholars in the Key Interpretive Debates." *Translating the Americas* 1: 47–95.

Heilman, Madeline. 2001. "Description and Prescription: How Gender Stereotypes Prevent Women's Ascent up the Organizational Ladder." *Journal of Social Issues* 57: 657–674.

Henig, Ruth, and Simon Henig. 2001. *Women and Political Power: Europe since 1945*. London: Routledge.

Hernández, Tanya Katerí. 2013. *Racial Subordination in Latin America: The Role of the State, Customary Law*. New York, NY: Cambridge University Press.

Hicken, Allen, and Erik Martinez Kuhonta. 2014. *Party System Institutionalization in Asia: Democracies, Autocracies, and the Shadows of the Past*. New York, NY: Cambridge University Press.

Hinojosa, Magda. 2009. "'Whatever the Party Asks of Me': Women's Political Representation in Chile's Unión Demócrata Independiente." *Politics & Gender* 5: 377–407.

2012. *Selecting Women, Electing Women: Political Representation and Candidate Selection in Latin America*. Philadelphia, PA: Temple University Press.

Holman, Mirya R., and Monica C. Schneider. 2016. "Gender, Race, and Political Ambition: How Intersectionality and Frames Influence Interest in Political

Office." *Politics, Groups, and Identities,* FirstView DOI: 10.1080/21565503.2016.1208105.

Holmsten, Stephanie, Robert Moser, and Mary Slosar. 2010. "Do Ethnic Parties Exclude Women?" *Comparative Political Studies* 43 (10): 1179–1201.

Honaker, James, Gary King, and Matthew Blackwell. 2010. *Amelia II: A Program for Missing Data.* Retrieved from http://gking.harvard.edu/amelia/ (Accessed May 12, 2015)

Hochschild, Arlie Russell, and Anne Machung. 1989. *The Second Shift: Working Parents and the Revolution at Home.* New York, NY: Penguin Books.

Hordge-Freeman, Elizabeth. 2015. *The Color of Love: Racial Features, Stigma & Socialization in Black Brazilian Families.* Austin: University of Texas Press.

Hox, Joop. 2002. *Multilevel Analysis: Techniques and Applications.* Mahwah, NJ: Psychology Press.

Htun, Mala. 2002. "Puzzles of Women's Rights in Brazil." *Social Research* 69 (3): 733–751.

2004. "From 'Racial Democracy' to Affirmative Action: Changing State Policy on Race in Brazil." *Latin American Research Review* 39 (February): 60–89.

2005. "Women, Political Parties, and Electoral Systems in Latin America." In Julie Ballington and Azza Karam (eds.) *Women in Parliament: Beyond Numbers (A Revised Edition).* Stockholm, Sweden: International Institute for Democracy and Electoral Assistance, 112–121.

2015. *Inclusion without Representation in Latin America: Gender Quotas and Ethnic Reservations.* New York, NY: Cambridge University Press.

Htun, Mala, and Mark Jones. 2002. "Engendering the Right to Participate in Decision-Making: Electoral Quotas and Women's Leadership in Latin America." In Nikki Craske and Maxine Molyneux (eds.) *Gender and Politics of Rights and Democracy in Latin America.* London: Palgrave, 32–56.

Htun, Mala, and Timothy Power. 2006. "Gender, Parties, and Support for Equal Rights in the Brazilian Congress." *Latin American Politics and Society* 48 (4): 83–104.

Hughes, Melanie. 2008. "Politics at the Intersection: A Cross-National Analysis of Minority Women's Legislative Representation." Ph.D. dissertation, Ohio State University.

2011. "Intersectionality, Quotas, and Minority Women's Political Representation Worldwide." *American Political Science Review* 105 (3): 604–620.

Hughes, Melanie, and Pamela Paxton. 2008. "Continuous Change, Episodes and Critical Periods: A Framework for Understanding Women's Political Representation over Time." *Politics & Gender* 4 (2): 233–264.

Hunter, Wendy. 2010. *The Transformation of the Workers' Party in Brazil: 1989–2009.* Cambridge, UK: Cambridge University Press.

Huntington, Samuel. 1968. *Political Order in Changing Societies.* New Haven, CT: Yale University Press.

Hurtado, Lourdes. 2005. "Abriendo Puertas: Cuotas y Participación Política de Mujeres en el Perú." In Magdalena León (ed.) *Nadando Contra la Corriente: Mujeres y Cuotas Políticas en los Países Andinos.* Quito, Ecuador: UNIFEM, 91–140.

Inglehart, Ronald, and Pippa Norris. 2003. *Rising Tide: Gender Equality and Cultural Change.* New York, NY: Cambridge University Press.

Índice de Vulnerabilidade Juvenil à Violência e Desigualdade Racial 2014–2015. Secretaria-Geral da Presidência da República, Secretaria Nacional de Juventude,

Ministério da Justiça, e Fórum Brasileiro de Segurança Pública. Brasília: Presidência da República. Retrieved from http://unesdoc.unesco.org/images/0023/002329/232972POR.pdf (Accessed December 12, 2015)

Institute for Applied Economic Research (IPEA).2010a. "Human Development Index." Retrieved from http://ipea.gov.br (Accessed March 8, 2018)

2010b. *Mercado de Trabalho: Conjuntura e Análise*. Retrieved from https://ipea.gov.br (Accessed March 8, 2018)

2011. *Retrato das Desigualdades de Gênero e Raça* (4th edn). Brasília, Brazil: Ipea.

2012. "Trabalho para o Mercado e Trabalho para Casa: Persistentes Desigualdades de Gênero." Comunicados do Ipea 149 (May). Retrieved from https://ipea.gov.br (Accessed July 24, 2015)

2014. *Retrato das Desigualdades de Gênero e Raça*. Retrieved from https://ipea. gov .br/retrato/apresentacao.html (Accessed July 13, 2015)

Institute of Socioeconomic Studies (INESC). 2009. *Sondagem de Opinião Parlamentar: Reforma Política*. Retrieved from https://inesc.org.br (Accessed March 8, 2018)

2014. *Perfil dos Candidatos às Eleições 2014; Sub-Representação de Negros, Indígenas, eMulheres: Desafio à Democracia*. Brasília: Inesc.

Inter-American Development Bank (IDB). 2012. *Gender and Political Parties in Latin America*. Retrieved from https://iadb.org/research/geppal (Accessed March 8, 2018)

2015. *Partidos Políticos y Paridad: Un Desafío de la Democracia en América Latina*. Washington, DC: IDB and IDEA International. Retrieved from http://publications .iadb.org/handle/11319/7356 (Accessed May 11, 2016)

Inter-American Dialogue. 2008. *Women in the Americas: Paths to Political Power*. Washington, DC: Inter-American Dialogue, Inter-American Development Bank, and League of Women Voters. Retrieved from http://archive.thedialogue.org (Accessed January 4, 2008)

International Institute for Democracy and Electoral Assistance (International IDEA). 2015. Democracy and Gender. Retrieved from https://idea.int/gender/ (Accessed July 18, 2015)

Inter-Parliamentary Union (IPU). 1994. *Plan of Action to Correct Present Imbalances in the Participation of Men and Women in Political Life*. Geneva: IPU.

2017. *Women in National Parliaments Database*. Retrieved from https://ipu.org/ wmn-e/classif.htm (Accessed July 5, 2017)

2000. *Politics: Women's Insight*. Geneva, Switzerland: Inter-Parliamentary Union.

Inter-Union Department of Socioeconomic Statistics and Studies (DIEESE). 2011. *Anuário das Mulheres Brasileiras*. São Paulo, Brazil. Retrieved from https://dieese .org.br (Accessed March 8, 2018)

Iversen, Torben, and David Soskice. 2006. "Electoral Institutions and the Politics of Coalitions: Why Some Democracies Redistribute More Than Others." *American Political Science Review* 100 (2): 165–181.

Jalalzai, Farida, and Pedro dos Santos. 2015. "The Dilma Effect? Women's Representation under Dilma Rousseff's Presidency." *Politics & Gender* 11 (1): 117–145.

Janda, Kenneth. 1980. *Political Parties: A Cross-National Survey*. London: Macmillan.

Johnson III, Ollie A. 1998. "Racial Representation and Brazilian Politics: Black Members of the National Congress, 1983–1999." *Journal of Interamerican Studies and World Affairs* 40 (4): 97–118.

2006. "Locating Blacks in Brazilian Politics: Afro-Brazilian Activism, New Political Parties, and Pro-Black Public Policies." *Interamerican Journal of Black Studies* 12 (2): 170–193.

2015. "Blacks in National Politics." In Ollie A. Johnson III and Rosana Heringer (eds.) *Race, Politics, and Education in Brazil: Affirmative Action in Higher Education.* New York, NY: Palgrave Macmillan, 17–58.

Johnson III, Ollie A., and Rosana Heringer (eds.). 2015. *Race, Politics, and Education in Brazil: Affirmative Action in Higher Education.* New York, NY: Palgrave Macmillan.

Jones, Bryan D. 1999. "Bounded Rationality." *Annual Review of Political Science* 2: 297–321.

Jones, Mark. 2005. "The Role of Parties and Party Systems in the Policymaking Process." Washington, DC: Inter-American Development Bank. Retrieved from https://iadb.org (Accessed May 15, 2012)

2009. "Gender Quotas, Electoral Laws, and the Election of Women: Evidence from the Latin American Vanguard." *Comparative Political Studies* 42 (1): 56–81.

2010. "Democracy in Latin America, Challenges and Solutions: Party and Party System Institutionalization and Women's Legislative Representation." In Bjørn Lomborg (ed.) *Latin American Development Priorities: Costs and Benefits.* New York, NY: Cambridge University Press, 13–44.

Jornal Cidade. 2008, July 20. "Cota Obrigatória para Candidaturas Femininas Ainda Não Foi Atingida." Retrieved from http://jornalcidade.uol.com.br/rioclaro (Accessed September 12, 2008)

Kahn, Kim Fridkin. 1996. *The Political Consequences of Being a Woman: How Stereotypes Influence the Conduct and Consequences of Political Campaigns.* New York, NY: Columbia University Press.

Kanter, Rosabeth Moss. 1977. "Some Effects of Proportions on Group Life." *American Journal of Sociology* 82 (5): 965–990.

Karolyne, Anne. 2017. "Partido sem Machismo." Retrieved from https://pt.org.br/anne-karolyne-partido-sem-machismo/ (Accessed June 19, 2017)

Katz, Richard S., and Peter Mair (eds.). 1994. *How Parties Organize: Change and Adaptation in Party Organizations in Western Democracies.* Thousand Oaks, CA: SAGE.

Keck, Margaret. 1995. *The Workers' Party and Democratization in Brazil* (Revised edn). New Haven, CT: Yale University Press.

Kenney, Sally J. 1996. "New Research on Gendered Political Institutions." *Political Research Quarterly* 49 (2): 445–466.

Kenny, Meryl. 2013. *Gender and Political Recruitment: Theorizing Institutional Change.* New York, NY: Palgrave Macmillan.

2014. "A Feminist Institutionalist Approach." *Politics & Gender* 10 (4): 679–684.

Kenny, Meryl, and Tania Verge. 2015. "Contagion Theory Revisited: When Do Political Parties Compete on Women's Representation." Presented at the Biannual Meeting of the European Conference on Politics & Gender, Uppsala, Sweden.

Kenworthy, Lane, and Melissa Malami. 1999. "Gender Inequality in Political Representation: A Worldwide Comparative Analysis." *Social Forces* 78 (1): 235–269.

King, Gary, Robert Keohane, and Sidney Verba. 1994. *Designing Social Inquiry: Scientific Inference in Qualitative Research.* Princeton, NJ: Princeton University Press.

Kitschelt, Herbert. 1994. *The Transformation of European Social Democracy.* Cambridge, UK: Cambridge University Press.

Kittilson, Miki Caul. 2006. *Challenging Parties, Changing Parliament: Women and Elected Office in Contemporary Western Europe.* Columbus, OH: Ohio State University Press.

2013. "Gender and Political Parties." In Georgina Waylen, Karen Celis, and Laurel Weldon (eds.) *The Oxford Handbook of Gender Politics.* New York, NY: Oxford University Press, 536–553.

Krook, Mona Lena. 2009. *Quotas for Women in Politics: Gender and Candidate Selection Reform Worldwide.* New York, NY: Oxford University Press.

2010a. "Why Are Fewer Women than Men Elected? Gender and the Dynamics of Candidate Selection." *Political Studies Review* 8 (2): 155–168.

2010b. "Women's Representation in Parliament: A Qualitative Comparative Analysis." *Political Studies* 58: 886–908.

2015a. "Contesting Gender Quotas: A Typology of Resistance." Presented at the 4th European Conference on Politics and Gender, Uppsala, Sweden.

2015b. "Empowerment Versus Backlash: Gender Quotas and Critical Mass Theory." *Politics, Groups, and Identities* 3 (1): 184–188.

Krook, Mona Lena, and Fiona Mackay (eds.). 2011. *Gender, Politics and Institutions: Towards a Feminist Institutionalism.* Basingstoke, UK: Palgrave Macmillan.

Krook, Mona Lena, and Diana Z. O'Brien. 2010. "The Politics of Group Representation: Quotas for Women and Minorities Worldwide." *Comparative Politics* 42 (3): 253–272.

Krook, Mona Lena, and Pär Zetterberg. 2014. "Electoral Quotas and Political Representation: Comparative Perspectives." *International Political Science Review* 35 (1): 3–11.

Kunovich, Sheri, and Pamela Paxton. 2005. "Pathways to Power: The Role of Political Parties in Women's National Political Representation." *American Journal of Sociology* 111 (2): 505–552.

Lamounier, Bolívar, and Octavio Amorim Neto. 2005. "Brazil." In Dieter Nohlen (ed.) *Elections in the Americas: A Data Handbook.* New York, NY: Oxford University Press, 163–252.

Landes, Ruth. 1947. *The City of Women.* New York, NY: Macmillan.

LAPOP. n.d. The AmericasBarometer by the Latin American Public Opinion Project. Retrieved from https://LapopSurveys.org (Accessed March 8, 2018)

Larserud, Stina, and Rita Taphorn. 2007. *Designing for Equality: Best-Fit, Medium-Fit and Non-Favourable Combinations of Electoral Systems and Gender Quotas.* Stockholm, Sweden: International IDEA.

Lawless, Jennifer, and Richard Fox. 2005. *It Takes a Candidate: Why Women Don't Run for Office.* Cambridge, UK: Cambridge University Press.

2010. *It Still Takes a Candidate: Why Women Don't Run for Office.* Cambridge, UK: Cambridge University Press.

Lemos, Leany (ed.). 2008. *O Senado Federal Brasileiro no Pós-Constituinte.* Brasília, Brazil: Senado Federal.

Lemos, Leany, and Sonia Rainicheksi. 2008. "Carreiras Políticas no Senado Brasileiro: Um Estudo das Composições do Plenário e da Comissão de Constituição, Justiça e Cidadania na Década de 90." In Leany Lemos (ed.) *O Senado Federal Brasileiro no Pós-Constituinte.* Brasília, Brazil: Senado Federal, 87–120.

Leonardi, Gisele. 2011, October 21. "Bolsa Família: 94% dos Beneficiários são Mulheres." *PT Macro ABC*. Retrieved from https://macroabc.com.br (Accessed March 1, 2012)

Levitsky, Steven. 1998. "Institutionalization and Peronism: The Concept, the Case and the Case for Unpacking the Concept." *Party Politics* 4: 77–92.

2013. "Peru: Challenges of a Democracy without Parties." In Michael Shifter and Jorge Dominguez (eds.) *Constructing Democratic Governance in Latin America* (4th edn). Baltimore, MD: The Johns Hopkins University Press, 282–315.

Lima, Luciana. 2014, September 25. "Cota Feminina é Insuficiente para Assegurar Eleição de Mulheres." *Último Segundo*. http://ultimosegundo.ig.com.br (Accessed August 14, 2015)

Lijphart, Arend. 1994. *Electoral Systems and Party Systems in Twenty-Seven Democracies, 1945–1990*. Oxford, UK: Oxford University Press.

Llanos, Beatriz, and Vivian Roza. 2015. *Partidos Políticos y Paridad: Un Desafío de la Democracia en América Latina*. Washington, DC: Inter-American Development Bank and International Institute for Democracy and Electoral Assistance.

Llanos, Beatriz, and Kristen Sample. 2008. *30 Years of Democracy: Riding the Wave? Women's Political Participation in Latin America*. Stockholm: International Institute for Democracy and Electoral Assistance.

Llanos, Mariana, and Francisco Sánchez. 2008. "Conselho da Anciãos? O Senado e Seus Membros no Cone Sul." In Leany Lemos (ed.) *O Senado Federal Brasileiro no Pós-Constituinte*. Brasília, Brazil: Senado Federal, 121–150.

Loveman, Mara, Jeronimo O. Muniz, and Stanley R. Bailey. 2012. "Brazil in Black and White? Race Categories, the Census, and the Study of Inequality." *Ethnic and Racial Studies* 35 (8): 1466–1483.

Lovenduski, Joni. 1998. "Gendering Research in Political Science." *Annual Review of Political Science* 1: 333–356.

2005. *Feminizing Politics*. Cambridge, UK: Polity Press.

Lovenduski, Joni, and Pippa Norris (eds.). 1993. *Gender and Party Politics*. London: Sage.

Luhiste, Maarja. 2015. "Party Gatekeepers' Support for Viable Female Candidacy in PR-List Systems." *Politics & Gender* 11 (1): 89–116.

Luke, Douglas. 2004. *Multilevel Modeling*. Thousand Oaks, CA: Sage.

Luna, Juan Pablo, and David Altman. 2011. "Uprooted but Stable: Chilean Parties and the Concept of Party System Institutionalization." *Latin American Politics and Society* 53 (2): 1–28.

Macaulay, Fiona. 2003. "Sexual Politics, Party Politics: The PT Government's Policies on Gender Equity and Equality." Centre for Brazilian Studies Working Paper CBS46-03, University of Oxford, UK.

2006. *Gender Politics in Brazil and Chile: The Role of Parties in National and Local Policymaking*. New York, NY: Palgrave Macmillan.

Macedo, Thyago. 2008, May 16. "Fátima Bezerra Tem Maior Índice de Rejeição entre os Candidatos a Prefeito de Natal." *Nominuto.com*. Retrieved from www .nominuto.com (Accessed September 8, 2008)

Machismo Mata. 2012. Blog. Retrieved from http://machismomata.wordpress.com/ (Accessed March 8, 2018)

Mackay, Fiona. 2014. "Nested Newness, Institutional Innovation, and the Gendered Limits of Change." *Politics & Gender* 10 (4): 549–571.

Mackay, Fiona, and Georgina Waylen. 2014. "Researching Gender and Institutions: Introduction." *Politics & Gender 10*(4):659–660.
Mackay, Fiona, Faith Armitage, and Rosa Malley. 2014. "Gender and Political Institutions." In Rosie Campbell and Sarah Childs (eds.) *Deeds and Words: Gendering Politics after Joni Lovenduski*. Colchester, UK: ECPR Press, 93–112.
Mackay, Fiona, Meryl Kenny, and Louise Chappell. 2010. "New Institutionalism Through a Gender Lens: Towards a Feminist Institutionalism?" *International Political Science Review* 31 (5): 573–588.
Magalhães, Alvaro. 2015, February 1. "Partidos Colocam Candidatas-Laranjas para Cumprir Cota Mínima de Mulheres, Afirma Estudioso." *R7 Notícias*. http:// noticias.r7.com (Accessed August 14, 2015)
Mainwaring, Scott. 1995. "Brazil: Weak Parties, Feckless Democracy." In Scott Mainwaring and Timothy Scully (eds.) *Building Democratic Institutions: Parties and Party Systems in Latin America*. Stanford, CA: Stanford University Press, 354–398.
  1999. *Rethinking Party Systems in the Third Wave of Democratization: The Case of Brazil*. Stanford, CA: Stanford University Press.
Mainwaring, Scott, and Timothy Scully (eds.). 1995. *Building Democratic Institutions: Parties and Party Systems in Latin America*. Stanford, CA: Stanford University Press.
Mainwaring, Scott, and Edurne Zoco. 2007. "Political Sequences and the Stabilization of Interparty Competition: Electoral Volatility in Old and New Democracies." *Party Politics 13* (2): 155–178.
Majic, Samantha. 2013. "Challenging Gender Norms? Feminist Institutionalism and the Nonprofit Sector." Presented at the annual Meeting of the Western Political Science Association, Hollywood, CA, March 28–30.
Mansbridge, Jane. 1999. "Should Blacks Represent Blacks and Women Represent Women? A Contingent 'Yes'." *The Journal of Politics* 61 (3): 628–657.
Manuela Ramos. 2008. *Pensamientos, Voces & Saberes de Mujeres: Una Apuesta por la Equidad, Manuela 1978 – 2008*. Retrieved from https://manuela.org.pe (Accessed August 9, 2017)
Marcelo, Jota. 2014, 12 December. "Raquel Teixeira Assumirá Super Pasta da Educação." *Jornal Cidade*. Retrieved from https://jotacidade.com (Accessed November 12, 2015)
Marcondes, Mariana Mazzini, Luana Pinheiro, Cristina Queiroz, Ana Carolina Querino, and Danielle Valverde (eds.). 2013. *Dossiê Mulheres Negras: Retrato das Condições de Vida das Mulheres Negras no Brasil*. Brasília: Institute of Applied Economic Research (IPEA).
Marx, Anthony W. 1998. *Making Race and Nation: A Comparison of South Africa, the United States, and Brazil*. New York, NY: Cambridge University Press.
Marx, Jutta, Jutta Borner, and Mariana Camionotti. 2007. *Las Legisladoras: Cupos de Género y Política en Argentina y Brasil*. Buenos Aires, Argentina: Siglo XXI Editora Iberoamericana.
Matland, Richard. 1993. "Institutional Variables Affecting Female Representation in National Legislatures: The Case of Norway." *Journal of Politics* 55 (3): 737–755.
  1998. "Women's Representation in National Legislatures: Developed and Developing Countries." *Legislative Studies Quarterly* 23 (1): 109–125.
  2005. "Enhancing Women's Political Participation: Legislative Recruitment and Electoral Systems." In Julie Ballington and Azza Karam (eds.) *Women in*

Parliament: Beyond Numbers (2nd edn). Stockholm, Sweden: International IDEA, 93–112.

Matland, Richard, and Dudley Studlar. 1996. "The Contagion of Women Candidates in Single-Member District and Proportional Representation Electoral Systems: Canada and Norway." *Journal of Politics 58* (3): 707–733.

Matland, Richard, and Michelle Taylor. 1997. "Electoral Systems' Effect on Women's Representation: Theoretical Arguments and Evidence from Costa Rica." *Comparative Political Studies 30* (2): 186–210.

Matos, Marlise. 2008. Professor and Chair of the Department of Political Science and Coordinator of the Working Group of Studies and Research on Women at the Federal University of Minas Gerais. Interviewed by Mais Mulheres no Poder. Retrieved from https://spm.gov.br/assuntos/poder-e-participacao-politica/referencias/entrevistas/entrevista_marlise_matos.pdf (Accessed March 8, 2018)

Mayhew, David. 1974. *Congress: The Electoral Connection.* New Haven, CT: Yale University Press.

McConnaughy, Corrine. 2007. "Seeing Gender over the Short and Long Haul." *Politics & Gender 3*: 378–386.

Mendonça, Ricardo, and Silvio Navarro. 2012, June 11. "Mulheres Recebem Apenas 8% dos Repasses dos Partidos." *Folha de São Paulo.* Retrieved from https://folha .uol.com.br (Accessed March 8, 2018)

Meneguello, Rachel. 1989. *PT: A Formação de um Partido, 1979–1982.* São Paulo, Brazil: Paz e Terra.

Miguel, Luis Felipe, and Flávia Biroli. 2009. "Mídia e Representação Política Feminina: Hipóteses de Pesquisa." *Opinão Pública 15* (1): 55–81.

2011. *Caleidoscópio Convexo: Mulheres, Política e Mídia.* São Paulo, Brazil: Editora da Universidade Estadual Paulista (Unesp).

Miguel, Luis Felipe, and Cristina Monteiro de Queiroz. 2006. "Diferenças Regionais e o Êxito Relativo de Mulheres em Eleições Municipais no Brasil." *Revista Estudos Feministas* 14:363–385.

Ministerio de la Mujer y Desarrollo Social. 2009. *50 años del Voto Femenino en el Perú: Historia y Realidad Actual.* Lima: Dirección General de la Mujer, MIMDES. Retrieved from https://mimp.gob.pe/webs/mimp/sispod/pdf/89.pdf (Accessed August 9, 2017)

Minority Rights. 2015. "Brazil – Afro-Brazilians." World Directory of Minorities and Indigenous Peoples. http://minorityrights.org/minorities/afro-brazilians/ (Accessed November 19, 2015)

Mitchell, Gladys L. 2009. "Afro-Brazilian Politicians and Campaign Strategies: A Preliminary Analysis." *Latin American Politics and Society 51* (3): 111–142.

2010. "Politicizing Blackness: Afro-Brazilian Color Identification and Candidate Preference." In Bernd Reiter and Gladys L. Mitchell (eds.) *Brazil's New Racial Politics.* Boulder, CO: Lynne Rienner, 35–50.

Money, Jeanette, and George Tsebelis. 1992. "Cicero's Puzzle: Upper House Power in Comparative Perspective." *International Political Review 13* (1): 25–43.

Montero, Alfred P. 2010. "No Country for Leftists? Clientelist Continuity and the 2006 Vote in the Brazilian Northeast." *Journal of Politics in Latin America 2* (2): 113–153.

Moore, Robert. 2005. "Religion, Race, and Gender Differences in Political Ambition." *Politics & Gender 1* (4): 577–596.

Morgenstern, Scott, and Peter Siavelis (eds.). 2008. *Pathways to Power: Political Recruitment and Candidate Selection in Latin America.* State College, PA: Pennsylvania State University Press.

Morgenstern, Scott, and Javier Vázquez-D'Elía. 2007. "Electoral Laws, Parties, and Party Systems in Latin America." *Annual Review of Political Science 10* (1): 143–168.

Moriére, Laisy. 2015, 2 October. "O PT, seus 35 Anos e sua Capacidade de Ousar." Retrieved from https://pt.org.br (Accessed March 8, 2018)

Moser, Robert. 2001a. "The Effects of Electoral Systems on Women's Representation in Post-Communist States." *Electoral Studies* 20 (3): 253–269.

2001b. *Unexpected Outcomes: Electoral Systems, Political Parties, and Representation in Russia.* Pittsburgh, PA: University of Pittsburgh Press.

2003. "Electoral Systems and Women's Representation: The Strange Case of Russia." In Richard Matland and Kathleen Montgomery (eds.) *Women's Access to Political Power in Post-Communist Europe.* Oxford, UK: Oxford University Press.

Moser, Robert, and Ethan Scheiner. 2004. "Mixed Electoral Systems and Electoral System Effects: Controlled Comparison and Cross-National Analysis." *Electoral Studies* 23 (4): 575–599.

2012. *Electoral Systems and Political Context: How Electoral System Effects Differ in New and Established Democracies.* Cambridge, UK: Cambridge University Press.

Moura, Paula. 2014, October 10. "Do Quotas for Female Politicians Work?" *The Atlantic.* Retrieved from https://theatlantic.com (Accessed March 8, 2018)

Mulholland, Timothy, and Lúcio Rennó. 2008. *Reforma Política em Questão.* Brasília, Brazil: Editora Universidade de Brasília.

Muñoz, Paula. 2013. Campaign Clientelism in Peru: An Informational Theory. University of Texas Ph.D. Dissertation.

2014. "An Informational Theory of Campaign Clientelism: The Case of Peru." *Comparative Politics* 47 (1/Oct): 79–98.

Murray, Rainbow. 2008. "The Power of Sex and Incumbency: A Longitudinal Study of Electoral Performance in France." *Party Politics* 14 (5): 539–554.

Murray, Rainbow (ed.). 2010. *Cracking the Highest Glass Ceiling: A Global Comparison of Women's Campaigns for Executive Office.* Santa Barbara, CA: Greenwood Publishing Group.

2016. "The Political Representation of Ethnic Minority Women in France." *Parliamentary Affairs* 69 (3): 586–602.

Murray, Rainbow, and Jennifer Piscopo. (n.d.). "Gendered Media Coverage of Candidates for Executive Office." Unpublished Manuscript.

Nicolau, Jairo. 2006. "O Sistema Eleitoral de Lista-Aberta no Brasil." *DADOS – Revista de Ciências Socias* 49 (4): 689–720.

Nicolau, Jairo, and Rogério Augusto Schmitt. 1995. "Sistema Eleitoral e Sistema Partidário." *Lua Nova* 36 (95): 129–47.

Norris, Pippa. 1987. *Politics and Sexual Equality: The Comparative Position of Women in Western Democracies.* Boulder, CO: Lynne Rienner.

1997. "Introduction: Theories of Recruitment." In Pippa Norris (ed.) *Passages to Power: Legislative Recruitment in Advanced Democracies.* New York, NY: Cambridge University Press, 1–14.

North, Douglass C. 1990. *Institutions, Institutional Change, and Economic Performance.* New York, NY: Cambridge University Press.

Notícias STF. 2015, September 17. "STF Conclui Julgamento sobre Financiamento de Campanhas Eleitorais." *Notícias STF.* Retrieved from https://stf.jus.br (Accessed August 21, 2017)

Novaes, Marina. 2015, October 1. "A Um Ano das Eleições, Partido de Marina Silva Embola Xadrez Político." *El País.* http://brasil.elpais.com/brasil.html (Accessed November 8, 2015)

O'Brien, Diana Z. 2015. "Rising to the Top: Gender, Political Performance, and Party Leadership in Parliamentary Democracies." *American Journal of Political Science* 59 (4): 1022–1039.

Oliveira, Mariana, and Vladimir Netto. 2017, June 6. "PGR Denuncia Aécio Neves ao STF por Corrupção Passiva e Obstrução de Justiça." *O Globo.* Retrieved from https://g1.globo.com (Accessed September 30, 2017)

PC do B. 2009a, September 9. "Escola do PC do B Marca Novo Curso e Quer Mais Presença Feminina." Retrieved from https://vermelho.org.br/noticia/115299-3 (Accessed March 8, 2018)

   2009b, November 30. "Escola Nacional Divulga Programa e Bibliografia do Próximo Curso." Retrieved from https://vermelho.org.br/noticia.php?id_secao=141&id_noticia=120379 (Accessed March 8, 2018)

   2010, January 28. "Escola Quer Formar Quadros e Estimular Cursos Locais para Eleição." Retrieved from https://vermelho.org.br/noticia/123360-1 (Accessed March 8, 2018)

   2011, December 6. "Fique Atento ao Curso de Nível III da Escola Nacional." Retrieved from https://pcdob.org.br (Accessed March 1, 2012)

   2012, May 23. "Liège: 'Devemos Perseguir a Emancipação na Perspectiva Humana.'" Retrieved from https://vermelho.org.br/noticia/184031-8 (Accessed March 8, 2018)

PMDB. 1986. "Mulheres, Jovens e Negros." São Paulo, Brazil: Fundaço Ulysses Guimarães.

   2015, June 20. "Participação das Mulheres na Política é Tema do Fórum das Vereadoras." http://pmdb-rs.org.br (Accessed July 16, 2015)

PMDB Mulher. 2012, June 18. "PMDB Fortalece o Núcleo Feminino do Partido." Retrieved from http://pmdbmulher.org.br/mdb-mulher-nacional/pmdb-fortalece-o-nucleo-feminino-do-partido/ (Accessed July 1, 2012)

PT. 2011, September 4. "Mulheres Petistas Vibram com a Aprovação da Paridade de Gênero para o Estatuto do PT." Retrieved from https://pt.org.br (Accessed June 1, 2017)

   2012a, May 10. "Resolução sobre Gastos de Recursos do Fundo Partidário com Mulheres." Meeting of the National Executive Commission, São Paulo. Retrieved from https://pt.org.br (Accessed June 1, 2017)

   2012b, March 8. "Secretária Nacional de Mulheres do PT Diz que Partido Vai Passar por Transformação com a Paridade de Gênero nos Cargos de Comando." Retrieved from https://pt.org.br (Accessed June 1, 2017)

   2017a, February 12. "PT Aprovou Cota de Mulheres no 1° Congresso, em 1991." Retrieved from https://pt.org.br (Accessed June 1, 2017)

   2017b, March 20. "Paridade no PT Ajuda a Empoderar as Mulheres, Afirma Maristella." Retrieved from https://pt.org.br (Accessed June 1, 2017)

   2017c, May 27. "Paridade Mudou Cultura Política no PT, Afirma Vivian Farias." Retrieved from https://pt.org.br (Accessed June 1, 2017)

   2017d, May 29. "Congresso do PT Será Momento de Reforçar Paridade, Diz Laisy." Retrieved from https://pt.org.br (Accessed June 1, 2017)

2017e, May 29. "Secretaria de Mulheres do PT Promove Seminário em Brasília." Retrieved from https://pt.org.br (Accessed June 1, 2017)

2017f, June, 3. "Gleisi: Ser Presidenta é Grande Responsabilidade com Companheiras." Retrieved from https://pt.org.br (Accessed June 4, 2017)

Paes, Dora Paula. 2014. "Luta Contra Candidata 'Laranja.'" *Folha da Manhã Online.* March 23. Retrieved from https://fmanha.com.br (Accessed August 14, 2015)

Paiva, Raquel. 2008. *Política: Palavra Feminina.* Rio de Janeiro, Brazil: Mauad Editora Ltda.

Paixão, Marcelo, and Luiz M. Carvano (eds.). 2008. *Relatório Anual das Desigualdades Raciais no Brasil; 2007–2008.* Rio de Janeiro, Brazil: Editora Garamond Ltda.

Paixão, Marcelo, Irene Rossetto, Fabiana Montovanele, and Luiz M. Carvano (eds.). 2010. *Relatório Anual das Desigualdades Raciais no Brasil; 2009–2010.* Rio de Janeiro: Editora Garamond Ltda.

Panebianco, Angelo. 1988. *Political Parties: Organization and Power.* Cambridge, UK: Cambridge University Press.

Paraguassu, Mara. 2008. As Eleições para a Câmara dos Deputados em 2002 e 2006: Grandes Partidos Elegendo Menos Mulheres. Master's Thesis. Universidade do Legislativo Brasileiro, Universidade Federal de Mato Grosso do Sul.

Parés, Luis Nicolau. 2013. *The Formation of Candomblé: Vodun History and Ritual in Brazil.* Chapel Hill: University of North Carolina Press.

Paschel, Tianna. 2011. States, Movements, and the New Politics of Blackness in Colombia and Brazil. Ph.D. dissertation. University of California.

2016. *Becoming Black Political Subjects: Movements and Ethno-Racial Rights in Colombia and Brazil.* Princeton, NJ: Princeton University Press.

Paxton, Pamela, Melanie Hughes, and Matthew Painter. 2011. "Growth in Women's Political Representation: A Longitudinal Exploration of Democracy, Electoral System and Gender Quotas." *European Journal of Political Research* 49: 25–52.

Paxton, Pamela and Sheri Kunovich. 2003. "Women's Political Representation: The Importance of Ideology." *Social Forces* 82 (1): 87–114.

Paxton, Pamela, Sheri Kunovich, and Melanie Hughes. 2007. "Gender in Politics." *Annual Review of Sociology* 33: 263–284.

Pedersen, Mogens N. 1979. "The Dynamics of European Party Systems: Changing Patterns of Electoral Volatility." *European Journal of Political Research* 7(1): 1–26.

Pérez Llosa, Valentina. 2016, April 4. "Qué Proponen los Partidos Políticos para las Mujeres?" *La Mula.* Retrieved from https://redaccion.lamula.pe (Accessed August 9, 2017)

Perissé, Gabriel. 2010. "Laranja Ingênua ... ou Não." *Palavras e Origens: Considerações Etimológicas.* Retrieved from http://palavraseorigens.blogspot.com (Accessed March 8, 2018)

Peron, Isadora. 2012, March 7. "80 Anos após o Voto Feminino, Papel das Mulheres na Política ainda é Pequeno." *Estado de São Paulo.* Retrieved from https://estadao.com.br (Accessed March 8, 2018)

Perondi, Regina Heurich. 2007. *Partidos Políticos e Terceiro Setor.* Brasília, Brazil: Fundaço Ulysses Guimarães.

Perú – Congreso de la República, Congresistas. 2017. Retrieved from https://congreso.gob.pe/Congresistas/ (Accessed August 14, 2017)

Peters, B. Guy. 2005. *Institutional Theory in Political Science: The 'New Institutionalism,'* (2nd edn). London: Continuum.

Phillips, Anne. 1995. *The Politics of Presence*. New York, NY: Oxford University Press.
Phillips, Tom. 2011, November 17. "Brazil Census Shows African-Brazilians in the Majority for the First Time." *The Guardian*. Retrieved from https://theguardian .com (Accessed June 27, 2015)
Piatti-Crocker, Adriana, Gregory D. Schmidt, and Clara Araújo. 2017. *Gender Quotas in South America's Big Three: National and Subnational Impacts*. Lanham, MD: Lexington Books.
Pinheiro, Luana Simões. 2007. *Vozes Femininas na Política*. Brasília, Brazil: Secretaria Especial de Políticas para as Mulheres.
Pinho, Patricia de Santana. 2010. *Mama Africa: Reinventing Blackness in Bahia*. Durham, NC: Duke University Press.
Pintat, Christine. 1998. "Democracy through Partnership: The Experience of the Inter-Parliamentary Union." In Azza Karam (ed.) *Women in Parliament: Beyond Numbers*. Stockholm: International IDEA, 159–173. http://archive.idea.int/ women/parl/index.htm (Accessed May 11, 2016)
Pinto, Céli Regina Jardim. 1994. "Mulher e Política no Brasil: Os Impasses do Feminismo, Enquanto Mmovimento Social, Face as Regras do Jogo da Democracia Representativa." *Estudos Feministas* 2 (2): 256–270.
Pinto, Céli Regina Jardim, Maria Lucia Moritz, and Rosangela M. Schulz. 2013. "O Desempenho das Mulheres nas Eleições Legislativas de 2010 no Rio Grande do Sul." *Revista Brasileira de Ciência Política* 10: 195–223.
Piscopo, Jennifer. 2014. "Female Leadership and Sexual Health Policy in Argentina." *Latin American Research Review* 49 (1): 104–127.
Piza, Edith, and Fúlvia Rosemberg. 1999. "Color in the Brazilian Census." In Rebecca Reichmann (ed.) *Race in Contemporary Brazil: From Indifference to Inequality*. University Park, PA: Penn State Press, 37–52.
Portal Brasil. 2014, April 10. "A Partir das Eleições deste Ano, Candidatos Devem Declarar Etnia." Brasília: Portal Brasil. Retrieved from https://brasil.gov.br/ cidadania-e-justica/2014/04/a-partir-da-eleicao-deste-ano-candidatos-devem-declarar-etnia (Accessed May 3, 2016)
  2015. "Mulheres São Maioria da População e Ocupam Mais Espaço no Mercado de Trabalho." Retrieved from https://brasil.gov.br/cidadania-e-justica (Accessed July 24, 2015)
Post, Colin. 2016, 17 July. "Peru President-elect Kuczynski's New Cabinet Ministers." *Peru Reports*, http://perureports.com/2016/07/17/peru-president-elect-kuczynskis-new-cabinet-ministers/ (Accessed August 9, 2017)
Power, Timothy. 2000. *The Political Right in Postauthoritarian Brazil: Elites, Institutions, and Democratization*. College Park: Pennsylvania State University Press.
Power, Timothy, and Cesar Zucco. 2009. "Estimating Ideology of Brazilian Legislative Parties, 1990–2005: A Research Communication." *Latin American Research Review* 44 (1): 218–246.
  2011. "Elite Preferences in a Consolidating Democracy: The Brazilian Legislative Surveys, 1990–2009." Unpublished Manuscript, Oxford University, UK.
Quinn, Sheila. 2009. *Gender Budgeting: Practical Implementation*. Strasbourg, France: Council of Europe.
Quota Project. 2017. Retrieved from http://quotaproject.org (Accessed September 6 2017)
Radio Primerisima. 2011. "FSLN Incorpora a Jóvenes y Mujeres a Todos sus Órganos." Retrieved from https://rlp.com.ni (Accessed March 8, 2018)

Rahat, Gideon, and Reuven Hazan. 2001. "Candidate Selection Methods: An Analytical Framework." *Party Politics* 7 (3): 297–322.

Randall, Vicky (ed.). 1988. *Political Parties in the Third World*. London: Sage.

Randall, Vicky, and Lars Svåsand. 2002. "Party Institutionalization in New Democracies." *Party Politics* 8 (1): 5–29.

Reiter, Bernd, and Gladys L. Mitchell. 2010. "The New Politics of Race in Brazil." In Bernd Reiter and Gladys L. Mitchell (eds.) *Brazil's New Racial Politics*. Boulder, CO: Lynne Rienner, 1–16.

Reynolds, Andrew. 1999. "Women in the Legislatures and Executives of the World: Knocking at the Highest Glass Ceiling." *World Politics* 51 (4): 547–572.

Ribeiro, Isaac. 2008, September 19. "Fátima – 13 – Comício com Lula – 19.09.2008 – Discurso do Presidente Retrieved from https://youtube.com/watch?v=xYx9dAozfwc (Accessed March 8, 2018)

Robinson, William. 1990. "Ecological Correlations and the Behavior of Individuals." *American Sociological Review* 15: 351–357.

Rodrigues, Leôncio Martins. 2002. *Partidos, Ideologia e Composição Social: Um Estudo das Bancadas Partidárias na Câmara dos Deputados*. São Paulo, Brazil: Editora da Universidade de São Paulo.

Rodrigues, Lima. 2012, June 19. "Bel Mesquita Anuncia Oficialmente que Compôs Chapa com o PT." *Jornal Successo – Panoramio Noturno de Parauapebas*. Retrieved from https://blogdofrancescocosta.blogspot.com (Accessed March 8, 2018)

Rodríguez, Victoria. 2003. *Women in Contemporary Mexican Politics*. Austin: The University of Texas Press.

Romio, Jackeline Aparecida Ferreira. 2013. "A Victimização de Mulheres por Agressão Física, Segundo Raça/Cor no Brasil." InMariana Mazzini Marcondes, Luana Pinheiro, Cristina Queiroz, Ana Carolina Querino, and Danielle Valverde (eds.) Dossiê Mulheres Negras: Retrato das Condições de Vida das Mulheres Negras no Brasil. Brasília, Brazil: Institute of Applied Economic Research (IPEA): 133–158.

Rosenbluth, Frances, Rob Salmond, and Michael Thies. 2006. "Welfare Works: Explaining Female Legislative Representation." *Politics & Gender* 2 (2): 163–192.

Rousseau, Stéfanie. 2009. *Women's Citizenship in Peru: The Paradoxes of Neopopulism in Latin America*. New York: Palgrave Macmillan.

Roza, Luiza Barros. 2009. Cotas para Negros nas Universidades Públicas e a Sua Inserção na Realidade Jurídica Brasileira: Por uma Nova Compreensão Epistemológica do Princípio Constitucional da Igualdade. Master's Thesis submitted to Universidade de São Paulo.

Roza, Vivian, Beatriz Llanos, and Gisela Garzón de la Roza. 2010. *Partidos Políticos y Paridad: La Ecuación Pendiente*. Washington, DC: Inter-American Development Bank.

2011. *Gender and Political Parties: Far from Parity*. Stockholm, Sweden: International IDEA and the Inter-American Development Bank.

Rudman, Laurie. 1998. "Self-Promotion as a Risk Factor for Women: The Costs and Benefits of Counterstereotypical Impression Management." *Journal of Personality and Social Psychology* 74: 629–645.

Rule, Wilma. 1987. "Electoral Systems, Contextual Factors and Women's Opportunity for Election to Parliament in Twenty-Three Democracies." *Western Political Quarterly* 40: 477–498.

Rule, Wilma, and Joseph Zimmerman. 1994. *Electoral Systems in Comparative Perspectives: Their Impact on Women and Minorities.* London: Greenwood Press.

Sacchet, Teresa. 2007. *"Political Parties and Women's Leadership in Latin America."* Prepared for the Inter-American Dialogue/Inter-American Development Bank/League of Women Voters/Organization of American States Conference, Women in the Americas: Paths to Political Power.

Salmond, Rob. 2006. "Proportional Representation and Female Parliamentarians." *Legislative Studies Quarterly* 31 (2): 175–204.

Samuels, David. 1999. "Incentives to Cultivate a Party Vote in Candidate-centric Electoral Systems: Evidence from Brazil." *Comparative Political Studies* 32 (4): 487–518.

2001a. "Money, Elections, and Democracy in Brazil." *Latin American Politics and Society* 43 (2): 27–48.

2001b. "Does Money Matter? Campaign Finance in Newly Democratic Countries: Theory and Evidence from Brazil." *Comparative Politics* 34: 23–42.

2003. *Ambition, Federalism and Legislative Politics in Brazil.* New York, NY: Cambridge University Press.

2006. "Sources of Mass Partisanship in Brazil." *Latin American Politics & Society* 48 (2): 1–27.

2008. "Political Ambition, Candidate Recruitment, and Legislative Politics in Brazil." In Scott Morgenstern and Peter Siavelis (eds.) *Pathways to Power: Political Recruitment and Candidate Selection in Latin America.* State College, PA: Pennsylvania State University Press, 76–91.

Sanbonmatsu, Kira. 2006. *Where Women Run: Gender & Party in the American States.* Ann Arbor: University of Michigan Press.

2015. "Electing Women of Color: The Role of Campaign Trainings." *Journal of Women, Politics & Policy* 36 (2): 137–160.

Santos, Fabiano. 2000. "Deputados Federais e Instituições Legislativas no Brasil: 1946–99." In Renato Boschi, Eli Diniz, and Fabio Santos (eds.) *Elites Políticas e Econômicas no Brasil Contemporâneo: A Desconstrução da Ordem Corporativa e o Papel do Legislativo no Cenário Pós-Reformas.* São Paulo, Brazil: Konrad Adenauer, 91–117.

dos Santos, João Marcelo Pereira. 2009. Identidade e Diferença: A Trajectória das Mulheres no Partido dos Trabalhadores. Retrieved from https://fpabramo.org.br/csbh/wp-content/uploads/sites/3/2017/04/T03perseu4.pdf (Accessed March 8, 2018)

Santos, Fabiano, and Fernando Guarnieri. 2016. "From Protest to Parliamentary Coup: An Overview of Brazil's Recent History." *Journal of Latin American Cultural Studies* 25 (4): 485–494.

Santos, Marcelo Barbosa. 2010. "Racismo e Política: Os Parlamentares Negros no Congresso Nacional Brasileiro na Legislatura 2007/2011. Uma Reflexão sobre a Dimensão da Ideologia, da Representação e da Participação." Rio de Janeiro, Brazil. Retrieved from https://secretariadegoverno.gov.br/.arquivos/monografias/Marcelo%20Barbosa%20Santos.pdf (Accessed May 3, 2016)

dos Santos, Pedro. 2012. "Gendering Representation: Parties, Institutions, and the Under-Representation of Women in Brazil's State Legislatures." Ph.D. Dissertation. University of Kansas.

Sartori, Giovani. 1976. *Parties and Party Systems: A Framework for Analysis.* Cambridge, UK: Cambridge University Press.

Scarrow, Susan E., Paul D. Webb, and Thomas Poguntke (eds.). 2017. *Organizing Political Parties: Representation, Participation, and Power.* New York, NY: Oxford University Press.

Schedler, Andreas. 1995. "Under- and Overinstitutionalization: Some Ideal Typical Propositions Concerning New and Old Party Systems." Kellogg Institute Working Paper #213, University of Notre Dame, IN.

Schelling, Thomas. 1978. *Micromotives and Macrobehavior.* New York, NY: W.W. Norton.

Schlesinger, Joseph. 1966. *Ambition and Politics: Political Careers in the United States.* Chicago, IL: Rand McNally.

Schmidt, Gregory D. 2003a. "Unanticipated Successes: Lessons from Peru's Experiences with Gender Quotas in Majoritarian Closed List and Open List PR Systems." Presented at International IDEA Workshop. Lima, Peru.

2003b. *Cuotas Efectivas, Magnitud Relativa del Partido, y El Éxito de Las Candidatas Mujeres: Una Evaluación Comparativa de las Elecciones Municipales Peruanas.* Lima, Peru: Movimiento Manuela Ramos.

2009. "The Election of Women in List PR Systems: Testing the Conventional Wisdom." *Electoral Studies* 28 (2): 190–203.

2012. "Success under Open List PR: The Election of Women to Congress." In Manon Tremblay (ed.) *Women and Legislative Representation: Electoral Systems, Political Parties, and Sex Quotas.* New York, NY: Palgrave Macmillan, 167–182.

2017. "Origins, Interactions with Electoral Rules, and Re-Election." In Adriana Piatti-Crocker, Gregory D. Schmidt, and Clara Araújo (eds.) *Gender Quotas in South America's Big Three: National and Subnational Impacts.* Lanham, MD: Lexington Books, 98–113.

n.d. "Gender Disparities in Re-Election: The 2006 and 2010–2011 Electoral Cycles in Peru." Working paper, 1–53.

Schmidt, Gregory D., and Kyle L. Saunders. 2004. "Effective Quotas, Relative Party Magnitude, and the Success of Female Candidates: Peruvian Municipal Elections In Comparative Perspective." *Comparative Political Studies* 37 (6): 704–724.

Schubert, Renate. 2006. "Analyzing and Managing Risks: On the Importance of Gender Differences in Risk Attitudes." *Managerial Finance* 32 (9): 706–715.

Schwindt-Bayer, Leslie. 2005. "The Incumbency Disadvantage and Women's Election to Legislative Office." *Electoral Studies* 24 (2): 227–244.

2006. "Still Supermadres? Gender and the Policy Priorities of Latin American Legislators." *American Journal of Political Science* 50 (3): 570–585.

2010. *Political Power and Women's Representation in Latin America.* New York, NY: Oxford University Press.

Schwindt-Bayer, Leslie, Michael Malecki, and Brian Crisp. 2010. "Candidate Gender and Electoral Success in Single Transferable Vote Systems." *British Journal of Political Science* 40 (3): 693–709.

Secco, Lincoln. 2011. *Historia do PT, 1978–2010.* Cotia, São Paulo: Atelie Editorial.

Smooth, Wendy. 2006. "Intersectionality in Electoral Politics: A Mess Worth Making." *Politics & Gender* 2 (3): 400–414.

2010. "African American Women and Electoral Politics: A Challenge to the Post-Race Rhetoric of the Obama Moment." In Susan J. Carroll and Richard Logan Fox (eds.) *Gender and Elections: Shaping the Future of American Politics.* New York, NY: Cambridge University Press, 165–186.

Special Secretariat for Policies Geared towards the Promotion of Racial Equality (SEPPIR). 2010. "A Participação das Mulheres Negras nos Espaços de Poder." Retrieved from https://seppir.gov.br/central-de-conteudos/publicacoes/pub-acoes -afirmativas/a-participacao-das-mulheres-negras-nos-espacos-de-poder (Accessed May 3, 2016)

Special Secretariat for Policies for Women (SPM). 2010. Evolução dos Indicadores Sociais sobre as Mulheres no Brasil. Retrieved from https://maismulheresnopoderbrasil.com.br (Accessed May 15, 2012)

2014. *Mais Mulheres no Poder: As Mulheres nas Eleições de 2014.* Retrieved from https://spm.gov.br (Accessed July 16, 2015)

Senado Federal. 2004. *As Senadoras: Dados Biográficos, 1979–2004.* Brasília, Brazil: Senado Federal.

2015. "Mais Mulheres na Política." Brasília, Brazil: Senado Federal. Retrieved from https://www12.senado.leg.br/institucional/procuradoria/proc-publicacoes/2a-edicao-do-livreto-mais-mulheres-na-politica (Accessed March 8, 2018)

Senado Notícias. 2017, September 26. "Plenário Aprova Fundo de R$ 1,7 Bilhão para Eleições." *Senado Notícias.* Retrieved from https://senado.leg.br (Accessed September 30, 2017)

Shugart, Matthew Soberg, and Scott Mainwaring. 1997. *Presidentialism and Democracy in Latin America.* New York, NY: Cambridge University Press.

Shugart, Matthew, Melody Valdini, and Kati Suominen. 2005. "Looking for Locals: Voter Information Demands and Personal Vote-Earning Attributes of Legislators Under Proportional Representation." *American Journal of Political Science* 49 (2): 437–449.

Silva, Tatiana Dias, and Fernanda Lira Goes (eds.). 2013. *Igualdade Racial no Brasil: Reflexões no Ano Internacional dos Afrodescendentes.* Brasília, Brazil: Institute of Applied Economic Research (IPEA).

Simmons, Beth. 1998. "Compliance with International Agreements." *Annual Review of Political Science* 1: 75–93.

Smith, Amy Erica. 2010. "Who Supports Affirmative Action in Brazil." *LAPOP Americas Barometer 2010 Insights* 49 (October): 1–8. Retrieved from https:// vanderbilt.edu/lapop/ (Accessed December 8, 2015)

Souza, Sílvia Rita. 2008. *A Mulher Candidata – Guia para Disputar Eleições.* Brasília, Brazil: Sílvia Souza.

Speck, Bruno Wilhelm, and Wagner Pralon Mancuso. 2015. "'Street Fighters' e 'Media Stars': Estratégias de Campanha e sua Eficácia nas Eleições Brasileiras de 2014." Presented at the Annual Meeting of the Latin American Studies Association, San Juan, Puerto Rico.

Stevens, Evelyn. 1973. "Machismo and Marianismo" *Society* 10 (6): 57–63.

Stokes, Susan C. 1997. "Are Parties What's Wrong with Democracy in Latin America?" Presented at the XX International Congress of the Latin American Studies Association. Guadalajara, Mexico.

Streb, Matthew, Barbara Burrell, Brian Frederick, and Michael Genovese. 2008. "Social Desirability Effects and Support for a Female American President." *Public Opinion Quarterly* 72 (1): 76–89.

Studlar, Dudley. 2008. "Feminist Society, Paternalist Politics: How the Electoral System Affects Women's Representation in the United States Congress." In Manon Tremblay (ed.) *Women and Legislative Representation: Electoral Systems, Political Parties, and Sex Quotas*. New York, NY: Palgrave Macmillan: 55–66.

Studlar, Dudley, and Ian McAllister. 1991. "Political Recruitment to the Australian Legislature: Towards an Explanation of Women's Electoral Disadvantages." *Western Political Quarterly* 44: 467–485.

2003. "Does a Critical Mass Exist? A Comparative Analysis of Women's Legislative Representation since 1950." *European Journal of Political Research* 41: 233–253.

Suplicy, Marta. 1996. "Novos Paradigmas nas Esferas de Poder." *Estudos Feministas* 4 (1): 126–137.

Svåsand, Lars. 1994. "Change and Adaptation in Norwegian Party Organizations." In Richard S. Katz and Peter Mair (eds.) *How Parties Organize: Change and Adaptation in Party Organizations in Western Democracies*. London: SAGE, 304–331.

Taagepera, Rein, and Matthew Soberg Shugart. 1989. *Seats and Votes: The Effects of Determinants of Electoral Systems*. New Haven, CT: Yale University Press.

Tarouco, Gabriela da Silva. 2010. "Institucionalização Partidária no Brasil (1982–2006)." *Revista Brasileira de Ciência Política* 4: 169–186.

Tavener, Ben. 2015, 19 November. "While Murders of Black Women in Brazil Rise Sharply: Murders of White Women Fall." https://news.vice.com (Accessed April 3, 2016)

Telles, Edward E. 2004. *Race in Another America: The Significance of Skin Color in Brazil*. Princeton, NJ: Princeton University Press.

2014. *Pigmentocracies: Ethnicity, Race, and Color in Latin America*. Chapel Hill, NC: University of North Carolina Press.

n.d. "Racial Ambiguity among the Brazilian Population." Retrieved from https://sscnet .ucla.edu/soc/faculty/telles/Paper_RacialAmbiguityBrazil.pdf (Accessed December 10, 2015)

Temer, Michel. 2009, March 11. "Ações Concretas para Ampliar a Participação Política das Mulheres." *Jornal da Câmara* 2210, 1–12. Retrieved from https://camara.gov .br/internet/jornal/jc20090311.pdf (Accessed March 8, 2018)

Thames, Frank. 2005. "A House Divided: Party Strength and the Mandate Divide in Hungary, Russian, and Ukraine." *Comparative Political Studies* 38 (3): 282–303.

Thames, Frank, and Margaret Williams. 2010. "Incentives for Personal Votes and Women's Representation in Legislatures." *Comparative Political Studies* 43 (12): 1575–1600.

Thelen, Kathleen. 1999. "Historical Institutionalism in Comparative Politics." *Annual Review of Political Science* 2 (June): 369–404.

Thomas, Melanee, and Marc André Bodet. 2013. "Sacrificial Lambs, Women Candidates, and District Competitiveness in Canada." *Electoral Studies* 32 (1): 153–66.

Toole, James. 2003. "Straddling the East-West Divide: Party Organisation and Communist Legacies in East Central Europe." *Europe-Asia Studies* 55 (1): 101–118.

Transparencia. 2013. "Retos para la Participación Política de las Mujeres en el Perú." Retrieved from http://transparencia.org.pe/documentos/retos_para_la_partici pacion_politica_de_la_mujer.pdf (Accessed August 9, 2017)

Tremblay, Manon. 2012. *Women and Legislative Representation: Electoral Systems, Political Parties, and Sex Quotas (2nd edn)*. New York, NY: Palgrave Macmillan.
Tribunal Regional Eleitoral de Alagoas (TRE-AL). 2017, July 20. "Justiça Eleitoral Reforçou Fiscalização de Contas de Partidos e Candidatos ao Longo de 2016." Tribunal Regional Eleitoral de Alagoas (TRE-AL). Retrieved from https://tre-al.jus.br/ imprensa/noticias-tre-al/2017/Julho/justica-eleitoral-reforcou-fiscalizacao-de-contas-de -partidos-e-candidatos-ao-longo-de-2016 (Accessed August 21, 2017)
Tribunal Superior Eleitoral (TSE). 1994–2016. Electoral Results and Statistics. Retrieved from https://tse.jus.br/eleitor-e-eleicoes/eleicoes/eleicoes (Accessed September 5, 2017)
Tripp, Aili, and Alice Kang. 2008. "The Global Impact of Quotas: On the Fast Track to Increased Female Legislative Representation." *Comparative Political Studies* 41: 338–361.
TV Seridó. 2009, March 27. "Conversa com Deputada Fátima Bezerra." Retrieved from https://youtube.com/watch?v=18u36y9wTAo (Accessed March 8, 2018)
United Nations Development Program (PNUD). 2013. *Atlas do Desenvolvimento Humano no Brasil*. Retrieved from https://pnud.org.br/atlas/ranking/Ranking-IDHM-UF-2010.aspx (Accessed July 20, 2015)
United Nations Human Development Report (UN HDR). 2009. *Overcoming Barriers: Human Mobility and Development*. New York, NY: Palgrave Macmillan. Retrieved from http://hdr.undp.org (Accessed March 8, 2018)
2010. *The Real Wealth of Nations: Pathways to Human Development*. New York, NY: Palgrave Macmillan. Retrieved from http://hdr.undp.org (Accessed March 8, 2018)
2014. *Sustaining Human Progress: Reducing Vulnerabilities and Building Resilience*. New York, NY: UN Development Programme. Retrieved from http://hdr.undp.org (Accessed March 8, 2018)
2016. *Human Development for Everyone. New York: UN Development Programme*. Retrieved from http://hdr.undp.org (Accessed March 8, 2018)
Valdini, Melody Ellis. 2012. "A Deterrent to Diversity: The Conditional Effect of Electoral Rules on the Nomination on Women Candidates." *Electoral Studies* 31 (4/Dec): 740–749.
2013a. "Electoral Institutions and the Manifestation of Bias: The Effect of the Personal Vote on the Representation of Women." *Politics & Gender* 9 (1): 76–92.
2013b. "A Stubborn Assumption of Innocence: The Effect of Corruption on Women's Representation." Presented at the Annual Meeting of the Midwest Political Science Association, Chicago.
van Biezen, Ingrid, and Daniela Romée Piccio. 2013. "Shaping Intra-Party Democracy: On the Legal Regulation of Internal Party Organizations." In William P. Cross and Richard S. Katz (eds.) *The Challenges of Intra-Party Democracy*. New York, NY: Oxford University Press, 27–48.
Verge, Tània, and Sílvia Claveria. 2016. "Gendered Political Resources: The Case of Party Office." *Party Politics*. OnlineFirst, doi:10.1177/1354068816663040: 1–13.
Verge, Tània, and Maria de la Fuente. 2014. "Playing with Different Cards: Party Politics, Gender Quotas, and Women's Empowerment." *International Political Science Review* 35 (1): 67–79.
Waiselfisz, Julio Jacobo. 2012. Mapa da Violência: Caderno Complentar 1: Homicídio de Mulheres no Brasil. São Paulo, Brazil: Instituto Sangari.

Retrieved from http://mapadaviolencia.org.br/pdf2012/mapa2012_mulher.pdf (Accessed March 8, 2018)

2015. *Mapa da Violência 2015: Homicídio de Mulheres no Brasil.* Brasília: Flasco Brasil.

Walsh, Denise. 2010. *Women's Rights in Democratizing States.* New York, NY: Cambridge University Press.

Waylen, Georgina. 2000. "Gender and Democratic Politics: A Comparative Analysis of Consolidation in Argentina and Chile." *Journal of Latin American Studies* 32 (3/ Oct): 765–793.

Waylen, Georgina (ed.). 2017. *Gender and Informal Institutions.* London: Rowman & Littlefield.

Weingast, Barry, and Kenneth Shepsle (eds.). 1995. *Positive Theories of Congressional Institutions.* Ann Arbor: University of Michigan Press.

Weyland, Kurt. 2002. "Limitations of Rational-Choice Institutionalism for the Study of Latin American Politics." *Studies in Comparative International Development* 37 (1): 57–85.

2006. *Bounded Rationality and Policy Diffusion: Social Sector Reform in Latin America.* Princeton, NJ: Princeton University Press.

Wiliarty, Sarah Elise. 2010. *The CDU and the Politics of Gender in Germany: Bringing Women to the Party.* New York, NY: Cambridge University Press.

Wolbrecht, Christina. 2000. *The Politics of Women's Rights: Parties, Positions, and Change.* Princeton, NJ: Princeton University Press.

Wolbrecht, Christina, and David E. Campbell. 2007. "Leading by Example: Female Members of Parliament as Political Role Models." *American Journal of Political Science* 51 (4): 921–939.

World Values Survey 1981–2014. Longitudinal Aggregate v.20150418. World Values Survey Association (https://worldvaluessurvey.org). Aggregate File Producer: JDS Systems, Madrid.

Wylie, Kristin. 2011. "Institutional Change and Sacrificial Lambs: Explaining the Underperformance of Female Candidates to the Brazilian Chamber of Deputies in 2010." Presented at the Annual Meeting of the Midwest Political Science Association, Chicago, IL.

2017. Disrupting the Good Ole Boys Club: Leadership Change and Inclusivity in the Brazilian Workers' Party, Presented at the Biannual Conference of the European Conference on Politics and Gender, Lausanne, Switzerland.

Wylie, Kristin, Daniel Marcelino, and Pedro dos Santos. 2015. "Non-viable Candidates and the Dynamics of Legislative Elections in Brazil." Presented at the Annual Meeting of the American Political Science Association, San Francisco, CA.

Wylie, Kristin, and Pedro dos Santos. 2016. "A Law on Paper Only: Electoral Rules, Parties, and the Persistent Underrepresentation of Women in Brazilian Legislatures." *Politics & Gender* 12 (3): 415–442.

Young, Iris Marion. 1989. "Polity and Group Difference: A Critique of the Ideal of Universal Citizenship." *Ethics* 99 (2): 250–274.

Index